COLLABORATIVE DAMAGE

An Experimental Ethnography
of Chinese Globalization

Mikkel Bunkenborg
Morten Nielsen
Morten Axel Pedersen

CORNELL UNIVERSITY PRESS   **ITHACA AND LONDON**

First published 2022 by Cornell University Press

Library of Congress Cataloging-in-Publication Data

Names: Bunkenborg, Mikkel, author. | Nielsen, Morten, 1971– author. | Pedersen, Morten Axel, 1969– author.
Title: Collaborative damage : an experimental ethnography of Chinese globalization / Mikkel Bunkenborg, Morten Nielsen, Morten Axel Pedersen.
Description: Ithaca [New York] : Cornell University Press, 2022. | Includes bibliographical references and index.
Identifiers: LCCN 2021033853 (print) | LCCN 2021033854 (ebook) | ISBN 9781501759802 (hardcover) | ISBN 9781501759833 (paperback) | ISBN 9781501759819 (pdf) | ISBN 9781501759826 (epub)
Subjects: LCSH: Globalization—Social aspects—Mongolia. | Globalization—Social aspects—Mozambique. | Globalization—Case studies. | Globalization—China. | Economic development projects—Social aspects. | Economic development projects—Political aspects.
Classification: LCC JZ1318 .B873 2022 (print) | LCC JZ1318 (ebook) | DDC 338.91/51—dc23
LC record available at https://lccn.loc.gov/2021033853
LC ebook record available at https://lccn.loc.gov/2021033854

COLLABORATIVE DAMAGE

It never ends (*nunca para*). We will never govern our own country. . . .
Now it's the Chinese, who are running Mozambique. . . . When you
come back here, you will have to talk to a Chinese community chief.

—Jaime Paguri, Mozambican tree scout, 2012

Whose side are you actually on?

—Pedersen to Bunkenborg, Eastern Mongolia, 2010

**Their misunderstanding of me was not the same as my
misunderstanding of them.**

—Roy Wagner, 1981

Contents

Acknowledgments

Many people have contributed to the making of this book. First of all, we would like to express a deep debt of gratitude to the individuals, communities, and institutions in Mozambique, Mongolia, and China who spent time answering our questions and giving us access to their workplaces and lives. Without them, this book would simply not exist.

In addition, we would also like to extend a very special thanks to Anna Tsing and George Marcus, whose work has inspired and informed many of the arguments of this book, and who have also both helped us at various crucial stages in the course of bringing this project to fruition. A big thank you also to the three anonymous peer reviewers, as well as to Jim Lance and other good people at Cornell University Press, for their detailed, insightful, and constructive suggestions and criticisms to the first version of this manuscript.

The following scholars have heard or read and shared their input to presentations, papers, and draft chapters: Bjørn Enge Bertelsen, Franck Billé, Lauren Bonilla, Susanne Bregnbæk, Uradyn Bulag, Manduhai Buyandelger, Matei Candea, Sérgio Chichava, Christopher Connery, Dimitris Dalakoglou, Filip de Boeck, Devon Dear, Grégory Delaplace, Jørgen Delman, Bumochir Dulam, Judith Farquhar, Anders Sybrandt Hansen, Thomas Blom Hansen, Donna Haraway, Penny Harvey, Martin Holbraad, Caroline Humphrey, Sara Jackson, Paul Jenkins, Casper Bruun Jensen, Hanna Knox, Peter Kragelund, Tanya Luhrmann, Christian Lund, Gordon Mathews, Sayana Namsaraeva, John Osburg, Ivan Peshkov, Ed Pulford, Andreas Roepstorff, Lisa Rofel, Danilyn Rutherford, István Sántha, AbdouMaliq Simone, Marissa Smith, David Sneath, Jason Sumich, Stig Thøgersen, Brit Winthereik, Matthew Wolf-Meyer. A big word of thanks also to our many colleagues from the Department of Anthropology, University of Copenhagen; the Department of Cross-cultural and Regional Studies, University of Copenhagen; and the Department of Anthropology, Aarhus University.

We would also like to acknowledge the many excellent questions, comments, and criticisms received in the context of papers presented by all or some of us at the Mongolia and Inner Asia Studies Unit, Cambridge University; the Inner Asian and Altaic Studies Seminar, Harvard University; the Department of Anthropology and the Center for Cultural Studies, University of California, Santa Cruz; the Department of Anthropology, University of Michigan; the Department of Anthropology, Stanford University; the Department of Anthropology, University of St. Andrews; the Department of Anthropology, University of Copenhagen; Nordic Institute of Asian Studies (NIAS) in Copenhagen; the Anthropological Megaseminar, Sandbjerg Denmark; the panel Borderline Intimacies: Sino-Xeno Encounters in Sub-Saharan Africa and Inner Asia at the 2012 Annual Meeting of the American Anthropological Association; the Center for East and South-East Asia Studies, Lund University; Department of Global Area Studies, Aarhus University; the Asian Dynamics Conferences held at the University of Copenhagen in 2013 and 2017; the University of Eduardo Mondlane, Mozambique, Instituto de Estudos Sociais e Económicos (IESE), Mozambique; the Institute of Anthropology, Renmin University; the University of Chicago Center in Beijing; and the Institute of Global Ethnology and Anthropology, Minzu University of China.

We would like to acknowledge the help and support in Mongolia from Zhenia ("Jenya") Boikov and B. Otgonchimeg. A special thanks to the late Mr. Bürneebat, who in addition to being a steady driver for Pedersen and Bunkenborg, also turned out to be an excellent assistant and a trusted discussion partner during their travels in Mongolia. Many thanks also to Bayarmaa Khalzaa and to Ms. Batdulam for help with the transcription and translation of interviews, and for linguistic and ethnographic assistance in the field. A big thanks also to Prof. D. Bumochir for his assistance in obtaining research permissions. In addition Pedersen and Bunkenborg would like to thank the following list of individuals in Mongolia: Ms. Altanlish, Mr. Amraa, D. Battulga, Nasan Bayar, Mr. Bayarsaihan, the late Slava Boikov, Mr. Chimedtseren, Nigamet Dastan, Rebecca Darling, D. Enhjargal, Robert Grayson, Tjalling Halbertsma, Pearly Jacob, Jia Xinsheng, Bolarmaa Luntan, Lao Luo, Laurenz Melchior, Mr. Mönhtör, Ms. Narantsetseg, Kirk Olson, N. Onon, B. Tsendsüren, T. Tumentsogt, and Ms. Ülzii Chimeg.

In Mozambique, Nielsen and Bunkenborg's individual and collective ethnographic research drew heavily on the tireless help of Cândido Jeque, whose work ethics and stamina always made them run a little faster. We are particularly grateful for the guidance and patience during extended discussions about all things Mozambique with Nelson Machava and his family, who have been dear friends to Nielsen for more than fifteen years. During research trips to the forests of Cabo Delgado, Nielsen in particular, but also Bunkenborg and Pedersen, relied on the assistance of Taquinha Manuel and Babo Chiauque, who made it possible to get a deep sense of the work and craftsmanship of local *olheiros* (tree scouts). A huge thanks also to Professors Anselmo Cani, Júlio Carrilho, Luís Lage, and João T. Tique from the faculty of Architecture, University of Eduardo Mondlane, for their enthusiastic support and for kindly hosting Nielsen and Bunkenborg during many research stays in Maputo. In addition, Bunkenborg and Nielsen would like to thank, Lars Buur, José Forjaz, Eva Tommerup Johnsen, Idalio Juvane, Pedro Nacuo, Daniel Ribeiro, Bento Sitoe, and Anne Witthøfft.

We would like to express our gratitude in China to Zhao Xudong for his extraordinary hospitality during our visit to the capital to present our work, to Bao Zhiming for his help, and to Gong Haoqun and Lai Lili for their support and insightful comments on many occasions.

For help with preparing the manuscript for publication, we would like to thank Karoline Husbond Andersen.

Finally, but not least, Mikkel would like to thank his wife, Cæcilie, and their two daughters, Frederikke and Johanne, for their patience with all the globe-trotting, for spending the summer of 2010 in Mozambique, and for keeping their cool when the four of us stuck in the sand on our way to Ponta do Ouro. Morten Nielsen hopes that his wife, Maria, and his two sons, Bertram and Pelle, have long forgotten the many times he was away on project field trips while more important things were going on at home, such as his son's learning to walk. Morten Axel Pedersen would like to thank his wife, Kimi, and his daughters, Sophie and Ines, for their enduring support, for accompanying him to Ulaanbaatar during the summers of 2010 and 2011, and for putting up with many hours of working on yet another book project.

A Note on Transliteration and Currencies

Chinese words in the text are mostly written with simplified Chinese characters only, but names and certain terms that may be familiar to an English speaking audience have been transliterated according to the pinyin system with tone markers omitted.

Except for widely used spellings of well-known historical names, such as Genghis Khan, the following system has been used when transliterating from the Mongolian Cyrillic alphabet:

A a	Л l	Х h	Б b	М m	Ц ts	В v	Н n	Ч ch
Г g	О o	Ш sh	Д d	Ө ö	Ъ "	Е ye	П p	Ы y
Ë yo	Р r	Ь '	Ж j	С s	Э e	З z	Т t	Ю yu
И i	У u	Я ya	Й i	Ү ü	К k	Ф f		

In a few cases we have followed Sneath (2000, viii) in adding a Roman "s" to the end of Mongolian words instead of using the Mongolian plural.

Transliteration of Changana done according to Bento Sitoe's dictionary *Dicionário Changana-Português* (2011) and subsequently verified through interviews with Sitoe.

Throughout the book, we regularly refer to four different currencies: the Chinese Renminbi (RMB), the Mongolian Tögrög (MT), the Mozambican Metical (MZM), and the US Dollar (US $). The rates fluctuated somewhat during the years 2009 to 2012, but on average, US $1 equalled approximately RMB 6.5, MT 1,300, and MZM 30.

COLLABORATIVE DAMAGE

There is only one method in social anthropology: the comparative method—and that's impossible.

—E. E. Evans-Pritchard

Western philosophy sees humanity through the eyes of subjectivity, while the Chinese sees it through the eyes of otherness.

—Zhao Tingyang, 2006

The well-worn asphalt road meandered through a lush green landscape. It was one of Mozambique's less traveled roads, and there was no apparent reason why the section ahead had been emblazoned with freshly painted white and yellow lines that curved, straightened, spattered, and jumped in a madly irregular scribble stretching over several kilometers to the top of a distant hill. It looked as if someone had used this quiet coastal road to illustrate a massive and improbable pileup by tracing out skid marks in white and yellow paint and then left the markings as a warning to future motorists. Puzzled by the disorderly stripes, Mikkel Bunkenborg and Morten Nielsen stopped their car to investigate the matter further, but a local man in his thirties was the only other person on the road, and he was equally mystified by the stripes that had recently appeared. Having snapped a few photos, the two ethnographers resumed their journey toward the main camp of a Chinese construction company that was currently rehabilitating a ninety-five-kilometer section of the National Highway (EN1) just north of the city of Xai-Xai in Gaza Province in southern Mozambique.

When Bunkenborg and Nielsen arrived at the compound of the Chinese company, the gates were closed for the night and guarded by Mozambican security guards with semiautomatic weapons. Feeling lucky to have met up with Edgar, the Zimbabwean resident engineer appointed to supervise the project by the Mozambican National Road Administration (Administracão Nacional de Estradas (ANE)), they waited patiently for the gate to be opened, and Edgar took the opportunity to ask Bunkenborg for a translation of the Chinese characters that

FIGURE 0.1.   Mozambican workers and Chinese managers, north of Xai-Xai, Mozambique. November 2010.

graced the entrance. The Mozambican officials, he remarked, were concerned about these incomprehensible signs. They could mean anything.[1] Inside the compound the headlights revealed that most of the space was occupied by long rows of trucks and heavy equipment, but along the edges decorative patches of banana trees lined the fronts of the prefabricated buildings that served as workshops, storage sheds, and living quarters for some forty Chinese employees. In the main office a handful of young Chinese men in beige uniforms were absorbed in the online game *World of Warcraft*, and it was only with some degree of reluctance that one of the interpreters and the man in charge of the camp, both in their late twenties, looked up from their computers to greet Edgar and the inquisitive visitors.

All the Chinese engineers seemed quite young, and it turned out that most of them had been plucked straight from the university and sent off to Mozambique. They had held internships on road projects in China, but this was the first time they were responsible for getting a road built themselves. It wasn't easy, some of them admitted, especially when the local workers were unreasonable and went on strike and the resident engineer forced them to redo sections of the road that did not meet the required standards. None of these young men, however, seemed overly concerned about the delays and added costs, and it took Bunkenborg a few days to find a middle-aged finance officer who could explain this mysterious lack of interest in the road between Xai-Xai and Chissibuca: The subcontracting company was a branch of China Railways, and being eager to move into construction projects overseas, the manager saw the project as a sort of training exercise. Instead of sending twenty people, which would have been enough for a project of this scale, he sent sixty. Some of them would prove incompetent and others would be unwilling to continue this sort of work, so it was just as well to send too many and pick the best of the bunch for further grooming in the company. The fact that they were building a substandard road and losing a lot of money in the process was not a concern for a company of this size. "We are just paying school fees," the manager had told the finance officer and dismissed the losses as small change.

The local workers interviewed by Nielsen were equally aware that they were not building a proper road, and they furtively pointed out some of the cracks that were already starting to appear on the surface. Their explanation, however, mainly hinged upon the improper terms of employment: Only a minority of the workers had contracts, the system for calculating wages was opaque, and the pay was hardly enough to live on. "When the workers are not treated as proper workers, how can you expect them to produce a proper road?" they asked Nielsen rhetorically.

While everyone agreed that the Chinese engineers and the Mozambican workers were busily constructing something that was not quite a road, no single explanation seemed to suffice. "The Chinese are probably convicts doing hard time in Africa," the Italian auto mechanic volunteered when Bunkenborg, Nielsen, and Edgar sat down for dinner in his roadside café close to the main camp. "I once tried to talk to one of the foremen working outside my place, and he just walked away. I went after him, but he kept walking, and in the end, the locals started laughing at me for chasing the Chinese into the bush." Smiling at the image of the fleeing Chinese, Edgar confessed that he himself remained mystified by his Chinese counterparts. The young men might be engineers, he said, but they failed to follow his instructions and constantly made costly mistakes. Even with the minimal wages paid to local workers, the Chinese company was losing money on this project, and no one really seemed to care. To illustrate the accumulation of errors, Edgar explained how all the paint for marking the road had partially dried out from being left in the burning sun for months. Having failed to report the arrival of the paint and its incorrect storage, the Chinese secretly ordered some of the local workers to salvage the liquid remains at the bottom of the drums, but as the reflective beads failed to adhere to the paint, it was immediately discovered that they were using damaged paint. "And it wasn't just the paint," Edgar chuckled. "The spraying machine they ordered looked like something you would use to mark up a tennis lawn and they couldn't make a straight line with it. They had to fly in a specialist from China to operate the thing, but it broke down after a hundred meters. I wouldn't let them work on the EN1 before they could make two hundred meters of perfect road marking, and I told them to go somewhere else and practice first."

Realizing that the long stretch of mysterious markings on the country road was in fact the trial section where the Chinese road workers had been obliged to hone their painting skills, the two anthropologists started laughing. They quickly agreed that Morten Pedersen, the third member of their newly launched comparative ethnographic investigation of Chinese globalization in Mozambique and Mongolia, would find their photos of the stripes hilarious. "If this road gives us any indication of where China is going, it must be that they're building a global empire of junk," Nielsen remarked, expecting Bunkenborg to concur. But he did not. Instead, Nielsen's facetious comment produced an awkward silence between the two ethnographers, exposing the first crack in their anthropological understanding of the road project. This crack only widened in the course of their ensuing discussions, as it became clear to both of them that they interpreted not just the stripes but the road project as a whole in different if not incommensurable ways. To Bunkenborg and the Chinese engineers, the project was a training exercise that would enable the company to move on to build real roads in other parts of the world; the errant stripes were just byproducts, the collateral damage of an otherwise meaningful and serious development process. For Nielsen, however, and especially for the Mozambicans, who would have to live with the uneven stripes, cracked surfaces, and loose reflective beads for years to come, there was an air of tragedy; for them, the outcome of all their efforts was a stretch of road that would rapidly become sheer junk.

The tragicomical tale of the not-quite-road, and the local Sino-Mozambican and our own disagreements about how to make sense of it, are emblematic of a much larger story of Chinese globalization in the early twenty-first century. Many of the elements from the above account—the endemic misunderstandings and the escalating tensions, the insulation of Chinese managers in walled container enclaves, and an increasingly disgruntled workforce and local community—recur again and again in the diverse cases of Chinese infrastructure investment and resource extraction projects encountered by the three of us of during a total of eighteen months of fieldwork in Mozambique and Mongolia. As such, the not-quite-road is iconic of this book's overarching theme: failed collaborations and their unpredictable social, economic, political, and cultural effects. Far from being avoidable mishaps on a path to seamless cooperation between Chinese and Mozambicans, it is our contention that the fortuitous mishaps on the EN1 road go to the very heart of Chinese globalization—not just in Mozambique, but also elsewhere in the Global South. We call this *collaborative damage*, by which we mean the social relations and the material infrastructures linking different participants in Chinese globalization processes—Mozambican workers, Chinese managers, as well as Danish anthropologists—in paradoxical partnerships of mutual incomprehension.

The increasing Chinese intervention in the Global South has been subject to much scholarly and public attention. As evident in two review articles (Siu and McGovern 2017; Alden and Large 2018), a growing number of scholars, journalists, and opinion makers have attempted to make sense of the emerging Chinese global polity. In the mid-2000s the first wave of scholarship on China's role in the world, almost exclusively focused on Africa, was informed by an explicit mission to rectify the "misinformation" and the "misunderstandings," that allegedly had proliferated in press reports about Chinese engagement with this continent (Alden 2007; Taylor 2006; Alden, Large, and Oliveira 2008; see also special issues of the *China Quarterly* in 2010, *African and Asian Studies* in 2010, and *African Studies Review* in 2013). Peppered with observations from fieldwork in many different sites, Deborah Brautigam's books *The Dragon's Gift: The Real Story of China in Africa* (2009) and *Will Africa Feed China?* (2015) argued that the Chinese embrace of Africa does grow out of a long-term strategic plan but that this Beijing blueprint is not necessarily as sinister as it has been portrayed by Western journalistic consensus. Barry Sautman and Yan Hairong have argued that the abuse of African laborers was an effect of the neoliberal economy and not something specific to Chinese companies (Yan and Sautman 2012; Sautman and Yan 2008; 2009; 2007). At the same time a growing body of fine-grained ethnographic descriptions has attested to the complexity of Sino-African relations, describing Chinese migrants in South Africa (Park 2008), Chinese shopowners in Cape Verde (Haugen and Carling 2005) and Namibia (Dobler 2009; 2008), the treatment of African employees in mines and factories run by Chinese in Zambia and Tanzania (Lee 2009), relations between African employees and Chinese shop-owners in Uganda, Ghana, and Nigeria (Arsene 2014; Giese 2013; Giese and Thiel 2012; 2015; Lampert and Mohan 2014), interpersonal relations in Tanzania (Sheridan 2018; 2019), perceptions of Chinese goods in Guinea (Fioratta 2019) and South Africa (Huang 2019), and African traders and communities in China (Bodomo 2010; Haugen 2012) (Mathews 2015; Lan 2017).

Valuable as this work has been, it also suffers from limitations. More precisely, we find that the tendency to frame the issue at hand as a question of "China in Africa," "the new Silk Road," (see below) or more recently "Africa in China" has led to both overgeneralization and hyperspecification: On the one hand, ongoing attempts by journalists, political scientists, and China hands to second-guess the intentions of political leaders in Beijing have, predictably, failed to provide reliable accounts about what is happening. On the other hand, the growing body of ethnographic studies has provided important empirical counterpoints to such lofty speculations, but their extreme specificity has made them too easy to dismiss as special cases and exceptions. What is needed, we therefore suggest, is a more distinct and more ambitious anthropological approach that is grounded in fieldwork while allowing for a more systematic comparison and theorization of China in the world. The present book aspires to fill this empirical and theoretical gap. Thus, while a number of anthropologists have been studying China's political-economic intervention abroad, few attempts have been made to compare these regional developments, let alone explore how such a comparison might contribute to wider social and political-science debates about globalization, empire, and late capitalism. Our ambition in this book is to provide precisely such a comparative anthropological study of Chinese globalization based on a collaborative ethnographic study of Chinese political-economic inventions in Mongolia and Mozambique, two countries selected not just because of our past fieldwork experience, regional knowledge, and linguistic skills, but also because, as we explain below, they both represent paradigmatic cases of Chinese globalization in sub-Saharan Africa and Inner Asia respectively.

But the book also has a second and more methodological and theoretical ambition. In addition to representing the first book-length comparative ethnographic study of Chinese globalization, it is also a chronicle of what happens when three ethnographers set out to conduct a collaborative study of something whose interpretation turns out to be impossible for them to agree on. What follows, then, is not only a comparative study of Chinese globalization from a bird's-eye perspective; it represents as well a concerted attempt to chronicle the fraught collaboration among three anthropologists during eighteen months of joint fieldwork and eight years of subsequent writing and analysis. In that sense the story of the EN1 highway offers not just an iconic example of the endemic misunderstandings between our Chinese and Mozambican/Mongolian interlocutors. It also provides an illustration of another and equally central theme of this book: our own failure to collaboratively study this failed collaboration. Crucially, in honing in on what we call "collaborative damage," we do not merely want to highlight the oftentimes fraught relationships between Chinese and local interlocutors in Mozambique and Mongolia. We also want to focus analytically on our own failed collaborations as researchers. As a serious attempt to recognize that failures of understanding are intrinsic to all collaborative work (Fabian 1995; Tsing 2005; Rabinow and Stavrianakis 2013)—from misunderstandings between Chinese managers and their Mozambican or Mongolian collaborators to the equally profound misunderstandings among three differently positioned ethnographers—this is a global ethnography, written from the inside out. Through in-depth case studies of friendship, hatred, jokes, misunderstandings, irresolvable differences, and carefully maintained mutual indifferences across disparate Sino-Mozambican and Sino-Mongolian worlds, this book explores the nature and the dynamics of a global form *from within*, as we witnessed, documented, and debated it in the course of a decade of collaborative research.

In what remains of this introduction, we lay out the empirical, methodological, and theoretical ground for our study. We begin by situating the present book within the bourgeoning social and political-science literature concerned with China's growing political and economic clout in the Global South over recent decades, including the increasing number of Chinese nationals engaged in trade, aid, infrastructure construction, and natural-resource extraction in Mozambique and Mongolia specifically. Next, we address the question of methodology and the (impossibly) rigorous comparative framework that we originally devised before setting out to conduct our joint fieldwork. We then present three central concepts—empire, enclaves, and intimate distances—that grew out of our attempts to analyze and theorize our ethnographic data. And finally we return to the question of collaborative damage, elaborating on the process by which the more or less productive misunderstandings so characteristic of many Sino-local encounters in Mozambique as well as Mongolia gradually began to inflict themselves upon and appear within our own collaboration as a team, setting in train the double process of collaborative intent and failure, the chronicling of which is this book's ultimate ambition.

A Chinese Century?

One of the things to emerge from the ashes of the 2008 financial crisis was an increasingly expansive and self-confident China. Accelerating Chinese political and economic interventions took place in Africa, Asia, Latin America, and other corners of the globe, including Western Europe, Australia, and Polynesia (see Kynge 2006; Taylor 2006; 2011; Alden 2007; Currier and Dorraj 2011). The driving force behind this global expansion was economic. As financial institutions collapsed and stock markets plummeted in the West with the onset of the great recession, the Chinese economy was buoyed up by governmental stimulus and bank credit packages financed by decades of trade surpluses and financial reserves in US dollars, and it was widely reported that Chinese companies scoured the globe for fire-sale bargains. "After a shopping spree for natural resources, the Chinese are shifting to automakers, high-tech firms, and real estate. Where will they strike next?" was the question posed by *Forbes Magazine* under the memorable headline "It's China's World (We Just Live in It)" (Powell 2009).[2] Indeed, the post-Mao Chinese economy has proven to be an extraordinary powerhouse. Growing by an average of 10 percent every year since 1979, the economy's size overtook that of Japan in 2009 as the world's second largest. Starting with manufacturing in special economic zones along the coast, China in the 1990s and 2000s became "the factory of the world," and many Chinese companies eventually also began investing outside China to gain access to natural resources and new technologies and to market their own increasingly high-tech goods. President Jiang Zemin launched the idea of "going out" (走出去) or "going global" (走向世界) in party seminars as early as 1992, but it took another decade before the surge in outward foreign direct investment (OFDI) really started. From 2002 to 2016, the flow of OFDI from China grew at an average annual rate of 35.8 percent, reaching a peak of US $192.8 billion in 2016 (Wang and Gao 2019). While several academics have presented the levelheaded message that China will hardly own the rest of the world in the foreseeable future,[3] it is not surprising that the acceleration of investments from China has raised more than a few eyebrows. Even if China does not "own the world" just yet, it has been playing a major role in the Global South by offering access to funds and what appears to be a highly efficient model of economic development.

As a political actor China has proclaimed itself a champion of the Third World and committed to a so-called multipolar world order. Integral to this process has been China's emphasis on the need to forge "multipolar" alliances across the world to curb US hegemony (Taylor 2006) and to foster what Chinese politicians under Xi Jinping's leadership have begun to refer to as the "Great Renaissance of the Chinese Nation" (中华民族伟大复兴). A reform of Chinese aid policy in 1995 coupled aid and trade, and the diplomatic efforts of Chinese leaders over the following years culminated in the year 2000 with the festive establishment of a platform for win-win economic cooperation, the Forum on China Africa Cooperation (FOCAC) (Taylor 2011). At a time when the so-called Washington consensus dictated conditional lending and structural adjustment programs, China stepped in to offer turn-key infrastructure and loans with no strings attached. This emphasis on noninterference, dubbed the "Beijing consensus" (Ramo 2004), proved attractive to many states in the Global South, and not surprisingly, Western-controlled international organizations and agencies like the World Bank were at odds about what to do with a country that offered huge loan-and-investment packages and infrastructure projects reminiscent of Western projects in the 1960 and 1970s, without caring about issues such as environmental standards or local participation. "So far," as Nyíri and Breidenbach write, "China's globalization looks in many ways like an earlier stage of Western capitalist globalization" (2008, 140).

In the specific case of Africa, China pointed to a long-standing commitment to south-south cooperation dating back to the 1955 Bandung conference, and a long history of support for socialist countries that included medical teams, agricultural projects, and infrastructure, most notably the icon of Sino-African friendship, the TAZARA railway (Brautigam 1998; Monson 2008; Snow 1989; Strauss 2009). China's strengthening of diplomatic and commercial ties to countries, especially in Africa, has been hotly debated in Western media and academia, and both the EU and the United States have expressed concern about "unfair" Chinese competition for influence on this continent from an adversary with "no political strings attached" in the context of both bilateral aid and foreign direct investment (Alden 2005).[4]

Taking Mozambique as an example, the effects of China's growing economic and geopolitical clout in sub-Saharan Africa have indeed been extraordinary. Unlike for instance Angola, where oil has been the focal point (Ferguson, J. 2005), Chinese interests in Mozambique are quite diverse and include construction, logging, agriculture, development of IT technologies, and trade (Alden and Chichava 2014). By 2014 China had become the number one export partner; it was second only to neighboring South Africa as an import partner; and bilateral trade had grown to US $3.6 billion, up from 120 million in 2004. The same gigantic leap can be read from the bilateral trade between Mozambique and China, which reached $284.11 million in 2007, eight times more than in 2001 (Chichava 2008, 9). With the Mozambican peace agreement in 1992, the destructive civil war between the ruling Frelimo party and the Renamo movement that had lasted since shortly after independence in 1975 was finally brought to an end. Faced with the overwhelming challenge of reviving a paralyzed state administration and rebuilding an infrastructure system in ruins, the Frelimo government turned to international lending institutions and political allies for support (Abrahamsson and Nilsson 1995; Hanlon 1991, 1996). Already during the protracted struggle against the Portuguese colonizers, Frelimo had established a collaborative relationship with China that involved military support and guerrilla training (Dinerman 2006, 21). Although the friendship cooled somewhat in the mid-1980s, when Mozambique made its "turn toward the West" by adopting a series of IMF-sponsored economic adjustment programs, China remained a potential political ally (Roque 2009, 16; Hanlon 2016). From the early 1990s onwards, the relationship has been massively reinvigorated through a series of intergovernmental agreements and memoranda preparing the way for China's intensified presence in Mozambique. And judging from statements by the political elite in Mozambique, their Chinese counterparts are being confronted by few hindrances (if any) on the road toward further economic involvement in the country. In a response to the increased Chinese presence in sub-Saharan Africa, Armando

Guebuza, Mozambique's president until 2015, stated that "*China é muito bem vinda em Mozambique*" (China is very welcome in Mozambique) (Revistamacau 2006). The cordial openness toward China is reflected in seemingly unlimited economic room for maneuver. Donations from the Chinese state and loans from the Exim Bank have financed a series of construction projects including the Parliament, the Ministry of Foreign Affairs, the High Court, the new presidential palace, the national football stadium, the airport in Maputo, and a suspension bridge connecting Maputo to the Catembe Peninsula. The Chinese construction companies involved in these projects have established themselves in Mozambique and are highly successful in their bids for public tenders for infrastructure projects. According to a high-level Mozambican official at ANE, nearly all public tenders have been won by Chinese companies, not least because of their highly competitive prices: "Despite the often poor quality, we need to accept the Chinese companies," he told Nielsen. "They are always the cheapest and we don't have a lot of money." There are concerns about Chinese companies causing environmental degradation, making infrastructure projects of very poor quality, and taking local labor regulations too lightly by importing workers from China, paying local workers less than minimal wages, or mistreating them in other ways, but on the surface, Sino-Mozambican relations are flourishing (Robinson 2012; Macauhub.com 2016).

As Western journalists and researchers began focusing on China's growing presence in Africa around a decade ago, the country's growing political and economic clout in other parts of the globe largely first took place under the radar. Take, for instance, the belated Western realization of the Chinese engagement in Latin America (Strauss and Armony 2012) and in Eastern Europe and the Balkans (Góralczyk 2017), or, above all, in Asia, including Central and Inner Asia, where a "New Great Game" took off in the 1990s as China, Russia, the United States, and Turkey began competing for influence in the strategically important but politically volatile underbelly of the former Soviet Union (Kleveman 2003). With the geopolitical realignment between Russia and China centered around the Shanghai Cooperation Organization and other economic, political, and military collaborations between the two Eurasian powers, China expanded its domestic "Go West Strategy" (西部大开发) into the "Belt and Road Initiative" (一带一路). Also referred to as the "New Silk Road," the Belt and Road Initiative includes new land and sea routes linking China, Inner Asia, Russia, and Europe (Freeman and Thomson 2011; Campi 2014; Radchenko 2013; Yeh 2016; Grant 2018; *Economist* 2020). In this context China has invested heavily in infrastructure projects across the region, with dramatic effects on local livelihoods and security politics, not just in China's western (and politically unstable) provinces of Xinjiang and Tibet (Fischer 2014; Han and Paik 2017), but also in neighboring states like Kazakhstan (Reeves 2011), Pakistan (Menhas et al. 2019), and, indeed, Mongolia (Soni 2009, 2018).

Scarcely populated and rich in natural resources, Mongolia—or "Mine-golia" as Bulag (2009) famously dubbed it—was disproportionally affected by the surge in Chinese demand for energy and minerals between 2005 and 2012. As an article in the *Economist* (2012) on Mongolia's so-called "wolf-economy" (a term coined by then vice minister of finance, Ganhuyag Chuluun Hutagtin) prophesied, "Put together Mongolian supply and Chinese demand, . . and Mongolia will be rich beyond the wildest dream."[5] What began as mostly informal economic links in the early 1990s rapidly grew into substantial bilateral trade that reached a volume of US $661 million in 2004 and 3.6 billion in 2014 (Davaakhuu et al 2014). Over approximately the same period, Mongolia's GDP tripled in size from US $3.4 billion to 11.5 billion (Lahiri-Dutt and Dondov 2017). By 2003 "cumulative FDI inflows had exceeded the US $1 billion mark, an amount equaling Mongolia's nominal GDP" (Demerbag et al 2005, 353). Between 1990 and 2010 10,709 foreign companies invested in Mongolia, and over the same period China's share of FDI by value was 51 percent. At the peak of the Mongolian mining boom in 2011, GDP grew at a staggering rate of 17.3 percent, making it the world's fastest-growing economy and the darling of international institutions and commentators. Roughly half the foreign companies registered in Mongolia that year were Chinese, and in terms of both trade and cumulative foreign investment, China trumps any other country in the Mongolian context.[6] Most of the Chinese investments in Mongolia have gone into the country's fast-growing mining sector (see chapter 2), but there have also been substantial investments in oil extraction (chapter 3), just as a wide range of smaller and medium-sized Chinese companies have been engaged in construction, trade, catering, and agriculture (chapter 1).[7]

Whereas Nielsen's Mozambican interlocutors were sometimes intrigued and on rare occasions even positive about the growing Chinese presence, Mongolian responses towards the Chinese engagement in their country since 1990 have been overwhelmingly negative, if not downright vitriolic, spurred by pervasive and deeply held fears of a Chinese economic, cultural, and territorial takeover (Billé 2014; Campi 2017). As a taxi driver told Pedersen in 2011, "The Chinese are the new bosses. Everything goes to the south. We depend on them for all things. All our raw materials and all our metals are extracted and shipped to the south. We are going to become a Chinese colony, an economic colony." Or, in the words of a female teacher from eastern Mongolia in 2012, "Because China controlled Mongolia economically for many years in the past, Mongolians and Chinese are careful of each other and know each other's traditions very well. That's why Mongolians don't like Chinese. A two- or three-hundred-years'-long historical relationship has been absorbed into Mongolians' blood and flesh. We used to get many things from China and to use all things from China. We depended on China economically and financially. Now people are afraid of being dependent on them again."[8] Indeed, toxic combinations of resource nationalism and xenophobia (especially Sinophobia) have been on the rise since foreign investments in mining began picking up around 2005 (Jackson 2015a). Among the more spectacular instances encountered by Bunkenborg and Pedersen was the abduction by dissatisfied locals of a Chinese worker from an iron mine in Central Gobi province (apparently, they put the man inside a big sack and told his bosses that they would keep him there until their demands were met), and an incident from Inner Mongolia, much debated in the Mongolian press, where a Chinese manager drove his car into a mob of angry Mongolian coal miners and killed one of them in what he insisted was a desperate act of self-defense (see also chapter 2).

Small wonder then that Chinese investments (and China's geopolitical influence more generally) has been at the top of Mongolia's political and public agenda since the 1990s. Yet, as Jackson and Dear (2016, 348) note, "Interpreting Mongolian fears as xenophobic resource nationalism elides a centuries-long history of unequal economic relations with Chinese merchants, and more directly, mining's connection to Chinese state-building in the early twentieth century." Far from being a new phenomenon, Mongolian Sinophobia is inflected by a long history: China was first ruled by Mongolian conquerors during the Yuan dynasty (1279–1368) and Mongolia was later incorporated into the Qing empire (1644–1911) (Bawden 1989; Di Cosmo 2010; Elverskog 2006). More recently, the increasingly repressive Chinese rule over Inner Mongolia and Mongolian minorities in other Chinese provinces (Bulag 1998), memories of economic domination during the Qing dynasty (Bawden 1989; Delaplace 2012), and vestiges of anti-Chinese sentiment whipped up by the Mongolian government during the Sino-Soviet conflict from 1960 to 1989, have made China a primary concern in Mongolian foreign policy from 1990 onwards (Campi 2004) and a highly contentious issue in current public debate and political life (Billé 2014). Much as with the case of Mozambique in Africa, then, Mongolia is an ideal test ground for an ethnographic study of Chinese political-economic engagements in Asia.

Studying Global China Ethnographically: The Dual Perspective Approach

Studying China's global expansion poses considerable challenges. How to go about designing and conducting an empirical ethnographic investigation of something as big and complex as globalizing China? How to anthropologically carry out and compare multiple ethnographic case studies from not just diverse locations and countries, but even continents? To address these questions, two things are needed. First, we need to identify a battery of concepts that are both precise and yet sufficiently open-ended to capture the diverse practices and encounters witnessed by us in Mozambique and Mongolia. Even more crucially, we need to engage head-on with a methodological and epistemological problem that anthropology shares with other disciplines that rely on qualitative data and methods, namely the question of how to conduct a proper comparison when there are no fixed scales and no objective external positions from which to compare. To tackle these questions, from the onset of the project in 2008 we developed the "Dual Perspective Approach" (DPA).

As a general blueprint for comparative and collaborative ethnographic research, the DPA was devised to allow for the planning, execution, and alignment of several individual fieldwork projects along an internal (intra-case) as well as an external (inter-case) comparative axis. As illustrated in figure 0.2, the DPA was meant to facilitate (1) an ethnographic study of Chinese infrastructure and resource projects in Mozambique from a "local" perspective, (2) a second study of similar Chinese interventions in Mongolia, also as seen from a "local" perspective, and (3) an ethnographic study at the same field sites in Mozambique and Mongolia, but from the "global" vantage of Chinese interlocutors. The DPA thus had a two-fold collaborative aspiration. Not only did it involve conducting ethnographic fieldwork in pairs (Bunkenborg and Nielsen in Mozambique, and Bunkenborg and Pedersen in Mongolia), it also entailed a collaboration among all three of us in the comparative analysis of this data. (To ensure that each of us gained basic knowledge of all the field sites, Pedersen visited Bunkenborg and Nielsen in Mozambique in 2011, just as Nielsen traveled to Mongolia and China with Bunkenborg and Pedersen in 2012.)

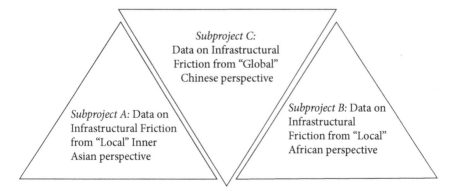

Subproject C:
Data on Infrastructural
Friction from "Global"
Chinese perspective

Subproject A: Data on
Infrastructural Friction
from "Local" Inner
Asian perspective

Subproject B: Data on
Infrastructural
Friction from "Local"
African perspective

FIGURE 0.2. The DPA design (photo taken from our 2008 application to the Danish Council for Social Science Research).

FIGURE 0.3.   Bunkenborg greeting Chinese mine manager, Central Gobi, Mongolia. August 2010.

The ambition behind the DPA, then, was to study and compare selected ethnographic sites as local variations of one global phenomenon. By doing joint ethnographic fieldwork in Mongolia and Mozambique, our objective was not only to gain insights about a number of particular Sino-local engagements in two countries and continents, but also, through comparison of these specific cases, to infer something more general about Chinese globalization that on a broader scale might also allow for comparison with other empires, past or present. Not surprisingly, things did not turn out exactly as planned. Yet, as we shall now show, our concerted attempt to deploy the (we knew from the start, overly) formalized DPA framework turned out to be obstructive and productive in equal measure. The DPA heuristic ended up providing a range of analytical opportunities that in retrospect are difficult to distinguish from the disadvantages. The two turned out to amplify one another, so that the methodological, epistemological, and ethical obstacles we encountered in implementing the DPA came to function as drivers in our ensuing analysis.

From the moment we first came up with the DPA design, we knew that, with its switches between different scales of enquiry—sites, cases, regions countries, and empires—it harked back to an old and, according to many contemporary anthropologists, obsolete model of anthropological knowledge production, where comparison is imagined to involve a process of zooming out from the specific to the general via ascending orders of abstraction, complexity, and generalization

(Kapferer 1989; Wastell 2001; Detienne 2008; Candea 2018). Dating back to the method of cross-cultural comparison developed by Radcliffe-Brown and other British social anthropologists during the first half of the twentieth century (Stocking 1995), comparison here is understood to take place between "substantive differences of content, framed by a formal similarity . . . undertaken either by the same ethnographer, or at least by trusted fellow members of an epistemic community which shares a set of methods as well as clearly formulated categories and research problems" (Candea 2015, 6). In many ways, the DPA reflected an equally positivistic ideal. Its three neatly arranged triangles not only promised identical objects of study and similar data, the triangles also indicated that the collection of these data sets and their subsequent analysis would not overlap. Of course, we were aware that the DPA's promises of fixed axes of comparison and self-similar data sets were hardly realizable, not just in terms of making the data obtained in different languages commensurable, but also in terms of making our case studies sufficiently symmetrical to allow for a controlled comparison. Still, we did imagine that some sort of integration was going to happen subsequent to our individual fieldwork: Once the subprojects had yielded three discrete and commensurable data sets, these were to be pooled into a larger data set which, that, or so the logic went, would amount to a shared pool of comparative data three times the size of each individual set.

Alas, our attempt to realize the DPA model gave rise to numerous methodological, epistemological, and (as we shall see below) ethical problems. Our first challenge was to find ethnographic cases that were characterized by "substantive differences of content, framed by a formal similarity" (Candea 2015). We soon discovered that identifying such "formally similar" cases across different settings in the same country, let alone between two countries or continents, was well-nigh impossible. It is one thing to identify a Chinese road construction project in Mozambique (chapter 4) and another one in Mongolia (chapter 3), or two Chinese resource extraction projects in these countries (chapters 2 and 5), as well as securing access to and rapport with key local gatekeepers and Chinese stakeholders, all of which we managed to do. It is quite another thing to uphold any viable reason why, simply by virtue of a "formal similarity," the study of these cases would in any meaningful sense amount to a comparison *of the same thing* (Strathern 2004; Holbraad and Pedersen 2017). Consider, for instance, the case of the ENI highway. Here, what had initially appeared as a single object of investigation to be studied by combining two ethnographic views on it slowly disintegrated into disparate parts as Nielsen and Bunkenborg's joint fieldwork progressed. Eventually, the only thing left for the two anthropologists to agree upon, after having spent time with their respective interlocutors, was that the "road project" at hand was not really about making a road at all. For Nielsen and his Mozambican interlocutors, the road was a piece of Chinese junk associated with dodgy economic practices and dubious moralities; for Bunkenborg and his Chinese informants, it was primarily a training ground and thus a means to a different end. As a result of these diverse perceptions, it proved almost impossible for Nielsen and Bunkenborg to work out a coherent ethnographic account—let alone a shared interpretation of their supposedly common object of study.

This turned out to be an unforeseen but extremely frequent consequence of the DPA design. Our ambition with this approach had been to bring together our jointly produced ethnographic data from different fieldwork sites so as to produce comparatively induced generalizations. Yet, in our eagerness to implement this comparative design we had ignored that doing so required an exterior vantage point from which to make these generalizations. In practice, doing fieldwork in pairs (and on two occasions, all three of us together) involved an array of overlapping collaborative activities, ranging from joint interviews with key informants and gatekeepers to the quotidian business of getting to places. Whenever we had the chance—in hotel rooms, en route to field sites, in bars, cafes, restaurants, and airports—and even while interviewing people—we would engage in intense discussions about our data and interpretations. Upon leaving joint visits to field sites in Mozambique, such as a Chinese logging compound (chapter 5), Nielsen and Bunkenborg would embark on prolonged but unsuccessful attempts

FIGURE 0.4.   Pedersen with Mongolian herders, Dornod Province, Mongolia. August 2010.

toward mutual exegesis of shared data sets so that for hours and sometimes days heated discussions or even shouting matches would ensue without the two of them being able to reach common ground. Similarly, in the course of their joint fieldwork in Mongolia, Pedersen and Bunkenborg also learned the hard way that what they had initially assumed would amount to straightforward data collection (such as a visit to a nomad's yurt inhabited by Chinese workers, chapter 2) became the starting point for profound epistemic divergence and conflicts of interpretation. Indeed, there is still much data for which we have not managed to reach a common understanding!

The lesson from these experiences of comparative failure is deeply disturbing for anyone clinging to the hope that ethnographic research can produce objective knowledge and generalizable findings in the ordinary naturalistic/positivistic sense. We gradually came to realize that the distinction between our project-internal relations as researchers and the project-external relations between Chinese and Mozambicans/Mongolians became increasingly muddled. Soon after embarking upon our two joint fieldwork projects in Mozambique and Mongolia, we realized that the ambition of maintaining a workable distance between individual subprojects was not only impossible but also counterproductive. As we gradually came to realize, however, this collapse of the DPA model was not a bad thing for our research, but a new opening in terms of achieving our goals. As our project progressed it gradually dawned upon us that our object of study was comprised of collaborative damage *in a double sense*. That is, we realized that our own internal disagreements were manifestations of the same tensions between Chinese and locals. Perhaps, we started asking ourselves, by taking our own failure to collaborate as ethnographically seriously as theirs, a new method and style of comparative anthropology might be laid bare—a radically experimental mode of reflexive ethnographic description and analysis that would allow teams of anthropologists to systematically examine their own discordances as *part of* the object of study. As such, it is the sum total of our interlocutors' disparate perspectives on Chinese globalization processes *and* our own equally divergent interpretations of this data that define the true object of investigation of this book. And it is just this hyperreflexive mode of inquiry, whereby a certain object of study fuses with the people who study it into a single analytical reality, that we denote as "collaborative damage."

To return to the question posed earlier, it *was* indeed possible to study ethnographically something as "big" as globalizing China, but only as long as one accepts that this object of study was present within our team all the time. It was *because*, and not in spite, of its positivist aspirations, that the DPA design facilitated a data set, where method, theory, and context were irrevocably intertwined. And it was *because* we stubbornly sought to structure our comparative collaborative efforts around a tripartite structure of separate fieldwork projects imagined to intersect only along their edges that we discovered a crucial analytical possibility at the heart of our joint research, namely that our own internal disagreements and misunderstandings were points of departure for new anthropological insights and forms of comparative analysis, as opposed to being merely unwanted aberrations best ignored and eradicated.

Theorizing Globalizing China: Empires, Enclaves, and Intimate Distances

As the constraining but also reassuringly rigid DPA framework gradually began collapsing, we found ourselves facing a considerable conceptual challenge: We were beginning to see the advantages of eliminating the analytical distance between our object of research and ourselves as researchers, but it was still unclear to us how to theorize the new ethnographic reality taking shape in the debris of the collapsed DPA edifice. Below, we recount the process by which we came to formulate a new conceptual apparatus and analytical framework.

Empire

Popular attempts to make sense of China's new role in the world often include comparisons to empires and colonies of the past. Western journalistic accounts of China in Africa have thus tended to invoke past European empires, hinting at the sinister colonial intentions that must lie behind the growing Chinese engagement in the continent: "In Africa it is as if the era of 19th century imperial expansion is happening all over again—but this time the freebies and open check books have replaced glass beads and pith helmets," as one *Guardian* article reporting on the 2006 FOCAC summit in Beijing concluded. In *China's Second Continent: How a Million Migrants are Building a new Empire in Africa*, Howard French (2014, 170) furthermore describes the "higgledy-piggledy cobbling together of a new Chinese realm of interest. Here were the beginnings of a new empire, a haphazard empire perhaps, but an empire nevertheless." Amid growing fears that the world was witnessing the rise of a new superpower, and for the first time (but as we now know, by no means the last) since Fukuyama foretold the end of history in 1989, mainstream Western media in the years after the financial crisis from 2008–2009 began expressing serious doubts about liberal democracy and free-market capitalism as the inevitable order of things. Autocracy and state capitalism seemed to be the winning hand, so what remained to be debated was not so much if US hegemony would come to an end, but when "the Chinese century" was set to begin and what sort of polity China would become on its way to global dominance.

Due probably to an understandable aversion among anthropologists and other critical social scientists to make essentialist claims, few Western scholars have wanted to take seriously the question of whether China is now about to become an empire again. To be sure, the totality of Sino-Mongolian and Sino-Mozambican engagements is unlikely to be the result of a colonial master plan drawn up by the Chinese Communist Party. On the other hand, it is equally oversimplified to reduce China's political-economic interventions abroad to mercenary attempts to strike deals "with no strings attached." Indeed, historically, Chinese empires have always justified their existence as a model of civilization held up to peoples on its edges (Wang 2006). Similar ideas can be found among contemporary Chinese political philosophers. For Zhao Tingyang (2006, 29) from the Chinese Academy of Sciences, the meaning and usefulness of the concept of empire has been "distorted" by the Western powers, who have been responsible "for the most terrible wars recorded in history." What is needed instead, he suggests, is to "introduce the Chinese traditional conception of world governance . . . to rethink the best Idea of an acceptable empire." The conception he has in mind is, perhaps not surprisingly, the Chinese "All-under-Heaven" (天下 tianxia), which, Zhao Tingyang (2006, 30) writes, "distinguishes itself from the pattern of the traditional military empire, for instance the Roman Empire, or that of an imperialist nation/state, for example the British Empire. The conceptually defined Empire of All-under-Heaven does *not* mean a country at all but . . . is a deep concept of the world, defined by the trinity of the geographical, psychological, and political worlds." Indeed, "whilst not even the strongest empires have controlled the entire world, it is not difficult to conceive of the world controlled by a conceptual empire" (2006, 31).

It is easy to dismiss such essentializing "Sino-speak," which uses ideas of the past to make teleological inferences about China's "natural" path to world rule (Callahan 2004). Yet, from the onset of our research, we have operated with the premise that the concept of empire would have an important role to play in our comparative study of Chinese globalization. After all, as is well known and has been well documented, the real-world effects of concepts are hardly predicated upon their historical accuracy. Indeed, as we see in the chapters to come, many Chinese abroad think of themselves and their public or private employers as bearers of civilizing, moral, and cultural ideas, and not as brute instruments of late-capitalist economic exploitation and resource extraction. According to Zhao Tingyang, one needs to distinguish between "conceptual empires," which he associates with past, present, and future Chinese polities, and "colonial empires," which in his view have been characteristic of the West. For Zhao Tingyang, one important way in which these two imperial modes differ is the higher degree of openness to and acceptance of irreducible otherness in the Chinese "All-under-Heaven." As Zhao Tingyang (2006, 31) summarizes his argument, "To see the world from its world-ness is different from seeing it from part of it."[9] Thus one perhaps may indeed speak of a "yellow man's burden" (Nyíri 2006), akin to the complex and often contradictory political imaginations that grew out of prerevolutionary Chinese imperial expansions in its southeast and Inner Asian fringes (Perdue 2006; Bulag 2010; Gladney 2004; Fiskesjö 2006).

Recent scholarship about empire has by no means been restricted to the case of China alone. The controversial British historian Niall Ferguson (2003), for example, has sparked heated discussions about European colonialism following his claims that the British Empire was, on balance, rather benign and that it was established not as the result of an imperial master plan, but rather as a largely unintended outcome of early capitalist adventures in Southern Africa. Writing from a more philosophical and, in political terms, very different perspective, Michael Hardt and Antonio Negri (2000, xii) have theorized the fundamental nature of late capitalism as made up of "rhizomic" imperial forms, which, unlike the state-controlled empires of the past, "establish no territorial center of power and do not rely on fixed boundaries or barriers" (see also Harvey 2005). Finally, coming from a more anthropological angle, Kathrine Lutz (2006) has argued that, like all other global forms, the contemporary "American empire" can only be studied "in the details." What all these and numerous other recent theorizations of empire (e.g., Cooper and Stoler 1989; Comaroff 1989; Smith, 2003; Bacevich 2002) agree about, however, is that imperial effects are not always predicated upon imperial intentions.

Thus, while it is important to investigate and to understand what different Chinese agents in China and abroad want their infrastructure and resource-extraction projects in the Global South to accomplish, what their local counterparts want these projects to do, and what they want to do with them, is quite another question. In keeping with social and political-scientific research on the "unintended effects" of state modernization schemes (Flyvbjerg 1999; Scott 1998; Murray Li 2007; 2014), we have from the onset of this project operated under the premise that China's interventions abroad cannot be analyzed by looking for linear links between plans and their degree of realization. Instead, we have conceived of them as inherently nonlinear processes, along the lines of what Anna Tsing has called "global friction" (2005). In particular, we have taken inspiration from Tsing's suggestion that the relationships between people who are more or less randomly coupled together from such transnational economic flows take the form of "productive misunderstandings," that give rise to volatile and frequently paradoxical assemblages of persons, things, and ideas. Far from representing the execution of sinister neocolonial blueprints cooked up in secret by

Beijing mandarins, then, the Sino-local encounters studied by us in Mozambique and Mongolia should be understood as "zones of awkward engagement," (2005, xi) where China's global economic and political aspirations intersect with local African and Asian lifeways as portents of a potential empire to be—an "imperial potentiality" if you like.

While the concept of empire takes us some of the way toward formulating a viable analytical language, we are not quite there. For even if globalizing China can be studied as an emerging empire, we still need to figure out how to analyze and theorize the distinct social and material forms of this global assemblage (Ong and Collier 2005). Over the next pages, we turn to anthropological and political-scientific work on zoning technologies in China and economic enclaves in Africa and elsewhere in the Global South. In doing so, we recount our attempt to translate the still rather abstract and generic concept of "imperial potentialities" into a more empirically applicable conceptual framework that can be implemented with data from specific settings to capture the concrete social and material forms by which Chinese agents abroad adapt to local imponderabilia and the wider dynamics of late capitalism.

Enclaves

One striking pattern that we observed across many sites ranging from guarded Chinese-owned shoe shops in downtown Maputo (chapter 5) to Mongolian yurts inhabited by Chinese mining workers (chapter 2) was the marked discontinuity between the outside and the inside, and between the external and the internal. As Pedersen remarked to Bunkenborg when the two ethnographers had been invited to spend the night in an air-conditioned container belonging to a Chinese oil field in the remote grasslands of far-eastern Mongolia: "Hmm, these people might want to put some windows and fresh air into these containers. . . . Perhaps that would make the Chinese notice that there are actually people living here in these lands." Yet, a Chinese worker's explanation to Bunkenborg that he had brought with him from China the precise amount of clothing, dental supplies, soap, and shampoo that he needed for a two-year stint in Mozambique and that he, by the way, hardly ever left the construction ground for fear of robbers suggested that these self-contained worlds were the result of deliberate attempts by the Chinese to separate themselves from the local context. Another sign of this "labor of division" (Pedersen 2017) were the numerous gardens set up by the Chinese in some of the most unlikely locations on the planet, such as the Gobi Desert (chapters 2 and 3). While these gardens in some cases served a concrete practical purpose, such as growing vegetables that could not be procured locally, it became clear that the importance attached to them by the Chinese reflected affects and logics that far exceeded their rational utility.

What these and many other similar instances suggested was that there was something distinct about the sites inhabited by Chinese nationals in Mongolia and Mozambique, something experienced as a claustrophobic stuffiness by Pedersen; as a cozy homeliness by Bunkenborg; and as a fundamentally alien way of being social by Nielsen. The question was what concept might best capture this characteristic ambiance and the associated spectrum of repulsion and attraction. How to theorize, in other words, the peculiar—and seemingly purposeful—insularity of these strange spaces? For a while, "container civilization" seemed to represent one good candidate for capturing the ambience of these sites as something simultaneously cozy, claustrophobic, and alien. Perhaps, we thought, the image of "the container" might allow for a theorization of Chinese globalization as a constellation of modular logics and units ready to be combined into whole cities or empires, while being capable of staying self-sufficient and self-contained in the most inhospitable and hostile surroundings (see also Haugen 2019). However, as our fieldwork progressed, it became clear that the characteristically insular quality of Chinese lifeways in Mozambique and Mongolia was manifest also in the absence of containers: It was there at walled construction sites in both countries, in gated compounds and guarded shops in downtown Maputo, and within refitted nomads' yurts in the Mongolian countryside. Clearly, what was going on was more than the carving out of container-sized pieces of China that were then set down in foreign sites and lands.

Eventually, we settled on the concept of the "enclave." In traditional sociological usage, this term has been used to denote geographical areas with a distinct cultural identity and a loosely integrated economy (Blandy 2006; Caldeira 2000; Low 2003). Essentially this is also how the concept has been used to describe urban zones of socioeconomic segregation in post-Maoist China, including gated communities as well as past and present Chinese living arrangements in "China-towns" and other sites of "self-segregation" within China and abroad (Wissink et al. 2012; Yan, Sautman, and Lu 2019; Zhang 2001; Zhou, M. 1992). As several scholars have pointed out (Thunø 2007; Wong and Tan 2013), the stereotypical notion of the China-town enclave captures the detachment from local culture and context often associated with transnational Chinese communities, both by the Chinese themselves and by local residents. Indeed, it is worth noting here that the Chinese term for enclave (飞地) may literally be translated as "flying land," a phrase that seems to communicate an almost magical disconnection, where the enclave hovers above a local terrain without touching it. Along with this image, in this book we use the concept to denote the social and material infrastructures that encompass and contain Chinese corporations and communities in ways that detach them from their surroundings (see also Ferguson, J. 2005). While similar patterns can also be found at construction sites inside mainland China (Swider 2015), it seems to us that the concept of the enclave provides a particularly apt way of theorizing the peculiarly self-contained quality and insular ambiance of Chinese projects in Mongolia, Mozambique, and other sites around the world. This is not just because it allows us to understand the export beyond China's borders of certain logics of late-communist authoritarian statecraft in post-Mao reform China. It is also because the enclave is emblematic of a general mode of late capitalist transnational extraction through corporate zones beyond sovereign control.

We are here reminded of Aihwa Ong's work on governmentality in China (2004, 2006). Particular interesting for our present purposes is her suggestion that the post-Mao Chinese state purposefully created "spaces of political and economic exception" within and around China, not only in the form of special economic zones that were meant to take the lead in the transformation from socialism to capitalism during the early years of reform, but also in the formation of special autonomous regions such as Hong Kong and Macau. "Zoning technologies," she writes, "provide the mechanisms for creating or accommodating islands of distinct governing regimes within the broader landscape of normalized rule, thus generating a pattern of variegated but linked sovereignty" (Ong 2004, 75). To be sure, descriptions like these call to mind what we have witnessed in Africa and Inner Asia. But Ong restricts her discussion to China only. This is somewhat odd, given that Ong herself makes clear that these forms of dominance can be traced back to Western colonial habits of setting up special treaty ports and customs areas in subjugated lands. We suggest that Chinese enterprises have exported and implemented these technologies of zoning to overseas territories in recent decades.

Several social and political scientists have written about extractive enclaves as a new modality of global capitalism. James Ferguson (2006, 2005), for example, has argued that foreign companies engaged in resource extraction in Africa carve out profit-generating zones, where they can operate with little concern for local communities or these countries as a whole: "Enclaves . . . are secured, policed, and, in a minimal sense, governed through private or semiprivate means. These enclaves are increasingly linked up, not in a continuous, territorial national grid, but in transnational networks that link dispersed spaces in a selective, point-to-point fashion." Writing about Chinese engagement in Angola, Albert Bergesen (2008) has coined the term "surgical colonialism" to capture the process of "resource extraction by a foreign power that involves a minimum of local disruption," suggesting that state-owned enterprises are at the forefront of these developments. A hypothetical sales pitch for such a project, Bergesen (2008, 7) wittily speculates, might go like this: "For the first time the exploiter will exploit himself, and further, to make sure there is no mess or social disruption made in getting the oil, copper, gold, diamonds, iron, and uranium we need, we will build—below cost—and completely finance, manage, and use our own labor (and even our own cement) to build hospitals, schools, sports stadiums, rail lines, highways, apartment buildings, government buildings. In short this is a neo-colonial extraction process that is purely surgical in nature. You won't even know we are there."

What we take from this discussion of the intersection between late-modern enclave capitalism and Chinese technologies of zoning is the image of a discontinuous patchwork, distributed across not just the Global South but also the so-called West, of differentially administered enclaves run by private companies, sometimes in collaboration with the Chinese state. There is no doubt that this aura of hyperinsulation can be recognized in many of the social and material forms encountered by us in Mongolia and Mozambique. Still, their many merits notwithstanding, desktop studies of China in Africa by political scientists such as Bergesen (2008; see also Alden 2007; Alden, Large, and Soares de Oliveira 2008; Asche 2008; French 2014; 2017; Kragelund 2012; Mohan 2013; Sautman and Yan 2007; Taylor 2006) are likely to overlook a great deal of complexity and specificity on the ground. Indeed, as the growing body of ethnographic studies of resource-extraction projects in the Global South makes amply clear, what was first intended as surgical interventions abroad by Western companies, always ends up becoming entangled with local social and cultural forms in highly unpredictable and sometimes deeply paradoxical ways. Consider Hannah Appel's work (2012a; 2012b). Based on fieldwork on offshore oil production in Equatorial Guinea, she has shown how US oil companies enforce their own rules, technologies, and labor regimes by systematically and deliberately distancing themselves from local norms and standards. Even offshore oil production requires an ongoing effort of disentanglement, Appel (2012a, 443) argues, citing Michael Callon (1998, 252): "Instead of regarding framing as something that happens of itself, and overflows as a kind of accident which must be put right, overflows are the rule and framing is a fragile, artificial result based on substantial investments . . . required to produce the effect of the separation itself."

And yet, the case of Chinese projects in Africa is even more complicated. As Giles Mohan (2013, 1265) has pointed out, "Much of the discussion of Chinese enclaves [has been] based on the activities of [State Owned Enterprises] that have some connections to the Chinese state. However, . . . a sizable majority [of Chinese firms in Africa] are privately owned and often quite small." "To what extent," he asks, "does the enclave model apply to these?" (1266). Clearly, Mohan is making an extremely important point when he calls for more empirical studies of concrete Chinese interventions in Africa that seek to "go beyond the enclave model." For what happens to the meaning of the concept of the enclave when it cannot be traced back to a master plan devised by Beijing mandarins, but rather seems to be the result of ongoing struggles to muddle through by scattered individuals and groups of freewheeling Chinese entrepreneurs and investors who are equipped with neither the capacity nor the desire to impose any "elevated control" or "surgical colonialism" over local people and communities? Could it be that the Chinese enclaves studied by us in Africa and Asia are not so much causes, but to a higher degree *effects*, of specific histories of failed Sino-local collaborations? If so, the insular ambience of these sites are less to be considered as loyal instantiations of a single and coercive imperial strategy than as momentary stabilizations of awkward encounters between people who remain largely incomprehensible to each other.

In our take on enclaves, then, we follow Appel (and actor-network-theorists like Callon) in focusing on the constant social and material boundary work that needs to be put into the production and reproduction of Chinese enclaves as specific stabilizations of economic networks, infrastructures and other sociotechnical components and dynamics. Still, while the materiality of walls, gates, and other technologies of enclaving are clearly important to take into account, the above story of the Chinese road worker running into the bush to avoid an inquisitive auto mechanic is a reminder that there is much more to enclaving than the separation of groups of actors into outsiders and insiders. We need, to an even greater extent than the existing scholarship on enclaves in Africa and elsewhere, an analytical vocabulary that will allow us to take seriously how diverse human and nonhuman agents, ranging from state cadres to day laborers, and from state-of-the-art infrastructures to forest spirits, partake in the making and unmaking of the social and material worlds under investigation.

Intimate Distances

"I just don't get it," sighed Mr. Wang, the manager of a Chinese fluorspar mine in the Gobi Desert. Slipping into a pair of Mickey Mouse slippers, he continued: "The Mongolians don't think ahead like we Chinese do. When they get their wages they disappear for days, get into drunken brawls, and only return when they have spent all their money on vodka. We try to be fair: they are provided with food and lodging, and we have built a proper dormitory for them, whereas we live in simple nomadic tents! But they are so ungrateful and childish!" Meters away from Mr. Wang in the same makeshift canteen situated in a refitted nomads' yurt sat two Mongolian workers. Displaying no outward interest in what their boss was saying to the Chinese-speaking foreigner (Bunkenborg), they turned to his Mongolian-speaking peer (Pedersen) and confided, "Look at those Chinks (*hujaa*). Some of them have stayed here for years, but they still haven't learned to eat our food or to speak our language. They are just eating stinking soups all day, flicking ash at the sacred fire, without showing respect for custom."

As this story illustrates, one of the most striking patterns that emerged from our joint fieldworks was the fact that Chinese and locals spent days, months, and sometimes even years working side by side, unable or unwilling to speak with one another. Perhaps as a substitute for this lack of connection and comprehension, certain material objects, ranging from the refitted nomadic yurts inhabited by the Chinese (chapter 2) to the envelopes with cash handed from Chinese bosses to Mozambican workers (chapter 4), seemed to assume a great deal of importance in the management of these relationships, tying people together while also keeping them apart. To our surprise, many Chinese and local people involved in such relationships seemed happy about this state of affairs, to a point where both of the two "sides" (as they often referred to themselves) seemed to make an effort to stay maximally—or could we say optimally—disconnected. To further add to our confusion, there were often profound disagreements between (and among) the two sides about what it meant to be (dis)connected in the first place.

But what kinds of connections do these relationships articulate—insofar as it makes sense to call this minimal sociality "a connection" in the first place? In order to unpack and answer this vital question, we need to delve into some of the ideas associated with the so-called relational or ontological turn in anthropology (Strathern 2020; Holbraad and Pedersen 2017). Over the last decade, some anthropologists have questioned the tacit assumption held by many social scientists that the more connections there are, the better—that is, the widespread, but seldom substantiated assumption that connections are somehow inherently good things, whereas disconnections are inherently bad things, in both a sociological, a psychological, and an ethical sense (see Pedersen 2013; Candea et al. 2015; Nielsen 2010). Partly overlapping with this "fetish of connectivity" (Pedersen 2013) among social scientists is an equally common and equally unsubstantiated tendency to confuse the concept of "the relation" with the concept of "the connection" as if the two concepts denoted the same thing and belonged to the same level of abstraction (Pedersen 2012; Nielsen 2012a).[10] Indeed one of the central ethnographic-cum-theoretical lessons from the relational or ontological turn in anthropology is that cutting connections does not necessarily involve a reduction of relationality. On the contrary, there are peoples in the world for whom it is of utmost moral, political, and cosmological importance to produce and reproduce social and material relations of "engaged separation" (Stasch 2003, 325) .

These discussions have far-reaching implications for our present purposes. Once we understand that the degree of relationality and indeed of sociality is not always a function of the degree of connection and proximity between actors, we have come a good way toward identifying a method for theorizing the oddly detached quality of Sino-local relationships. At least in the case of Chinese engagements in Mozambique and Mongolia, these relationships seem to be driven by a widespread and unabashed desire for maintaining a minimal degree of connection. Yet, we are still left with the tricky question of how to conceive of these relations in more concrete terms: exactly how are we to characterize them, and what are we to call them?

One good candidate is Matei Candea's concept of "inter-patience" (2010). Based on fieldwork among field primatologists studying meerkats in the Kalahari Desert, Candea points out that the "central theoretical question raised by the recent focus on social relations between species is, in effect, what counts as a social relationship and who can participate?" (243). In a formulation uncanny in its resemblance to our own attempts to verbalize our fieldwork experiences from Mozambique and Mongolia, Candea argues that "maintaining proper distance is a project that meerkats and scientists have in common" (246). Suspended between the perceived warmth of connection and the coldness of its absence is a distinct relation characterized by a "mutual suspension of action, a ceasefire of sorts" between the agents involved that therefore prompts an "extension of the meaning of relationship beyond intersubjectivity, and even beyond interaction" (249). It is this quality of certain interspecies relationships that Candea coins "inter-patience."

Like other recent attempts to capture and convey the nature of irreducible ambivalent relationships that straddle and conjoin mutually opposing forces and affects (such as Singh (2011) on "agonistic intimacies" in Rajasthan and Segal (2016) on "ambivalent attachments" in Palestine), Candea's concept of inter-patience seems to provide us with a path toward theorizing the strangely detached or "hollow" relationships between many Chinese and local people in Mozambique and Mongolia. It is, of course, highly questionable whether it is epistemologically (not to say, ethically) viable to directly compare human-meerkat relations in Africa with Sino-local ones. Even if the relationships encountered by the three us in the field might look those studied by Candea, it makes for a fundamentally different ethnographic situation that these are relations among individual human beings with thoughts, desires, and agendas (that they, to the extent that they wished do so and their respondents understood them, could communicate and share, not just within and between these two sides, but also with us). Furthermore, while it may be accurate to say that the only thing all almost our interlocutors agreed about was the importance of "maintaining proper distance" (cf. Candea 2010), this did not imply that they were in agreement about what the term meant, or how to do so. On the contrary, both within groups of Chinese, Mozambicans, and Mongolians, and to an even greater extent between them, there was vast disagreement about what might constitute and how to maintain relationships of distance as well as of proximity.

Rupert Stasch has also been at the very forefront of recent anthropological attempts to theorize relationships of detachment and distance. Like Candea, Stasch's (2009) explorations of social relations are motivated by a lacuna that he identifies in the existing anthropological scholarship with respect to the "question . . . of what a particular relation of otherness actually is, as a relation of *otherness*. How is it built? Of what does it consist?" (14). Based on fieldwork in West Papua, Stasch argues that any given relation—say, a marriage—in this ethnographic context is best conceived as "a kind of edge at the meeting point of multiple other relational states" (18) and is "less an assumed unit than a ratcheting into tensility of a problem of connection-and-disconnection" (73). In fact, Stasch goes as far as suggesting that uncertainty is so ingrained in all relationships at his field site that, in any given situation, "two persons do not know where they stand with each other" (18).

Stash's ideas offer a potential analytical vantage point from which to conceptualize the fraught relations between Chinese and locals in our field sites—as well as the often equally tense relationships among the three of us as a research team. For our Chinese, Mozambican, and Mongolians interlocutors as much as for the three of us, many of the relationships that came into being as a result of the more or less failed efforts to collaborate were experienced like "systematic mismatches of closeness and strangeness" (21), which neither they nor we were able to predict beforehand. The only thing certain was that each collaboration would inevitably involve new "relations of otherness," whose awkwardness and tensions would vary in degree and intensity depending on the concrete encounter, but would never reach zero.

Still, there are two senses in which our ethnography is not fully captured by Stasch's sophisticated analytical framework. The first sense is empirical. Unlike the cases described by Stasch, the Sino-local relations of otherness investigated by us were deeply asymmetrical in several senses. For example, there was a strong degree of inequality and hegemony at play between the Chinese employers at the above mentioned road construction site near Xai-Xai and their workforce of local Mozambicans. But we also detected a longing among some Chinese interlocutors to be friends with their Mozambican and Mongolian collaborators. Alas, this desire was seldom reciprocated and so resulted in a form of "unrequited love" (see chapter 1). Of course, such asymmetries oscillating between attraction and repulsion are common in colonial contexts, whether in the case of the Western imperial powers or past Chinese ones (see also chapter 1). But the lesson we take with us here is a more general one, namely the fact that an irreducible asymmetry was at play in the relations of otherness investigated by us in sub-Saharan Africa and Inner Asia. For while our Chinese interlocutors and their Mozambican and Mongolians counterparts seemed to an equal extent to perceive one another as radically different and thus fundamentally unknowable, there was an unequal distribution of both intent and effort when it came to trying to overcome these perceived differences.

The second problem is theoretical. Notwithstanding Stasch's theoretical sophistication, the forms of detachment he discusses are posited as fulfilling a certain *function*, namely a "balancing out" of opposing social dynamics and affective states. From this perspective the social is imagined as a space in which heterogeneous forces are pitted against each other in a fight between detachment and intimacy, repulsion and attraction, understanding and ignorance. Yet, as several of the above ethnographic vignettes make clear, the relations of distantiation encountered by us cannot really be theorized as ways of mediating contrasting forces, but as sui generis relational forms that, far from performing any function within a purported social whole or cultural logic, are instead the basic building blocks of the social as such. Instead of relying on the functionalist logic of balancing acts between opposing but symmetrical agents and forces, as Stasch does, we need to treat the relationships at hand as intrinsically asymmetrical and inherently ambiguous forms, whose "tensility" (cf. Stasch 2009), so to speak, erupts from the inside out, and not, as with Candea and Stasch, from the outside in.

Recent postcolonial scholarship offers a possible way of solving both of these problems. As part of a broader attempt to rethink European colonialism from a critical feminist vantage, Ann Stoler (2002) has posited "intimacy" as a productive concept for bringing together seemingly separate arenas and scales of imperial life and imaginaries. As she explains of nineteenth- and twentieth-century English and French discourses about *métissage*, these "expressed . . . pervasive if inchoate dilemmas of colonial rule and a fundamental contradiction of imperial domination: the tension between a form of authority simultaneously predicated on incorporation and distancing . . . in an unstable and uneven set of discourses in which certain institutional authorities claimed priority of one over another in accordance with other authorities' attempts to designate how political boundaries were to be protected and assigned" (2002, 84). Stoler's concept of "imperial intimacies" provides just what we have been looking for: a way of theorizing how relations of otherness are perpetually suspended between the poles of proximity and distance, attachment and detachment, connection and disconnection, in a context of political and economic hegemony. For Stoler, it is the term's dual meaning of "'sexual relations' and 'familiarity'" that "locates intimacy so strategically in imperial politics" (9). Conversely, "intimacy" in our understanding does not only or even primarily refer to relations of sexual desire and their politics in various contexts, including post- or neocolonial ones (although, as we see in chapters 1 and 2, our ethnographic material also comprises examples of such relationships too). Indeed, we suggest that the postcolonial concept of imperial intimacy from Stoler and others may usefully be extended to encompass a more general power dynamic, namely the fact that many hegemonic relationships that are felt to be the most intimate are not necessarily those relations that are perceived to involve the highest degree of proximity. Instead, some of the most intense relations combine or transcend the binary between proximity and distance in optimal or "sublime" ways.

We use the term "intimate distances" to describe this quality of the Sino-local relationships at hand. Drawing on Stoler's work as well as on Michael Herzfeld's (2005) notion of "cultural intimacy" and on Elizabeth Povinelli's writings on "intimate events" (2006; see also 2016), we define as intimately distant those relations that cannot meaningfully be described as close, yet are infused with an intensity that equals and in some cases even surpasses what arises from connections of proximity. Neither denoting a binary between nor a unity of connection and disconnection, the concept of the intimately distant bespeaks a unique relational form: the permanent state of awkward suspense in which Chinese expats and their local collaborators are irreversibly trapped, as if caught in a global spider's net.[11] As such, the concept is meant to capture the totality of imperial relations that hover between the personal and the political, between attraction and repulsion, between curiosity and ignorance, and of which it is characteristic that gaps, chasms, and fissures are imbued with as much social efficacy—and as much moral virtue—as unisons, sympathies, and connections. In that sense the intimate distances that linked our interlocutors in paradoxical liaisons of mutual misrecognition emerge as the elementary building blocks of the social and material worlds studied by the three of us. They are the closest we can come to studying what globalizing China *is*—the totality of intimately distant relations that can be found in different Chinese enclaves across the globe, including the ones investigated by us.

The Politics and Ethics of Collaborative Damage

It is important to engage with one still outstanding issue before proceeding to the ethnographic chapters. We are referring to yet another problem pertaining to doing a collaborative study of Chinese globalization, namely the question of how to coauthor an anthropological monograph based on ethnographic data whose interpretation the authors do not agree about—an experiment that, as we shall now elaborate upon, has not only involved ongoing and challenging questions about how to conduct collaborative fieldwork and analysis, but also how to write a book about it. We have already on several occasions indicated that the challenges we faced in implementing the DPA were not just methodological and epistemological, but also ethical and political. On the one hand, these challenges pertain to the ways in which we have chosen to portray our own doings and sayings in the field, including our mutual disagreements and conflicts. But of even higher importance is the question of the potential ramifications of our decision to include and focus on our interlocutors' conflicts, tensions, and disagreements in our ethnographic account.

At the outset of the research project on which this book is based, what seemed worrying was not the potential for tensions between us as ethnographers but rather the many similarities among the three of us in terms of gender, age, educational background, class, and ethnicity. Being white middle-aged, male anthropologists from Denmark, we no doubt shared a particular perspective on the world that was simultaneously privileged and limited; if anyone could agree upon a shared interpretation of globalizing China, it was surely such a nondiverse team of ethnographers, or so we assumed. It was thus with some surprise that we gradually registered how some of the conflicts pertaining to our object of study were absorbed and reenacted within our own research team, and this prompted us to include our own positional divergences and biases as part of the ethnographic object studied.

FIGURE 0.5. Nielsen with Mozambican workers and "tree scouts," Pemba, Mozambique. May 2011.

Writing a book that included our own disagreements has been no simple task, and the first steps echoed our division of labor in the field. The three chapters on Chinese globalization in Mongolia and elsewhere in Inner Asia have been coauthored by Pedersen and Bunkenborg, while the following three chapters based on fieldwork in Mozambique have been written by Nielsen and Bunkenborg. More specifically, Bunkenborg drafted chapters 1 and 5, Pedersen chapters 2 and 3, and Nielsen chapters 4 and 6. In a long process during which all three of us discussed, rewrote, and edited the chapters several times, Pedersen revised chapter 1, just as Nielsen revised chapter 5, and Bunkenborg chapters 2, 3, 4, and 6. Furthermore, Nielsen and Pedersen read and commented on the three Mongolia and Mozambique chapters respectively. These details about the writing process are included here in the interest of transparency and explication of the research process, but the fact is that substantial parts of the book have been rewritten so many times that we cannot truthfully say that a single person authored them. Allowing authorial control to shift elusively between us this way strikes us as the form of writing and the style of presentation that best corresponds to the overarching methodological, analytical, epistemological, and ethical challenges that arise from conducting an anthropological comparison that does not have (or pretend to have) any neutral external vantage. Rather than engaging in speculation about the original author of a particular passage, we hope the reader will approach the text as if it were an instantiation of collaborative damage in its own right. Much as the crazy stripes on the road in Mozambique never led back to a single culprit but forward into a sociomaterial assemblage of misunderstandings and conflicts, this book does not reflect a singular authorial intention, but follows the emergence of disagreements and intimate distances between its three authors from the inside out.

With these general considerations in mind, we can now hone in on a number of interrelated questions that have consistently been on our minds during fieldwork and the subsequent writing process: How should a book like this be written, and why did we end up writing it in the way we did? What were, and are, the epistemological and ethical ramifications of our failure to agree about a common reading of our interlocutors' collaborations? In confronting these questions, we have been faced, in a rather specific and urgent sense, with many of the dilemmas that were originally identified by the so-called postmodern anthropologists, who were among the first to put the problem of "writing culture" on the disciplinary map (cf. Clifford 1983; 1986; 1988; Clifford and Marcus 1986; Marcus 1986; Marcus and Fischer 1986a; 1986b; Rabinow 1986). In keeping with their overarching ambition of bringing "anthropology forcefully into line with its twentieth century promises of authentically representing cultural differences and using this knowledge as a critical probe into our own ways of life and thought" (Marcus and Fischer 1986b, 42–43), this implied, among other things, destabilizing ethnographic authority by giving voice to new subjectivities and critical perspectives that had hitherto been suppressed by more or less tacit literary conventions of traditional ethnographic writing (Clifford 1986). Accordingly, these scholars began experimenting with different forms of "dialogue" and "polyphonic ethnography" as potentially productive ways of forging an "active communicative process with another culture" (30) in the ethnographic field and in the production of anthropological knowledge as a whole (see also Gottlieb 1995).

In the chapters that follow, we seek to heed the central lessons from this important moment in the maturation of anthropology as a professional discipline and as a community of scholars who are aware of and reflexive about the ethical, cultural, and political responsibilities and ramifications of not just what they write, but also how it is written. Yet, the particular way in which we will do so will differ quite substantially from other recent experiments with collaborative anthropological writing.[12] Rather than striking an explicitly normative (and one might say, moralizing) tone, we will instead pursue what might on the surface look like the opposite strategy. In keeping with the time-honored anthropological tradition of using one's own embarrassing mishaps in the field as a narrative ploy in the construction of ethnographic prose, we will make no effort to hide the personal biases from which some of our starkest practical and analytical disagreements arose. In concrete terms this means that when we recount an interview with a strongly anti-Chinese Mongolian journalist with a penchant for "fake news" (chapter 1), or when describing a violent encounter or even a racist attack involving a Chinese manager and a Mozambican foreman (chapter 6), we will not seek to downplay the degree to which Bunkenborg and Pedersen (in the first instance) and Nielsen and Bunkenborg (in the latter) in the heat of the moment and its aftermath took sides with their interlocutors, and more generally the groups (i.e., Mongolian, Mozambican, and Chinese) that the three ethnographers saw them as representing. On the contrary, in chronicling these and other instances of collaborative damage in the dual sense of the word discussed above, we seek to highlight—indeed, make a virtue of—our failure to always adhere to what many anthropologists would consider a professional obligation—the capacity to remain partly detached from, and thus reflexive and critical about, one's interlocutors' reflections and opinions about others and the world more generally.

Clearly this particular writing strategy (as all writing strategies in their specific ways) raises a number of ethical—and epistemological—challenges. First, due caution is necessary when the author(s) of an anthropological text makes the decision to include "naked portrayals of its interviewees" in the ethnography. Given the radically collaborative nature of our research design as well as our object of research, particular attention must be given to the acute challenge of working with the same interlocutors across several interconnected fieldwork

projects and, in particular, of ensuring that the politically, socially, and culturally fraught issues that we raise in our empirical analyses will have no negative
repercussions for them. Apart from the importance of abiding to the overarching
ethical and legal principles for good social science research practice, including
the European Data Protection Regulation (see Corsín Jiménez 2018) and other
EU-defined standards (European Commission 2018; Iphofen 2013), as well as
Danish national guidelines, several more specific ethical questions need to be
considered within the context of ethnographic research and data, especially
when, as in the present case, the topic of research is a subject of controversy and
potential conflict (American Anthropological Association 2009; Oates 2006; see
also Pels 2018). When it comes to the writing of this book, the urgency of these
questions has led to a systematic attempt to disguise and thus protect the identity
of our interlocutors by using pseudonyms and blurring or omitting references to
specific localities. In the few cases where this has not proved a possible strategy
(when, say, life histories or cases focusing on particular individuals are the basis
of whole chapters or parts of them), oral or verbal consent has been solicited
from the interlocutors at hand, just as we have carefully reflected upon whether
the individuals in question were in a position to sufficiently understand and fore-
see the potential consequences of revealing their identities.

The second set of ethical (and epistemological) questions arising from this
book's experimental style has less to do with protecting the privacy and the
safety of individual interlocutors and more to do with the way in which various categories of people are represented by us. For precisely how can one—and
indeed should one—write about collaborative damage in the double, recursive
meaning of this term proposed by us? What are the aesthetics—as well as the
ethics—of ethnographic writing when the overarching objective is to produce
and publish a jointly authored anthropological monograph with one overarching
argument, while at the same time remaining faithful to, and thus explicitly incor-
porating, our own recurrent failures to find mutual agreement in the interpretation of ethnographic data and encounters? As we hope will become progressively
clearer in the six chapters that follow, apart from raising a number of represen-
tational challenges, the way in which this book has been written also brings with
it a number of progressive ethical and epistemological possibilities when held up
against other experimental attempts to write anthropologically about comparison and collaboration. Indeed, we will go as far as suggesting in the conclusion
that this superficially naïve but actually highly controlled form of ethnographic
writing may point toward a viable way of "writing culture" in twenty-first century
anthropology.

FRIENDSHIP EMPIRE

How a Chinese Entrepreneur Failed to Make
Friends in Mongolia

The impressive display of agricultural technology looked like a peaceful invasion of Chinese agricultural machinery to Bunkenborg and Pedersen. Fifteen
brand-new tractors lined up on the Mongolian grassland, harvesters decked
out with festive, colored banners, and long-haul trucks loaded with Chinese
equipment. "Promote Sino-Mongolian Friendship," a red banner on one of the
trucks proclaimed in Chinese and Mongolian. Another banner, this one only in
Chinese, offered a convoluted explanation of the whole exercise: "Aid Mongolian grain production in response to the central government's call to realize the
developmental strategy of making agriculture go abroad." Despite the reference
to the Chinese central government, it was a private entrepreneur from Shandong
province, Mr. Jia, who was behind this martial deployment of productive forces.
A vivacious man in his late fifties, Mr. Jia had moved to Eastern Mongolia in 2007
to establish the amicable relations with local partners that he saw as a precondition for starting up an agribusiness in Dornod Province. On this particular day in
the summer of 2010, he was having second thoughts about that decision. Sitting
at a computer screen in his messy office in the provincial capital of Choibalsan,
Mr. Jia was reviewing the digital images that documented the beginnings of his
large agricultural project. With a mixture of resignation and anger, he described
how his local friends were proving to be less than trustworthy and how his vision-
ary scheme for grain production was running into one obstacle after another. It
wasn't just a question of fuel and spare parts being stolen, Mr. Jia claimed, the
machines were being deliberately destroyed, and he suspected that members of

FIGURE 1.1.   "Promote Sino-Mongolian Friendship." Mr. Jia's harvesters on parade. May 2010.

the Democratic Party were instigating acts of sabotage against him because they thought he was allied to the Revolutionary Party. Mr. Jia was not happy with his situation, and things went from bad to worse over the next few days when a local television station aired a damaging reportage on the Chinese entrepreneur. Accusing Mr. Jia of running a brothel, the broadcast set off a train of events that eventually forced Mr. Jia to abandon his residence in Choibalsan and pursue his frustrated desire for Sino-Mongolian friendship in other parts of the country.

Imagining Mongolia to be a new frontier for Chinese agriculture, a virgin country full of unexploited resources, Mr. Jia had worked hard to cultivate personal relationships with local political leaders, and he had managed to secure a lease on the fertile land of a former state farm in eastern Mongolia. Yet, as Mr. Jia's projects unfolded, he became increasingly disappointed by his failure to elicit the expected responses from his local collaborators and eventually he lost his way in the opaque politics and anti-Chinese sentiments of provincial Mongolia. "A hot face against cold buttocks" (热脸贴冷屁股) was the idiom that Mr. Jia used to express his sense of rejection when his attempts to court friendship in Mongolia failed one after the other. Mr. Jia's ideas of friendship (友谊) seemed to be a concatenation of different normative repertoires: As has been shown in ethnographies of *guanxi* (关系) in post-Mao China (Kipnis 1997; Osburg 2013; Wank 1999; Yan 1996; Yang 1994), friendship is simultaneously a business strategy shaped by the uncertainties of postsocialist economic reforms, a framework for understanding politics and foreign relations inspired by Maoism, and a fundamental way of relating to non-kin that seems to be modeled on brotherhood. Mr. Jia appeared to think of friendship as a multipurpose relation that was simultaneously instrumental and sentimental and that covered the full range of relational distances, from the allied strangers who were called friends under Maoism to the sworn brothers of precommunist China. Mr. Jia's ideas of friendship found little resonance in Mongolia, but his perpetually disappointed desire to impose his version of friendship on everyone around him seemed to be a key driver in his business projects, and it provided us with a case study to explore how interpersonal relations are caught up in expansive projects of empire and how China's interventions abroad give rise to unexpected relational imbrications between detachment and proximity, or indeed "intimate distances" in the sense we have described.

The intimate relations and affective ties that emerged from colonization and past projects of empire have become a topic in the fields of history and ethnography in recent decades, and a number of anthropological studies of European colonialism have emphasized relations involving carnal intimacy and romantic love (Stoler 2002; Povinelli 2006). While this chapter follows a similar trajectory in the attempt to document and theorize the interpersonal relations between Chinese and Mongolians that are now taking shape along with China's increasing presence in Mongolia, the focus is on another kind of relation, namely friendship, which would also appear to have played a significant role in past colonial projects and imperial imaginaries. Paul Burton (2011), for example, argues that notions of friendship played a vital role in the early Roman empire's foreign policy, where *amicitia* was more than just a polite gloss for domination over client states, while Vanessa Smith (2010) suggests that notions of friendship were central to British colonial encounters in the Pacific: When Captain Cook reached Tahiti in 1769, his primary instruction to the crew was "to endeavour by every fair means to cultivate a friendship with the Natives and to treat them with all imaginable humanity" (61). Friendship is probably a common political technology of empires in the making, and Uradyn Bulag's (2010) account of the Chinese state's discursive construction of a sentimental Sino-Mongolian friendship suggests that friendship has a particular cachet in Sino-Mongolian relations. As evident from the harsh accusations leveled against Mr. Jia, carnal love was certainly an issue in Sino-Mongolian relations, but because friendship remains a recurrent theme in Chinese political discourse on relations to foreign countries and their inhabitants and because Mr. Jia constantly talked about friendship, and not love or sex, Bunkenborg and Pedersen were prompted to explore what Mr. Jia actually meant when he talked about friendship and what type of relations emerged from this attempt to make money and friends in Mongolia. As we shall see, Mr. Jia's attempt to cast all relations around his agricultural project as friendship not only failed to bring Mr. Jia closer to his local collaborators, but actually worked as a wedge that prized the two sides farther apart as the Mongolians responded negatively to Mr. Jia's assumption of an intimacy they found excessive. By trying to configure all his relations as friendship, Mr. Jia appeared to trigger a feedback loop in which his desire to be friendly and make friends was perceived as an annoying, if not downright hostile, gesture, and relations between the Chinese entrepreneur and his local contacts thus seemed to be oddly stitched together by too much and too little desire for relationship, a paradoxical and fraught type of situation that we came to see as an example of the intimate distances that emerge with the globalization of Chinese business ventures.

Together with the tragicomical story of Mr. Jia's failed attempt to set up a large agricultural business in far eastern Mongolia, this chapter chronicles Bunkenborg and Pedersen's equally fraught attempt to make sense of this case of Sino-Mongolian collaborative damage. Having embarked upon their joint fieldwork with the naïve assumption that they would reach a common understanding about what was going on between the Mongolians and the Chinese, Bunkenborg and Pedersen discovered that the conflicts between their respective interlocutors were increasingly mirrored in their own interpretative disagreements. When Pedersen came to see Bunkenborg's insistence on joint fieldwork and analytical synthesis as a project of empire building that bore an uncanny resemblance to Mr. Jia's attempt to impose friendship as a standard for all relations, their collaboration ground to a halt. As we will see, however, it was precisely because the object of study (Sino-Mongolian collaboration) was "folded into" the relationship between the two subjects doing the study (the collaborating ethnographers) that it was possible to reach new insights regarding the nature of Chinese global forms and practices in Mongolia. We would argue that the ramshackle logic and often unintended ramifications of empires past and present (Stoler 2002; Lutz 2006) are best investigated and theorized at this little-studied and understood vanishing point between social engagement and social detachment, so instead of trying to provide a general overview of globalizing China from a bird's-eye perspective—an endeavor that we consider neither methodologically nor analytically feasible—our ambition in this first chapter is to begin unearthing *from within* the often incidental and always complex and capricious relational dynamics of an emerging empire, as Bunkenborg and Pedersen discussed and experienced its paradoxical effects over years of collaborative research.

"Let's Go! To Farm the Land in Mongolia!"

Bunkenborg and Pedersen first met Mr. Jia in 2009. En route to Ulaanbaatar from Petrochina's oilfields in the Tamsag basin (see chapter 3), the two passed through Choibalsan and met Mr. Luo, an elderly Chinese man who had moved to Mongolia in the late 1950s to work on a railroad. Back then, Choibalsan had a community of a few hundred Chinese nationals, but most of them had returned to China in the 1980s due to the increasingly restrictive policies adopted by the Mongolian state in the wake of the Sino-Soviet split that began in the late 1950s (see Bawden 1989). Mr. Luo was married to a Mongolian woman, and his four children spoke no Chinese, but even so, the family also tried to leave Mongolia when more than two decades of anti-Chinese propaganda and sentiment culminated in the early 1980s. However, Mr. Luo had no living relatives in his native village, and the authorities there accordingly claimed to be unable to provide him with land and grain, so the Chinese embassy in Ulaanbaatar refused his request for repatriation. Mr. Luo then renounced his Chinese citizenship and applied for Mongolian citizenship. It took more than seven years before he was finally naturalized and provided with proper documents, an identification card he proudly showed Bunkenborg and Pedersen when they admired the astonishing variety of vegetables he had managed to grow within the walls of his *hashaa*. Like some ethnically Chinese Mongolians who were born and raised in Mongolia, Mr. Luo was completely bilingual, and over the years he had occasionally worked as a translator. Most recently, he told Bunkenborg and Pedersen, he had been helping out as an interpreter for a Chinese investor in Choibalsam. Needless to say, the two anthropologists immediately became eager to learn more, and Mr. Luo kindly offered to take them to visit this Chinese entrepreneur who was currently renovating an old building close by.

The building proved to be the former provincial headquarters of the People's Revolutionary Party, a beautiful two-story edifice from the 1920s that was located in the westernmost part of Choibalsan, close to the ruins of a former Soviet army base. The roof and the windows looked new, but the inside contained nothing but bare walls. Threading their way upstairs between bricks, tools, and discarded bottles, Bunkenborg and Pedersen found Mr. Jia in the spacious room that served simultaneously as main office, dining room, and bedroom. The remains of a meal sat on a folding table next to the bed, and although Mr. Jia was neatly dressed in a white shirt and a dark-blue jacket, he looked somewhat flushed and disheveled as if the meal might have included a certain measure of alcohol (certainly, the shelf of paired bottles of expensive Chinese liquor suggested that his business in Mongolia involved the frequent giving and consumption of alcohol). It was clearly an inconvenient moment, but Mr. Jia rose to the occasion immediately and received the two anthropologists cordially. Learning that Bunkenborg and Pedersen were interested in the experiences of foreign investors in Mongolia, Mr. Jia launched into a long description of the obstacles he had encountered in his attempt to start an agribusiness in

Mongolia. "The political leaders are corrupt," he complained, "and the rules are constantly changing." He had already spent millions of RMB, but the officials were insatiable; one could "easily spend hundreds of millions in this country and still have nothing to show for it." And then there were the incompetent workers: "The Mongolians are herders; they haven't got a clue about this sort of work. You give them a job, and they will finish the tools." Opening the door to a storage room full of broken Chinese power tools to prove his point, Mr. Jia confessed that he had been on the verge of exploding that morning. "Yesterday, I showed the Mongolian workers how to dig a proper ditch for an electric cable," Mr. Jia explained. "But today, when I asked them to finish the job, they just put the cable on top of the ground and covered it with a bit of dirt."

Mr. Jia was born in 1954 in China's northeastern Heilongjiang Province. His father was labeled a rightist in the political campaigns of the late 1950s, but despite this problematic background, Mr. Jia managed to get an education in forestry and became recognized as a model worker. Having joined the Communist party, he became a cadre and was later assigned to work in a bank in the booming trading port of Dalian. As a banker, Mr. Jia was in a position to grant loans to expansive Chinese enterprises, and thus he became friends with a number of officials and businessmen who made a fortune in the messy transition from a planned economy to a market economy. Having acquired sufficient capital, Mr. Jia set up his own business in the beginning of the 1990s and started trading in furs, traveling to auctions in Scandinavia and setting up a fur factory in China. By the late 1990s the fur business was no longer as profitable as it had been, so Mr. Jia sold his company and invested the capital in a number of different enterprises focusing on agricultural production.

When accounting for his success as a businessman and entrepreneur,[1] Mr. Jia generally emphasized connections rather than money, and he claimed to be the poorest among his old friends from Dalian, many of whom had become billionaires. He always gave the impression of being extremely well connected, and while his agricultural project in Mongolia required substantial economic investments, it really hinged upon political contacts. While doing business in Inner Mongolia in 2005, he ran into the leader of Halhgol District, located in the far eastern corner of Dornod Province (and Mongolia generally), who told him that it might be possible to lease the land of a former state farm that had not been used for farming since the bankruptcy of most of the former socialist collective and state farms in the early 1990s (Sneath 1993; Bruun and Odgaard 1996; Pedersen 2011, 20–29). While visiting Mongolia in 2006, Mr. Jia learned that the state policies encouraging the development of agriculture in Mongolia (ironically implemented to make the country less dependent on the import of flour from or via China) would ensure a minimal price for grain, so he decided to make a bid for the sixty-year lease on the land, and in 2007 he moved to Mongolia. While working to clinch a deal on the land with the leaders of Halhgol District, he managed to befriend the mayor of Choibalsan and purchased the somewhat dilapidated historical building that used to house the provincial branch of the People's Revolutionary Party but would now serve as the headquarters of his company. In 2008 Mr. Jia registered a company in Mongolia with US $1.45 million in capital and three branches: an agricultural branch with a sixty-year lease on 460,000 mu (30,667 hectares) of land situated in Halhgol; a pastoral branch with a twenty-year lease on 600,000 mu (40,000 hectares) of grassland in Herlen District outside Choibalsan, and a meat processing branch with 160 mu (10.7 hectares) in Choibalsan itself.

Mr. Jia's agricultural venture in Mongolia was sizable enough to be described in a number of newspaper articles in China (Li 2009; Shi and Chang 2009; Zang 2008). One article describes Mr. Jia flourishing reports of Heilongjiang farmers going abroad and Zhejiang farmers growing soybeans in Brazil as he encourages Shandong farmers to go to Mongolia where the Mongolians, he claims, are "calling out for Chinese farmers to teach them modern farming techniques" (Shi and Chang 2009). Under the headline "Let's go, to farm the land in Mongolia," Mr. Jia describes how Mongolia is like the three northeastern provinces of China in the 1950s: "A Great Northern Wilderness (北大荒) with black soil so rich that it practically drips with fat when you pick up a handful, a place where one can still apply the saying 'wave a club and you will hit a deer, scoop up water and you will catch a fish, wild birds will fly into your cooking pot by themselves" (Shi and Chang 2009). Portraying Mongolia as an undiscovered frontier zone, Mr. Jia also emphasizes the need to cultivate good relations with the Mongolians. For example, as part of the aforementioned negotiations to lease the land of the former state farm in Halhgol, he invited all the local political leaders on a trip to China to see his company in Dalian. One of the visiting Mongolian officials is quoted as saying, "In our country, grain is imported from abroad. We like to eat eggs, but we don't know how to raise chickens, we like pork, but no one rears pigs. We welcome more enterprises like Mr. Jia's to come to our country and set up farms and businesses" (Shi and Chang 2009).

While the Chinese newspaper articles present the Mongolian officials as somewhat childish and technologically backward in their inability to raise chickens, they also emphasize Mongolians' emotional response to their hosts. The visiting Mongolian leader, for instance, is quoted as saying, "We are really good friends with Director Jia, his sincerity and enthusiasm moves everyone he meets. Collaborating with him, we feel at ease" (Li 2009). This emphasis on the affective dimension of doing business in Mongolia is equally evident in Mr. Jia's account of his business adventure: "The most important thing was to get their recognition by displaying sufficient competitive strength, to win their trust with an investment of sincere emotion" (Li 2009).

The stories in the Chinese media of Mr. Jia's relations to his Mongolian collaborators present Sino-Mongolian relations as being both emotional and involved. This is quite the opposite from Western media outlets, which typically describe relations between Chinese investors and locals as ultrapragmatic, if not downright cynical in Africa and elsewhere, where they supposedly conduct their business without any strings attached (Mawdsley 2008). All the nice words employed to describe Sino-Mongolian relations—recognition, trust, emotions, friendship, sincerity, enthusiasm, being moved, feeling at ease—could obviously be mere rhetorical wrappings for purely economic relations and neocolonial profit-seeking abroad, and Pedersen was quick to point out that some of the themes in Mr. Jia's discourse on investments in Mongolia were eerily reminiscent of well-worn colonial and neocolonial tropes.[2] Pedersen was never entirely convinced of the earnestness of the sentiments at stake here, but Bunkenborg was intrigued by the sentimental quality attributed to the relations between the Chinese businessman and the Mongolian officials who travelled to China to ask for investments. Surely, Bunkenborg insisted in the ongoing discussions with Pedersen about the evolving case of Mr. Jia and his Mongolian business adventure, surely it was possible that there really was an effusive sense of goodwill at this early stage of Mr. Jia's romance with Mongolia. The reporters no doubt exaggerated the Mongolian officials' admiration for Mr. Jia, but the fact that the articles so clearly expressed a desire for friendship and an expectation that the Mongolians would respond with appropriate emotions, was interesting in itself. And if there were no "earnest sentiments" involved, as Pedersen suggested, this actually made the insistence on friendship as the template for Sino-Mongolian relations even more intriguing.

Before Bunkenborg and Pedersen left Choibalsan after their first visit in 2009, they posed for a group photo together with Mr. Luo and Mr. Jia outside the latter's half-renovated headquarters. Mr. Jia first took them on a tour of the small vegetable plot in front of the building to point out the broad variety of greens he and his employees had planted for their own consumption, and he was so enthusiastic about the sunflowers that he could hardly stand still long enough to let his son take the photos. Presenting Bunkenborg with a business card printed on gold paper to match the elaborate gold casing on his cell phone, Mr. Jia first pointed to the logo of his company on the business card and then upward to a massive bronze ornament fitted into the building above the entrance (figure 1.2). Only then did the two ethnographers realize that the ornament bore the company logo. Mr. Jia explained that he had replaced the red star of the Revolutionary Party with his logo to mark the building as the headquarters of his operations in

FIGURE 1.2.   Mr. Jia's headquarters in Choibalsan. October 2009.

Mongolia. Having waved goodbye to his newfound Chinese friend, Bunkenborg was enthused by the possibility that some sort of successful Sino-Mongolian collaboration might actually emerge from Mr. Jia's substantial and seemingly genuine economic and affective investment in Mongolia. Pedersen, on his side, was less optimistic about the prospects for Mr. Jia's empire of friendship. And indeed, Mr. Jia had chosen to look for friends in a tough place.

Mongolia's Last Communist Bastion

Unbeknownst to him, Mr. Jia had chosen a particularly tricky spot for his Mongolian business venture. After all, as both natives and newcomers to this city told Pedersen, Choibalsan is more old-fashioned than other big Mongolian cities, not just in the sense that doing business was different, but also by virtue of the city's general look and feel. As the site of one of Mongolia's largest Soviet army bases and a regional hub for the country's heavy industry that had essentially closed down overnight, Choibalsan was particularly affected by the collapse of state socialism in 1990 and the transition to market capitalism over the following decades. The departure of thousands of Red Army soldiers in combination with local Mongolians' migration to Ulaanbaatar meant that, unlike most other provincial capitals in Mongolia, the city had not experienced any population growth during the two first decades of postsocialist transition, but rather hovered around 40,000 inhabitants. During socialism Choibalsan had been divided into a "new town" of concrete apartment blocks and an "old town" with yurts and wooden shacks, the former reserved for army personnel and other VIPs while the latter served as a residual slum for the majority of the Mongolians. After 1990 many of these Mongolians suddenly had the opportunity to move to proper housing in one of Mongolia's model socialist residential developments where Choibalsan's power plant ensured a lavish supply of free boiling-hot water in the pipes all year round. This had left the "old town" slum rather small and insignificant compared to other Mongolian cities. The eerie mechanical hum from the power plant, the crumbling statues of revolutionary heroes, and the traces of Communist iconography, all added to the general sensation that life in Mongolia's far-eastern capital had been unfolding in a sort of time bubble, strangely untouched by the mining craze and the investment boom that had unfolded in Ulaanbaatar and the Gobi since 2000.

Choibalsan's landscape of factory ruins and scattered industrial debris constituted a perfect conduit for the experience of bittersweet "expectations of modernity" (Ferguson, J. 1999) and "nostalgia for the future" (Piot 2010) of the sort that anthropological scholars have described in African contexts. Not even these desires, however, were strong enough to curb the anti-Chinese anxieties among the local population. Something happened in, and to, the sleepy, run-down, postcommunist city over the four years that Pedersen and Bunkenborg visited, from 2009 to 2012. Economic activity was gradually beginning to pick up, partly as a result of the general improvement of the Mongolian economy around 2005, but also because of an increasing number of medium-sized mining developments in the Dornod region, including a Chinese-owned zinc mine, a Canadian uranium mine (de facto nationalized in 2009 after having been designated a "strategic resource" by the Mongolian government) and the PetroChina oil field in the southeastern corner of the country.

Politicians and officials from various agencies were fighting to take credit for this development. As Mr. B. Ganzorig, chairman of Mongolia's Foreign Investment and Foreign Trade Agency, explained during a lavish foreign investors' conference that Pedersen attended in Choibalsan in August 2009, eastern Mongolia had largely been ignored by foreign investors, making this new interest all the more welcome. "Indeed," Mr. Ganzorig stressed in his opening comments, "the eastern region has many opportunities: mining, light industry, tourism, husbandry, agriculture, production of food and fruits, that may attract your attention and initiatives" (Ganzorig 2009). And, "needless to say," all foreign investors would "receive treatment equal to that enjoyed by domestic investors as regards rights to own, utilize and exploit assets and capital." In fact, he stressed, a "fifty percent income tax credit shall be granted for the production or cultivation of cereals, potato, vegetables, dairy products, fruits, and foraging products" (2009). While this wooing was undoubtedly targeted at representatives from the Korean-German agricultural consortium at the gathering, as well as the different Russian and Chinese officials from state-owned industries who were also present, it is reasonable to assume that the message was not lost on the numerous private Chinese investors attending the meeting.

Even though most of these business activities took place in the countryside, hundreds of kilometers away, Choibalsan's status as regional capital and transportation hub (the site of the only airport in the region) was resulting in ever more visible trickle-down effects, ranging from the opening of new hotels and restaurants replete with "new European design" and "international menus" to the increasing volume of traffic and trade across the border with China toward the east and south. An increasing number of shops were accepting Chinese *renminbi* alongside the Mongolian *tögrög* (as one man noted, "It is almost as if we have two currencies"); public and private educational institutions were offering lessons in Chinese from primary school to university level; and occasionally, ever so incrementally, one might hear Chinese spoken on the street and notice the presence of Chinese-owned restaurants and shops, even if these were usually tucked away in side streets and hidden behind grim concrete facades with billboards in Mongolian letters only. And then, of course, there was Mr. Jia, whose enterprise stood out, not just because of its size and the fact that it was located in Choibalsan itself, but also because the owner was making no effort to hide the scale of his investment, let alone his own presence in the town.

While it was hard to find anyone in town who did not appreciate or take a certain pride in the fact that Choibalsan was "finally developing" as several people expressed to Pedersen, such nascent optimism was often accompanied by an undercurrent of uncertainty, fear, and even bigotry. And while these negative sentiments toward outsiders were not restricted to the Chinese—corrupt officials and other foreign investors were the targets of a fair share of angry bickering too—it was inevitably the Chinese who bore the brunt of it. Because of widespread skepticism, if not fear toward the Chinese in Mongolia, and because of Choibalsan's prominent place in peoples' recollection of the Communist past, it was perhaps not strategically wise to buy up the former headquarters of the Revolutionary Party. "At the very least, Mr. Jia might have refrained from discarding the number one symbol of former Communist glory, the red star on the building's front wall!" Pedersen remarked as he and his collaborator sat down to dine in the faded Soviet-style splendor of the almost deserted restaurant in the Herlen Gol Hotel after their first visit to Mr. Jia's headquarters. Surely, Pedersen elaborated as the waiter brought them their beefsteak with egg, mashed potatoes, and Russian salad (another reminder of once ubiquitous Soviet tastes), no matter how well meaning and genuine all his talk about "friendship," this was not the best starting point for striking up an amiable and trusting relationship with local people. And even Bunkenborg had to admit that, for all the eloquence and foresight that Mr. Jia had invested in his plans for making friends and money in the Mongolian frontier zone, he had failed to consider the powerful symbolism of an important historical building adorned with Chinese characters being sold to a Chinese businessman. With the benefit of hindsight, it was not hard to discern, in Mr. Jia's lack of consideration for local interpretations of his actions and in his impatience with his Mongolian partners, the first telltale signs of impending disaster.

Imperial Intimacies

Mr. Jia had a knack for storytelling and a seemingly inexhaustible stock of stories about his experiences in Mongolia, so Bunkenborg was happy to drink tea in the messy office and to accept the role of Mr. Jia's "foreign friend" (外国朋友). The Chinese Communist Party traditionally applied the epithets "foreign friend" or "international friend," (国际友人), to foreigners who supported the party line. Critics of the party would no doubt argue that the term was an honorific for useful idiots. Bunkenborg did not particularly mind this ambiguity, and previous fieldwork experiences in China had proven that the position of foreign friend was often a good starting point for interesting exchanges. Not only was Mr. Jia quick to invoke friendship as the explicit name and template for his relation to Bunkenborg, whom he had only just met, he also talked constantly about the way he had tried, and failed, to make friends with Mongolians and to promote friendship more generally. Having first learned Chinese from textbooks and dictionaries produced in the late 1970s, Bunkenborg had been trained to dismiss such ubiquitous mentioning of friendship as a mere rhetorical flourish appropriate to all dealings with foreigners. For instance, the department store in Beijing where foreigners could spend their hard currency back in the seventies and eighties was known as the Friendship Store, not because the cashiers were particularly friendly, but simply because the store dealt with foreigners. In Chinese descriptions of foreign countries and persons, the word "friendly" seemed to suggest a polite detachment rather than an intimate relation. No doubt this is part of the reason why scholarly literature on Chinese politics tends to dismiss Chinese appeals to friendship as insincere:

After more than fifty years of assiduous propaganda work on Sino-foreign relations, both foreigners and Chinese alike now frequently find themselves wittingly or not enmeshed in a worldview which evaluates Sino-foreign interactions in terms of whether they are friendly or not to China, a "China" which implicitly means that ruled by the CCP. Breaking through such a paradigm to establish genuine interaction and a genuine exchange of ideas and opinions is one of the challenges of Sino-foreign interactions in the future. (Brady 2003, 251)

Pedersen, as well as Nielsen, was puzzled, even irritated, by the constant references to friendship and by Bunkenborg's interest in them. It might not be particularly strange that the Chinese-built bridge in central Ulaanbaatar, a gift from the People's Republic of China in 1963, was called Friendship Bridge, but why would a Chinese company building an airport in Maputo put up signs claiming that the friendship between Mozambique and China was everlasting? Why would Chinese managers speak of local employees as friends? And why, Pedersen kept asking with mounting suspicion, would a private entrepreneur like Mr. Jia decorate his trucks with exhortations to promote Sino-Mongolian friendship? Thoroughly annoyed that his colleagues seemed to be as automatically suspicious of any Chinese appeal to friendship as he himself had been, Bunkenborg decided to take the calls for friendship more seriously. Mr. Jia's attempts to invoke and produce friendship involved not only persons but also ethnic groups, cities, provinces, and nations, and to Bunkenborg this suggested that friendship, to him, had implications far beyond a commonsense notion of friendship as mutual affection and voluntary obligation between non-kin.

It soon became clear that Mr. Jia, as part of his attempt to "win their trust with an investment of sincere emotion," had not only toured China with Mongolian officials but also organized visits from China to Mongolia. The mayor of Mr. Jia's hometown of Heze found Mr. Jia's project important, and as Mr. Jia was also on "very good terms with the female mayor of Choibalsan," as he proudly put it to Bunkenborg during one of their first meetings, an official visit was arranged. It was Mr. Jia's intention to have the two towns designated as friendship towns. It wasn't an even match, Mr. Jia admitted, as the municipality of Heze had a population of eight million, while the entire population of Dornod hardly numbered eighty thousand, but then a little help from the Chinese municipality would go a long way toward developing the sparsely populated Mongolian province. Mr. Jia needed political backing in Choibalsan to establish his headquarters and the meat processing plant, but he also needed leverage at the provincial level to secure his hold on the farmland in Halhgol. Thus he started working on a plan to establish a province-level friendship between Shandong and Dornod. The governor of Shandong was favorably inclined and sent the leader of the agricultural department on a reconnaissance mission:

> MR. JIA: The year before last, a head of department from Shandong province came over on a preliminary visit to see what the Mongolians were like. After that, the governor of Shandong was supposed to come over. The head of department brought an introductory gift of 30 million.[3] The plan was to meet the governor of Dornod, but he wouldn't meet with us. I was staying with the head of department in a small hotel, but he flew home the next day. When they heard how much money he had brought, they said, "Come on over, come on over," but the head of department refused.
>
> BUNKENBORG: Was the money intended as an investment?
>
> MR. JIA: It was to protect us. The reason he brought so much money was this: Xianglong Company is from Shandong Province and my company is from Shandong. So, in order to protect us, our government brought some money as aid to their government. As a sort of gift. Just like Wen Jiabao brought 500 million dollars.

Mr. Jia believed that the Dornod governor had failed to consider the size of Shandong. The visitor may have been a mere head of department and formally junior to the Dornod governor, but leading a department in a province with more than a 100 million people was actually a very powerful position. Mr. Jia was shocked at the arrogance of the Dornod governor. Not surprisingly, he went on to explain, the governor of Shandong decided to stay away from Dornod, and relations between Heze and Choibalsan were likewise stalled before they could develop into a formalized friendship. Mr. Jia's attempt to transfer political influence from China to Mongolia thus came to nothing, but the attempt in itself suggests a particular emphasis on friendship as a form of relation that can operate on multiple levels. The difference between China's relation to Mongolia, Shandong's relation to Dornod, Heze's relation to Choibalsan, and Mr. Jia's relation to a Mongolian friend is quantitative. The size of the gifts may differ, but friendship is imagined to be similar at all levels and thus operates as a universal scale that establishes China and Mongolia as separate but commensurable entities at all levels ranging from person and municipality to province and nation. For Mr. Jia, friendship appeared to be the universal type of relation that allowed him to discern and assess the constituent parts of Mongolia in terms of their potential for friendly relations to similar entities in China, and friendship was thus imposed as a universal scale to connect and construct both Mongolia and China. But while Mr. Jia presented friendship as a universal and ahistorical type of relation that should be understood and honored in the same way in China and Mongolia, it would appear that Mr. Jia's ideas about friendship were actually a synthesis of shifting and possibly even contradictory takes on friendship in recent Chinese history.

Mr. Jia had learned to do business in China during the 1980s, when market forces were introduced in a piecemeal fashion while the redistributive economy remained dominant. It is easy to forget that many goods in China were rationed even in the 1990s and that governmental bureaucracies controlled access to education, jobs, and housing in a way that made personal relations the only way of obtaining goods and services that could not be bought for money. In an economy of scarcity, the cultivation of social relations becomes an art as evident in Mayfair Yang's (1989; 1994) classic description of the subversive economy of gifts, favors, and banquets that enabled ordinary people to cultivate social relations (关系) and win tactical battles against the coercive state that controlled many aspects of their lives. The gifts presented in the course of cultivating relations are clearly not disinterested, but Mayfair Yang insists that they are not simply a camouflaged form of market exchange, as they refer to a relational ethics of reciprocity. Ethnographies of gift giving in rural China emphasize that the construction and maintenance of social relations involve both instrumentality and affect (Yan 1996; Kipnis 1997). In discussions of guanxi, social relations may be cast as instruments, but they are also viewed as sentiments and described as "feelings" (感情) or "human emotions" (人情). As Andrew Kipnis points out, material obligation and sentimental attachment appear to be inseparable. This is neatly reflected in the expression *zuo ge renqing* (做个人情), which is used in the sense of "giving a gift" but literally means "enacting human emotions" (Kipnis 1996, 288). Similar understandings of social relations as both instrument and sentiment are at work in David Wank's (1996; 1999) description of patron-client ties between officials and businessmen in the city of Xiamen. It is fairly easy to discern this in Mr. Jia's efforts to build relations of trust with political leaders in Mongolia by appealing to an ethics of reciprocity, where social relations can be simultaneously useful and emotionally gratifying for both sides. In a context where material obligation and sentimental attachment are seen as inseparable, it is even possible to think of instrumentality and affect as two aspects of friendship that deepen and amplify each other (Strickland 2010). It is against this background that Mr. Jia's claims about investments of capital and emotion make sense. Why he imagined that this approach would work in Mongolia is a mystery, but it seems quite possible that the constant references to friendship in socialist rhetoric about international relations led him to believe that friendship was an internationally recognized social form and that he could simply continue to make friends on the same terms that he did in China.

Friendship was a general template for the way relations between China and foreign countries were conceptualized in the socialist era. Maoist philosophy and propaganda emphasized the need to draw a clear line between friends and enemies and presented relations between China and other socialist countries in terms of friendship, one that extended to the laboring masses across the globe regardless of their nationality or ethnicity. Friendship has accordingly played an important role in Chinese discourse on Africa. While it is easy to dismiss this as mere rhetoric, the more interesting question is whether this rhetoric may actually have contributed to structure patterns of affect in encounters between Chinese and Africans. Julia Strauss notes that this discourse has been remarkably stable since the early 1960s: China's relation to Africa is traced back to Zheng He's peaceful visits to east Africa in the fifteenth century; a common background in the struggle against imperialism is emphasized; and China is cast as the "all-weather friend" of Africa, a country that offers noninterference, nonconditional aid, and friendship. In particular, the construction of the TAZARA railroad project seems to have cemented this discourse.

> The success of the railroad was ascribed to elements that were in microcosm projections of China's best revolutionary self: the commitment and selflessness of individuals both "red and expert," devoted to service and sacrifice, working with close links to the people, reliance on human will to achieve extraordinary and quick results, and above all *an investment as much emotional as practical* (Strauss 2009, 787, emphasis added).

Here again, investments are emotional, and the peculiar affective quality of this early engagement with Africa may still lend a particular hue to the way Chinese politicians and entrepreneurs perceive and present their activities in Africa, even when they seem very business-like to an outside observer. Relations between China and Mongolia, of course, are historically far more complicated, intense, and long-lasting than relationships between China and more geographically distant nations in Africa, but since the withdrawal of Soviet troops, Mongolia has been rhetorically embraced as a particularly close friend of China. This presumption of intimacy is connected to the population of ethnic Mongolians who live as a recognized minority group in China proper (Bulag 1998, 234). However, the idea of a particularly close relation between China and Mongolia is generally frowned upon in Mongolia, and the same is true for the idea of a close relation between Han Chinese and the Mongolians. Writing from the perspective of Inner Mongolians, Uradyn Bulag (2010, 244) has described relations between Han Chinese and minority peoples in China as a "regime of intimacy":

> It is not the Chinese space that is being invaded now, but rather the reverse, the expansion of the Chinese into Inner Asian Lands. And this expansion has been achieved as much by the barrel of the gun as by

means of friendship and hospitality. What China has been emphasizing in recent decades is interethnic cooperation, unity among nationalities, forming what I have called the regime of intimacy. In the process, the Chinese project themselves as cosmopolitan while pressuring minorities to reciprocate by showing friendship and hospitality to the Chinese.

For Bulag, then, Chinese offers of friendship are a way to pressure Mongolians and other ethnic minorities in mainland China. Seen as instrumental rather than affective, such gestures are dismissed as insincere. The underlying assumption seems to be that friendship is *either* affective and genuine *or* instrumental and false. Such a binary conception of friendship clashes with the notion of social relations as both instruments and sentiments. Perhaps here, in Bulag's frustration with the interested friendship offered by China, there is a rehearsal, on the scale of grand politics, of the kind of problems faced by Mr. Jia in his attempts to make friends in Choibalsan. Having started his business with an initial assumption of a special potential for friendship between Chinese and Mongolians, Mr. Jia was repeatedly and increasingly disappointed in his attempts to cultivate friendly relations with his Mongolian collaborators. Instead of getting closer to his local contacts as the years went by, Mr. Jia was discovering distances within relations he had assumed to be intimate. He seems to have operated on the assumption that the supposed intimacy between Han Chinese and Mongolians in China would also apply to Sino-Mongolian relations in Mongolia, and his attempts to make friends abroad grew from a "regime of intimacy" in the sense that he brought a set of assumptions about Han-Mongolian relations from China and continued to act upon them in a foreign country. If so, the ramifications of what Bulag describes as a "regime of intimacy" potentially extend far beyond the borders of China proper and may well offer a key to understanding not only Sino-Mongolian interactions, but also "Sino-Xeno" relations more generally. Indeed, the activation and problematization of friendship—in the particular form where friendship becomes hegemonic and imperial because it serves as a standard for all relations—was gradually starting to assert itself in the internal dynamics of the research project, and Bunkenborg and Pedersen increasingly found themselves weighing sympathies for their respective informants against the friendship that undergirded their collaborative endeavor.

Split Sympathies

In the summer of 2011, exactly a year after Mr. Jia's controversy with the local media started, Bunkenborg and Pedersen found themselves back in Choibalsan, this time mingling with eastern Mongolia's nouveau riche elite in the fanciest restaurant in town, the Azure, and trying to conduct a joint interview with a senior journalist from a local news provider, who had been involved in breaking the story about Mr. Jia's business. As one of the people responsible for the controversial reportage that dragged the news provider into a legal battle with Mr. Jia, the woman was adamant that she had done nothing wrong. It was the first time anyone had filed a lawsuit against her, she told Pedersen, remarking that it was annoying to be repeatedly summoned to appear in court. In her view the court case was a farce—a waste of time that sapped unnecessary energy and resources from her employer's role as protector of the weak and as eastern Mongolia's primary public watchdog. Worst of all, the case meant being forced to deal with "that Chinese liar": "They told me to stand up. I was dressed very fancy and was wearing high heels. Eventually, as the case against [Mr. Jia] was presented to the court, he looked into my eyes and said, 'This woman came to me and asked whether the two of us could come to an agreement.' He continued, now directly to me, 'You and I sat down. I offered you tea.' It was so terrible, I almost passed out. To lie like that! I never even asked him to meet. All I ever wanted was to fight him!"

Despite her confident appearance, the journalist had been rattled by the court case. Mr. Jia, had managed to mobilize several powerful local helpers and backers in his attempt to clear his name and disprove the allegations made against his company. First, he had employed a Mongolian law firm to litigate against the news provider who employed her. Secondly, during his ongoing conflict with the local press and authorities, he had also called upon the Chinese embassy in Ulaanbaatar to intervene on his behalf and had even had the audacity to make a distress call to Interpol, successfully putting a stop to a nightly search of his premises instigated by the Choibalsan police.

"I always get into trouble because of Chinese companies," murmured the journalist. "Actually," she continued as she lit up a cigarette, "we Mongolians don't like Chinese. So if we were to praise a Chinese company in our news, people would get angry." Pedersen could easily imagine how these words would be used against him by Bunkenborg in their internal discussions after returning to the hotel that same evening—"Aha, so Mr. Jia is perhaps not paranoid after all!" his fellow ethnographer might justifiably ask. So Pedersen quickly went on to ask, "But surely, if you find cases of Chinese who are doing good, then you also report this and praise them, right?" To which she replied:

> The Chinese here do nothing praiseworthy. But of course, if they did, then we would also be telling it. When Chinese come here in big numbers, they break laws and ignore and patronize Mongolians, so people don't like it. For example, regarding that disgusting company, there are

so many things to tell. There has been a lot of talk about prostitutes and alcoholics. But the most important thing is that the building [from which Mr. Jia ran his business] is a historical building. It is devoted to war and has a very big tunnel under it. That is a very great building, and there are few buildings like it in Mongolia; in fact, there are only three. Yet, it was sold for only MT 100 something million and to a Chinese, not a Mongolian! People here felt very sorry about that building.

But what was it, Bunkenborg and Pedersen wanted to know, that first prompted an investigation of Mr. Jia's business in Choibalsan? The journalist took another drag of her Davidoff cigarette and explained, "Well, people kept calling us with information. So we decided to go but were not allowed to ask questions. Then one day we returned with a hidden camera." The journalist paused and turned her head to look Pedersen directly in the eye. (Bunkenborg, on his side, double-checked the recorder for although he did not understand what was being said, he sensed that a key break in the two ethnographers' reconstruction was imminent.) "As we entered the director's office, he shouted, 'You Mongolians are lazy, and I have done things you could never have done!' To check whether the director was telling the truth we called the district governor to enquire if the company had planted trees on their land or if they were doing other agricultural activities." At this point, the journalist raised her voice to relay the governor's words: "The governor replied 'For three years, that company has tried to obtain land, but we haven't given them any. They didn't plant 4,000 trees; in fact, they don't have a single square meter of land.' Such are the lies he tells. At this point, his female translator lashed out after our camera so we dropped it. And the director was mumbling something to himself. I didn't understand what he was saying, but he was walking back and forth."

To Bunkenborg and Pedersen's discomfort, other people in the restaurant were beginning to stare at their table, but the journalist didn't seem to care. Pedersen pushed on, now asking if she could perhaps elaborate on what in their reporting about Mr. Jia's business had made him so angry that he decided to take them to court? "Well," she said, extinguishing the cigarette in an overly ornamented ashtray, "we just told the story of how we visited the place four times and how on the last occasion we were beaten up. Foreign people were hitting our camera! The story of how a Chinese company bought a historical building and then made it look like a terrible storage place. How the neighbors came to dislike the Chinese because they threw their garbage outside, and they were not allowed to enter the fence or doors. The only thing going on there was people drinking vodka. The director's room was full of empty bottles everywhere, and it was very disgusting. Prostitutes came there a lot."

A pattern began to emerge in the journalist's engagement with the two ethnographers. While she readily answered Pedersen's questions, her coldness toward Bunkenborg indicated that she saw him as a hostile presence—a friend of the Chinese, perhaps?—and she doggedly refused to look him in the eye throughout the interview, despite his awkward efforts to establish at least a minimal rapport with her. Having been studiously ignored for almost an hour, Bunkenborg finally came up with an excuse to walk away from the restaurant, leaving Pedersen to finish the interview.

When Bunkenborg returned to the Azure half an hour later, Pedersen and the journalist were still embroiled in a discussion from which he felt estranged. Indeed, the journalist had ended up spending the bulk of the time after Bunkenborg's departure complaining about "that Chinese director," who, she told Pedersen, had also "broken immigration laws." In fact, she continued, "those Chinese did so many illegal things. They brought animals there and built a slaughtering house without permission. There was blood all over!" There really was "nothing they did according to the law." Pedersen and she began discussing other Chinese investments in eastern Mongolia and the different challenges generated by these projects, such as the environmental problems allegedly caused by the PetroChina Daqing Tamsag oil company's drilling in southeast Dornod Province. To Bunkenborg's consternation, Pedersen voiced his support for the struggle against what he saw as Chinese political-economic hegemony over eastern Mongolia and concluded the interview by encouraging the woman to join forces with Mr. Shagdar, the famous Dornod herdsman, who had made a name for himself as an incorruptible local activist fighting a Chinese oil company.

Running Out of Neutral Ground

The moment that Pedersen returned to the hotel, the two ethnographers began quarrelling among themselves. Bunkenborg strongly disagreed with Pedersen's attempt to facilitate an alliance between Mr. Shagdar and the journalist, objecting that the legitimate environmentalist concerns of the former and his community would drown in anti-Chinese propaganda from a populist local news media that evidently did not strive to be balanced in its reporting of Sino-Mongolian relations. Pedersen shot back that, while he acknowledged that the local journalists might not adhere to the (utopian) ideals of reporting propagandized by elite media in the West, the local journalists still seemed to be onto something, even if the rumors about prostitution and drugs were likely to have been blown out of proportion. After all, he objected to Bunkenborg, the journalist was hardly alone in her concerns; many people, including several leading formal and informal leaders in the Choibalsan community, worried that there was something fishy about Mr. Jia's business. "Just consider this," Pedersen exclaimed, tapping his finger on an interview transcript, "from no other than the local chief justice."

> It's possible there may be human trafficking here because of our location on the border between two countries. You know how times are today. People's lives are bad. Someone tried doing business. And some end up as prostitutes. I don't know about that news story. Maybe after the court decision, we will know who lied and who told the truth. I don't know. Because of that incident, maybe in the future they [Mr. Jia] will start to give higher salaries. And to provide a canteen where workers can eat Mongolian food so they don't have to eat Chinese. Maybe it will be possible that Mongolian workers and professionals can have their own separate places to live. If so and if they get higher wages, things will change, I think. Then maybe the *aimag* and the country will begin to develop.

As the evening wore on, the argument between the two collaborators became more heated, reaching a low point with Pedersen's parting salvo before going to bed: "Don't be so bloody naïve, Mikkel! Do you think local NGOs will succeed in their fight against Chinese multinationals by being nuanced and balanced? As far as I am concerned, they can say anything they damn well like. It's their country!"

Having initially assumed that friendly conversation would make it possible for Bunkenborg and Pedersen to reconcile Chinese stories of anti-Chinese prejudice and violence in Mongolia with Mongolian tales of Chinese encroachment and exploitation of Mongolians, it was increasingly clear that the cracks between these incommensurable social, political, and cultural realities, the distances imposed between Mongolians and Chinese, extended into the collaborative research project, cracking it open and exposing an intimate distance within it. By speaking to Pedersen while ignoring Bunkenborg, the journalist had made it abundantly clear that the Chinese and their friends (including Chinese-speaking ethnographers from abroad) had no place in a conversation between Mongolians and *their* friends, including Mongolian-speaking foreign scholars.

By treating the two ethnographers so differently, the female journalist not only drove a wedge between them, she also undermined a key premise of the collaborative project, namely the Dual Perspective Approach, which rested on the assumption that joint fieldwork would enable them to reach a common understanding of the ethnographic reality on the ground regardless of the perspectives afforded by our respective Chinese, Mongolian, and Mozambican informants. Having involved themselves in the conflict between the local news corporation and Mr. Jia, Bunkenborg and Pedersen rapidly found themselves running out of neutral ground for dispassionate discussion. The very idea of trying to align not just two but three different perspectives suddenly seemed like madness. It wasn't that Pedersen and Bunkenborg were prepared to follow their interlocutors all the way in their often vitriolic and racist representations of one another, or that they engaged fully in the mutually enforcing dynamic of mistrust, accusations, and hostility between Chinese and Mongolians in Mongolia more generally, but even so, the two ethnographers' ideal of anthropological collaboration had clearly reached a dead end. No amount of friendly dinner chats and earnest scholarly deliberation about anthropology's methodological and epistemological challenges could hide the grim realization than an unbridgeable gap existed between their basic perceptions and understandings of the ethnographic reality under investigation and the fact that it was going to be difficult, perhaps impossible, for Bunkenborg and Pedersen to reach a real consensus on their project.

What prompted Bunkenborg's reaction to Pedersen's collusion with the journalist at hand was not just a childish irritation at being ignored but also a certain liking for Mr. Jia and a sympathy with his struggles. The image of Mr. Jia as a "lying Chinese whoremonger" that the journalist and other locals sought to propagate (and which Pedersen, in his view, was not doing enough to question) was clearly a threat, not just to Mr. Jia's business but also to his personal safety. To Bunkenborg, the image seemed a gross and almost willful misrepresentation of the man's aims and intentions. Having followed his adventures and setbacks through intermittent interviews over a period of two years, Bunkenborg had come to appreciate Mr. Jia's friendliness, his reckless yet rather endearing entrepreneurship, and his gutsy attempt to start up a business in Mongolia. Finding Pedersen's suspicious view of Mr. Jia unwarranted, Bunkenborg insisted on a more balanced understanding of the case, but Pedersen found it ironic that Bunkenborg would make a plea for covering all the angles since he had obviously chosen to work for the Chinese side from the beginning. Taking his cue from the journalist, Pedersen hinted that Bunkenborg had been recruited to help Mr. Jia when the libel case first erupted in 2010. From Pedersen's point of view, Bunkenborg's attempts to follow the case as it unfolded looked less like an even-handed investigation and more like an attempt at aiding and abetting Mr. Jia.

Damage Control

On his 2010 visit to Choibalsan, Bunkenborg was surprised to be woken up by a phone call very early in the morning. It turned out to be Mr. Jia, who sounded agitated and asked for advice. The local police had just left his building. They had taken his car, his driver's license, and all the passports of the Chinese workers.

The police had stopped his car in the evening, but uncertain about their motives, Mr. Jia had driven off and then refused to let the police into his building. As the police were getting ready to enter the building by force, Mr. Jia informed Interpol that he was afraid the Mongolian police might molest him. Worrying that an international incident would reflect badly on the Mongolian police, the commanding officer ordered his men to stand down and wait till morning. Mr. Jia was convinced that the visit from the police was connected to the television program and suspected that he was being targeted as part of a local political struggle. "Is the television program a criminal offense? Is it a case of libel? Should I call the Chinese embassy?" Mr. Jia asked. Then he hung up, calling back twenty minutes later to inform Bunkenborg that the Chinese ambassador was very concerned about the incident. It was obviously necessary to obtain the footage as evidence. "We also need to discover who is behind this reportage," Mr. Jia said, suggesting that Bunkenborg would be in a good position to find out.

The ethics and risks of getting involved in an ongoing dispute with local Mongolians as a sort of secret agent for Mr. Jia seemed tricky, but in the end Bunkenborg was so curious to know what was going on that he went to the television station with a Mongolian interpreter. It turned out that a woman and two female reporters ran the television station. One of the reporters spoke a little Chinese, and she explained that they had visited Mr. Jia because some of his neighbors had asked them to find out what he was doing. The first time they went to the building, they were sent away. When they came back a few days later, the Chinese boss was there, but he refused to be interviewed and would not let them film inside the building. When they did so anyway, there was a bit of a scuffle, and Mr. Jia had shouted and pushed the reporter with the camera. The journalists came away without a proper interview, but having seen Mongolian prostitutes in the building and Chinese workers installing bathrooms, they felt pretty sure that Mr. Jia was transforming the historical building into a brothel. Bunkenborg asked whether he might be allowed to see the program, but the reporter insisted that it had already been deleted. She revealed that they were considering a follow-up to the story since one of Mr. Jia's neighbors had called after the broadcast and complained that Mr. Jia wasn't paying the Mongolian workers properly. Mr. Jia deducted the price of the tools the workers destroyed, and the workers ended up with nothing. The reporter didn't seem particularly proud of the program, but she was adamant that it wasn't a complete misrepresentation. The interpreter, a well-educated woman in her thirties, also thought that the reporters were right in depicting the Chinese boss as a bad person. She was puzzled that Bunkenborg had come to a different conclusion. He explained that Mr. Jia was setting up an agribusiness and showed her a photo from Premier Wen Jiabao's visit to Mongolia a few months earlier, depicting Mr. Jia among the prominent Chinese businessmen standing around Wen Jiabao. Bunkenborg argued that it was unlikely that Mr. Jia would be allowed to pose for a photo with the Chinese Premier if he were just a small-time pimp running a prostitution racket. The interpreter remained unconvinced, but she agreed that there was a real chance that Mr. Jia and the Chinese workers might get beaten up because of the unbalanced reporting in the television program. "Yes," she said with a smile that Bunkenborg found highly disconcerting, "they might even get killed."

Later that day, Bunkenborg called Mr. Jia to tell him that it was not possible to obtain the broadcast since the reporter claimed it was already deleted. The police had returned his car, his driver's license, and the passports of the Chinese workers, but he was still upset about the incident and convinced that someone had set him up. Bunkenborg told him that the television station was a small commercial enterprise run by an energetic but not particularly well-educated woman and that in all likelihood a Chinese businessman in the former headquarters of the Revolutionary Party was simply an easy target for a news-hungry local journalist looking for a sensational story. Mr. Jia refused to believe it. Even the dumbest reporters would have to know exactly whom they targeted with such a story, and they would also make sure they had political backing. While Mr. Jia suspected that Bunkenborg had only managed to scratch the surface of a larger conspiracy, he used some of Bunkenborg's information in a letter of complaint to the Chinese embassy, characterizing the television channel as "a private and highly irregular station, consisting of just a few persons." His five-page letter set out the legitimate goals and friendly ways of the company and then described the infuriating injustice it had suffered:

> We came to invest in Mongolia with the goal of self-development, but at the same time, we have stimulated Mongolia's economic development and greatly contributed to the Mongolian People by supplying large quantities of grain every year, by alleviating the country's grain shortage to a significant extent, and by providing many job opportunities. In Mongolia, we abide by Mongolian law, we respect local customs, we take environmental protection seriously, and the company employees have never engaged in any illegal or undisciplined activity. In order to cultivate close relations to the local government and people, we frequently take part in welfare activities, and as far as possible, we have extended a helping hand to the Mongolians residing near the company. The company has thus established a correct and positive image in Mongolia, and it has a good reputation among the Mongolian masses.

Noting that a Chinese company operating abroad must consider not only its own reputation but also that of China as a whole, the letter described in some detail Mr. Jia's painstaking efforts to project the image of a dynamic, helpful, clean, law-abiding, and genuinely friendly enterprise, but then it proceeded to the heart of the matter, describing a different, more conflictual reality:

> Though our company has been welcomed and supported by the great majority of the local Mongolian people, there are a few unfriendly characters who believe that we have come to their country to plunder their resources and they act as our enemies in all respects. Again and again, we have been treated unfairly, but chosen to remain silent because we simply wanted to mind our own business and had no wish to make enemies in a foreign country. However, the incident that recently befell us is extremely infuriating, it exceeds the limits of our tolerance, and thus we turn to the embassy for help in the hope of reclaiming our dignity and rights.

Even while Mr. Jia had been busy putting together this letter, describing how the company's employees were collectively infuriated "from top to bottom" and united in their opposition to these "groundless fabrications," his company had already started to unravel from within, and he was facing a new crisis. The twelve Chinese workers employed to renovate the company headquarters were concerned with the possible implications of the reportage, and they suspected that the police would manage to find fault with their passports and work permits. Having lost faith in Mr. Jia's ability to fix such things with the local authorities, they wanted to leave Choibalsan immediately. Mr. Jia refused to pay them anything because they had not finished the renovations as agreed. The workers, however, insisted on being paid for the time they had already spent in Choibalsan. In the heated discussion that followed, the foreman threatened to kill Mr. Jia if he didn't pay up. Things were about to turn uglier when old Mr. Luo intervened. Throwing his Mongolian identity card on the table, Mr. Luo warned the workers that he was a Mongolian citizen and would not countenance any talk of killing people. In the end no one was hurt, but the Chinese workers packed their tools and belongings and departed, leaving Mr. Jia with a few trusted employees in a building shorn of its former grandeur and resembling little more than an abandoned construction site.

Mr. Jia's attempt to make friends had clearly become a spectacular failure, and the proper regulation of the messy Sino-Mongolian relations surrounding him now became a judicial matter. The case never reached a definite conclusion, but the material presented in the Mongolian court suggests that Mr. Jia's calls for friendship, his wealth, and his erratic use of gifts to forge intimate relations to various Mongolian partners elicited suspicion and even revulsion in Mongolia's last communist bastion.

Lost in Litigation

Mr. Jia employed a Mongolian lawyer and initiated a suit for libel against the television channel for broadcasting the damaging report. The bone of contention itself, however, the broadcast about Mr. Jia's company, proved to be missing and despite repeated efforts to procure a copy through different networks, neither Bunkenborg nor Pedersen managed to obtain it. Indeed, even the Mongolian courts failed in their efforts to secure the version actually broadcast. While the transmission itself remained elusive, the web of conflicting explanations and interpretations spun around the missing core of the controversy became ever denser. Through letters, interviews, and court records that accumulated around the case, it is possible to sketch out both the contents of the broadcast and some of the emerging fault lines between the Chinese and the Mongolians. Mr. Jia had seen the broadcast together with an interpreter, and judging by Mr. Jia's description, the broadcast primarily presented the company as being exploitative, rehearsing themes from a stock of urban myths and paranoid tales that substantiate Mongolian fears of Chinese encroachment. Based on statements made by the journalist and Mr. Jia's interpreter, however, it can also be interpreted as an attempt to impose a proper distance between Mongolians and Chinese and to recalibrate relations where money and affect were deemed to be mixed in disturbing ways.

In his letter of complaint to the Chinese embassy, Mr. Jia claimed that the report consisted entirely of frames of the building and close-ups of the employees. There was not a single interview with a member of the Mongolian masses to substantiate the story, and the recorded interview with Mr. Jia—where he explained the purpose of the company and presented relevant legal documents to the reporters—was not used at all. Instead, there was a voice-over accusing Mr. Jia and his company of a variety of wrongdoings. Mr. Jia summarized the libelous allegations made in the voice-over as follows:

1. That there were backdoor dealings and secret manipulation involved when the building that originally belonged to the Mongolian People's Party was sold at a low price to serve as the Mongolian headquarters of our company.
2. That there is constant traffic of prostitutes in and out of the company, and that it serves as a venue for prostitution.
3. That we [the company] are unfriendly toward our neighbors; that we do not even allow them to enter the yard, but chase everyone out; that we are arrogant toward people; and that our neighbors feel disgusted and maintain a hostile attitude toward us.
4. That the women in the neighborhood are so often harassed by the Chinese workers that they take a detour instead of walking past the company.

5. That we are a fake company; that we have been in Mongolia for three years and achieved absolutely nothing; that even the building remains in the original state; and that our real purpose in coming to Mongolia remains unclear.
6. That we do not give our Mongolian employees proper wages but just hand out a little money once a month.
7. That we completely refuse to give interviews and even scold and beat reporters.

While some of these allegations deal with instances where the Chinese are perceived to be disrespectful and unfriendly towards neighbors and journalists, the most damaging accusations are the ones that address an excessive proximity, either in sexual relations, or in secret economic transactions. It is evident from the transcripts that the journalist was not intimidated when she appeared in the court of Herlen district on October 8, 2010 and responded to Mr. Jia's complaint in the following way:

> No one has spoken unheard things or written things based on rumors. As the official who manages the operation of this organization, I do not have reason to accuse or blame our reporters who prepare stories and reports based on real pictures and facts. The fact that these Chinese people have decided to address the Court complaining about actions of our media organization, instead of reasonably receiving critiques concerning their wrongdoings and mistakes, could be understood as a demonstration of their insolent and disrespectful attitude. Upon the ending of this court procedure, we shall continue our struggle with these kinds of foreigners' attitude and deliberate ignorance of Mongolian laws. Also, we are ready to support their good intentions as well.

Making strident appeals to nationalist sentiment and describing the Chinese as insolent and disrespectful, the female journalist in question quite evidently got off to a running start during the first court hearing. But Mr. Jia managed to throw a spanner in the works by claiming that he had tried to resolve the matter amicably by sending an official from the UN to negotiate with the television station, saying, "The reportage does not match with reality; the tone of the explanation had an insulting manner. This was made known to the Chinese Embassy and the international community. After the broadcast, an official of the United Nations responsible for Asian matters came to New Channel television and told them to stop this broadcasting."

It was at this point that the journalist on the witness stand recalled that she had, in fact, spoken to "a foreigner." Judging from the court transcript this made both her senior peer and herself confused and incoherent in their testimony, perhaps because they were unsure who this foreigner was and what had been said. It may, of course, be that "an official from the United Nations responsible for Asian matters" had been present in Choibalsan at the time. But it seems rather more likely that this mysterious foreigner, who supposedly visited the media corporation after the infamous broadcast, was actually Bunkenborg, the meddlesome anthropologist! In any case, the mention of a foreigner caused so much confusion on the witness stand that the court decided that further investigation was required and the news corporation was ordered to hand over a copy of the broadcast as evidence.

When the court reconvened on November 18, the news corporation had provided the court with a version of the broadcast and offered a more substantial rationale for their visit to Mr. Jia's company:

> There are three types of complaints from the citizens in regard to their company. Firstly, complaints as to why the only building that was built with a military purpose—the building of the former headquarters of the party, was given to Chinese. Secondly, these Chinese came in March 2008. We do not know what they are doing. During the three-year period, there is information that one year they slaughtered over 1,000 animals and soiled the headquarter building with the blood. Thirdly, there are complaints that Mongolian employees are not given their wages; instead, they are fired and removed. Also, according to neighboring residents, they drink a lot of alcohol inside their premises, and since the doors are always closed, the possibility that the Chinese bring in prostitutes cannot be excluded. In general, these people think that they can do anything they want, and they are not pleasant for neighboring people. Thus, we decided to verify the information. We went there three times; the son of the director Jia Xinsheng and his daughter-in-law were there. When the reporters visited the place, they got arrogant and said, "Get out, we will not give an interview," and even hit the camera.

The female journalist's more or less explicit hints as to the sinister motives that might have prompted Mr. Jia to acquire a former military building and use the blood of slaughtered animals for renovations serve as "evocative transcripts" that reference a stock of popular Mongolian stories about China and the Chinese. In these stories China is invariably cast as an evil force involved in various machinations and ploys ranging from the plausible—the Chinese would like to take control of Mongolia—to the paranoid—the Chinese government is trying to eliminate the entire Mongolian population by exporting shoddy goods and foodstuffs poisoned with pesticides (Billé 2008). "We do not know what they are doing," the journalist states. Yet, far from giving Mr. Jia the benefit of the doubt, she then invokes popular paranoia about the Chinese in Mongolia, hinting that the fact that she does not know what the company is up to is only an additional indication that they surely must have something to hide: "Since the doors are always closed, the possibility that the Chinese bring in prostitutes cannot be excluded."

Interestingly, the journalist managed to convince the court that the burden of proof should be reversed so after the second hearing the judge decided to dismiss Mr. Jia's suit on the grounds that he had not produced evidence to disprove the claims presented in the broadcast. Mr. Jia protested that the witness had given the court a doctored version of the report that differed significantly from the original broadcast, but the judge ignored his protests. Mr. Jia was left with no other recourse than to appeal the decision to the provincial court.

During the court hearings it was Mr. Jia's Mongolian interpreter who presented his complaints. A comparison between the Mongolian interpretation presented in court and the Chinese interpretation of the reportage that was sent to the embassy reveals an interesting discrepancy. The Mongolian reading repeatedly mentions how the reportage refers to the wealth of the Chinese. The reportage claims that Mr. Jia and his employees "treat people without respect and offend them with wealth," that these "wealthy Chinese" should be kept in their place, that they "use pressure on people who like money and make them work for low wages," and that when the television reporters came, "they insulted them, demonstrated their wealth, and almost beat them." Considering that both versions of what was said in the report must be based on information from Mr. Jia's interpreter, it is striking that the Mongolian version repeatedly emphasizes the offensive wealth of the Chinese, while this is not even mentioned in the version that Mr. Jia wrote up and sent to the embassy. It is almost as if the very idea that his wealth could be regarded as offensive is so outlandish to Mr. Jia that it doesn't really register even though his interpreter is well aware that it is one of the main issues in the report. The picture is not entirely clear-cut, as Mr. Jia is also presented as a miser who makes people work for low wages, but the odd claim that Mr. Jia will "use pressure on people who like money" and "offend them with wealth" may well suggest that it is not so much his stinginess as his generosity that makes his wealth offensive. What is understood as reprehensible about Mr. Jia's behavior, then, is not just the way he underpays workers, but the way he throws money around, giving gifts, indebting people, and making them do things they would not otherwise have done. While the report definitely presents a critique of the way Mr. Jia paid his Mongolian employees, what really provoked the journalists may not have been the economic exploitation—after all, that is only what one might expect from a Chinese, they perhaps assumed. Rather, it is fair to venture, it was Mr. Jia's erratic use of wealth to forge relations of economic, emotional, and sexual intimacy in Mongolia. On the surface, the report worked as a simple exposé of Chinese economic exploitation, but on a deeper level it was also a more disturbing and inchoate call for a recalibration of unseemly and excessively intimate relations, demanding an end to promiscuity and backdoor deals, and calling for properly structured interactions where workers are paid on time, neighbors are received politely, and reporters are treated respectfully. The report and the court case made it perfectly clear that despite his calls for friendship and his apparent willingness to invest both money and sentiment in relations with local collaborators, Mr. Jia had made no friends in Choibalsan. Instead, he had made people deeply suspicious of his motives and triggered the chain of events that forced him to abandon his plans in Dornod.

The Divisive Bridge of Friendship

When Bunkenborg and Pedersen returned to Choibalsan in the summer of 2012, they found the headquarters of Mr. Jia's business deserted. The building was locked; the vegetable garden in front was untended; and many of the new windows had been smashed. The neighbors didn't really know what was going on, though one had heard a rumor that the Chinese owner had been arrested for dealing drugs or something of that nature. Luckily, Mr. Luo was at home tending his garden, and he explained that Mr. Jia had decided to stay away from Choibalsan but was still in Mongolia. He continued to push on with the lawsuit against the local media organization. Puzzled by Mr. Jia's persistence, Bunkenborg asked Mr. Luo to explain his take on Mr. Jia's motives:

> BUNKENBORG: Why does he want to stay in Mongolia? He ran into so many problems, so much trouble. Why doesn't he go back to China?
>
> MR. LUO: Things would have been so much easier, if he had invited all the leaders of Dornod Province for a meal and explained to them what he wanted to accomplish when he first arrived. You can't just rely on backdoor dealings, and no matter how much money you have, you don't just give it away for nothing. He is that kind of man. He doesn't spend money when he should, then he tries to go by the back door, and spends more money than he should.
>
> BUNKENBORG: Why doesn't he go back to China? He has money and a good position in China. Surely it would be easier for him to make money there?

MR. LUO: He would make more money in China, but he is making a
name for himself in Mongolia, and when he stays in Mongolia, it's
for his reputation.

Many of the popular stories that circulate in Mongolia mirror historical narratives about the Chinese as exploitative merchants and usurious lenders (Billé
2014, 72), and the miserliness attributed to the Chinese is equally reflected in
contemporary ghost stories featuring the souls of rich Chinese merchants who
cannot bear to depart from their hoarded wealth and so haunt the place where
they buried their treasure (Delaplace 2010; 2012). If Mr. Luo's assessment is correct, Mr. Jia was more concerned with his reputation than his profits, and his
erratic shifts between miserliness and generosity do not fit the stereotypical
Mongolian image of a calculating Chinese businessman. "He is the kind of man
who will gladly give you a thousand RMB one day, and then ask you to sign a
receipt for ten RMB the day after," Mr. Luo said, shaking his head at the recollection of Mr. Jia's unpredictable behavior.

On the plane back to Ulaanbaatar, Pedersen revealed that he had made other
arrangements and would not be returning to the Wenzhou, a cheap Chinese
hotel in a somewhat dodgy neighborhood in Ulaanbaatar. "Where are you
going?" Bunkenborg asked, somewhat taken aback by this development. "Well,
I think it's really important that you keep up the good work and hang out with
the Chinese," Pedersen responded. "You said so yourself. The Wenzhou is a fan-
tastic place to meet the Chinese miners and investors passing through Ulaanbaatar, and it is also really convenient for you that you can talk to the hotel
staff in Chinese." Pedersen paused to let it sink in how perfectly the Wenzhou
suited Bunkenborg before he continued. "But I usually arrange meetings with
my Ulaanbaatar informants in the cafes around the city center, you know. Many
of them are state officials or representatives from various organizations so staying out there would be really inconvenient for me." Noticing the look of disbelief
on Bunkenborg's face, Pedersen hastened to add, "But let's meet up for lunch
tomorrow. Just give me a ring. Oh, and don't forget to watch your back if you go
out at night in that area."

The Wenzhou, it appeared, was undergoing major renovations, and Bunkenborg was thoroughly annoyed, not just with the din of jackhammers but also with
Pedersen who seemed to be distancing himself from the form of collaborative
research that had hitherto been the norm. However, Bunkenborg's reflections on
Pedersen's unusual behavior were cut short when Mr. Jia finally responded to his
cell phone. It turned out that he was still in Mongolia, and having temporarily
abandoned his projects in Dornod, he was now engaged in setting up an abattoir
in the capital. After some ten minutes of conversation, it became apparent that

Mr. Jia was in fact staying at the very same hotel, so Bunkenborg walked down the corridor to knock on his door. Laughing loudly at this strange coincidence, Mr. Jia uncorked a bottle of Chinese red wine and placed Bunkenborg in a chair for a long day of drinking, smoking, and talking.

Neatly dressed and constantly puffing away on the slim cigarettes he preferred, Mr. Jia seemed to be his usual dapper self. He was very enthusiastic about his new project. On the one hand, he was setting up an abattoir on the outskirts of Ulaanbaatar with a small group of Chinese investors, and on the other hand, he was trying to pull strings in the Chinese Ministry of Commerce to get the border opened for trade in livestock and meat. Also, one of his sons had recently bought a share in a fluorspar mine in Sükhbaatar province, and they were buying new computers as a gift to the local district administration to ensure amicable relations. There seemed to be little change in Mr. Jia's fundamental approach to business, but he became visibly worked up as he explained how the district court had rejected his suit against the local media organization. Mr. Jia insisted that this had been a political rather than a legal decision:

> MR. JIA: When the provincial governor heard about this case, he intervened. He called the court, and said that it would not do to have a Mongolian paying damages and apologizing to a Chinese. . . .
>
> BUNKENBORG: How do you know?
>
> MR. JIA: The lawyer I found is a man with a sense of justice. After the ruling, I asked him how it had come to this, and he told me. He had asked people at court. He said that I should forget about it and be satisfied that the television station wouldn't do it again in the future. Such appeasement! "Don't carry on." He said the provincial governor telephoned in person. I was furious at the time and said, "You claim that Mongolia is ruled by law, so how can power be greater than the law? How can you just do what he says?"

Having lost the case at the district court, Mr. Jia chose to ignore the advice of his Mongolian lawyer and appealed to the provincial court. In January 2011 the provincial court decided to censure the district court because it had failed to secure and consider the reportage as it was actually broadcast. With this important evidence missing, the provincial court reasoned, the actual case could not be decided, and it was accordingly sent back to the district court. For Mr. Jia, this was a useless victory, and he was having second thoughts about pursuing the matter at the district court again as there was a very real possibility of a legal battle would drag on for years in one court after another. Also, Mr. Jia had heard that a Korean investor had given the provincial governor a number of apartments to take over the land in Halhgol that had been originally promised to Mr. Jia. If true, Mr. Jia would be an embarrassment to the governor, and his various business projects in Dornod were unlikely to prosper before a new governor came to power. So Mr. Jia had decided to leave the building under the care of a single caretaker and pause his ongoing projects in Dornod while he awaited the results of the next election.

Mr. Jia still thought it was possible for him to succeed as a businessman in Mongolia, but his talk of Mongolians had an angry edge that Bunkenborg had not noticed in their conversations a year earlier. Mongolians did not appear to respond in the way Mr. Jia had expected, and this experience was something he shared with a number of Chinese business associates. Over dinner in an upscale restaurant that evening, a Chinese businessman recounted a similar story of disappointed expectations. Rather than speculating that Mongolians might simply have a different approach or questioning the universality of "human emotions," (人情), he seemed inclined to draw the conclusion that the Mongolians were not fully human, but more like children, saying, "It's difficult sometimes with the Mongolians. They're like children. The children will cry and throw tantrums, and then the Chinese hand out candy and tell them not to cry. After a while, the children are no longer satisfied with candy; now they want toys, expensive toys. Then the Chinese will think about it and hand out toys. After all, they're just children. And then it just gets worse and worse. Actually, when children throw tantrums like that, you should smack them twice and tell them they're not getting anything."

Late that evening Mr. Jia's Chinese chauffeur took him and Bunkenborg from the Chinese restaurant back to the Wenzhou hotel. On the way through the dimly lit streets of Ulaanbaatar, Mr. Jia pointed out darkened construction sites and half-finished buildings where Chinese investors had been stalled by conflicts and political machinations. By the time they reached the bridge known in Mongolian as Enhtaivan Güür (Peace Bridge), Mr. Jia had worked up a strong sense of the accumulated injustices suffered by the Chinese. He exclaimed loudly, "Do you know this bridge? It's actually called Friendship Bridge (友谊桥), and it was built by the Chinese. But not so much as a thank you did we get in return. The day after, they were saying 'What a lousy bridge the Chinese have built. They should have built it in marble, but they used cement and it will go to pieces in a few decades.' They even said that on television, seven or eight years ago. The staff at the embassy was furious."

In Mr. Jia's reading, the Chinese friendship bridge was a gift intended to establish a practical and symbolic connection between China and Mongolia, and the fact that the Mongolians rejected it out of hand as an inferior piece of infrastructure clearly resonated with Mr. Jia's own experience of trying to forge connections and being rejected.

Totalizing Friendship

If the common image of the Chinese entrepreneur presented in Western media and academic literature is that of an ultrapragmatic economic man with little desire to establish lasting ties in the places targeted for investment, the story of Mr. Jia's failed attempt to make friends in Mongolia may serve to question such simplistic assumptions. The controversy in this case sprang not from indifference towards Mongolians but from Mr. Jia's overeager efforts to combine economic and affective investment and from his attempts to be intimate in ways that local people perceived as excessive and patronizing, if not downright imperial. As Mr. Jia invested ever more capital and emotion in cultivating ties to the Mongolians, the rumors of his unseemly sexual and economic relations grew stronger. The issue came to a head in a widely disseminated and much discussed news story and an ensuing court case where the social relations between Mr. Jia and the local Mongolians were presented not as friendships but as the impossibly messy outcomes of his offensive wealth. In the context of Sinophobia and apprehension about Chinese investors buying up the whole country, Jia's attempts to make friends among the Mongolians set off a process of complementary schismogenesis, in Bateson's sense (1958). While he continued to intensify his economic and affective engagement in Mongolia, Mr. Jia's local counterparts became ever more suspicious about the real motives behind these lavish gifts and offers of friendship. The imposition of friendship triggered a messy web of relations surrounding Mr. Jia and activated a contractive mode of sociality, where his effusive protestations of friendship were met with increasing skepticism. Mr. Jia's endeavors may prove successful in the future, but his frustrated insistence on friendship seemed to be more than just beginner's difficulties. Though he seemed increasingly bitter, he continued to launch new projects in which his approach to other Mongolian collaborators was not so different from what he had attempted in Choibalsan. Mr. Jia made few friends in Mongolia, but his misguided efforts were highly productive in the sense that they contributed to the configuration of a form of intimate distance, where one side operated on the suspicion that the relation was pure business while the other was perpetually disappointed at the misrecognition of what it saw as a genuine attempt to make money and friends.

Friendship presents itself in this chapter as a desire that remains perpetually unfulfilled, but also as a relational form that drives the production of a particular type of intimate distance in Sino-Mongolian relations. We would suggest that it is possible to discern, in the fraught relations produced around this disappointed desire for friendship, the contours of a more general form of intimate distance that does not occur just in this particular case or exclusively in Mongolia but that may well be an integral part of an emerging relational infrastructure of globalizing China, where friendship and its disappointments play a central role.

The day after meeting Mr. Jia at the Wenzhou, Bunkenborg joined Pedersen for lunch in a traditional Mongolian café. Working his way through yet another heavy soup of mutton fat and noodles, Bunkenborg relayed the news of Mr. Jia's relocation and his continued attempts to make friends with the Mongolians. However, it soon became apparent that Pedersen was losing interest in Mr. Jia and his Mongolian adventures. At some point Bunkenborg had had enough and expressed in no uncertain terms that he was displeased about the direction their collaboration was taking. Having sat through endless conversations in Mongolian and consumed inordinate amounts of salty tea and mutton fat in a bid to see things from the perspective of Pedersen and his interlocutors, Bunkenborg found it unfair that Pedersen was now refusing to make the slightest effort to see things from a Chinese perspective. From the outset the whole idea of conducting fieldwork in pairs had been to see things from both sides so as to reach a common understanding that would be better and more comprehensive (at least twice as good and twice as comprehensive) as anything they could have achieved on their own. Initially, Bunkenborg conceded, Pedersen had in fact made an effort to partake in conversations with the Chinese, but more recently he seemed to be changing the parameters—and lowering the ambitions—of their collaboration by avoiding the Chinese informants, deliberately excluding Bunkenborg from interaction with his own Mongolian ones, and more generally resisting Bunkenborg's attempt to establish common analytical ground. "We were supposed to work on this together," Bunkenborg complained, "but Nielsen is doing his thing in Mozambique, you have started doing your own thing here, and it seems I am the only one who feels compelled to actually try to bloody collaborate!"

In the long and awkward silence that followed Bunkenborg's plea for collaboration, the relation between him and Pedersen suddenly appeared eerily similar to that between Mr. Jia and his Mongolian collaborators. With an almost audible click, a new line of interpretation sprang open. Was it possible that the growing appearance of obstacles in their own collaboration was not a random fluke that could be settled over a couple of beers and a good night's sleep, but an indication that the fraught relations between the Chinese and the locals were starting to emerge in the internal relationship between themselves as researchers? If so, was there a sense in which the emerging Chinese empire they had set out to investigate in Mongolia had begun to manifest itself within the dynamics and frictions of their own collaboration? If the imposition of friendship in relations to locals was a Chinese logic of empire, and if locals were generally skeptical towards such patronizing gestures of "friendship" and "understanding," then Bunkenborg's constant attempts to maintain friendly relations with not just the Chinese and Mongolian interlocutors, but also with Pedersen, his almost compulsive desire to present a balanced account and to incorporate the perspectives of his colleagues in a total analytical synthesis, could be interpreted as an imperial strategy in its own right, and Pedersen's rejection as an equally predictable anticolonial response.

WHOSE WALLS?

A Chinese Mining Enclave in the Gobi Desert

"It's just to improve the environment. When we first started planted the seedlings, someone in our group said, 'Let's make things pretty and orderly around here,' and we decided to make two rows with ample space for each of the trees to grow tall and strong." Such were the words of the manager of the Bountiful Nature Mine, a wiry, bespectacled mining engineer known as Professor Guo, in response to Bunkenborg's query into the contours of a square enclosure around this mine, which he and Pedersen were visiting for the second year in a row (see Figure 2.1). Using some of the rocks that had been chipped clean of fluorspar, it was Professor Guo's predecessor, Mr. Lin, who had first traced the outline of a wall in the perimeter of the camp and planted two rows of saplings. Mr. Lin's wife and his ten-year-old son had come to spend part of the summer in Mongolia, and perhaps the presence of his son, who complained that there was absolutely nothing to do, was part of the reason why Mr. Lin had tried to produce a semblance of domesticity. But Mr. Lin did not return to Mongolia, and all but one of his saplings died (placed close to a rusty cart used to accumulate rainwater, the single tree that did make it probably survived because of the occasional splash of water from the cart).

Professor Guo was dismissive of his predecessor's gardening skills, but he outlined a far more ambitious plan: A wire fence surrounded a new building, and he envisioned the installation of an irrigation system that would allow him to grow trees and flowers inside the perimeter of the fence. "It would be so nice," he mused, "if I could sit in my office and look out upon a garden full of flowers instead of this colorless and boring landscape."

It was Pedersen who first noticed the Chinese garden-in-the-making. To him and Bürneebat, the Mongolian driver of the two Danish ethnographers, the contours of a walled courtyard with trees was not only an incongruous sight in the wild, windswept Mongolian desert, it was yet another sign that the Chinese were more or less intentionally—and more or less violently— imposing a radically different landscape aesthetic if not a neo-imperial logic upon their former colony of Outer Mongolia. Bunkenborg, stepping on the row of stones and plants without taking note of them (and thus ironically contributing to the garden's shabby and not very threatening appearance), was unimpressed by Pedersen's discovery and calmly tried to reassure his collaborator that the Chinese managers were just trying to make things look a bit nicer for themselves and their visiting relatives. Alas, this did not reassure Pedersen or Bürneebat, who reminded Bunkenborg about the several other instances of conspicuous Chinese gardening encountered during their travels in the Mongolian countryside. The most ambitious gardening project they had come across so far had been at a zinc mine, a Mongolian-Chinese joint venture located outside Baruun-Urt, the provincial capital of Sükhbaatar Province in southeastern Mongolia. There it had clearly been of great importance to the Chinese CEO, who took the two ethnographers on a guided tour of the shiningly new and well-ordered factory complex, that the mine was not only producing top-grade zinc ore but also high-quality vegetables. Walking around the muddy fields amid enormous piles of potatoes and carrots, he bragged to Bunkenborg that the potato harvest that year amounted to ten tons and that the largest potato weighed 1.6 kilograms. In addition to the fields, there were four large, heated greenhouses where a group of Chinese technicians managed to grow more than twenty different vegetables. The CEO picked a cucumber and munched it while explaining that it wasn't even necessary to wash the vegetables since they were grown organically. Having sampled a variety of greens and commenting that the strong ultraviolet light in Mongolia made the chili peppers and bitter melons grown from Chinese seed unusually pungent, the CEO explained to Bunkenborg that his dream was to make a "flower-garden–style mine" (花园式的矿场).

For this Chinese manager, and possibly some of his peers at other Mongolian mines, the ambition of establishing a "flower-garden mine" complete with trees, flowers, and vegetables seemed to involve more than a simple question of beauty, but a larger cosmological vision of "creating a small society" (创造一个小社会), as he put it. Thus, the future "flower-garden mine" would not just provide the workers with vegetables produced on site. As in the former state socialist collective farms and factories studied by anthropologists in Mongolia, the former Soviet Union, and China (Bray 2005; Bruun 2006; Humphrey 1998; Kotkin 1997; Lu and Perry 1997; Ssorin-Chaikov 2003; Pedersen 2011; Smith, M. 2015), the mine would also take care of housing, leisure activities, and education for the workers and their families in the style of an all-encompassing socialist "work unit" or *danwei* (单位). Having noted several instances of marriage and children among the coworkers, he was even considering the possibility of opening a kindergarten. "Maybe we could even open our own university," he joked. "Then we could hire Bunkenborg to teach the Mongolian workers Chinese!" When Bunkenborg translated for Pedersen and Bürneebat, the joke fell totally flat. Indeed, it made the two of them uneasy and worried, as if an invisible danger had suddenly become manifest in their most everyday surroundings. This uncomfortable sensation of an *unheimlich*, potentially malevolent alien force lurking behind seemingly innocent flowers and vegetables was brought back full scale when it dawned on Bürneebat that the Bountiful Nature Mine was also seen as a "flower-garden mine" and, more alarmingly still, a future "small society" by Professor Guo and his compatriots.

As the two ethnographers sat down that evening to talk about their day, Bunkenborg could not help responding to—and perhaps, against his better will, start becoming influenced by—the postcolonial passion (or, he could not help thinking, paranoia) drummed up by his fellow travelers. To be sure, it was unlikely that Professor Guo or the zinc mine manager thought of themselves as a secret vanguard of Chinese territorial expansion cleverly masked behind the innocent garb of gardening and environmental protection. But then again, he conceded, imperial effects are not always predicated upon imperial intentions. It was not entirely impossible that the almost subliminal aesthetics of gardening were imbued with effects reaching far beyond local affairs. Certainly, as a seemingly frivolous practice irrelevant to the business of resource extraction, the potential implications of gardening could easily be overlooked. So perhaps Pedersen was on to something with his assertion that gardening was doubly insidious precisely because it was construed as an unremarkable and almost natural side effect of Chinese life.

In *The World in Miniature: Container Gardens and Dwellings in Far Eastern Religious Thought* (1990), Rolf Stein suggests that the Chinese garden has traditionally been imagined as "a miniaturization of the world," imbued with magical power. In this view, a Chinese garden is not a representation of the cosmos but a magic act of world-making that renders the universe malleable: "Whenever hermits draw or cultivate dwarf plants in a miniature landscape, they create for themselves, as does a magician-illusionist, a separate world in miniature" (52). Without necessarily subscribing to Stein's notion of a timeless Chinese cosmology, it seemed to Bunkenborg just possible that the real intervention of the Chinese miners in Mongolia took place just as much through extracurricular gardening activities as through the more mundane business of extracting fluorspar and zinc. As anthropologists Katherine Lutz (2006) and Anne Stoler (2002) have shown, sites of imperial power and colonial intervention are located as much in the nitty-gritty details of everyday life as in large and imposing material and political structures. Perhaps there was a sense in which the withering saplings encircling the mine were the seeds of an empire to be.

China's global expansion has been theorized as a form of "enclave capitalism" (Ferguson, 2005). Yet, as we discussed in this book's introduction, it is pertinent to ask what might happen when the enclave is not the result of a centralized master plan but results from scattered groups of private Chinese? Is the "enclave" here not so much a precondition but the *product* of a specific instance of collaborative damage? If so, what can that reveal about our concept of intimate distances and its purchase in this and other ethnographic contexts?

These are some of the questions we address over the following pages. Accordingly, we chronicle Pedersen and Bunkenborg's case study of the Bountiful Nature Mine, a small, privately owned Chinese fluorspar mine located deep in Mongolia's Central Gobi Province. Considering three arenas of Sino-Mongolian relationships and conflicts—environmental damage, work conditions, and métissage—we tell a tragicomic tale from a small mining enclave in one of Mongolia's most mineral-rich and sparsely populated provinces, where the increasingly fraught relationships between Chinese and Mongolians reached a low point when gangs of self-proclaimed Mongolian Nazis accused and attacked Chinese workers for engaging in sexual liaisons with local women, "polluting the purity of the Mongolian blood" and the nation state. In doing so, we continue our exploration of Chinese and Mongolian perceptions and conceptualizations of what constitutes the right kind of social relationship in a given situation, understood as an optimal balancing between engagement and detachment, intimacy and distance.

How Not To Respect Local Customs

Having landed for the first time in Ulaanbaatar a few days before, Bunkenborg was still punch-drunk from the unfamiliar sights and incomprehensible language of the Mongolian capital, where he scanned in vain for signs and sounds in Chinese.

But the real shock occurred when he and Pedersen left the city on a snowy September morning. The bridge leading south was under repair, and a long line of cars was waiting. Instead of slowing down and getting in line, Bürneebat, their driver, swerved onto the grass and took them along the river until they reached a stony patch with shallow water. With a gleeful expression, the driver floored the accelerator and rammed the car through the waist-deep water with a splash. Both Pedersen and Bürneebat were laughing maniacally when they made it to the southern bank, and Bunkenborg realized that this was a landscape and a mode of relating to it entirely different from what he had become accustomed to after years of fieldwork in the pear growing districts of rural Hebei deep in the Chinese heartland. As they headed south, Bunkenborg had the impression that roads were not strictly necessary and that driving a car was more like riding a horse that might be urged to swim through a river or whipped up a hill to get a view of the terrain. In the end, this was how they spotted the mine. Driving along and between the parallel dirt tracks that cut through the sparse desert vegetation, their driver sped to the top of a hill and located the mine with a pair of binoculars. To Bunkenborg, what met them was a very strange sight. A blockhouse in cement, a wooden shed, half a dozen yurts, rusty metal winches placed above what seemed

FIGURE 2.1.   The Bountiful Nature Mine, Central Gobi Province. September 2009.

to be two shafts, pushcarts, and metal tracks—a seemingly random assemblage of structures without clear boundaries or center in a vast and empty landscape.

As they approached the shaft closest to the yurts, Bunkenborg trailed behind while the driver and Pedersen greeted a group of bulky Mongolian men in canvas outfits and helmets, who were smoking next to the winch. Noticing an awkwardly smiling man in a cheap suit who looked just as displaced as himself, Bunkenborg relaxed. Clearly, this was a Chinese person with whom he could communicate, and judging from the stolen looks the man received from the Mongolian workers, he was also the holder of significant authority in the camp. As for Pedersen, things were very much the other way around: an initial sense of familiarity and routine was replaced by one of strangeness and alienation as he realized this was no ordinary visit to a Mongolian *ger* (the traditional nomadic dwelling of Mongolia's nomadic peoples). He had already felt a first twinge of discomfort when noticing the stones around its perimeter, as if someone were trying to physically demarcate a spatial boundary between inside and outside. But things got worse when Mr. Hao, as the man introduced himself, invited the two foreign visitors inside. Bunkenborg, as oblivious of correct bodily deportment in Mongolian yurts as the Chinese clearly were, immediately felt at home and found the set-up rather nice, a bit like a Chinese home in a tent. It was only after a prolonged session of talking and chain-smoking with the Chinese managers that he noticed that Pedersen was somewhat surprised and troubled at what he saw.

What from the outside looked like any other ger in a male-dominated Mongolian work setting—small, dirty, without ornamentation, but otherwise essentially identical to the homes inhabited by thousands of herding households across Mongolia—immediately appeared to Pedersen as a veritable tableau of Otherness. From the perspective of Mongolian *yos* (custom), the interior space of the ger was organized in the *buruu* ("wrong") way: a huge bunk bed occupied the entire *hoimor* (north section) of the ger where, under normal circumstances, one would expect to find the family altar and seating for the senior men. Instead of various tools and washing facilities, the southwest corner was filled by a battered computer table and a worn office chair. Even more shocking and downright offensive to Pedersen and the Mongolian workers he spoke to was the blatant failure of the Chinese to abide by "the 100 rules" for behavior within a ger (Humphrey 1987), ranging from the taboo about touching or even passing any object through the two central poles (*bagana*) to the notion that the fireplace (*gal golomt*) is pure and should thus be treated with appropriate respect. In fact, as Pedersen pointed out to Bunkenborg once they stepped outside, the sight of a worker with a cigarette in his hand slung across an unkempt bed in the sacred hoimor was a moral aberration from the perspective of all Mongolians, especially when this worker happened to be from China, the historical arch-enemy and primary current foreign investor. Why, Pedersen asked, could the Chinese not make an effort to learn some basic yos?

It is hardly a coincidence that the ger stood out as a central arena of failed Sino-Mongolian collaboration at the mine. In many parts of Mongolia, it is still the most common form of dwelling for pastoralists, especially in the grasslands and deserts of southern and eastern Mongolia, where trees are scarce and herders nomadize up to eight times a year (Humphrey and Sneath 1999). But even in Inner Mongolia inside China on the other side of the border, where much land is fenced as the herding economy has shifted from nomadism to ranging (Sneath 2000; White 2020), Mongolians attach enormous importance to the ger, even if they do not live in one for most of the year, or at all. Conversely, even the Chinese living as herders in Inner Mongolia do not show any affection toward it.[1] In fact, as several scholars have observed (e.g., Pasternak and Salaff 1993), in Inner as much as in Outer Mongolia, the ger and one's behavior around and inside it has come to symbolize what being Mongolian is all about—as perhaps, walled compounds materialize the Confucian values behind the traditional patriarchal household in Chinese contexts (Dutton 1998). Small wonder, therefore, that the Mongolian workers (and Pedersen, who had spent years living among hunters and pastoralists in northern Mongolia; cf. Pedersen 2011) reacted so strongly to the Chinese flipping ash in all directions from their cigarettes with no regard for hoimor, gal golomt, or any other sacred spaces inside the ger. Behaving in such a disorderly (*zambaaraigüi*) and uncivilized (*yosgüi*) manner, the Chinese were not just sending an impolite and disrespectful message to the Mongolian workers and the local herders, they were quite literally soiling Mongolian custom and its associated ideal of a balanced and orderly cosmos celebrated in ancient lore as well as in contemporary public culture.

Bunkenborg thought something crucial was missing from the oft-repeated lament about Chinese disrespect for Mongolian ways of life. "Actually," he told Pedersen as they set up camp for the night, "some of the Chinese here would like to learn more about Mongolian culture." The problem was that no Mongolian had ever told the Chinese anything about yos, even though some of them had lived in the camp, working, eating, and resting together, for weeks, months, or even years. Mr. Hao, the manager of the Bountiful Nature Mine, had told Bunkenborg earlier, "I just don't get these people! We try to be fair to them, but get nothing in return." So, Bunkenborg tried to convince Pedersen, from the Chinese perspective, it was just as much the Mongolians themselves who were acting disrespectfully by responding so coldly to what was actually an earnest attempt on the part of the Chinese to respect the local people and improve their lives. As we are going to see, there was more than a glimmer of truth to this depiction of Chinese motivations, even if their effects were not met with the cheers from workers and locals that people like Mr. Hao thought they deserved.

Collaborative Complaining

The story of the Bountiful Nature Mine resembles other accounts collected by Pedersen and Bunkenborg of how small- and medium-sized Mongolian mines ended up in Chinese hands via processes that are often opaque and therefore lend themselves to conspiracy theories and rumors among locals. In the present case, the owner of the mine was a man from Hangzhou with a degree in mining. Having travelled around Mongolia after the turn of the millennium looking for promising mining licenses to purchase, he decided to buy this particular mine from a Mongolian artisanal miner (called *ninjas* from their colorful hard-plastic helmets) based on a geological survey undertaken by Soviet technicians in 1986. The survey indicated that there were sizable deposits of fluorspar, but the mine had not been developed. It was still a small operation when he bought it from the ninja in 2004. The man also owned another fluorspar mine in the Central Gobi province and was investing some US $6 million to set up a processing facility in the regional economic and railway hub of Choir, where he and the company planned to process the fluorspar ore from his two mines as well as additional ore purchased from other mines in the region.[2]

Developing the mine was a slow process, the Chinese frequently reminded Bunkenborg, but small, incremental steps took place each year. On Pedersen and Bunkenborg's first visits, the fluorspar was washed on site, but this process was later moved to Choir, where water quality was less problematic. The original, hand-drawn survey maps were checked and digitalized by a Chinese technician, who also drew up a plan for new and improved shafts underground. New buildings were being added, and the designated ger, which contained explosives, eventually became surrounded by earthen ramparts to prevent mishaps from flattening the whole camp. Nevertheless, while the physical structures of the mine did indeed seem to improve between each of Pedersen and Bunkenborg's visits, there was always a rapid turnover of staff. Because a provision in Mongolian labor and mining law dictated that all mines must have ten Mongolian employees for every foreigner—a regulation that in many cases proved impossible to abide by in practice (Jackson 2015b; Batbuyan and Fernández-Giménez 2012)—it was difficult for Bunkenborg to obtain precise staffing figures from the Chinese managers, who seemed to exaggerate the number of Mongolian workers and understate the number of Chinese. Judging from Pedersen and Bunkenborg's five visits

FIGURE 2.2.   Mongolian workers, Bountiful Nature Mine, Central Gobi. October 2010.

to the mine over a four-year period, the staff averaged ten Chinese and some thirty Mongolians, all of whom worked together from early spring until the mine closed down for the winter around 1 November. There was always a muscular Mongolian guard from a security company in Ulaanbaatar posted at the mine to keep tabs on the explosives, intervene in conflicts among the workers, and prevent arguments with visiting locals from getting out of hand. All the other Mongolians employed at the mine were manual laborers, the men generally working in the shafts and the women chipping and cleaning the fluorspar ore that was brought out.[3] Apparently, the Chinese managers at some point had tried to solicit help from the local district to identify suitable local employees, but most of them had eventually been deemed unfit or simply unwilling to work underground, so the mine instead employed Mongolians from a variety of places, including both the local district and Ulaanbaatar.

   The Chinese contingent was made up of managers, technicians, and foremen, a few of whom had brought their wives along to do odd jobs around the camp. They hailed from many different provinces in China: Guangxi, Sichuan, Hubei, and Inner Mongolia, but the owner of the Bountiful Nature Mine seemed to have a preference for people from his own native province of Zhejiang. They had no means of transportation, and except for meat—which the Chinese cook sometimes purchased from local herders—they had to ask the head office in Ulaanbaatar to send a truck when they needed supplies, though sometimes, Mongolian workers could be persuaded to fetch items from the nearest village on their motorbikes. Because of poor reception a cell phone had been permanently affixed to the top of a pole in one of the gers, so while it was possible to reach the outside world, it was necessary to stand on a chair for the duration of the conversation. Small wonder that the Chinese felt alone, deserted, and vulnerable. Their sense of abandonment and isolation was accentuated by their limited opportunities to communicate with and get to know their Mongolian coworkers and the locals. Necessary daily communication the employees relied on sign language and a few simple phrases in Chinese and Mongolian; the foremen called upon their Inner Mongolian interpreter only to explain basic emergency procedures to new workers.

The mid-level Chinese staff worked on one-year contracts with a salary of RMB 3000–4000 a month. They typically arrived in late March, stayed on site for the duration of their contract, and when the mine closed down for the winter in December, they returned home and received their entire salary as a lump sum. The Mongolian workers, conversely, were typically paid twice per month and earned much less than their Chinese peers, ranging from MT 200,000 a month for beginners to MT 300,000 a month for workers with some experience. According to Professor Guo, they "often asked for advances," which he saw as an indication of their "inability to plan ahead." Thus, he complained, on each salary day some Mongolian workers would disappear and only come back days later with enormous hangovers, remorsefully begging to get their jobs back. To this, the Chinese cook added that he had also noticed that on the twice-monthly payday, only one or two of the Mongolian workers would go shopping for flour, salt, toilet paper, and other daily necessities while the rest of them discussed where to drink. "I try to persuade them to drink less," he explained with a tired voice. "'You've got children and parents at home,' I say. They all understand but still won't listen." The Mongolian workers, on their side, were equally puzzled about the way in which the Chinese spent (or rather, did not spend) the money they earned. Unsure how much the Chinese were actually making, they knew it was saved up and hidden, which reinforced pervasive Mongolian stereotypes about the Chinese hoarding their wealth, hiding it underground, and refusing to pass it on, even to their own children (Delaplace 2012).[4]

Still, if there was one thing that the Chinese and Mongolian workers did seem to have very much in common, it was the fact that they did not like being there. No matter whether one was a middle-class mining engineer from Chengdu on a two-year contract in Mongolia or a former Mongolian state socialist factory worker from the provincial capital, now employed as a day-laborer, one was stuck in the middle of the desert a long way from home without loved ones (often not even via telephone), long hours of hard and dangerous work six and (depending how much ore the miners dug out per day) sometimes seven days a week, with little choice in food, and an extremely limited range of possibilities for spending one's precious time off. Apparently, the only thing that made people stay was the money.

Pedersen was witness to a constant murmur of dissatisfaction from the Mongolian workers at the Bountiful Nature Mine, a murmur that occasionally rose to a chorus of collective complaint. Indeed, it was striking how differently the Chinese and the Mongolians understood why things went wrong, who was blamed for it, and how they vented their frustrations. The Mongolians drew on an extensive repertoire of ethnic stereotypes, many of which have circulated in Mongolia for centuries, the subject of detailed and critical anthropological analyses (Bulag 1998; Billé 2014). Some of the most widespread include the notion that Chinese people are hardworking but stingy and cunning, as opposed to Mongolians who are lazy but also honest and generous; the idea that Chinese men are unmanly wimps, unable to fight, who like to gossip "like women", unlike Mongolian men who know how to fight and speak straight; and the widespread conception that Chinese love vegetables (which they grow right next to their toilets!) in opposition to "real Mongols," whose ideal diet consists of meat and milk products from sheep, goats, and cows. What most bothered the Mongolians at the mine—apart from the fact that the Chinese did not know how to behave inside a nomadic ger—was the inadequate working conditions, especially (1) what they considered to be unreasonably low wages and the lack of breaks, and (2) the lack of proper equipment (clothes, helmets, tools, etc.) necessary for them to not only perform their jobs safely, efficiently, and in accordance with regulations, but also to be the "real workers" (*jinhene ajilchid*) they wanted to be. Indeed, the issue of rights was at the heart of Mongolian complaints, both formal rights as stipulated in national labor laws (and in contracts between companies and workers, and between companies and authorities), and in the more informal sense of workers' expectations of a proper relationship between employer and employees.

The Chinese were less univocally negative in their views of the Mongolians. Professor Guo, found it hard to accept that the "bad habits" of his Mongolian workers had anything to do with Mongolian culture as such and speculated that modern Mongolians might have been affected by the spendthrift habits of Westerners and Russians (after all, he reminded Bunkenborg, one should not forget that the Mongolians were once the rulers of China). In making this comment, he displayed the sensibility (and the biases) of an educated mandarin doing his best to rationalize the particularities of the Mongol workers with reference to a unique culture worthy of the same measured respect accorded to non-Han Chinese "minority nationalities" (少数民族) inside China. But his attempted tolerance was constantly interrupted, and trumped, by more straight-talking Chinese from less priviledged class backgrounds such as the cook, who simply saw Mongolia as "underdeveloped" (不发达). As far as he and his peers were concerned, Mongolians were "primitive" (野蛮), "childish," (幼稚), and "backwards" (落后). Having spent more time in Mongolia than his boss, he felt that he drew upon a wider range of experiences to back up this conclusion.

The disagreement between Professor Guo and his Chinese employee was emblematic of the attempt by Chinese managers and workers to reconcile more or less genuine respect for certain aspects of Mongolian way of life with a more or less explicit, nagging sense that Mongolian people were plain and simply backwards, if not downright barbarian. Stressing their respect for local ways and traditions in the abstract while becoming repeatedly irritated and angry in their concrete encounters with workers and locals, the Chinese managers slid between tolerant relativism and impatient developmentalism in a way that called to mind liberal Western voices in nineteenth-century empires (Mehta 1999) as well as many contemporary development projects (see e.g. Ferguson 1994; Escobar 1995). Yes, Bunkenborg admitted in response to Pedersen's complaints about Chinese racism, there was a clear sense among his Chinese interlocutors in which the "wild Mongolian landscape" and its "backward, savage inhabitants" needed help in order to be made "modern and productive," but it would be a mistake to see this imperializing and patronizing notion as a purely economic endeavor. More than simply cold calculation, there was an aesthetic sensibility of civilized existence involved in the Chinese understanding of their role and impact in Mongolia. And nowhere, Bunkenborg reminded Pedersen, was this noninstrumental imperial aesthetics more visible than in the Chinese attempt to cultivate a "flower-garden mine" in the middle of the desert.

Pedersen could feel his patience with the Chinese (and Bunkenborg) running dangerously low. Why, he asked Bunkenborg, were the Chinese so obsessed with "developing" and "civilizing" a proud country and people who were far from a cultural and economic *tabula rasa* onto which the Chinese could impose their own tastes and more or less repressed colonial desires? He decided that they needed to visit some local herders living in the vicinity of the mine. Perhaps this would teach Bunkenborg and his Chinese pals a thing or two about life in the inner Asian desert. His hope was that, in doing to, Bunkenborg would come to understand that the allegedly "empty" and "wild" space upon which the Chinese had imposed their walled compounds and exploitative neoliberal regimes, was, in fact, a place of immense human complexity and natural beauty.

From Aliens to Adversaries

From Pedersen's conversations with a number of local herders, it eventually transpired that their experiences with the Chinese in and around the Bountiful Nature Mine had undergone significant changes over the years. When the Chinese first arrived around the turn of the millennium, their motivations for turning up in the homeland of the Mongolian herders seemed opaque and mysterious to the latter. Only one thing was clear, they told Pedersen, namely that "the Chinese loved to work, and to make other people work too." As a middle-aged household head, who arrived every spring with his family, belongings, and livestock to spend the summer at a designated spot a few kilometers east of the mine, explained to Pedersen: "I remember that when I used to bring my sheep to the pond next to the mine, the Chinese were always chattering. None of us local people had a clue about what they were saying. But it was clear that they made people work very hard. To work according to schedule and to rest according to schedule. The Chinese were always on time. Everything they did was on time."

As the years passed, the presence of the Chinese became a known and predictable to the locals, although some aspects of their lives (e.g., money) were still felt to be couched in a cloud of radical alterity. This transformation from unfamiliar strangers to familiar others involved trading partnerships and other business friendships that, however, gradually deteriorated between Chinese workers and the herders, and increasing tension and competition between the mine owners and the herders about scarce water resources. As three of the herders explained to Pedersen:

> HERDER 1: Herders from around here don't like the mine anymore. Our drinking water is being depleted. There was a spring three kilometers from here, and another around four to five kilometers in that direction [points in direction of the mine]. Both used to be full of water, but now they are dried out. It is because they are pumping out so much ground water from the ground. We think it's because of the mine.
>
> HERDER 2: Since 2000 animals began to die. Not right away, but over time. As long as the herds do not graze in this area for too long, it is okay. But animals belonging to families who water their livestock here become sick all the time.

HERDER 3: Some years back, things were not bad. Now water levels have dropped, and the wells are poisoned. If the animals drink this water for more than a month, their livers and lungs become destroyed. Maybe it's because of chemicals used in the explosives. People here say that when the lambs grow up, they sometimes start running like they are drunk. . . . It has become like a war zone around here. I just wish the Chinese would go away. Every time officials come from the provincial government, we here try to tell them, but to no avail. And now I am sure that the springs have dried out for good.

Later that same day, in the windswept district center some ten kilometers away, the secretary of the district council, a stern-looking, bespectacled woman in her late thirties, gave Pedersen her version of the environmental situation in and around the mine:

I don't know about any wells that have actually dried out. But the ground water level has dropped several meters. Their shafts and tunnels reach all the way down to the ground water. So, they have to pump all this water out to work. A muddy lake of drain water has emerged north of the mine. This is why the water levels in the wells are falling. According to the water department at the Aimag [the provincial government office around one hundred kilometers away], the water level is going down because of global warming, not because of any pumping. But the local herders think that the wells dried out because the mine is pumping water out, and they continue to complain about it.

For several years, the interactions between the mine managers and local cadres were relatively cordial, stable, and predictable. But this businesslike relationship was not to last. When Pedersen and Bunkenborg returned to the Bountiful Nature Mine in August 2011, they were faced with a different tone and new complaints about the Chinese mine. As the secretary of the district council lamented to Pedersen, in a rare outburst of emotion for someone in her position:

This May the members went on a monitoring trip to all mines in the district. As you know, the district council is the highest level of authority at the local level. Out of fifteen members of the council, thirteen of us went, including the head. In total, we visited ten mines. By far the worst case was the [Bountiful Nature] Mine. The working conditions are very bad. For safety measures, workers are just provided with rubber boots and nothing else. They are not given any special clothes even though they have to go down deep. Even dirt-poor people do not live like that in such shabby gers! The food is bad, and the conditions are poor; even the containers for storing the food are dirty.

At this point, the secretary lifted the receiver of her bulky black phone to call one of the lower-ranking staff members at the district administration, instructing her to find the "demand for action" (*shaadlaga hürgüüleh tuhai*) so that Pedersen and Bunkenborg could see it. While they waited, the secretary explained that if the Chinese failed to solve the problems raised in the letter, the district council would take them to court, a rather dreaded scenario, judging from her expression. Before Pedersen could enquire any further, a young man wearing a suit and nomadic boots knocked on the door and entered the room. The secretary gave him a silent nod, and he presented Pedersen with the following letter signed by the head of the district council from July 2011:

> For the director [of the Bountiful Nature Mine] and its manager
> Demand for Action
>
> The District Council monitors the activities of the thirteen companies that have exploration and extraction licenses in this district. As part of our supervision, we found out that enhancement, environmental hygiene, the comfort of workers' places to live, workers' social issues, and order in the [Bountiful Nature] Mine were very bad compared to other mines. So we are issuing this demand to solve the following problems.
>
> 1. Provide safety clothes (like pants and coats) to workers every season (every three months).
> 2. Register the premium of social insurance and health insurance in the workers' insurance books every month; and have workers keep their insurance books on hand. Pay workers' salaries through cards and get their signatures for approval.
> 3. Starting from June 1, 2011, register part-time workers' social insurance premiums and income taxes in the district office.
> 4. Improve the appearance and style of the mine compound and establish a fixed road between the rest and work areas. Improve conditions for the workers during their free time (by building a square for basketball, volleyball, and billiards; and a pavilion).
> 5. Plant trees, bushes, pasture perennials and grasses in order to protect the soil and stop desertification.
> 6. Dig a special channel of no less than 1.5 kilometers long to ensure the channeling of wastewater from the mine to the artificial lake.
> 7. Keep foodstuffs in a special storage place that meets the requirements for health and hygiene.

8. Keep gers used for cooking and eating very clean and make them comfortable. (Separate the place to prepare food from the place to eat).

9. Prepare a proper menu and increase the amount of food served.

10. Solve the problem about the road from the mine to Choir and stop using the dirt road for transport and ruining nature.

11. Build a comfortable place for the workers to live and a hot shower.

12. There are 26 Mongolians and 5 foreign workers at the mine. This is not in accordance with § 9:1, provision 43.1 in the Mineral Law. Therefore, according to provision 43.2 of the Mineral Law, a fine must be paid for two foreign workers for the last two months to the district's account in the Toriin San Bank before June 25, 2011.

13. Manage the mine properly, and stop crimes and vodka drinking. Organize training and produce leaflets in consultation with relevant officials from the district to prevent on-site crimes.

We require you to fulfill this demand fully and give us an official report by July 1, 2011.

"So," Pedersen concluded, turning his head to Bunkenborg with an assertive look as Pedersen and Bayarmaa (his research assistant and teacher who had joined them on this trip) finished translating the petition that evening, "all this pretty much corroborates what I had predicted when we discussed this yesterday." Pedersen was referring to the fact that neither the form nor the content of the document contained any surprises compared to other complaints and litigation by officials and NGOs against the Chinese companies that he and Bunkenborg had come across in southeastern Mongolia. But Bunkenborg tapped his finger meaningfully on the fifth demand in the letter, and Pedersen paused mid-sentence as he took in the full meaning: "Plant trees, bushes, pasture perennials and grasses in order to protect soil and stop desertification." Could it be that the Chinese had planted saplings around the mine not because of some cultural proclivity for trees and gardening but simply because they were threatened with litigation? If this was really the case, as Pedersen grudgingly agreed with Bunkenborg could be a possibility when they discussed the issue, then it would not only force them to question their hypothesis that the "flower-garden mine" was a "seed of empire," but it might also force them to reevaluate their understanding of the Sino-Mongolian relationship more generally.

A Not-So-Productive Misunderstanding

When the two returned to the mine the following year, they immediately noticed a large, prefabricated building with white metal walls and a blue roof, which had been erected on the site. Assuming that the Chinese had finally grown tired of the gers, they were surprised to learn that the Mongolian workers had moved into dormitories in the new building. The manager who had made this decision was Professor Guo, the constant Chinese gardener. Happy to speak to an audience with more education than his employees, he eagerly explained what had happened:

> PROF. GUO: When I arrived, the Mongolians moved in here, and the Chinese moved into the gers.
>
> BUNKENBORG: What? You switched things around? Why?
>
> PROF. GUO: We do our best to offer the Mongolians the best conditions. You know the Chinese. Even if they come from a place where conditions are better, they can make do. We want to take better care of the Mongolians, so here it is the Chinese who live in yurts. Even I live in one. This is my office, but the rest are over there (pointing towards the other gers).
>
> BUNKENBORG: That's really interesting. Do the Chinese workers accept the gers? Do they mind?
>
> PROF. GUO: No, because the Chinese know this country. Originally the Mongolians were like the Chinese. But China's development has been somewhat faster, while their development has been somewhat slower. So they have a bit of a psychological issue and think the Chinese disrespect them. The first step is that all Chinese must learn to respect them, and when we have learned to respect them, they might feel better about us. For historical reasons there is still some enmity against the Chinese, so we need to express cultural respect. We are trying to respect them as much as we can from our standpoint.

When the Chinese cook joined the conversation, it became clear that living in gers was not a terribly efficient way of instilling cultural respect in the Chinese workers. He grumbled, "Have you ever done research here during the winter? I have been to the grasslands a couple of times. Old and young in one ger, a grandmother and her grandchildren with nothing to drink and nothing to eat. . . . They don't know where the next meal will come from. And the fuel they use is just cow shit they pick up. It's cold during the winter, and when I go there to buy sheep, they have their quilts draped around them, and the children's faces are all red with frostbite. I don't know if people live such bitter lives in Africa, but as for Asian countries, Mongolia is really uncaring." Professor Guo also expressed doubts about the ger and wondered why Mongolians were so conservative. It would be easy, he opined, to design an improved, prefabricated ger with a round covering in plastic or nylon to keep out rain. "No one here seems to use their imagination; it's such a simple thing, but they can't do it."

Gradually, it began to dawn on the two ethnographers what had happened since their last visit. In an attempt to respond to the critique of the conditions at the mine raised informally by its Mongolian workers and in the formal demand from the local district, Professor Guo had built "a comfortable place for workers to live and a hot shower" (per demand #11); he had made efforts to "improve the appearance and style of the mine compounds and establish a fixed road between the rest and work areas" and to "make good conditions for the workers to spend their free time . . . (by building a square for basketball, volleyball, and billiards; and a pavilion)" (per demand # 4), and endeavored to "keep gers used for cooking and eating very clean and make them more comfortable" by separating "the place to prepare food from the place to eat" (per demand #8). To underscore how seriously Professor Guo took the Mongolian workers, it had been decided that they (and not the Chinese) would move into the "modern" facilities, while the Chinese contingent would stay on in the old and "primitive" gers.

Alas, the Chinese attempt to show respect by offering the Mongolians what they considered the best accommodation backfired. Far from feeling that their problems had been alleviated, the Mongolian workers' criticism of the Chinese (and the latter's frustration with this critique) had only escalated compared with Pedersen and Bunkenborg's earlier visits to the Bountiful Nature Mine. Contrary to the intention of the Chinese, the fact that they had chosen to remain in the gers—aided by the fact that they missed no opportunity to stress their sacrifice in doing so—only accentuated the message that they did not respect the local yos.[5] After all, the workers had not been bothered about staying in gers (most of them also lived in gers with their families back home), and while gers are not associated with wealth in contemporary Mongolia, they are emphatically not a symbol of poverty and backwardness either, as many Chinese in Mongolia and Inner Mongolia seem to think. On the contrary, the ger is one of the most salient cultural forms across the Mongolian cultural zone; in places like Inner Mongolia, it has become a potent symbol of Mongolian nationalism and resistance.

It is hard to find a better example of an intimate distance, which is a very different kind of intimacy than the tacit acknowledgment of shared cultural knowledge (including imperfections) that Michael Herzfeld (2005) calls "cultural intimacies." By moving into what they considered the "backwards nomadic dwelling" while leaving the "modern and superior" accommodation to the Mongolian workers, the Chinese were too outspoken and perfectionist in their attempt to facilitate the "development" of Mongolian culture by leaving past "imperfections" behind. Just like Mr. Jia's failed business adventure in eastern Mongolia described in chapter 1, it was almost as if the Chinese were trying too hard—they were so eager and insistent in their attempt to please the Mongolians by meeting their needs that they ended up making the problem worse, not unlike someone in an unhappy relationship who is desperately trying to bring it back on track by overcompensating for the partner's lack of love. But this leaves the question of the wider effects of such misunderstandings on the Sino-Mongolian relationship. As described in this book's introduction, one of our original hypotheses was that new social, economic, and cultural forms are emerging as a result of China's recent political-economic expansion in the Global South, not in spite of misunderstandings between Chinese and locals but *because* of them. Influenced by Anna Tsing's (2005) influential study of the intended and unintended social, economic, and environmental consequences of wild capitalism in the margins of the postcolonial Indonesian state, from the onset of our collaborative research, we had operated with the hypothesis that the Chinese political-economic interventions in Mozambique and Mongolia that we studied might be theorized as "zones of awkward engagement," which may give rise to various kinds of "socially productive engagement" as opposed to necessarily always "leading to inaction" (xi). Our plan was thus to study Sino-local misunderstandings, not as aberrations from an ideal of mutual comprehension, but as instances of such awkward engagements at the very heart of the neocolonial global encounters.

While this initial hypothesis in many ways turned out to hold water, it also became increasingly clear as our joint fieldwork progressed that there was good ethnographic reason to ask whether misunderstandings between groups of people can become so entrenched and protracted that they cease to allow for any "socially productive engagement." This would seem to have been the case at the Bountiful Nature Mine. For both Tsing and other scholars who have theorized "failure as an endpoint" (e.g., Miyazaki and Riles 2005), there seems to be a mostly tacit assumption that at least a minimum of the "unintended effects" resulting from such miscomprehensions will be socially positive in the sense of giving rise to increasing interaction, communication, and perhaps even trust between peoples. And yet, the sad truth about the Bountiful Nature Mine was that, with each visit Pedersen and Bunkenborg made, it was becoming more difficult to uphold this hopeful image. Instead, they found a conflict and a looming sense of disaster that seemed ever closer to the surface, an impression that strife or even violence was almost on the verge of breaking out. And nowhere was this sense of imminent calamity more present than in the contested arena of real or imagined sexual encounters between Chinese men and Mongolian women.

"He Took a Mongolian Wife and Now He Is Dead"

Consider the following incident from Pedersen and Bunkenborg's first visit to the Bountiful Nature Mine in 2009. It was late afternoon, and the two of them had at this point spoken to several managers and workers working in or close to the fluorspar pits. Having secured permission from the Chinese boss, they walked a few hundred meters away from the mine proper, to the other section of the encampment. Initially, no one seemed to be around, but then they noticed a little boy playing outside what appeared to be his home (a few moments after the picture was taken, a female Mongolian voice called him inside the ger). Upon returning to his newfound Chinese friends, Bunkenborg was told that the gers they had just seen were the living quarters of two Chinese technicians who came from the same province and therefore preferred to stay together in their own corner of the mine. Leaving aside the surprising (and yet also rather telling and human) fact that a contingent of ten Chinese living in a remote desert in a country of people widely known to detest them would choose to split into two moieties, Pedersen and Bunkenborg were mystified by the small boy playing with his red toy car next to the open fluorspar pits. Whose child was he, and how had he and (presumably) his mother ended up at the mine?

According to the local herdsmen mentioned above, the boy was the illegitimate child of one of the Chinese managers of the mine and a Mongolian woman from the neighboring city of Choir, who had first worked as his cook. "Everyone knows," one of the men calmly observed, as he held out his cup so that the other's wife could refill it with salty milk tea, "that there are many *erliiz* ("mixed race", lit. "half-breeds"—the term is also used for animals) children around here." Not wanting to miss the opportunity to gather information (or gossip, as Bunkenborg suspected) about a sensitive topic of great significance, Pedersen asked the two herders if they had heard of other romances between Mongolians and Chinese in the area. "Well," said the herder after a long hesitation, "there is the story of Mr. Ping." Exchanging a knowing look with his friend, he continued.

> HERDER 1: Ping was a Chinese who used to come here to buy meat. Some of the cooks and other Chinese stayed for a while, so we got to know them. He stayed here a long time, perhaps two or three years, working as a sort of boss. He only had one person above him. Sometimes, he would buy cows from me. But then suddenly, he disappeared.
> HERDER 2: Yes, Ping is gone now. He died, I heard.
> HERDER 1: I heard that there was some kind of problem and that he died.
> HERDER 2: Maybe he was caught while transporting explosives [for expanding the mine shafts]. I don't know what happened.
> HERDER 1: Apparently, it was the relatives. A guy beat him up and almost killed him.
> HERDER 2: Really?

HERDER 1: Well, I mean, it was the relatives of his Mongolian wife.

HERDER 2: Ah yes, so he took a Mongolian wife and now he is dead?

HERDER 1: Yes, I am quite sure that it was his wife's relatives who beat him up.

HERDER 2: I am not sure. I heard that Ping beat up a Mongolian worker in a state of anger and affect. And then perhaps the other Mongolians tried to protect their friend, I don't know. But after this, Ping was gone. And the mine was closed for a while. The government shut it for down for two or three months. Luckily, all of a sudden the mine was closed.

HERDER 1: The mine was closed. And Ping died. So all our problems were gone.

Even in a cultural context where significant degrees of violence—especially male violence—is expected and accepted, if not morally sanctioned (Benwell 2009; Pedersen 2011; Delaplace 2009; Højer 2019), there is something disturbing about the offhand way in which the two Mongolian herders discussed the fate of their Chinese acquaintance. To quote Franck Billé (2013, 17), the underlying assumption here and elsewhere "is that . . . Mongols . . . have the natural desire to kill the Chinese, thereby indirectly equating Mongolness with Sinophobia." Indeed, as Billé (2013, 2) also points out, in the course of "the past decade, Mongolian public discourse has been saturated with anti-Chinese statements and acts of violence against Chinese citizens, but also against Mongols fraternizing with Chinese, have become an increasingly common occurrence," including when "the leader of the nationalist group *Höh Mongol* was imprisoned for murdering her daughter's boyfriend, who allegedly had studied Chinese and had established cultural links with China" (2013, 11). Certainly, Pedersen had heard countless stories about Chinese men allegedly involved in short or long relationships with single mothers from rural communities or with "prostitutes from the city." Yet, when enquiring about these matters, both Chinese managers and local officials tended to give vague and evasive answers. It is telling that the two ethnographers never met a Mongolian woman who "admitted" to a romantic engagement with a Chinese man, though they spoke to several who had been accused of such. On several occasions, however, Pedersen and Bunkenborg were presented with possible "smoking guns," such as the presence of a Mongolian woman on the premises of a Chinese boss or suspicions about Chinese individual's knowledge of Mongolian language and customs ("how otherwise would he have learned to speak Mongolian like that?"). Or the telltale indication of such Chinese-Mongolian unions—the sight of an *erliiz* child.

What is the source of these intense affects towards a sexualized and racialized Other that oscillate uneasily between animosity and attraction, similarity and alterity? According to Stoler (2002, 79–80), "in linking domestic arrangements to the public order, family to the state, sex to subversion, and psychological essence to racial type, *métissage* might be read as a metonym for the biopolitics of empire at large" (see also Povinelli 2006). Mongolia is a case in point. Both as a Qing colony (1668–1911) and a Soviet satellite (1924–1990), *erliiz* were at the heart of racialized and oftentimes racist discourses and practices. This is clear in nineteenth-century reports on intermarriage between Mongolian and Manchu nobility (Bawden 1989), in socialist-era debates about the political and cultural status of marriages between (male) "specialists" from the USSR and Mongolian (female) citizens (Pedersen and Højer 2008), and in considerations of the citizenship of the offspring of the allegedly thousands of "Chinese Mongolians" (ethnic Chinese born in Ulaanbaatar and elsewhere in Mongolia from Chinese migrants who arrived before or after the revolution).

According to Billé (2013, 20), "Because in the Mongolian cultural region ethnicity is conceptualized as being transmitted through the father's line, intimacy with the Chinese is particularly problematic for women" (see also Bulag 1998). Accordingly, "perceived as sexual predators taking advantage of naïve and/or impoverished girls, or as agents of the Chinese state, Chinese men are one of the main dangers facing the Mongolian nation, it is held" (Billé 2013, 26). As the eerie story about Mr. Ping indicates, such fears of métissage have not subsided in recent years. Indeed, combinations between resource nationalism and xeno- (especially Sino-) phobia have been on the rise in Mongolia since foreign (including Chinese) interest and investments in mining started picking up in 2005 (Billé 2014; Jackson 2015b), as epitomized by the emergence of self-ascribed "Mongolian Nazis" and other ultranationalist movements in Ulaanbaatar and by the increasing popularity of resource-nationalist discourse and Sinophobia among broad segments of the Mongolian population (Bulag 1998; Billé 2014; Dulam 2020). Although some government officials and businessmen try to strike a more balanced and less nationalist chord in their public discourse about Chinese and other foreign investment and people in the country, these xenophobic fears are not restricted to marginalized and impoverished segments of the population. Indeed, high-ranking officials, policy makers, and senior academics stressed to Pedersen that the increasing number of Chinese in Mongolia, and the purported increase in Sino-Mongolian métissage and birth of erliiz offspring in particular, constitutes a "gigantic problem," given that the recent influx of unaccompanied male Chinese expats and the high number of poverty-stricken Mongolian women (many of whom are single mothers divorced or widowed from

alcoholic and violent men) offer fertile conditions for interethnic sexual relations, marriages, and children.

In the course of the four years that Pedersen and Bunkenborg travelled in
Mongolia, they heard about numerous incidents of Sinophobic violence. Among
the more spectacular was the reported abduction by a group of dissatisfied locals
of a Chinese worker from an iron mine north in the Central Gobi province;
apparently, they put the man inside a big leather sack and told his Chinese bosses
that they would keep him there until their demands were met. In another incident from Inner Mongolia, much debated in the Mongolian press, a Chinese
manager drove his car into a mob of angry Mongolian coal miners and killed one
of them in what he insisted was a desperate act of self-defense. The victims of this
escalating xenophobia were not only Chinese citizens; even ethnic Chinese born
and living in Mongolia, as well as vulnerable Mongolian minorities such as poor
single mothers, were targeted.

In the summer of 2011, Mongolian right-wing extremism also featured very
prominently in Bunkenborg's interviews with Chinese residents. For example,
over a meal in a Chinese restaurant in Ulaanbaatar, Mr. Liu, an ethnic Chinese
man in his early forties recounted how his wife had been killed and his thirteen-
year-old daughter strangled and left for dead. The police treated the incident as a
robbery, but the man was sure it had been a politically motivated killing carried
out by members of the Dayan Mongols ("the Nazis"). Though he was fluent in
Mongolian and had lived all his life in Ulaanbaatar, he found it far too dangerous to move about the city on his own. As Mr. Liu was telling Bunkenborg how
dangerous Ulaanbaatar was, a muscular Mongolian with a shaved head and visible tattoos entered the restaurant and insisted that he wanted the chair that Mr.
Liu's equally muscular friend was sitting on. The friend deflated the situation by
moving to another chair, but the two Chinese remarked that the man was clearly
trying to pick a fight with them and they kept a wary eye on him all evening.

During their last visit to the Central Gobi province in the autumn of 2012,
Pedersen and Bunkenborg witnessed some of the concrete effects of this dramatic surge in Sinophobia and ultranationalist sentiments across Mongolia.
According to several of Pedersen's interlocutors in the area, that same summer
two Land Cruisers packed with members of the Dayan Mongols had toured
the Gobi desert looking for Chinese-owned mines. One Mongolian man,
who had met and spoken to them, explained to Pedersen with more than a
hint of admiration, that they were out "to teach them a lesson." Until 2012
the Bountiful Nature Mine had not been on the itinerary of these or other
ultranationalist groups but Pedersen and Bunkenborg did pay a brief visit to
another Chinese fluorspar mine some hundred kilometers away a few weeks

after a group of self-ascribed Nazis had paid a visit. Equipped with baseball bats, they had demanded "taxes" and beat up some of the Chinese. The Chinese were frightened and decided that it would be futile and probably even detrimental to report the incident to the local authorities. Even Bunkenborg only got the Chinese to talk about the incident after a Mongolian worker had hinted at the incident. According to a local guard, a man from Mongolia's Kazakh minority, they had left with the words, "We will return three weeks from now to check whether you have raised the salaries of the Mongolian workers to the same level as the Chinese. If not, then we will kill you!"

Until then, Pedersen had always found it hard to take the stories about "Mongolian Nazis" seriously (see also Højer 2020). It was, he thought, a passing fad that had been blown up by news-hungry foreign journalists and represented a small bunch of Mongolian losers who loved to pose in German WWII uniforms purchased from used-army shops in the former Soviet Union. As Pedersen had told Bunkenborg whenever the latter had brought up the topic, it just did not make sense for Mongolian nationalists to justify their violence toward the Chinese through Third Reich racism. The paradox that would seem to stand in the way of any theory of Mongolian "Nazism," namely the fact that it is often difficult to distinguish Mongolians and Chinese from each other, is a fact that many Mongolians are ready (albeit not happy and typically reluctant) to recognize. Indeed, as several Mongolians have confided to Pedersen, "Chinese and Mongolians have similar bodies"—even if, people hasten to add, it is not just possible but easy to distinguish individual members of the two "peoples" (*yastan*) by how they carry their bodies when, for example, walking, talking, and dancing. Nonetheless, as the angst and paranoia about a secret and invisible vanguard of Chinese-fathered offspring in Mongolia suggest, this method was not infallible either, for why otherwise be so worried about the erliiz?

"Racism," Stoler (2002, 84) writes, "is not really a visual ideology at all. Physiological attributes only signal the nonvisual and more salient distinctions of exclusion on which racisms rest. . . . This convergence of national and racial thinking achieves particular clarity in the colonial legal and social debates that linked parenting styles and domestic arrangements to the hidden psychological requirements for access to French and Dutch citizenship in the period." This, we suggest, is the reason why the seemingly oxymoronic "Mongolian Nazis" was not just locally meaningful, but came to attract the most ardent and extreme exponents of the widespread Sinophobia that spread across Mongolia at the height of the foreign investment boom in Mongolia in the years between 2005 and 2012. At the heart of this more or less overtly racist and more or less explicitly violent outburst of Sinophobia was the claustrophobic and paranoia-inducing awareness that, on the one hand, "Mongolian modern identity is contingent on a formal and absolute separation from China" (Billé 2013), while, on the other, this perceived radical otherness is not always distinguishable from you and your peers, and may thus potentially be present in your midst.

Pedersen and Bunkenborg were not surprised, then, on their last visit to the Bountiful Nature Mine in 2012, that what Professor Guo described as "a new and very strict set of rules" had been introduced concerning personal and private relationships between Chinese and Mongolians. "Does this mean that Chinese workers are not allowed to interact with Mongolian women at all?" Bunkenborg enquired. To which Professor Guo responded,

> Prof. Guo: They can interact, but there can be no sexual relations, that's not allowed.
> Bunkenborg: But there were before, right?
> Prof. Guo: Yes.
> Bunkenborg: That wasn't much of problem, was it?
> Prof. Guo: It was. After that happened, there was something about the way the Mongolian men saw the Chinese, something collective, as if all the Mongolians were saying, "You did so and so with a Mongolian woman." To different extents, they all hold it against you, and that is a problem for the whole company. There are small contradictions as it is, and when you add this, it may easily become a big problem. So now it's like this, we made it a strict rule for all Chinese workers. If you can't abide by that, you can't work here. It's a strict rule, so now we don't allow the Chinese here to do that sort of thing. If the Chinese are looking for girls, they can go home, they can't do it in Mongolia.

Apparently, the new rules had worked. Certainly, Pedersen and Bunkenborg were left with the clear impression during their last visit to the mine that there were no more amorous relations between Chinese men and Mongolian women—or indeed any close social relations between the two groups. As the two herders had told Pedersen during his last visit, with smirking grins:

> Herder 1: Generally, the Chinese never leave their compound anymore. They just stay in their holes.
> Herder 2: Oh, poor poor things! Ha! They know that the moment they leave, the Mongolians will come after them. So they stay inside the camps and buy what they need. They don't dare come to close to the herding households.
> Herder 1: Before the Chinese hired a watchman, two or three locals used to take turns to protect them in the night. They were paid 5000 per night for sleeping in their gers.

HERDER 2: Yes, and the Chinese have also tried to build a big fence around the mine for protection.

Faced with the threat of gangs of Nazis acting as self-appointed union leaders for a pan-Mongolian workforce, and with the danger of Chinese employees being abducted for ransom or simply disappearing, it is not hard to understand the Chinese need for protection and for "staying in their holes."

Whose Walls?

Few stereotypes have proven as persistent as the contrast between the "wide open steppes of Mongolian nomads" and the "walled enclosures of Chinese peasants." As the famous British geographer Owen Lattimore (1962, 39) put it, "A decisive choice [has been demanded] of every people and state that in the course of history overlapped the Great Wall Frontier . . .—the choice between agriculture of a notably intensive form and nomadism of an especially dispersed form. Of the repeated attempts to create societies or states that could integrate both orders not one succeeded." Over recent decades a number of prominent anthropologists and historians specializing in Mongolia and Inner Asia have done an important job in deconstructing and historizing this essentialized binary between nomadic Mongols and sedentary Chinese (see, e.g., Bulag 1998, 2002, 2009; Humphrey and Sneath 1999; Billé 2013, 2014; Myadar 2011). We have pursued a different strategy in this chapter. Instead of contributing to the laudable task of critical debunking of cultural stereotypes, we have attempted to strategically and deliberately play along with some of them. We have done this, of course, not so as to affirm these stereotypes, but to repurpose them for particular analytical and methodological ends distinct to the analytical predicament of conducting the present study and producing the present book whilst being mindful about the potential risk and the moral responsibility involved in doing so. In keeping with our overarching ambition of writing a comparative ethnography of globalizing China "from the inside out," we have thus constructed much of our account around a number of ethnographic differences experienced, interpreted and evaluated differently by Pedersen and Bunkenborg. In so doing, we have sought to unearth from within certain forms of intimate distances encountered by Bunkenborg and Pedersen in the course of their joint fieldwork.

For a long time Pedersen and Bunkenborg assumed that the Bountiful Nature Mine was a perfect example of a "Chinese enclave," understood as "distinct territorial, cultural, or social units enclosed within or as if within foreign territory" (Lee 2009, 653). In Africa and elsewhere in the world; "[e]ven when brought to work on projects that required prolonged stays in non-urban, remote parts of the country, Chinese workers, almost exclusively male, lived together out of sight of the local population, in walled compounds, which they seldom left. They imported all their food and requirements and when they left their compounds they did so as a group" (Ferme and Schmitz 2014, 385). As such, Pedersen and Bunkenborg's early musings concerning a "flower-garden mine" and other "miniature worlds" not only tapped into but served to bring to the fore and greatly intensify local and scholarly imaginaries about China's neocolonial ambitions abroad. In the eyes of both Pedersen and Bunkenborg (as well their Mongolian friends and Mongolian academics later shown these images), the different Chinese gardens, repurposed gers, and compounds encountered by the two ethnographers in the course of their travels in southeastern Mongolia were indeed the seeds of a new empire in the making.

But whose creation were these enclaves? As we have shown in this chapter, Pedersen and Bunkenborg learned in the course of their fieldwork of several cases where groups of Chinese had quite literally walled themselves in as protection from violent groups of Mongolian "Nazis" and other ultranationalist groups—almost like a new Great Wall (or many such walls) was in the process being built, but this time inside Mongolia itself. Indeed, we suggest that this image of many new Chinese walls goes to the heart of the particular kinds of intimate distance and relational infrastructures that were brought to the fore in Pedersen and Bunkenborg's joint fieldwork. At issue is the unnerving experience of unwanted closeness and awkward attachment that one has with people whom one would prefer to remain forever radically Other, but who force one to recognize that the Otherness at hand originates as much from within as from a place existing on the outside of one's person/group/tribe/nation (Harrison, S. 2003; Højer 2019)—a form of intimate distance overflowing and undermining all binaries between Self and Other, Us and Them. In Mongolian understandings of that sense, the Chinese have become a vanishing point in a Mongolian cultural imagination. In Mongolian understandings of their minds and bodies, perceived physical similarities and psychological differences come together in a paradoxical, optimal or sublime Other who is both radically familiar and radically alien at the same time.

Accordingly, as Pedersen's and Bunkenborg's study of the Bountiful Nature Mine progressed, the two ethnographers were forced to revise deeply held stereotypes about both Mongolians and Chinese as well as their mutual relation. Professor Guo and the other Chinese managers did not decide to build walls or to "stay in their holes" due to a deep "cultural logic" that celebrated bounded spaces, walled compounds, and floral empires; nor did the Mongolian resistance toward the Chinese spring from an innate proclivity for open spaces, free movements, and a corresponding aversion to walls, compounds, and enclosures. Whether the wish expressed by Professor Guo and his Chinese peers to "learn more about" and "better respect" Mongolian traditions and laws was actually sincere (Pedersen and Bunkenborg have yet to agree on this), it is safe to surmise that it was not just the Chinese but also the Mongolians who were the cause of the former's desperate attempts to wall themselves off from the surroundings. As shown by the tale of Mr. Ping—not to mention the disturbing touring of the Mongolian countryside by groups of right-wing, ultranationalist vigilantes—it was the actions of the Mongolians as much as the Chinese that forced the latter into isolation, socially, spatially, and emotionally.

ROADS THAT SEPARATE

How a Chinese Oil Company Failed to Detach
Itself from Its Mongolian Surroundings

"We don't know anything about those Chinese over there, and we don't have any interest in them," said the elderly Mongolian herdsman. Pedersen and Bunkenborg had stopped at his *ail* (household) to ask directions during their first trip in southern and eastern Mongolia looking for Chinese resource extraction projects in the Gobi Desert (the "Chinese safari" as Bürneebat, their driver, mockingly called their endeavor). As they entered the ger, Bunkenborg and Pedersen caught a glimpse of an oil tower flickering in the desert horizon several kilometers away. Over a serving of salty tea, the head of the household, a man in his late fifties, grumpily confirmed, "Yes, some Chinese are apparently drilling for oil over there." He quickly went on to stress that neither he nor the rest of the family knew anything about that place. Indeed, throughout the visit, the herdsman missed no chance to emphasize his total lack of interest in "those Chinese over there."

The herdsman's response came as a surprise to Pedersen and Bunkenborg. After all, the Chinese oil field was the closest neighbor to this isolated household, the nearest nomadic *ail* being located at least a dozen kilometers away. Surely, the two ethnographers asked themselves as they waved goodbye to the family from their car, even taking into consideration that many Mongolians are suspicious of if not downright hostile toward the presence of Chinese in their country, such a remotely located household would be interested in a new and strange neighbor like this. Might there not be money to be made from the Chinese, as hired hands or via informal trade? At the very least, one would expect the children to be curious.

Pedersen and Bunkenborg's musings were brought to an abrupt halt as the rear axle of their four-wheel drive snapped. The fact that they were some 150 kilometers from the nearest town explained Bürneebat's unusually glum countenance as he examined the fractured axle. It dawned upon the two novice collaborative ethnographers that they would be in this particular patch of the Gobi desert for a while. There was no one in sight, but on the horizon they could glimpse the Chinese drilling tower for which they had originally been heading. They had literally though accidentally become stuck in the no-man's-land between the two groups of people they had set out to study, with the Mongolian ger and the Chinese oil rig separated by ten kilometers of desert.

It was only natural, Bunkenborg and Pedersen decided, that they pay the Chinese a visit. There they found three dozen oil Chinese engineers, geologists, and workers living in camps around two drilling rigs with a few kilometers between them. The camps consisted of neat rows of white containers, each equipped with bunk beds, electric heating, and air-conditioning, in addition to a shared bathroom and a common kitchen. All supplies were trucked in from China, the workers claimed, and the food was prepared by a Chinese cook. Asked whether they had any interaction with the local Mongolians, they responded, "There is no one here!" and gestured at the undulating desert that stretched to the horizon without any sign of human habitation. Indeed, the oil workers ensconced in their snug containers seemed entirely disconnected from the pastoralists and their herds. Caught midway between what came across as two radically different worlds, Pedersen and Bunkenborg's immediate thought was that everything fitted into the stereotypical image of sedentary Chinese and nomadic Mongols living radically disparate lives (see chapter 2).

Things were not what they seemed, however. Early next morning they were woken up in their tents as a battered Nissan pickup passed by. It was only the second car they had seen for two days, and much to their surprise, it turned out to be the head of the herders' *ail* and two of his sons, with a full-grown goat in the back. "Where are you going?" Pedersen quizzed unnecessarily. "Over there, to the oil field," was the curt reply. Ever so slowly and only through very persistent questioning, Pedersen ascertained—between half-finished sentences, forlorn looks, and downcast eyes—that the Mongolian family was a regular supplier of meat to the Chinese oil workers, who apparently purchased "a couple of goats every fortnight," delivered and paid for at the gates of their container compound via the mediation of the single Mongolian there (a young man employed as security guard, who described himself as the loneliest person in the world). Naturally, Pedersen and Bunkenborg very much wanted to ask the herdsman and his sons, in a minimally awkward way, how this information squared with what they had been told a few days earlier. Alas, the possibility never arose, for the herdsman stepped on the gas pedal, and the pickup vanished in a cloud of Gobi dust.

Many anthropologists would no doubt take this anecdote as a reminder of the basic sociological dictum to always distinguish between what people say that they do and what they actually do. Indeed, this was very much the conclusion Pedersen and Bunkenborg reached in the aftermath of the event. "Okay!" they told each other with the self-satisfaction of professionals convinced that they have discovered something about their informants that has been kept secret from them. "That was the reason behind the old man's striking indifference toward his Chinese neighbors during our visit to his *ail* a few days before." Evidently, he had not wished to disclose what was clearly a convenient business arrangement, just as, very possibly, he had also felt ashamed about his friendly relations with the mistrusted Chinese. Yet over the following days, as the two ethnographers gathered sheep droppings to heat water for coffee and waited for the spare parts from Ulaanbaatar that would allow them to proceed to their next destination, the much larger PetroChina oil field located 750 kilometers to the east, a nagging sensation began growing in their minds and between them that an alternative interpretation of the herdsman's "lies" might have escaped them.

In 2006 PetroChina Daqing Tamsag, a subsidiary of PetroChina (中国石油), the global energy giant, bought a partly developed oilfield in far eastern Mongolia from the US exploration firm SOCO Oil, which had been drilling in the Tamsag Basin since 1998. By 2008 the field was producing one million barrels of crude oil from the four concession blocks for which the company had acquired exploration and extraction rights. With a US $511 million investment and an annual tax of US $19 million in 2009, PetroChina Daqing Tamsag is tiny by international standards—"a million barrels per year? That's a drop in the ocean!" an energy consultant in Ulaanbaatar remarked to Pedersen in 2010. Nonetheless, it was eastern Mongolia's biggest foreign direct investment at the time of Bunkenborg and Pedersen's fieldwork, probably even the largest single Chinese investment in Mongolia as a whole back then. Certainly, with a work force fluctuating between 2500 and 6000 workers, more than 90 percent of whom were Chinese nationals in 2009, the oil field loomed large in local peoples' lives. In 2007 the approximately 3000 herders and villagers making up the population of the Matad district (where most wells and the central headquarters are located) were outnumbered by Chinese nationals, and the district had Mongolia's highest concentration of foreign workers in absolute and relative terms.[1] The oil field is located in the Tamsagbulag Basin, a remote corner of Mongolia's Dornod Province. The region is known not just for its low population density even by Mongolian standards (below 0.5 persons/km^2) but also for its pancake-flat grass steppe, which is one of the largest temperate grass wildernesses in the world and home to many endangered species, including several hundred thousand Mongolian gazelles.

This chapter explores the material, economic, and social forms through which a Chinese oil company over a five-year period worked hard—but nevertheless failed—to maintain an "optimal distance" from local peoples and lands. By chronicling the story of how PetroChina Daqing Tamsag became embroiled in still more conflicts and misunderstandings around polluted pastureland and ground water and other legal, economic, and political issues, we show how this state-owned Chinese company slowly but steadily evolved into an epicenter of complex tensions between its predominantly Chinese workforce, its Mongolian workers, and a range of other local, regional, and national stakeholders (herders, politicians, cadres, and NGOs). We first provide an overview of the oil company as a distinct ethnographic site as it presented itself to Pedersen and Bunkenborg during their first days of joint fieldwork there. Then our storyline bifurcates into two analytical tracks corresponding to the separate ethnographic paths pursued by the two researchers. After detailing Bunkenborg's attempts to make sense of the rather particular local form assumed by PetroChina's global CSR policies in the Tamsag context, we turn to Pedersen's concurrent visits to local community leaders and cadres, some of whom were engaged in high-profile disputes with the Chinese.

Finally, these two ethnographic-cum-analytical trajectories are stitched back together again in keeping with the ongoing process by which Pedersen and Bunkenborg continually have sought to combine, compare, and integrate their respective ethnographic data and findings. We will see how infrastructure as a general theoretical concept and as a specific matter of ethnographic concern gradually emerged as a gathering point for a constellation of fraught collaborations and misunderstandings centered in and around the oil field—an attractor around which different scales and relations assembled and gradually solidified into a single, material form. The most critical infrastructure in question was roads, more specifically, the much-contested political, economic, technical, and environmental problem of how many—and what kinds of—roads should link the oil field with local herder households, the district center of Matad, the provincial capital of Choibalsan, and various border crossings to China. As we are going to argue, roads thus played the role of "technologies of distantiation," which, due to material affordances and political-economic structures, worked to outstretch relations between the Chinese and the Mongolians so that they remained minimally connected.

Parallel Worlds

"The relationship between the oil firm and the local people is flawless." Such was the self-assured verdict of a high-ranking representative from the Mongolian Ministry of Oil, whom Pedersen and Bunkenborg met on a hilltop overlooking the vast swath of land occupied by the oil field in the autumn of 2009. The official—who came from a local family of ex-communist leaders and nouveaux riches businessmen—was not alone in presenting relations between the Chinese-owned company and the local community in rosy terms. Mr. Chimedtseren a spectacled former mayor of the Matad district, who for several years oversaw and negotiated relations between local residents and foreign mining companies working in the district's territory, concurred. "This company wants to protect nature. Drivers are not allowed to make roads where there are no roads. If so, they will hurt the vegetation. There are Mongolian laws for nature protection. The Chinese work according to our country's laws and regulations."

At first blush Pedersen and Bunkenborg were indeed impressed with what they saw at the oil field. Compared to the scruffy appearance of the privately owned fluorspar and coal mines that the two ethnographers had visited elsewhere Mongolia, PetroChina Daqing Tamsag felt overwhelmingly big and well organized. The operation included not just the head camp but also a handful of adjacent Chinese oil companies subcontracted by the mother company. Pedersen and Bunkenborg could not help admiring its sheer size, the long rows of air-conditioned containers, the neat lines of Land Cruisers parked outside the company entrance. In contrast to the Bountiful Nature Mine explored in the previous chapter, the place seemed to adhere to the standards that Mongolians expected from foreign investments in their resource extraction industry. Indeed, the place called to mind the state socialist workplaces once found across the former Soviet Union and still found today in China, complete with basketball court, sports hall, reception room, etc. In addition, even the mostly unskilled Mongolian workers employed at the oil field seemed to receive stable and fairly high salaries (around US $500 per month, not a bad figure back then, prior to the 2012 increase in labor costs due to rising demand in the mining sector). The workers were also provided with decent pension schemes and health insurance, at least compared to Mongolian standards. The living spaces and the bathroom facilities—situated in air-conditioned purpose-built containers—were clean, spacious, and functional. Subsidized plentiful meals were served three times a day and seemed geared towards the oftentimes very different tastes of Chinese and Mongolians.

Perhaps, Pedersen and Bunkenborg asked themselves, they had found a Sino-Mongolian collaboration that was a success story. Prior to his first visit to Tamsag in 2009, Pedersen had read reports in the Mongolian media about the oil field, which conveyed a picture of ample suspicions and occasional fights between Mongolians and Chinese (Önöödör 2001; UB Post 2008), just as he was familiar with more general concerns about the economic, political, and environmental ramifications of the oil field, which had been voiced by Mongolian and foreign activists and scholars. In the course of their four visits to Tamsag from 2009 to 2012, Pedersen and Bunkenborg also themselves heard about and witnessed numerous conflicts and incidents between Chinese and Mongolians. Pedersen learned, for example, that Mongolian workers on more than one occasion had engaged in labor disputes, including a strike for higher salaries in 2012, even if this action seemingly had no cultural/nationalist component.[2] Still, they came across only few examples of explicitly racist violence—and nothing nearly as serious as what they had encountered in the Central Gobi Province. In fact, as Pedersen and Bunkenborg began probing further into what the Mongolians and Chinese workers said about one another and their work conditions more generally, they found it surprising that the two sides spoke positively of each other, as both individuals and groups. Undraa, a female graduate in Chinese language from Choibalsan's Technical College, who used to work as a translator for a Chinese manager at the oil field, told Pedersen, "Some Chinese used to visit the Mongolian workers. They would finish work at 4:00 pm, take a shower, and eat their food and then walk over towards the gers in their free time. Mostly, the Mongolians would invite them inside to talk. Some Chinese were very interested in the gers because they came from somewhere deep in China and had never seen one before. They used sign language to communicate. Mongolians even referred to them as friends. These Chinese had more respect for traditions than other people."

Positively surprised by Undraa's descriptions—so perhaps it really was, after all, possible for Chinese and Mongolians to become friends?—Pedersen asked how this "respect for traditions" had been reciprocated? Did Mongolian workers also sometimes pay social visits to their Chinese peers?

> UNDRAA: Well, Mongolians don't go [to the Chinese containers] much. But there is a big TV in the [Chinese] canteen and some like to go there to watch TV in the evenings, sitting with the Chinese.
>
> PEDERSEN: Why don't the Mongolians visit the Chinese in their containers?
>
> UNDRAA: Well, maybe there is nothing to be interested in. Most people work in shifts. Maybe when Mongolians ask to visit the container of the Chinese, the Chinese say that there are people sleeping in there. Maybe for this reason. Or perhaps Mongolians are not used to [container homes]. Chinese also go to bed early. Mostly, their doors are closed.

Once again, then, closer inspection exposed limitations to the Sino-Mongolian collaboration. The investment from the two sides did not seem to be symmetrical. As Undraa noted, some Chinese were "very interested in" their Mongolian coworkers, but most of the latter apparently acted as if "there was nothing at all" to learn from the Chinese. Moreover, she and the other translators were having many problems with what seemed to be an insurmountable wall of misunderstandings:

> People forget that I can't tell the Chinese what to do, nor can I command the Mongolian workers. So both sides complain that I don't speak on their behalf. . . . For example, a Chinese might enter a ger with Mongolian workers who have just been cooking, but when they then ask them, "please eat," they will say "no" with reference to their traditions and how they don't touch other's things and don't like sitting on other's beds in their dirty clothes. So they stand up and refuse to eat. This makes the Mongolians angry. Then the Chinese explain their traditions and the Mongolians explain our tradition, and my role is to translate, so I try to stay in the middle. But sometimes it is really hard.

Undraa was not alone in her concerns. Virtually every local person that Pedersen met and talked to during his five visits to the oil field in Tamsagbulag Basin—young or old, male or female, and rich or poor—expressed profound doubt and skepticism if not downright hostility and animosity towards PetroChina's oil adventure, even as they disagreed about how to deal with, profit from, or resist the presence of a foreign oil company in their homeland. This hardly comes as a surprise. The relationship between multinational energy firms and local communities is often fraught with conflict, as documented in the extensive ethnographic literature on mining and other resource extraction projects and their often detrimental impact on local livelihoods (e.g., Kirsch 2014; Gledhill 2008). To make matters worse, PetroChina was one of the largest foreign companies operating in Mongolia (for a period after the 2008 financial crisis, it was the most valuable company in the world), bringing most of its workers, equipment, and provisions from abroad—something that seemed like a de facto invasion to many Mongolian eyes. Like numerous other places in Mongolia, including as we have seen Choibalsan (chapter 1) and Central Gobi (chapter 2), the locals were convinced that the Chinese company harbour[ed] "sinister intents" and was "plotting to destroy the Mongols' existence" (Billé 2008). Without the slightest hint of irony, several people told Pedersen that the toxic level of chemical pollution detected around some oil wells reflected a secret sinister attempt to "make local Mongolians die prematurely and become unable to have children." Another equally prevailing concern was that the many Chinese companies—as well as other foreign ones, even if these were seldom mentioned—who were investing in Mongolian resource extraction were depleting the homeland of its beauty and wealth (*bayan*). While such sentiments were ubiquitous in Mongolia at the time of our fieldwork (Bulag 2009; Jackson 2015a; Jackson and Dear 2016), what made the PetroChina oil field come across as especially sinister was that, unlike coal, iron, and fluorspar mining, the depletion of the land's deposits of oil was largely invisible to local people. "Clearly," as one local resident confided to Pedersen in a conspiratorial tone, "it is only a fraction of the oil extracted from our *nutag* that is being transported overland by truck. Most of it runs beneath our feet in underground pipes that have been secretly dug all the way from China."

Gradually, Pedersen and Bunkenborg realized that the level of interaction between the Chinese and the Mongolians in and around the camp was, in fact, very limited. Although the two groups worked together in drilling teams, they ate their meals in different rooms. After 2011 the Chinese and the Mongolians ate under the same roof inside a newly built dining hall, but they were nevertheless discretely separated by a screen wall. They were hanging out in separate groups when having a smoke outside, playing basketball, or engaging in other pastime activities (alcohol was strictly banned on the premises, but there were rumors of numerous breaches of this rule by both Chinese and Mongolian workers). It was as if the door for trusting Sino-Mongolian relationships that had still seemed partly open during Pedersen and Bunkenborg's first trip in 2009 was gradually closing over each of their subsequent three visits from 2010 to 2012. A local man, who had been employed as a drilling assistant for a few months in 2011, tersely responded to Pedersen's question about how he interacted with the Chinese: "I didn't. Since I didn't know the language, I just looked at them, and nothing else. When I said, 'I'm thirsty,' they gave me water. That was it." The interaction that did take place between the Chinese and the Mongolians, when lining up for the shower after a long day at the wells or waiting for one's turn at the ping-pong table in the sports hall, seemed perfectly polite, friendly, and amiable. Recalling Isabel Stengers's (2010) rhetorical question, "Who wants to be just tolerated?" it almost seemed as if the two sides had become so "tolerant" (read: indifferent) that they were able to work and live side by side for years without getting to know much about each other.

But how and why did things get this way? Had the Chinese and the Mongolians always wanted to stay detached, or was their mutual indifference perhaps the result of particular events and processes over time? Possibly, Bunkenborg wondered, he and Pedersen were faced with another case of "unrequited love" from well-meaning but naïve Chinese bosses of the sort described in the two previous chapters. Or, as Pedersen was more inclined to think, perhaps the two ethnographers were faced with a different variation of the wider Sino-Mongolian encounter, calling for the deployment and development of new analytical concepts and theoretical frameworks. These were some of the questions that Pedersen and Bunkenborg debated between themselves during the evenings as they rested on the comfortable mattresses in their deluxe containers. (Only managers and VIP guests were provided four-bed containers with private bathrooms. Ordinary workers had been allocated a more basic model with eight bunk beds, with access to a single common bath.) In order to further investigate these questions and ideally align their divergent preliminary interpretations, Bunkenborg and Pedersen decided to split up their ethnographic research activities. Over the coming days Bunkenborg would stay around the main camp, striking up conversations with Chinese managers, engineers, cooks and drivers. Meanwhile, Pedersen would travel in the direction of the Matad district center, hoping to interview different local stakeholders, including officials, herders, and activists.

The Corporate Construction of Ecological Civilization

As Bunkenborg soon learned, the Chinese bosses—several of whom had previously been stationed with PetroChina in countries like Angola and Sudan—were all too aware of the widespread antagonism in Mongolia toward Chinese people and Chinese investments. However, they were convinced that this negative image reflected the misbehavior of those "uneducated" Chinese individuals, who, they told Bunkenborg, "had flocked into Mongolia to make money" when the Soviet army pulled out in the early 1990s. In order to distance themselves as much as possible from these "low-quality" (素质差) countrymen and the negative image associated with them, they put great efforts into making the head camp look tidy and well equipped, and to projecting an air of professionalism, reliability, and accountability. The managers stressed how important it was that they themselves and their employees always wore company uniforms. They gave frequent reminders, to Pedersen and Bunkenborg as well as to their Chinese and Mongolian staff, about the many regulations (concerning, e.g., fire hazards) imposed by PetroChina as well as by the Mongolian authorities. One of PetroChina Daqing Tamsag's top managers emphasized to Bunkenborg that his company was doing more for the "development" (发展) and the "modernization" (现代化) of the local economy and infrastructure than it was legally required to do under the terms of its contract with the Mongolian government. "You mustn't forget," the chain-smoking manager instructed Bunkenborg in his overheated container, "that PetroChina is committed to high standards of corporate social responsibility and publishes annual reports on sustainability and HSE." While a quick glance at the reports reveals that they do not include any specific information on Mongolia,[3] the manager did list a number of ways in which the oil company sought to contribute to local community development and to minimize negative environmental impact. In addition to providing jobs to Mongolians, he stressed, the company had also financed a US $1 million water processing facility in Matad, offered scholarships to students at the technical college in Choibalsan, and boosted the local economy by purchasing livestock from herders.

The same upbeat message was echoed by PetroChina Daqing Tamsag's vice president, Zhao Zhenglun, in a keynote lecture at the Eastern Mongolian Investors Forum, held in Choibalsan's fanciest hotel in August 2009, which Pedersen together with a motley crew of Russian officials, Japanese investors, and not least, the Mongolian foreign minister and many regional and national notaries. As befitted one of the leaders of the then biggest Chinese investment in Mongolia, the vice president gave the impression of someone extremely well educated, well connected, and well groomed. He explained in polished English, "The company is taking effective actions used by world leading oil companies for environmental protection and restoration." In Tamsag, he went on, this took the form of five principles: "(1) transparency, (2) respect for the law, (3) close cooperation with the Mongolian government, (4) environmental protection, and (5) benefits for regional administration and citizens." The principles of bringing "benefits to regional administration and citizens" were elaborated as: "(1) the provision of jobs and training for local citizens, (2) the purchase of goods from local markets, (3), the rental of vehicles from local citizens, (4) the purchase of cattle and agricultural products from herdsmen, (5) the installation of electric lines from the Choibalsan power station, and (6) donations."[4]

One morning in the fall of 2009, Bunkenborg witnessed one such concrete instance of corporate social responsibility in the spirit of President Hu Jintao's 2007 call to "construct ecological civilization" (创造生态文明). Just outside the canteen of the main camp, he ran into Ms. Cao, a university student from Daqing across the border, who had spent the summer as an intern at the oil field. She was trying to mobilize a couple of Mongolian workers to drive an excavator, explaining that they were going to plant some trees in the compound. The two Mongolians appeared to be incapable of understanding her gestures and phrases in Chinese or broken Mongolian. Increasingly exasperated, Ms. Cao told Bunkenborg that they were probably just pretending not to understand her. She checked their nametags as if preparing to make a formal complaint about their obstinacy, but then an Inner Mongolian interpreter arrived; within two minutes, the excavator was on its way. The interpreter was an obnoxious person, Ms. Cao confided to Bunkenborg; in fact, she had been arguing with him all summer. More generally, she concluded, the Mongolians were "unreliable, rude, and primitive." Had she not spent all her summer restoring grasslands damaged by spillage and successfully replanted the area with a superior type of grass? And yet, those local Mongolians were ungrateful! They just wanted the original vegetation back, "even though it wasn't particularly good." Before Bunkenborg could ask Ms. Cao why she found her blend of grass species superior, they arrived at an open square with containers on three sides. The stout, middle-aged Mongolian driving the excavator impatiently revved up his engine and started digging. Mr. Shu, the young manager in charge of HSE, had not actually finished explaining where he wanted the holes, and he started pacing about, gesticulating frantically, waving a measuring rod, and shouting at the top of his voice to make it clear that he wanted two rows of evenly spaced holes (see Figure 3.1). The Mongolian man in the excavator could not be bothered with the niceties of measuring and started to dig an irregular series of enormous holes along the cement walkway. Realizing that the holes were so big that they would nonetheless allow for a uniform spacing between the saplings, Mr. Shu gave up shouting at the runaway excavator and squatted down with his measuring rod to show the workers with shovels that he wanted the saplings exactly one meter from the cement walkway.

Having satisfied himself that the workers understood the plan, Mr. Shu turned to Bunkenborg, proudly explaining that the planting of trees around the containers was part of the company's comprehensive HSE (Health, Society,

FIGURE 3.1.   "Constructing Ecological Civilization," Tamsagbulag Basin. October 2009.

and Environment) strategy, which aimed to mitigate the adverse environmental effects of oil extraction (a comment that only seems to confirm our previous observation made in the foregoing chapter that Chinese attempts to make gardens in Mongolia and elsewhere are somewhat overdetermined with civilizing if not imperial imaginaries). The Mongolian workers, on their side, seemed to find the day's exercise in so-called environmental beautification very silly, and Bunkenborg couldn't help remarking to his new Chinese friends that trees were rather unusual on the grasslands. In fact, the newly planted saplings were quite probably the only trees within a radius of two hundred kilometers. "That may be so," Mr. Shu retorted, "but the species is indigenous. To show our respect for Mongolian culture, we spared no effort to procure Mongolian trees, and these saplings have come straight from Ulaanbaatar!" (This was apparently considered a guarantee that the trees originated from Mongolia and not China —as is the case with the majority of products at Mongolian markets.) Mr. Shu walked off in a huff in response to what he clearly considered to be Bunkenborg's unjustified skepticism, so there was no opportunity to quiz him or Ms. Cao on their views on CSR policy more generally. Still, the carefully optimized blends of grass species and the planting of saplings imported from 900 kilometers away and placed with military precision suggested to Bunkenborg that the issue was not just environmental "protection" as "improvement" of land and people more generally.

To Bunkenborg the PetroChina CSR policy in Tamsag represented yet another example of the phenomenon of "enclaving" described by James Ferguson (2005) and other scholars studying foreign intervention on the African continent. Specifically, case of Chinese investments in Mongolia calls to mind Appel's (2012b, see also 2012a) work on American offshore oil companies in Equatorial Africa. Appel's fieldwork made her increasingly "interested in the oil industry's efforts to disentangle the production of profit from the place in which it happens to find itself, to structure liability and responsibility in such a way that the industry can remove itself from the social, legal, political and environmental entanglements in which it is so deeply immersed" (442). Perhaps, Bunkenborg asked himself, there was a sense in which the "work-intensive building of spatial and phenomenological distance" made the Chinese tree-planting project on the arid Eastern Mongolian steppe into "a form of violence," as Appel calls it (442). Certainly, it seemed to him, what made her analysis so apt for his and Pedersen's ongoing collaborative research was the central role allocated by her to infrastructure in the "framing work . . . required to produce the effect of the separation itself" (443; cf. Callon 1998). Could it be, Bunkenborg wondered while recalling his and Pedersen's experiences from the Beautiful Nature Mine, that the efforts of Ms. Cao and Mr. Shu toward the "construction of ecological civilization" was tantamount to the imposition of imperial logic?

The Hero of Matad

Meanwhile, eighty kilometers to the south, Pedersen was doing his first ethnographic rounds in the district center. Even compared to the run-down look of many other district centers in postsocialist Mongolia (see Pedersen 2011), the place looked desolate and deprived, with its rusty relics from high modernist socialist architecture in a more or less full state of ruination and its lack of big wooden houses and the Japanese or Korean four-wheels drives that had become a ubiquitous feature in wealthier rural settings in Mongolia. "This truly feels like Mongolia's most forgotten outpost," Bürneebat the driver gloomily remarked, and Pedersen could only concur. It was hard to imagine that this place figured so prominently in PetroChina's CSR program, including its "principles of bringing benefits to regional administration and citizens." As already noted, most local groups that he spoke to expressed reservations about the Chinese oil field.[5] Consider his interview with Ms. Narantsetseg, Matad's mayor, an energetic woman who used to work for the educational office in Choibalsan until her Democratic Union Party beat Mr. Chimedtseren's Revolutionary Party in the 2008 elections:

> When people from the Daqing company came here for the first time in 2005, they told the local people that they were going to make Matad into a real town. But this was just talk and lies. In reality, they have done very little. Please write about social responsibilities in your book! Resource extraction companies are supposed to have social responsibilities. But this company has weak social responsibilities. It is one thing to develop a relationship with the state, but they should establish relations with the local district and offer their help. And they are not offering training or providing jobs to our young people. They need to do this too. Local people only do menial jobs for them, because they haven't received any education.

Another prominent critique of PetroChina Daqing Tamsag was Mr. Shagdar, a local herdsman who became something of a figurehead in regional, national, and even international media for his local resistance to and fight against the Chinese oil company. Indeed, Mr. Shagdar was one of six prominent Matad residents who in 2008 submitted a formal petition to Mongolia's parliament in which they complained about not just the oil firm but also the national government. It was above all this petition that eventually brought Mr. Shagdar into direct conflict with representatives from PetroChina Daqing Tamsag and also the local government. As we shall now describe, these events made Mr. Shagdar into a figure of fame—and, crucially, an instrument for political ends beyond his control—not just in the local community but also to different audiences in Ulaanbaatar as well as in international contexts ranging from Western-sponsored environmental NGOs to ultranationalist groupings.

> The Americans started drilling in 1989. I was the person who first took them here. Then in 1994 they brought in a special drill that could go down to 3,000 meters. I didn't go this time, but my brother and sisters went. I was watching it on TV. Suddenly, oil was struck with such force that it hit Ochirbat [then president of Mongolia] on his *deel* [traditional Mongolian clothing]. An old general—I forgot his name—wanted to invest in it. Big airplanes arrived from abroad. I also forgot which countries, but I do remember the dust that blew from our dirt roads when they landed. A big factory was going to be constructed, and in ten years a whole city would be built. People were so happy because oil had been discovered in Mongolia. They thought that their lives would blossom.
>
> But then, in August 2006, PetroChina was allowed in, and things started to change. Since then, the Chinese have invaded this place. Their wells are everywhere. If a horseman tries to cross, guards will arrive. They use binoculars and come in big cars, so the horses become scared. The Chinese dump waste anywhere they wish. And they drive their trucks everywhere. Because the Chinese like to go straight to places, many new roads have appeared. The American oil workers didn't roam around everywhere. When they went to a well, they used an existing road to go there. And they took the same way back. Now, workers arrive from one direction and leave in another. Before, there were only a small number of wells along a few roads. Now, there are too many wells and roads everywhere.

Mr. Shagdar—or "the hero of Matad," as the head of an Ulaanbaatar-based NGO called him in an interview with Pedersen—was well aware of his fame and the powers that came with it. Around 2010 the story about his resistance against PetroChina featured in regional, national, and even international media. When Pedersen finally managed to locate him at his autumn camp, some sixty kilometers off the road between the oil field's headquarters and the district center, the famous herdsman explained, "Honestly, I think they are afraid of me. That's why they are so wary of me. They have seen me on TV. I have been on Mongolian state TV and also on TV9. And some foreign stations. Once, I gave an interview about how they break the law. Ten days later, the minister sent some people here, instructing them to meet the person called Shagdar personally to find out what was true or not true about this whole case."

Mr. Shagdar might qualify as the most dangerous adversary one could imagine for multinational resource extraction companies such as PetroChina. He is not rich, he does not have any powerful connections, and he is no urban intellectual or organized activist (though no one doubts that he is very smart). Precisely for these reasons, in his struggles with the oil company and other hegemonic actors such as the Mongolian state, he came to embody all the dissatisfaction and pent-up anger vis-à-vis this Chinese oil company, the local government, and Mongolian politicians as a whole. In keeping with Mongolian custom, Pedersen was offered a seat in the family's modest, traditional, and spotless ger and served a cup of boiling-hot salty milk tea. When Mr. Shagdar began talking with a friendly yet confident expression on his rugged face, Pedersen could not help thinking that the herdsman was the perfect ethnographic subject: one who, when asked a general question like, "so, how did it all begin?" always starts talking, engaged and entertainingly, for hours on end. Small wonder that the journalists, the activists, and the anthropologists adore him: Mr. Shagdar was the perfect interviewee.

Mr. Shagdar's fame can be traced back to an otherwise quiet day when he was returning with a flock of horses along a dirt road connecting the Matad-PetroChina road with the grasslands where he and other herders from the area spent their autumns. As he crossed a hilltop, he suddenly noticed,

> Eight or ten trucks. All with Chinese drivers. They were coming from the south, transporting sand. They had been digging in a place that was outside their land. That's why I decided to stop them. First, I scolded one Chinese man. But he didn't obey me, so I held up my whip. The man got scared, ran into his truck and took off. Soon after he returned with his translator, who told me that they [the Chinese] were afraid of me. They stopped working, and I said, "I won't let you guys go." Then the man who was in charge came to me. People called him Dania. It was he who later died. So that man came to me and said, "Brother, these people told me that they are very afraid of you." I replied that they weren't supposed to dig gravel here, that they could not come with their big truck and begin digging things five kilometers outside their limit. They should stay inside the boundary and fill up the hole [they had already dug]. This is what I told them. All night we argued like that.
>
> My ger was very close to that place. Well, at first, they were to the north of my home, but I then moved very close to them. Perhaps that is why they were thinking that I would shoot them and became so afraid of me. And perhaps that is the reason why they stopped their work for three days and later for another seven days. Many things happened

there. The story was featured in the newspaper *Önöödör* last year. In the article it says that a man called N. Shagdar at gunpoint stopped a big Chinese investor from transporting gravel. But I didn't have any gun, and they wrote that I was holding a gun. I'm just an old man from this place who stopped them for three days by not allowing them to work.

The environmental inspector of our district arrived and told me, "You held a gun against them! You scared them! We are going to take you to court." I said, "I don't care if you take me to court. All that I did was to tell them that they should stay inside the limit that was agreed upon when they made their contract." The next morning when I arrived, the man [Dania] had begun filling the hole assisted by the translator. And just in the middle of this, a car arrived. It was one woman and two men who introduced themselves with name cards and said that they had come because of environmental concerns. I think that it was those people who later told the story to the newspapers. That man [Dania] fell into the hole and died. But holes are supposed to be fenced off for protection. A drunken man fell into the hole and died. The hole didn't have protection.

During his time in Tamsag, Pedersen had heard several alternative accounts of the incident from different members of the community and various people from outside the district. None of the accounts corresponded fully to each other, nor did they all depict Mr. Shagdar in a flattering light. What everyone agreed upon was that Mr. Shagdar had singlehandedly brought the construction of a paved road to China (for that is what all the sand was going to be used for) by a group of Chinese workers from PetroChina Daqing Tamsag to days of standstill, by proclaiming a moral right—as a herder and citizen of the Matad district—to intervene in what he considered a breach of the company's arrangements with the Mongolian authorities. Mr. Shagdar was also complaining about graft among Matad officials. "Just look at the Land Cruisers our leaders are suddenly driving around in, and how they've been sending their daughters to university in the city. How do you think they can afford this?" ran an often overheard rhetorical question posed by him and other locals (see also Jackson 2014). Initially the local implications of Mr. Shagdar's actions, some of which were clearly unintended, were not at the forefront of his mind at this point. The presence of the Chinese oil field in his *nutag* was all that mattered to him. But gradually his activism became more directed towards the local authorities. Partly because, as he put it, "I feel as if I have been forgotten" by the environmental NGOs who had first taken such an interest in him, promising to "come here and help," and partly because of his views about politics, Mr. Shagdar became more interested in the internal fissures within the Matad community itself:

> Last year around June 20, a jeep came. It was [a senior Mongolian official from the district]. She had brought a judge or something. Maybe he works for [the oil company] as an attorney, I don't know. There were also two other lawyers there. They had brought many papers with them. "We have come to take you with us," they said. "You have committed a crime against the company! We are taking you to court for false testimony." They asked me to sign a paper saying, "I hereby take back the testimony I gave to [another judge]." I told them that I wouldn't do it. "I have no reason to sign this, I'm protecting my place, not yours. I'm protecting my homeland." Then they showed me the paper again and pointed to the seal of the mayor, who had signed the paper. Also [two of the co-signers of the petition] had signed. Only [another co-signer] and I hadn't. So, they told me they were going to meet [the other co-signer] and left. Four days later they returned: "So, now [the co-signer at hand] has signed the paper, and only you are left." Indeed, out of six people who signed the petition, only I was left. Then we had a long discussion. They were talking law, and I was telling them to fix the road. It's not possible for me to know all the laws. But I do know some.

Strongly insinuating that some of the local leaders were in the pockets of the Chinese, Mr. Shagdar concluded the interview by stressing his willingness to stand his ground and remain the last bastion, in spite of all the trouble and attention it entailed. "Of course," Mr. Shagdar commented as he escorted Pedersen to the waiting car, "had I been the first to sign [the new letter], they wouldn't have cared about me."

"The Problem Has To Do with the Law"

So this, Pedersen told Bunkenborg later, might be the reason why he had been receiving such mixed reports and ambivalent signals every time he had mentioned "the hero from Matad" to officials in Matad. Back when Ms. Narantsetseg had signed the petition with Mr. Shagdar and other community activists, he represented a perfect ally for her and her party. But as the complexities surrounding the presence of the Chinese oil firm in her constituency gradually became clear to the new mayor and her entourage—including the tricky fact that the state apparatus itself seemed part of the problem rather than simply a path toward its solution—the petition, as well as everyone and everything surrounding it, started to represent an embarrassing obstacle. Before the 2009 election, when Ms. Narantsetseg and her Democratic Party had been in opposition, she had seldom missed an opportunity to criticize PetroChina Daqing Tamsag and what she claimed to be her opponent's suspiciously cozy relationship with its Chinese managers. But things changed after she took over as mayor of Matad and assumed the responsibility for managing the official relationship with the oil company. Formerly one of its most ardent critics, appearing frequently on regional as well as national media complaining about the oil field, she changed her approach and—judging from what she told Pedersen—her mind. The mayor accounted for this change by claiming that becoming an official had given her better knowledge and therefore a deeper understanding of the legal issues pertaining to a foreign oil company operating on Mongolian soil. The crux of the problem, as she explained, was the oil law, not the oil firm. And while there were many problems—cultural, economic, and environmental—pertaining to this company in her district, all forces and efforts should from now on be put into making the national parliament amend the oil law so that a fixed percentage of the tax and profit share from oil production on Mongolian soil would be sent to the district—as well as the region—where the oil extraction took place. As she told Pedersen in 2012,

> Actually, we don't have too many problems communicating with the company. Our main problem is that they paid MT 80–100 billion [US $65–81 million at 2011 rates] to the Mongolian state over the last years. The problem has to do with the law. Actually, [PetroChina Daqing Tamsag] pays all the money they are supposed to according to the product-sharing contract, but no money is paid directly to the region or the district. There are no legal grounds for doing so. We are not benefiting from [the oil field]. That's how the system is. Some officials and politicians in Ulaanbaatar have talked about amending the oil law so that 10 percent will be given to districts and 10 percent for the regions. They have talked about this for several years, but it has never been made into law. Officials are well aware that this is the core of the problem, but [the local] people [here] don't understand it. Last year, the company extracted 5.2 million barrels of oil and gave US $7.9 million to the state, but our district didn't get anything. We are like "beggars sitting on gold." This is such a very strange law. What's the use of having such a company operating here? We don't have even

light and the village is dark! It is true that they paid more than MNT 200 million for a water purification machine in the village. And during holidays, like Lunar New Year or Children's Day, they give presents to the children. But these are small things. Instead, if the law was changed to specify how much the company should pay to us, the money question would be clear. Then we would not have to keep asking them for money. As long as this problem is not solved, of course, people here will be angry.

Not surprisingly, the Chinese (as well as the Mongolian) managers from the oil company shared this view: in their eyes, it was not they and their ability to act in accordance with established PetroChina CSR standards that was the problem; rather, it was an inability on the side of the Mongolians to create a proper legal and regulatory framework that would allow them to actually abide by these standards. In a grave illustration of this problem, the aforementioned CSR manager highlighted the question of environmental protection, which, he insisted, had been built into the very design of the PetroChina Daqing Tamsag's Mongolian operation from the start. As he explained to Bunkenborg, the clustering of wells and the expensive slanted drill holes were intended to minimize traffic on the grass, and the company had applied for permission to install pipes between the wells. The pipes would make it possible to operate with a staff of fifty workers, obviating the traffic of heavy vehicles and thus reducing the environmental impact significantly. The authorities, however, had procrastinated for years, and the issue was still not resolved. As for the problem with the open pits, the company had long since offered to build a facility to clean the water properly. The Mongolian authorities, however, were skeptical about the Chinese specifications. At the same time, they lacked the technical expertise and the resources to formulate and specify precisely what they wanted instead, and the negotiations dragged on for years. According to another Chinese manager, a great deal had been done to resolve the inevitable environmental challenges that arise from large-scale resource extraction, but the problems had been blown out of proportion by the Mongolian media. To minimize damage to the vegetation, drivers had been ordered to follow existing wheel ruts, markers had been set up along the tracks, and drivers who took short cuts over unspoiled grass were fined. As for the open pits with waste, the manager claimed that the locals had no realistic appreciation of the toxicity. Once the waste was treated with appropriate chemicals and covered with earth, there "really is no danger to humans or animals."

When Pedersen and Bunkenborg returned to the oil field in 2011, the level of activity had been visibly reduced. The container towns that had previously been home to subsidiary companies of several hundred employees each had disappeared or seemed empty, and the heavy truck traffic, so striking during previous years, had been brought to a near standstill. A frustrated Chinese manager told Bunkenborg that the company was barely maintaining production and that the number of Chinese employees had been cut to a mere dozen. A levy on foreign workers had been introduced; the cost of taking a truck across the border had quadrupled; and an outbreak of hand, foot, and mouth disease had complicated things further (see InfoMongolia.com 2010b). The subsidiary companies that had been contracted for the summer had been called off. Passing Bunkenborg a cigarette and gesturing at the dangerously full ashtray atop his aluminum desk, the manager inhaled deeply, emitted a smoky sigh, and lamented that the "local activists and journalists" who had incited the government to take action against the company displayed "a profound ignorance of scientific oil production." As he saw it, the main difficulty with oil extraction in Mongolia was the uncertain legal framework and the arbitrary manner with which bureaucrats issued fines without reference to or knowledge of legislation. The next year, during Bunkenborg and Pedersen's last visit, the oil field was back at full capacity, including thousands of subcontracted Chinese engineers, technicians, and workers. Because Russia had shut down the export of diesel oil to Mongolia for several months during the spring of 2011 (as part of ongoing Russian power games in the region), the Mongolian government had decreed that domestic oil production had "strategic significance" for the country. The prime minister had visited PetroChina Daqing Tamsag, and, possibly as a result of this, the oil company had been allowed to boost the number of Chinese workers and proceed with the stalled plans for establishing pipelines and electrical cables between its wells. In fact, according to a persistent rumor in the Matad community, a handful of state inspection officers had been fired following the PM's visit; they, in turn, had sued the head of the state inspection office for having been unlawfully laid off their jobs to please the Chinese. "These people simply did their jobs in closing down several illegal operations last year," complained one environmental activist in Choibalsan, "and this is what they got in return!"

According to Ferme and Schmitz (2014, 4), "It is critical to place the recent Chinese forays in Africa . . . within the context of a longer material history that . . . traces of China's historical presence in . . . multiple landscapes ..[to reveal].. how what is superficially described as a relationship between two states or two groups of people is in fact a contested domain with several competing actors" (2014, 7–8). As Pedersen and Bunkenborg gradually understood, these insights can be extended to Inner Asia too. Not all tension and conflict surrounding

PetroChina Daqing Tamsag was the result of cultural differences between "Chinese" and "Mongols," but was also the product of internal divergences and compering fractions within these groups. It was due to numerous and only partly overlapping agendas and conflicts not just between the Chinese and the Mongolians, but also *among* the latter, that Mr. Shagdar had ended up being at odds with the Chinese as well as with Mongolian leaders and government officials too. Gradually, he had become an instrument of political maneuverings and intrigues orchestrated by local leaders in tandem with ethnonationalist groups and NGOs from the capital.

Optimally Distant

In the course of their four trips to Eastern Mongolia, a pattern had begun to crystalize across the diverse ethnographic materials that Pedersen and Bunkenborg were collecting. The social relations between Chinese and Mongolians over the years were becoming increasingly shallow, and not—as one might have expected from a small group of coworkers and business partners working by side in a remote location—deeper. Far from engaging in and forging a complex, durable, and trusting relationship, dispelling whatever stereotypes might have existed, the sociality between the Chinese and the Mongolians seemed to have become increasingly hollowed out in the period between the Chinese purchase in 2006 and Pedersen and Bunkenborg's last visit in 2012. What is more, this was not a development that people seemed to mind—or at least not everyone. The oil company managers and also many locals preferred that the interaction between the Chinese and the Mongolians was kept to an absolute minimum, which in some instances could barely be deemed "social." Perhaps more than any other insight pressing itself upon the two ethnographers, it was the systematic manner in which the increasing Sino-Mongolian social disconnect they had identified had been actively promoted by core stakeholders from both sides. Nowhere was this clearer than in the debacle about meat trading between locals and Chinese:

> We used to sell our animals to Daqing company at a good price. To the Hobe unit [one of the subcontracted companies]. It improved our lives a great deal. We could sell our animals for a good price because the buyers were so close to us. If we don't sell our animals, we cannot live. These days, animals cannot be sold at a good price. With Daqing we had a company to sell to that was close by and it made it very easy. If our

family sold just two or three sheep, we would make enough money to send our kids to school.

From the perspective of many local people, one positive thing about the presence of a large Chinese oil field in their *nutag* was the fact that, probably for the first time since the collapse of socialism (Sneath 1993; Bruun and Odgaard 1996; Humphrey and Sneath 1999; Bruun 2006), local herders had access to a profitable local supply chain through which they could sell their animal products. But something happened a few years after the Chinese purchased the oil field from SOCO Oil. As another herdsman told Pedersen in 2011, "There are now more [Chinese] people working at the oil field than there are Mongolians living here. Yet, they hardly buy anything from us. Everything is brought in by truck from China or from Ulaanbaatar. We are not even allowed to sell meat to them individually anymore!" The herder was referring to a formal set of principles for the interaction between Chinese workers at the oil field and the local population that was reached at a meeting around 2007 between the managers of the company, the police chief from Choibalsan, and Mr. Chimedtseren. As the latter explained, without making any attempt to hide his pride in what he clearly considered one of the major legacies from his time as mayor of Matad:

> First, [Chinese] workers from Daqing company came directly to [Mongolian herder] families trying to buy meat. But it caused confusion. People said that the Chinese were up to something with their wives and children. And there was a rumor that the Chinese were roaming around freely in the landscape. As you know, husbands are often out looking after animals. So when the Chinese came to visit the herder households, only wives and children were home. The wives could not understand what the Chinese were saying, so they were wondering if they were talking about them, and became so afraid that they escaped from their gers. Then the Chinese tried to tell them, "Don't be afraid. We just want to buy meat," and ran after them. . . . Oh such a mess! It was like a big joke.

Mr. Chimedtseren clearly enjoyed telling this anecdote, probably perfected during countless rehearsals. The story aptly conveys the uncertainty or "chaos" characteristic of the Sino-local encounters during the first years after PetroChina's purchase of the oil field, not just within the company in terms of the daily interactions and tensions between Chinese and Mongolian workers, but also externally between Chinese employees from the company and local Mongolian herders and villagers. As Undraa, the former female translator from Choibalsan told Pedersen, "The relationship between Chinese people from the company was pretty good back then. Sometimes, when local people wanted to sell meat to the Chinese, they simply went there [to the head camp of the oil company]. The Chinese would buy the meat at a higher price than usual. Back then, people liked it [the company]. On a couple of occasions, herders' cars ran out of gas so they came there with their canisters and had them filled for free."

From the perspective of Mr. Chimedtseren and other managers and officials, however, such unregulated social and economic encounters between Mongolians and Chinese were a recipe for disaster. "Chaos" had to be replaced with order. "In 2007, I decided something had to be done. Chinese were haggling about meat prices, and drunken people wanted to fight them. So I told the Chinese workers not to visit Mongolian families anymore. From then onward, we only allowed the Chinese to travel between their own sites. Their trucks couldn't go anywhere else. If they did, then they would be fined. The regional police issued the rules after discussing with foreign companies how to better organize the relationship between local people and the company."

As part of these new rules and restrictions, the Chinese employed at Petro-China Daqing Tamsag were forbidden to leave the company premises without permission from the managers (who, in keeping with standard practice among companies employing Chinese nationals in Mongolia, were in possession of their employees' passports), just as Chinese truck drivers, who had sometimes visited herding households for business and other purposes en route to the border, were instructed to stick to the roads even in case of mechanical or other problems. Local people were banned from carrying out informal trade with anyone from the company; instead a nonprofit firm was set up by the district administration through which all meat trade with the Chinese had to be conducted at a fixed price renegotiated once annually between company representatives and Mr. Chimedtseren—which explains the abovementioned meat trader's dissatisfaction with the local officials.[6] "Soon after," Mr. Chimedtseren proudly concluded, "all the disorder and the strife disappeared and was replaced by an orderly trade arrangement." Pedersen could not help but ask the retired mayor, "You said the new rules were implemented to better manage relations between locals and people from the company. But didn't the rules cut off all relations?"

> Well, here is the thing. There was so much false information in the press. They claimed that the Chinese had taken over and now owned the entire Matad district; that the Chinese were roaming freely about the land, soiling it with dirt; and that white gazelles were becoming extinct. Even if none of this was true, what we did was because of it—it was a way to solve it. It may look as if these rules separate people, but we can't

have Mongolian and Chinese mix too much and become closer because of the way their social relationships are. These rules organize things. It is not to separate people, but to make them organized and not having them argue with each other. Because if they don't argue, their relationship will be peaceful, and they will not have any negative impact on each other.

It is hard to find a better illustration of the wish, shared by so many Chinese and Mongolians alike, to forge an optimal distance between them. In another example of this deliberate "building of spatial and phenomenological distance" (Appel 2012b, 442), a Chinese engineer told Bunkenborg that they had been obliged by the Mongolian government to upgrade the power plant in Choibalsan 250 kilometers away and to pay for power cables to the oil field. In any other country, he said, the electricity company would provide the infrastructure and set up a meter, and all people would have to do would be to pay the bills. To him, the best model for relations between different stakeholders was simple, predictable, and automated, a meter that went tick-tock as the supplier's kilowatt-hours poured into the Chinese headquarters. With an appropriate infrastructure of roads, pipelines, and cables serving to minimize friction, spillages, and conflicts, such an "automated" relationship was both conceivable and desirable from his perspective; the only thing that prevented its realization was the interminable red tape of Mongolian bureaucrats.

Evidently, what both company managers and local officials wanted was a form of relationship that would largely keep the two sides separate. During their last visit to Tamsag in 2012, Pedersen and Bunkenborg were left with the clear impression that the leaders from both sides believed they were finally about to achieve what they had been striving for.[7] For the Chinese managers, as much as for Mr. Chimedtseren and (at the end of the day) Ms. Narantsetseg, the perfect business relationship between the company and the local community was not one in which Chinese workers and Mongolian herders would over time become trusted partners sharing a deep intersubjective space. Rather, what the leaders hoped for was the forging, or the framing, of a perfectly predictable relationship regulated by various technical "solutions," ranging from a centrally planned meat-trading company over a system of pipes to the distribution of individual electricity meters, all serving to reduce to an absolute minimum the interactions between Chinese and Mongolians in and around the oil field. Perhaps one could call this the dream of "optimal distance"—the quintessentially communist dream that social life can be planned and organized to such detail and perfection that no "chaos" in the form of strife or its opposite (trust, friendship, love) will erupt. Certainly Mongolian cadres and Chinese managers expressed equal pride in having accomplished this: the carving out of a maximum workable distance between the supposedly disparate worlds of Chinese and Mongolians who, while remaining just sufficiently connected to perform the collaborative tasks required of them, could, and should, be kept apart at all costs. As we shall now see, nowhere was this desire for optimal distance more visible than in the case of roads.

Technologies of Distantiation

Over the last few decades mainland China itself has seen massive public and private investments in roads. The slogan "Want to get rich? Build a road first!" has been a common sight in the countryside (Nyíri and Breidenbach 2008, 128), signaling that roads and other infrastructures are built with the express purpose of stimulating economic development in the backward hinterlands. Indeed, while China has a long imperial tradition of public works, present discourses on infrastructure or "basic installations" (基础设施) bear the imprint of Marxist materialism. Much as in the Soviet Union (Humphrey 2005; Ssorin-Chaikov 2003; see also Pedersen 2011, 44–47), infrastructure is regarded not just as a precondition, but an agent of modernization in its own right, and the engineering of "material civilization" (物质文明) to boost "spiritual civilization" (精神文明) has been a central concern to successive politburos dominated by engineers. This intertwinement of the material and spiritual dimensions of infrastructure is also evident in the wider discourse centered around jiaotong (交通), which signifies both transportation and communication. Composed of characters that mean respectively "hand over, meet, associate with, have sexual intercourse with" and "connect with, join, understand, and open up," jiaotong has been a key term in the drive to modernize China and built infrastructure—roads, railroads, telecommunication networks, etc.—that will open isolated places and "backward people" for development. The high-modernist promise of jiaotong is evident not only in numerous ethnographic studies of road projects in the Chinese hinterlands (Joniak-Lüthi 2016; Flower 2004; Wu, K. 2020, Zhou, Y. 2013) but also in descriptions of borderlands where Chinese infrastructure extends into neighboring countries such as Nepal (Campbell 2010), the Altai Republic (Nyíri and Breidenbach 2008), and Kazakhstan (Reeves 2017). The Chinese state's promotion of connectivity as a panacea that opens the world for development is reflected not only in the increasing number of road and railway projects on either side of the country's northwestern and southwestern borders but also in the massive construction projects associated with the Belt and Road Initiative and throughout the Third World where infrastructure has been a dominant feature of Chinese investment.

Mongolia is a case in point. Its road infrastructure is famously inadequate and is often highlighted as a significant constraint by the growing number of foreign companies extracting natural resources in the country. While the total length of roads was almost 50,000 kilometers by the millennium, only some 2,000 kilometers were paved. As of 2011 the only paved road from the capital, Ulaanbaatar, to an international border crossing was the main highway leading north to Russia, but a new paved highway leading south to the Chinese border at Zamyn Üüd was approaching completion, and there were also plans for a north–south transport corridor through Western Mongolia and an east–west corridor. Indeed, a not insignificant share of the Chinese FDI [Foreign Direct Investment] in Mongolia since 2005 has been spent on roads, either as bilateral aid from the Chinese state and regions aimed at upgrading Mongolia's existing highway system (several such projects have taken place in different parts of the Gobi region) or in the form of new roads privately built by Chinese companies to service mines and other remotely located resource extraction adventures. To be sure, as noted in a World Bank study, "The massive increase in trade with China . . . will impact on the pattern of demands for transport infrastructure and services in the next decades."[8] There has been concern whether the many new roads to the southern and eastern borders might result in increasing Chinese influence, as well as health risks to humans and livestock caused by the dust and pollution generated by the trucks used to transport coal and other minerals (Jackson 2015b). Yet it is also recognized that increasing integration with the Chinese road network is inevitable.

FIGURE 3.2. Oil trucks en route to China, Dornod Province, eastern Mongolia. September 2011.

Certainly, the operation of PetroChina Daqing Tamsag has been utterly dependent on roads. Since Mongolia had no oil refinery at the time of Pedersen and Bunkenborg's fieldwork and the oil field is relatively close to the Chinese border, all the oil produced was transported directly to China by truck. According to one manager Bunkenborg spoke to, PetroChina Daqing Tamsag was the largest oil field in the world to transport its crude oil over land by truck rather than through pipelines.[9] The drivers doing the transporting were almost exclusively Chinese, unable to communicate with the locals they might encounter. Perhaps for the same reason, Tamsag had become riddled with roads and tracks, not only between different wells, the production headquarters, and the local district center of Matad, but also connecting the main roads (still nothing more than gravel roads) from Matad to Choibalsan and the three closest border crossings with China. This picture was not wholly new and by no means unique to this area— other rural Mongolian landscapes, including regions with no significant resource extraction, are also crosscut by gravel roads and dirt tracks reflecting decades of truck and car use for trade and motorized pastoral migration— but it was clear that the number of roads in Tamsag had increased along with the influx of Chinese people and Chinese investment in the area.

From the perspective of the local people, these new roads were not simply of the wrong width and quality but also in the wrong places and going in the wrong directions.[10] Mr. Shagdar and other herders complained that, unlike what the former American owners supposedly did, the Chinese ignored the restrictions on movement that roads are supposed to effectuate. For example, instead of following the existing path from Camp A to a newly opened oil well, B, via an already operational oil well, the Chinese drove trucks in a straight line between A and B, creating a new track and permanently damaging the fragile grassland. Or, as Matad's environmental inspector told Pedersen in 2011, where the land does not allow vehicular transport (because of rocks, swampy bog, or other natural obstacles), the Chinese would instead make new tracks parallel to the existing ones, causing no less environmental disruption. "This January, I fined them MNT 8.640.000 for polluting the land with roads," he said. "When they make roads, it damages the soil. If thirty to forty trucks weighing thirty to forty tons drive back and forth all day and night, then the soil is damaged. When it snows, they make new roads next to existing ones because they say that the existing road is blocked. It is the same down in the Erdenetsagaan district [southwest of Matad], I heard."

Having spent the previous days driving along and across what looked like a major road under construction, Pedersen asked whether the Chinese had made any positive steps toward environmental protection. "I think that they have," the environmental inspector replied. "The main thing is that they are now fixing the roads. It is not possible for cars to drive on them yet, but now they really are building that paved road they promised from Daqing to Bichigt via Erdenet-sagaan." Pedersen asked, "Will this road be beneficial to citizens from Matad?" The environmental inspector responded, "If herders wish to go to [the border] for some reason, probably they will use that road. But actually, it has no real benefit to them. The main thing is that the new road will be beneficial to nature because there will not be so many roads going here and there and everywhere anymore."

Soon after the stretch of road at hand had been constructed and was ready to be put to use, a delegation of officials from the Mongolian state inspection bureau's regional headquarter in Choibalsan found that they were still unhappy with it, complaining that its gauge was too narrow to allow two cars to pass each other and that it did not conform to Mongolian technical standards (see also InfoMongolia.com 2010a). While the Chinese engineers that Bunkenborg spoke to dismissed this criticism as yet another example of "Mongolian unprofession-alism" and lack of coordination between different government agencies, several local herders told Pedersen that there was something fundamentally wrong with the new road that would have to be fixed in order to protect not just the natural environment but also pastoral and nomadic livelihoods from negative impact. A number of state inspection officers had reportedly been fired at the behest of higher-ranking officials who answered to the prime minister. With regard to that rumor, Mr. Shagdar explained:

> The new road was closed this spring. Experts demanded it. But then the head of the state property office fired those people. Apparently he said, "That new road is paved, and it is of a quality unparalleled elsewhere in Mongolia. This company is being accused of too many things, and too many obstacles are put on their work." But he couldn't just fire them. He didn't come here to see the road himself. Local people know what kind of road the Chinese use. Its width is only 5 meters, which means that Russian jeeps [GAZ 4WD, the most commonly used vehicle in rural Mongolia] can't pass when meeting their trucks. That new road is simply too narrow. I went there myself by horse and saw it. I told them, "Listen, the way that you have constructed this road [by elevating it on a gravel bed] makes it difficult for horsemen to use it. And motorcycles or cars can't travel on it either. So at least you need to make some pass-way so that herders can cross the road. At the moment we have to travel more than ten extra kilometers so as to pass north of the company. It's very difficult."

One of the central insights to emerge from recent work on infrastructure in anthropology and science and technology studies is that infrastructures are imbued with tacit social, political, and cultural ontological conventions and assumptions that are materially built into their framings, standards, and configurations.[11] In that sense infrastructures may be described as "anti-politics machines" (Ferguson, 1994). The specific case of roads is a good example. It is common among policymakers and developers to think of roads as vehicles of social, political, economic, and cultural connections—harbingers of future networks that will enchain places, things, and people not previously as directly, or intensely, linked (see also Dalakoglou 2010). But Penny Harvey and Hannah Knox (2008, 80) note that this "historical desire for 'connectivity'" inheres in the fantasy that infrastructures offer a technical solution to problems of economic and social integration. A less ideological and more nuanced ethnographic approach, they suggest, would be to think of roads as "sites of passionate engagement holding the promise of transformative potential in ways that create an unlikely and unpredictable convergence of interest" (80).

The building of new roads in Tamsag is a case in point. As we have just seen, a single paved road was constructed in order to replace the many dirt roads accused of cutting up the Tamsag landscape. But the new road was (and perhaps only could be) used by the Chinese and their own trucks, either because only they are allowed on it or because only their vehicles fit on it, causing the local people to continue using all the previous small roads in a sort of parallel, "Mongolian" road network existing alongside the "Chinese" one. Indeed, it is safe to surmise that—as we saw with the other legal, economic, and infrastructural interventions by company managers and governmental officials—the road construction in Tamsag was fueled by an explicit desire on the part of these managers and officials for increased social and physical disconnection (as opposed to increased connection) between Chinese and Mongolians. For all the celebration of universal connectivity that accompanied the construction of infrastructure, the roads, pipes, and electric cables around the oil field could only facilitate particular flows by disallowing others.

The goal, it seems, was Chinese construction of enough roads of sufficient quality to extract and export oil with as little friction as possible. Indeed, the dominant assumption among Mongolian and Chinese officials and managers alike seemed to be that the better the roads on which the (Chinese) drivers took their loads, the less interaction they would have with local Mongolians thereby minimizing the risk of unplanned interactions between the two sides, whether in the form of unpredictable sexual liaisons, unregulated trade, or freak roadside encounters, all of which carried the potential for strife and dangerous escalation. Small wonder, then, that Mr. Chimedtseren always stressed that only after a "proper road" was built between the oil field, the district centers, the border crossings—along with legal, economic, and political regulation by oil company managers and local leaders—could the "chaotic" social and economic relations between Chinese workers and locals become an "orderly trade arrangement." If there was one thing that officials and their adversaries like Mr. Shagdar—and, in fact, everyone Pedersen and Bunkenborg spoke to during their five visits to Matad—all agreed on, it was that the new road detaches people more than it connects them. Its ultimate purpose was to reduce an unpredictable multiplicity of Sino-local relations to a predictable, single "business connection".

Rather than facilitating social and material interaction between Mongolians and Chinese in this remote but strategically important corner of Mongolia, then, the roads built to transport personnel, oil, equipment, and commodities between China and Mongolia and within Mongolia, ended up curbing both the quantity and quality of such relationships. Roads do not just connect Chinese and Mongolians, they also separate them by enabling new modes of social, economic, and cultural disconnect not previously present, or at least not as explicit and outspoken. In that sense, we suggest, roads and other infrastructure developments around the PetroChina oil field are "technologies of distantiation," imbued with the capacity to extend, and if you like, "stretch out" Sino-Mongolian relations while allowing them to remain just barely connected (see also Pedersen and Bunkenborg 2012). Crucially this detachment is equally desired by company managers and local officials alike, both of whom were eager to maintain an optimal distance between Chinese and Mongolians in order to stabilize and reduce what they considered an inherently volatile and conflictual relationship between radically different peoples. Roads, then, not only hide asymmetrical social and political relations beneath ostensibly technical solutions; they are imbued with the capacity to create as well as curtail the basis and context of relationality as such.

Roads That Separate

A late summer thunderstorm had broken out over the desert plains, and neither the two anthropologists nor their driver were quite sure where they were. Eventually, Bürneebat stopped to ask for directions at a lonely ger he spotted in the mist. Set within a ravine, it was shielded from snow or sand stirred up by the constant wind. It was late September, moderately cold, and there was no other sign of human habitation. The ger was small and sparsely furnished, giving the impression of a household with few pennies to spare. In keeping with *yos*, the visitors sat in silence as the apparent sole occupant, an elderly woman in a ragged *deel*, handed out cups of *süütei-tsai* [salty milk tea] to them. Since the old spinster showed no interest in conversation (of which there is no expectation on such occasions), Pedersen and Bunkenborg started chatting. "This reminds me a lot of the shamans' homes I used to visit up north," Pedersen said, referring to Hövsgöl Province in northwestern Mongolia, where he had done several years of fieldwork in the 1990s (see Pedersen 2011). "Do you think this woman might be a shaman too?" Bunkenborg quizzed. "She certainly looks the part!" With a slurping sound, Pedersen took a gulp of the salty brew and paused. "No, no," he retorted, embarking on a long lecture—beginning with Buddhist missionizing in unison with Manchu colonization in the sixteenth and seventeenth centuries and culminating with the state socialist repression of religion in the twentieth century—that explained the virtual eradication of shamanism from southern Mongolia, including the eastern Gobi. For a while, no further words were exchanged, and Pedersen considered the matter closed. It was therefore with a certain amount of irritation that he eventually sensed that his colleague was not entirely satisfied with his conclusion. Gently tapping Pedersen's shoulder, a mischievous smile on his face, Bunkenborg asked innocently, "Well, in that case, what *is* this thing hanging up there, I wonder?" Looking up, Pedersen realized that, suspended under the roof of the ger, less than one meter from the tip of his nose, was a full shamanic attire complete with eagle-feather–decorated boots, and a drum that, judging from the smooth wrinkles on its leather skin, was in regular use.

Returning to another of the numerous instances in which Pedersen and Bunkenborg managed to overlook the blindingly obvious during their joint travails in the Gobi Desert, let us now reconsider the story of the Mongolian herdsman caught red-handed selling goats to the Chinese oil workers he claimed to know nothing about. Can Pedersen and Bunkenborg's later insights into the role of roads in the Tamsag be used to reinterpret this incident in a more ethnographically satisfactory manner than the crude sociological distinction between what people say they do and what they really do? Such an analytical revision is not just possible and desirable, it is imbued with wider methodological and theoretical ramifications beyond our concerns in this book. When one realizes that roads are not just connectors but also infrastructures through which relationships are cut—as Pedersen and Bunkenborg gradually understood as their investigation progressed—it becomes possible to interpret this and similar incidents in more subtle and novel ways. As a technology of distantiation, the road between the Mongolian herders and the Chinese oil rig allowed the two sides to be optimally distant, while still engaging in a mutually beneficial trading partnership "without any strings attached," to borrow a characterization of China's approach to bilateral aid and trade (Alden 2005). In this interpretation, the herdsman's seemingly contradictory claim that he and the rest of the household did "not know anything about those Chinese" can be taken seriously as a genuine attempt to capture the nature of this Sino-Mongolian encounter. Perhaps he actually did mean what he answered in response to Pedersen and Bunkenborg's query. Perhaps his words discursively enacted the very optimal distance between him and his Chinese neighbors that the stretch of road between them materially demarcated. Thus understood, roads and words acted in tandem to truncate a multitude of potential Sino-Mongolian relations into a singular relationship, one that Mr. Shagdar might have called "real business."

This brings us to a final twist to the story with which we began this chapter. There is a sense in which the central concept that allowed Bunkenborg and Pedersen to reinterpret their encounter with the Gobi herdsman was present in front of their noses all the time in the form of the road between the Chinese oil rig and the herder's household, next to which they were accidentally forced to camp. Perhaps roads, in addition to representing material models of social connectivity in their capacity for bringing people and places together, are also visualizations or material conceptualizations of an often overlooked aspect of all infrastructures, namely their capacity to transform and transmute social and material relations into maximally hollowed-out relationships. In that sense, the length of a given stretch of road might be imagined as the visible depiction of an otherwise invisible capacity of material forms, namely that of interpolating optimal distances into relations whose terms may otherwise be perceived to be too close to or too far from one another: the longer the road, the more simplistic the nature of the connections between its endpoints, or so at least in the ethnographic case study we have explored in this chapter. In that sense, the materiality of the road traversed by Bunkenborg and Pedersen can be understood as an ethnographically derived scale for anthropological analyses (Strathern 2004; Holbraad and Pedersen 2009) that allowed the two ethnographers in first conceiving of and subsequently writing this chapter, to treat the herder's claim of not knowing anything about the oil rig as a unique source of insight into the social and material relations under investigation. Unbeknownst to them, Pedersen and Bunkenborg had from the onset been driving on the very thing—that is, the road—that eventually became a key concept in their analysis.[12]

Once again, as we also saw in the two previous chapters, certain contingencies arising from their joint fieldwork forced Bunkenborg and Pedersen to gradually modify their assumptions and interpretations. This time the analytical friction did not take the form of an irreducible difference between their respective understanding of the ethnographic data; on the contrary, in this particular case their interpretations were brought in closer alignment with one another via the complexities and contradictions in their data. Rather than being faced with two groups already separated from one another by different social, cultural, and economic relations and a long, bloody history of warfare, as they had expected when beginning their journey, what emerged was a subtle but importantly different understanding of the Sino-Mongolian encounter. Nowhere was this clearer than in the initial attempts by Chinese workers and local herders to forge trading partnerships of an informal, short-term nature and the subsequent decision by Chinese and Mongolian leaders to centralize and formalize all economic transactions in order to stabilize purportedly volatile ethnic relationships. Here and elsewhere in and around PetroChina Daqing Tamsag, infrastructures like roads and institutions like CSR worked in tandem to uphold certain kinds of "intimate distances" in the sense discussed in this book's introduction. Indeed, as technologies of distantiation, roads not only reduced multiple, informal, and emergent Sino-Mongolian chance encounters and relations to reified and ossified sociomaterial forms, they also bifurcated Bunkenborg and Pedersen's joint fieldwork into separate ethnographic paths that were only minimally connected.

STRATEGIES OF UNSEEING

The Possible Superimposition of a "Chinatown" on the Catembe Peninsula

"Well, . . . I can't really see what it says. Let me try to clean it." Lourdes Simango, local community chief (*secretário do bairro*) in the Catembe Peninsula across the Maputo Bay, took off her right shoe and used it to wipe the surface of the cement marker that was partly covered in sand. "I suppose you can read it if you are Chinese." Simango bent down over the cement marker in order to properly read the mysterious markings (see figure 4.1). After a few unsuccessful attempts to decipher the meaning, she got up and shook her head. "It's impossible to read! Anyway, it doesn't matter. The Chinese were here, and they left these markers in the ground without consulting me!" José, her soft-spoken assistant, nodded and pointed at the small two-room cement building at the other side of the dirt road, where a large hand-painted sign above the wooden door frame indicated that this was the headquarters for the local community council. "I was sitting in there watching the whole thing," José explained. "And they didn't even introduce themselves; they just starting putting down the markers. . . . But we don't worry about these things. The Chinese do what they have to do, and we mind our own business."

In June 2011 Nielsen visited the Catembe Peninsula, now part of the broader Maputo urban region in order to discuss with local community chiefs the recently announced plans for improving and "upgrading" the area. Earlier that year the Maputo municipality had launched the new "partial plan" (*plano parcial*) for Catembe, outlining the ordering and upgrading of hitherto informal habitational zones and describing in detail the ambitious plans for improving the weak

FIGURE 4.1.   Lourdes Simango, community chief in Catembe, cleaning the "Chinese'" road marker with her shoe. June 2011.

infrastructure, i.e., the street lights, sanitation, and the road system. In KweKwe, a small neighborhood that stretches across the peninsula, Nielsen met with Lourdes Simango, an outspoken community chief, who never seemed to miss an opportunity to voice her opinion on the need for improving Catembe's infrastructure. Obviously. Simango was delighted that the Maputo municipality would finally take seriously the residents' persistent demands for "development" (*desenvolvimento*). "Catembe is so close to the Maputo city center," Simango explained with a raised voice, "and we need development. There is no justification for people still having to live a life in the city during the day while, during the night, they have to live a semi-rural life (*vida semi-rural*) in Catembe. It's almost as if a person shifts from being sick with fever (during the night) to being normal (during the day)." Standing outside the community council's headquarters in KweKwe, it was hard not to agree with Simango about the glaring difference between Catembe and the city center. Across beautiful Maputo Bay, the skyline of high-rise buildings was silhouetted against a dark blue horizon. Turning around and looking toward the interior of Catembe, the sight was remarkably different. Along the dirt road that followed the seaside toward Maputo Bay, parallel rows of reed huts and small cement houses constituted the center of KweKwe. On the other side of the small housing area, vast fields of dry grass and bushes continued along the peninsula and onto the mainland. "Although Catembe is close to Maputo, it is also very far away," Simango concluded with a sigh and nodded toward José, who had apparently fallen asleep while reading the newspaper. "José has to take the ferry across the bay to go to the bank. That's not right, you know."[1] During her term of office, Simango had made it a monthly habit to approach relevant officials at the Maputo municipality to demand immediate improvement of the untenable situation in Catembe. Although it was impossible to know whether her proactive approach had been effective, the tides seemed to be changing. According to local municipal officials, residents in Catembe would soon enjoy the benefits of a functional roadnet, electricity, and sanitation and, most importantly, a bridge that would connect the peninsula with the city center. "Have you shown him the cement marker?" José suddenly asked; he had probably been disturbed in his sleep when hearing the sound of his name. Simango gave an irritated toss of the head. "Ah! But we don't know for sure what they wanted," the community chief sneered without looking at her drowsy assistant. Simango noticed Nielsen's bewildered look and began to elaborate on her exchange with José. A few weeks prior to Nielsen's visit, a group of Asian engineers had arrived in Catembe and spent two days inspecting the roadnet. This unannounced visit had worried Simango. Official inspections are rarely made without prior notice by relevant state or municipal departments, but this time the Asians seemed to have simply arrived in Catembe and started laying cement markers in the ground along the peninsula's main road. Nielsen asked Simango if she had actually met the foreign visitors. While responding, Simango got up from her chair behind the wooden desk and indicated they were leaving the office.

> People saw them early in the morning, but it was late afternoon before they arrived in my neighborhood. I approached them and introduced myself and asked if there was anyone from their team who could speak Portuguese. They pointed at the car where a young man was sitting. I asked him what company they worked for, and he told me that they weren't part of Maputo Sul but that they were a Chinese company responsible for building the bridge between Catembe and Maputo.[2] You see what I mean, Morten? It wasn't my administrator who told me about the Chinese. As a person, I have to believe (*eu como pessoa é que tenho que acreditar*) that, yes, they were Chinese and that they were involved in building the bridge because I saw that they laid down the markers. So I know that it is true.

Having shown Nielsen the cement markers with the indecipherable markings, Simango took Nielsen to the ferry berth in Guachene. While waiting for the small ferry to return from the city center, Simango told Nielsen about the "real plan" for Catembe. "You know that they are going to build a 'Chinatown' in Catembe, Morten?"[3] Simango looked Nielsen directly in the eyes, awaiting her interlocutor's response. "Build a 'Chinatown'?" Nielsen tried hesitantly. "Yes!" Simango nodded enthusiastically. "We discovered that the Chinese want to build a town. . . . It is going to be almost like a private town for one particular race. A Chinese town in Mozambique! Can you imagine that? This shouldn't be happening. We have surpassed such colonial nonsense, and we don't want to go back. But, you know, . . . I don't want to get involved in that. That's for them [i.e., the Maputo municipality] to decide (*fica para eles*)."

Sitting on the ferry on his way back to the city center, Nielsen wondered about Simango's disconcerting account. Gazing back at the ferry berth where the street vendors' afternoon activities seemed to be gradually slowing down, it was hard to imagine that social life in the peninsula would soon be undergoing radical changes. Could it really be that Simango was correct that a bridge and a "Chinatown" were about to be built? Maputo was always overflowing with rumors of the erratic maneuvers of the ruling Frelimo party, and this sounded much like yet another story that depicted the murky underworld of Mozambican politics. In general (often rightfully so), political life in Mozambique is portrayed as having little regard for the concerns of local citizens, such as Lourdes Simango and her fellow residents in Catembe, who would have to be relocated if a "Chinatown" were to be built. Without writing off the community chief's account as merely unsubstantiated political rumor, Nielsen nevertheless remained skeptical.

Here, we explore a particular form of Sino-Mozambican relationality that manifested itself in the "intimately distant" way people positioned themselves to make the most of the future bridge from Maputo to Catembe and the plans for a "Chinatown" associated with it. In line with our overall hypothesis that relations between Chinese workers and managers and their local counterparts may be conceived of as "intimate distances," Nielsen and Bunkenborg originally set out to chart the peculiar relations forged between people forced to spend extended periods of time with those they perceive as radical others whose intentions and opinions remain unknown. On the face of it, the notion that intimate distances emerge between radical others spending time together suggests that these parties are physically positioned within coterminous spaces, such as remote oil fields and mines in Mongolia or fenced-off construction sites and sawmills in Mozambique (as in the next two chapters). As we will see, however, our ethnographic material from Catembe forced us to reconsider the assumption that intimate distances can only exist between people who are forced to spend extended periods of time together. In this chapter we explore the relational dynamics and intimate distances forged between people when the crucial counterpart is a physically distant other whose perspectives and opinions remain unknown. Based on an in-depth analysis of the infrastructural "upgrading" of Catembe, we outline how relations to radical others may be figured as a process that takes its point of departure in the "unseeing" of the other, by which we mean individual and collective attempts at gradually eradicating the social and practical significance of a significant Other—even when this Other might continue to greatly impact one's everyday life. Indeed, as we will see, the Chinese engineers seemed to strategically disregard the fact that the area designated as construction site was already occupied by hundreds of local families. At the same time, while local Catembe residents illegally occupying land within the boundaries of the construction site were significantly affected by the encroaching construction project, they seemed to almost strategically avoid information about these foreign actors, opting instead to focus almost exclusively on the sociopolitical landscape they already knew.

Bergesen (2008) has described Chinese interventions in Africa as a form of "surgical colonialism" that "involves a minimum of local disruption, making the extraction almost surgical in nature." As he suggests, a key characteristic of surgical colonialism is that particular interventions, such as resource extraction or infrastructure projects, are concentrated in restricted areas with little or no economic benefit to the wider society. From this perspective it is the place rather than the people that is useful to broader socioeconomic processes of extraction; thus a process of dispossession in the form of land grabs, say, or extensive export of hardwood might occur without any significant involvement of the local population (Tsing 2000; Murray Li 2007). Here we consider whether such processes, where the other is from the outset "unseen" (e.g., by emphasizing the area's potential for infrastructure rather than residential), might also occur inversely, that is, from the perspective of those who are exposed to the effects of "surgical colonialism." In other words, could it be that the dispossessed also seek to remove agents of dispossession from having any importance in their daily doings? If so, how might that be done? Secondly, we also consider whether such processes are necessarily predicated on physical interactions. Consider again Simango and José's reflections on the strange visit by the Chinese engineers. During their conversation with Nielsen, they emphasized several times that minimal information regarding Chinese involvement in Catembe was a desirable thing in their eyes. (Recall Jose's argument that "we don't worry about these things. The Chinese do what they have to do and we mind our own business" and, later, Simango's concluding comment that "I don't want to get involved in that. That's for them to decide".) If we take into account Simango's habit of regularly discussing the need for improved infrastructure in Catembe with municipal officials, her reluctance to make further inquiries regarding the purpose of the Chinese visit seems odd. In this chapter, then, we examine the mutual process of canceling out and "unseeing" the Other that is undertaken not only by the mostly Chinese agents of dispossession but also by the Mozambican dispossessed in the process of "upgrading" the Catembe Peninsula. It was predictable that the plans for developing Catembe largely ignored the residents in order to present the peninsula as *terra nullius* ready for development, but it was a surprise that the residents were engaged in a similar operation. By annulling the importance of their Chinese counterparts, we argue, Mozambican residents assumed the position of equal counterparts to those state agencies that presumably control the provision of state services to the peninsula. This does not mean, of course, that the impact of the Chinese construction agents was not immediately felt by the Catembe residents. The effects of the possible construction projects were widely debated and gave rise to anxiety and concern, but their explanation or cause was left an open question, which was exactly the point. Here we suggest that an intimate distance becomes a relational space for configuring a significant other as an absent cause with very present effects.

Let us begin by outlining the internal collaboration of Nielsen and Bunkenborg as it played out during their joint fieldwork in and around Maputo. The heated discussions between the two anthropologists about whether a "Chinatown" might be built in Catembe eventually led to new insights about the Sino-Mozambican relationship under investigation, a relationship that was rapidly changing the living conditions for a large number of inhabitants in the Catembe peninsula. Not unlike the Chinese and Mozambican interlocutors who were disregarding each other to the extent that they appeared to have lost all immediate significance, the two anthropologists stubbornly ignored each other's findings from the outset, and the reflexive discovery of these overlapping processes of "unseeing" eventually informed the analysis. To the Chinese engineers managing the construction project, it was the place rather than the people that was imbued with value. In parallel with but opposite to the developmental ambition of "rescaling" the area as a site for urban property investments, the residents who were illegally occupying land in the projected construction zone also conjured up an imaginary of the peninsula in which it was locality rather than the "people" (in this case, the Chinese engineers) that was imbued with value. From years of frustrating encounters and futile negotiations with an almost paralyzed state machinery, the Catembe residents knew that the most productive and feasible strategy was to ignore what could not be controlled and instead focus on consolidating and securing one's position as best as possible. Where one's counterpart always makes larger promises than can be kept, it can be a viable strategy to proceed as if nothing new will happen. Taking our cue from David Harvey (2005), we argue that these simultaneous strategies of unseeing can be considered as a doubled version of "accumulation by dispossession." Not only the Chinese engineers but also the Mozambican residents were trying to capitalize on the process by strategically devaluing an "outside" other.

White-Collar Ethnography

After leaving the Catembe Peninsula, Nielsen returned to the flat he was sharing with Bunkenborg. Having spent the day in Catembe walking around in the ruthless sun, Nielsen was looking forward to a relaxing evening where he and Bunkenborg would discuss the spurious news regarding the alleged building of a "Chinatown" and compare the data that Bunkenborg would probably have collected during the day from his local Chinese informants. In the living room Bunkenborg was busy ironing one of his many white shirts. Wearing only shorts and slippers, Bunkenborg did not look as if he had been out during the afternoon. "Oh no," he told Nielsen with a serious look on his face. "I spent most of the day here! I did an internet search in Chinese and discovered that the China Road and Bridge Corporation has just announced that they're going to build the bridge to Catembe. I found the office of Maputo Sul and zipped down to confirm the news, but the director wasn't there, and the secretary wouldn't say whether the documents were signed. But I am certain they are. The secretary gave me such a knowing smile when I asked, and then she explained that they would be hiring more staff in the near future. I was so thrilled by my discovery that I treated myself to a nice lunch on the way home."

Although he did not admit it, Nielsen was slightly annoyed that Bunkenborg had managed to get crucial information about the bridge to Catembe without even leaving the apartment. For Nielsen, tired and dirty after an exhaustingly warm day talking to residents in Catembe, it did not seem quite fair that Bunkenborg had carried out his part of the research wearing shorts and slippers and lounging in air-conditioned apartments and restaurants in the city center. Equipped with two cold Laurentina beers, Nielsen and Bunkenborg went to the shady balcony where the slow afternoon traffic on the street below could be observed. Nielsen immediately started to narrate everything that had happened during the day in Catembe. "I wonder if Simango *really* believed it herself," he concluded with a laugh. "I mean, . . . a bridge and then a 'Chinatown' in Catembe? That's ludicrous!" Bunkenborg took a sip of his beer and cleared his throat. "Well, it's not all that insane. I just told you that I'm now confident that a Chinese company will build the bridge, and obviously other Chinese companies will be interested in developing the prime real estate on the far side of the bridge. I agree that the Chinatown plans associated with the Shanghai-based Tongjian investment company have seemed overly speculative, and that's what my Chinese informants have been telling me. This particular investment company has no real financial muscle; they're just throwing money around in five-star hotels in Shanghai and Maputo to sign MoUs with high-ranking officials and have their pictures taken in the hope of attracting more capital. But now that the bridge is being built, something is bound to happen."

Nielsen was dumbfounded. Clearly, his colleague found a spurious news item that was only available in Chinese more convincing than Nielsen's hard-earned understanding gained from engaging with flesh-and-blood Mozambicans on the Catembe Peninsula. Bunkenborg actually believed that the Chinese were going to build a bridge and a "Chinatown" in Catembe! As pedagogically as he could, Nielsen explained that Mozambican politics operated precisely on the basis of such rumors. At its core was nothing but a multiplicity of collapsed visions about what could be done with the necessary financial resources and human capacities (Nielsen 2011; see also Sanders and West 2003). Bunkenborg, however, remained steadfast, and they continued to discuss the probability of building a Chinatown in Catembe well into the night without reaching agreement on the truth of Simango's disconcerting account. Having worked in Maputo since 2004, Nielsen was convinced that his account of the questionable workings of Mozambican politics was accurate. Furthermore, when compared with his good friend and colleague's thin information (based on a Chinese construction company's website!), it seemed likely that his own meticulously collected data was more trustworthy.

Building a Chinatown the Catembe Way

While having never totally abandoned urban areas, at the time of our fieldwork, the once-socialist Frelimo government continued to prioritize rural development (Jenkins 2013; see also Dinerman 2006; Trindade 2006). Resources for improving Maputo's dilapidated infrastructure were restricted, and there was still no overall urban development policy guiding the municipality's ill-coordinated planning initiatives (Andersen et al. 2015a). Despite the lack of administrative coordination, however, urban areas continued to grow, not least in the predominantly informal peri-urban zones on the fringes of the city, what is still referred to as the "reed city." Of 86,300 new housing units built from 1980 to 1997, as few as 7 percent were provided by the state or the private sector (4,000 and 1,500, respectively). The remaining 80,000 plus housing units were built without state assistance (Jenkins 2001, 637). Despite constant promises by Frelimo cadres at the Maputo municipality to implement viable urban planning mechanisms, recent studies show that more than half the city's total area is still formally "unplanned" (Andersen et al. 2015a; 2015b). In this unstable socioeconomic context where urban development continues to be a low priority for the central government, Catembe constituted a constantly deferred future ideal activated by Frelimo politicians to assure their constituencies that the full potential of the city would be realized once the peninsula was urbanized. It is undoubtedly also for this very reason that the Catembe Bridge seemed to be constantly at the center of political debates on urban development in Mozambique at the time of Nielsen and Bunkenborg's fieldwork. Nielsen himself originally started doing doctoral ethnographic research in Maputo in 2004 when Armando Guebuza was first elected president; he vividly recalls daily debates on TVM, the national television station, on the importance of connecting the city center with the Catembe Peninsula. Limited access to Catembe had proven again and again to be a serious impediment, not only to the 22,065 inhabitants who lived on the peninsula (Betar Consultores 2012, 3) and commuted regularly to the city center, but equally to an increasing number of economically oriented political agents within and beyond the ruling Frelimo party who viewed Catembe as the next financial hub. As Nielsen was told in 2009 by an up-and-coming real estate agent from Maputo, "Catembe is virgin land, and it is there to be taken by anyone with a clever mind and friends in the right places."

From the mid-1980s and until approximately 2009, it was a widely held assumption among officials and private investors that the bridge would eventually be financed and built with Portuguese money through an administrative and economic setup similar to that established for the building of the Cahora Bassa dam in the Tete region, which opened in 1974 (Isaacman and Isaacman 2013). By early 2009, however, it was becoming increasingly clear to the Mozambican officials involved in the project that their Portuguese counterparts would not be able to fulfill the promised commitment in the wake of the 2008 financial crisis. They therefore started looking toward Asia for new financial collaborators capable of realizing the ambitious project of connecting the city center with the Catembe Peninsula and making a roadnet stretching from Maputo to Boane and Ponto d'Ouro.

Over the last two decades Chinese expansion in sub-Saharan Africa in general and in Mozambique in particular has increased its pace at a staggering rate. If we focus only on the most recent period, China's increasing economic presence is even more pronounced. Not all construction projects are realized through intergovernmental agreements, however, and the dozens of Chinese companies currently active in Mozambique also work for municipalities, international donor organizations, and private enterprises (Macauhub.com 2018; see also Jansson and Kiala 2009). Though modest in comparison with other African states, Mozambique's economic collaboration with China is worth noticing because of its accelerating pace, which represents one of the fastest growing rates for a single nation trading with China. In 2018 trade between the two countries reached US $2.515 billion, an increase of more than 35 percent over 2017 (allAfrica.com 2019). Dwarfed only by Brazil, Angola, and Portugal, this massive trade increase makes Mozambique the fourth largest trading partner with China in the Lusophone world.

A particularly visible manifestation of increased economic Sino-Mozambican ties is the now completed national stadium on the outskirts of Maputo, which was inaugurated in 2011. In 2005 the Chinese government proposed the donation of a football stadium to Mozambique to be located in Zimpeto, a neighborhood on the northern periphery of Maputo. Less than six years later, on April 23, 2011, the new national stadium, with seating for 42,000 spectators, was inaugurated by the Mozambican president, Armando Guebuza, and a delegation from the Chinese Embassy. Another spectacular example was the planned construction of a suspension bridge connecting the Catembe Peninsula to the city center, which we have mentioned earlier in this chapter. In 2011 Lourenco Sambo, the Mozambican general director of the Mozambican Investment Promotion Center, announced that the search for investors in Asia had proven successful. Representatives of the ruling Frelimo government had signed a memorandum with the Chinese government for financing of the bridge and a ring road around the city center, whose fragile roadnet was on the verge of breakdown. A year later the official loan agreement was signed by the Mozambican finance minister, Manuel Chang, and representatives of the Chinese Exim Bank, outlining overall costs that would add up to US $725 million, with the Exim Bank subsidizing 95 percent and the Mozambican state putting in 5 percent. On September 20, 2012, the first brick of the bridge was laid in the ground; with an expected construction period of three years, the inauguration of the Catembe Bridge was planned for the fall of 2015. Due to a number of setbacks, the completion of the project was postponed several times, but on November 10, 2018, Mozambique's President Filipe Nyusi finally announced the opening of the bridge.

A few months before Lourenco Sambo's public announcement, Nielsen had visited the Catembe Peninsula to meet with Alberto Costa, the head of the local municipal urbanization department. As Nielsen was told during the hour-long meeting, the Chinese government would fund not merely the construction of the bridge but, quite surprisingly, also the building of a "Chinatown" (in Costa's words). "Now, they are looking at Catembe as the future of Maputo city," Costa told Nielsen in a soft voice. He made a small rhetorical pause and shook his head before continuing. "And they are already talking about moving the National Parliament (*Assembleia da República*) to Catembe, you know, with a cultural city center and a Heroes' Square (*Praca dos Heróis*)." Nielsen was somewhat puzzled about the issues raised by Costa. Although Nielsen knew a few of the state officials involved in the project relatively well from his previous studies on urban planning in Maputo, no one had told him anything about the building of a Chinatown in Catembe or the plans to move the National Parliament to the peninsula. Since Nielsen couldn't confirm Costa's statements, he didn't push the matter further and proceeded instead to focus on the planned relocation of 245 families who would be affected by the building of the bridge.

When he and Bunkenborg returned to Mozambique in 2012, Nielsen visited Catembe once again to resume conversations with residents living on the peninsula. By that time the information that Bunkenborg had managed to find in Chinese the previous year had become public knowledge in Mozambique as the media had announced that the construction project was to be undertaken by the China Roads and Bridges Corporation (CRBC), which would also be responsible for building the ring road around the Mozambican capital. As Nielsen was returning to the city center with the small ferry, he noticed a black Toyota RAV4 with four Asian-looking men dressed in elegant black suits, their eyes covered by huge dark sunglasses. Feeling as if he were about to play a part in a Hong Kong gangster movie, Nielsen approached the car and tried to look as friendly and unassuming as possible. The young man sitting next to the driver rolled down the window; they exchanged a few civil comments about the brutal heat and the overcrowded ferry. After a few minutes Nielsen mustered the courage to ask what they were doing. The young man's low voice was constantly being drowned by the noise from the ferry's motor so Nielsen had to put his head halfway into the car in order to hear. "We are building a Chinatown," the young man replied without hesitation. "CRBC invited us here, and we have been at Catembe to locate a suitable place to build two thousand houses." Before he could continue, a portly man sitting in the back seat pulled the young man's arm, and Nielsen's interlocutor signaled that the conversation would be momentarily interrupted. The young man listened in silence for a few minutes to the man in the back seat before he turned toward Nielsen again. "My boss wants to know if you are in the construction business," he said, nodding toward the back of the car. "We are also considering building one or two cement factories in Catembe, and we want to collaborate with someone who speaks the language." Nielsen politely declined the offer, and after a few more cordial exchanges, the conversation was over. The young man handed Nielsen his company card, from the Henan Province Dengfeng City Songji Group, and rolled up the window.

Less than a week later, a good friend of Nielsen, who was working in the Ministry of Public Works and Housing (MOPH), forwarded a collection of internal documents describing the involvement of private Chinese companies in ongoing and projected infrastructure projects in Mozambique in general and in Catembe in particular. It appeared from these documents that by 2011 a project had been drafted to build a new city center in Catembe. Estimated at a total cost of US $2 billion, the project would be carried out by the China Tongjian Investment Corporation and consist of the construction of a new seat for the National Parliament and several additional public buildings and squares. Hence, while Nielsen was reluctant to admit it (and acknowledge the accuracy of Bunkenborg's information), it seemed that the head of the local urbanization department had been correct in stating that a town would be built in Catembe. Although a new company had apparently been selected to carry out the ambitious construction project, Costa was not entirely off the mark when he characterized the urban plan as the making of a "Chinatown." Though it was not initially clear to Nielsen what the young man in the black Toyota RAV4 had meant when he claimed that they would be building a "Chinatown," it now seemed that he was probably referring to the ambitious project of making a new city almost entirely of whole cloth, the plan that Nielsen's friend had found in MOPH's internal documents.

The Benefits of Illegal Land Invasions

As Nielsen's visit to Costa's office had indicated, the plans to build a bridge between the city center and Catembe had not gone unnoticed among residents living in the peninsula. While it was widely acknowledged that access to and from the city center was in dire need of improvement, many residents soon realized that building a viable roadnet between Maputo and Boane would eventually require the relocation of a considerable number of families currently living in the projected construction zones. According to Costa, as soon as news of the planned construction project started to spread, worried residents lined up outside his small office waiting to be informed about the consequences of the project. Since the urban plans for Catembe seemed to undergo continuous changes, however, it was impossible for Costa to give reliable information to the concerned residents regarding the consequences of the projects on their continued occupancy in the peninsula.

Not everyone was as frustrated about the lack of precise information as Costa clearly was. Many of the residents illegally occupying land in the projected construction zone were not at all against the expected relocation process. Relocation offered the possibility of transforming current illegal occupancies into formal property rights since residents occupying land in the designated construction areas would be relocated to areas laid out in accordance with state-authored urban plans. Even if it meant moving to a different part of Maputo, relocation was considered by many as worth the trouble. Of the 22,065 inhabitants registered as residents in Catembe in 2012, very few had legal property rights to their plots; people lived in constant uncertainty about whether they would eventually be forcibly removed by corrupt state officials wanting to sell the land to members of the party elite or to one of the many real estate agencies trying to make a profit on the expected increase in land values arising from improved accessibility to and from Catembe.

According to residents living in the projected construction zones near the seaside, the area had previously been owned by Emodraga, a state-owned company responsible for dredging the national harbors and rivers. When Emodraga moved its headquarters to Beira in the early 2000s, its Maputo workforce was made redundant. By way of compensation, the laid-off workers were allocated plots of land previously owned by the company in Catembe although, crucially, without receiving land use rights, the so-called DUATs (*direito de uso e aproveitamento da terra*), to the plots. At the time the Mozambican government had not yet established what Armando Guebuza, Mozambique's president, later described as its "eternal friendship" with China (Revistamacau 2006), and the bridge to Catembe was not on the political radar as a realistic priority. Hence, neither the Emodraga company nor its dismissed employees had found it worthwhile to legalize the occupancies in Catembe.

Although Nielsen had heard this historical account several times from residents occupying land in the projected construction zone, it was quite rare that he actually met former Emodraga employees who had been allocated land as compensation for lost jobs. Apparently the large majority of residents living in the area had bought their plots from former Emodraga employees, many of whom had used the allocated land merely as *machambas* (cultivated fields) to grow crops for their households, who were living elsewhere in Catembe. Perhaps somewhat naïvely, Nielsen initially assumed that these land transactions had taken place prior to the spreading of news of the Catembe Bridge and the new "Chinatown" projects. Surely, he surmised, such major investments of human and financial resources would be made only if and when occupancy was relatively secure. Considering the increased uncertainty surrounding occupancy in the projected construction zone, Nielsen found it quite unlikely that anyone would invest in land—or start building a cement house—knowing that it would most probably be removed. However, meeting Felizardo, a retired war veteran living in the projected construction zone, in a two-room cement house with his teenage daughter, Nielsen was forced to reconsider his initial assumptions.

Nielsen had first heard about Felizardo from Lourdes Simango in 2012. During a prolonged discussion about the increasing number of outside investors attempting to purchase land in Catembe, Simango commented that a certain Felizardo had acted as middleman between former Emodraga employees and some unidentified real estate agent. According to Simango, the transaction had been unsuccessful, but Felizardo apparently ended up buying land in the area himself. After Nielsen's conversation with the community chief, he went out to look for Felizardo and managed to locate his house in a fertile grove not far from the seaside. As Nielsen later learned from the blueprints of the construction project, it was in this area that the pillars of the Catembe Bridge were to be located. Nielsen explained that he was interested in knowing more about the ongoing transactions with the Emodraga plots, and Felizardo immediately agreed to provide all possible information. Felizardo had, indeed, acted as middleman in some recent land transactions, but the potential buyers were not outside real estate agents planning to make a profit from the booming land market in Catembe. Rather, the majority of interested buyers were people already occupying land illegally elsewhere in the peninsula. As soon as it was announced that the area was likely to be projected as construction zone, Felizardo was approached by numerous residents who wanted to buy land from former Emodraga employees. Having lived in the area for more than a decade, he was considered by the locals as an expert on the genealogies of land ownership in Catembe, and he was therefore used as a middleman in several transactions between former Emodraga employees and potential buyers.

Felizardo and Nielsen visited several plots that had been recently purchased by Catembe residents who had moved there from elsewhere in the peninsula. Although many were living in small one- or two-room reed huts, a few occupants had already laid the foundation for their future cement houses; in one instance a one-room cement house had been nearly completed. With zinc plates covering the roof and the wooden door and window frames already in place, the house only needed plastering on the outside walls and tiles laid as a front terrace. Somewhat bewildered, Nielsen asked these newcomers to explain why they had bought the land knowing they would most likely be relocated within the next few years. As expected, the initial responses revolved around the prospects of acquiring formal property rights to land through a state-authored relocation process. However, as Nielsen pushed the matter further, it was clear that to many of the newcomers who were now occupying land in the projected construction zone, relocation did not necessarily entail a physical move to another area in Catembe: Although the magnitude of the planned construction project was without precedent in post-independence Mozambique, residents in Catembe and elsewhere had vivid recollections of being exposed to the modernizing aspirations of the governing Frelimo party, something that had often resulted in striking failures and a consequential worsening of an already fragile socioeconomic situation.

Thus, by occupying a territory as politically saturated as the construction site in Catembe, the threat of relocation paradoxically indicated a momentary stabilization of the situation by steering toward an ordering of space that the government was clearly incapable of realizing. By illegally occupying land in the construction zone, residents were making themselves strategically visible to the state agencies overseeing the construction project in Catembe. This immediate visibility could potentially resolve the residents' current problems in one of two ways. The state agencies in charge of the project were not at all interested in prolonged discussions with stubborn residents refusing to leave the construction site. Lacking both time and resources to commence a legal procedure for dealing with the squatters who had invaded the construction site, chances were that all residents would be relocated to other areas in Catembe where they would be allocated formal use rights to their plots. Another way of resolving the situation, however—slightly more complicated but no less realistic—was the possibility, as had been the case with infrastructure projects many times before, that the construction project might never be realized. Although the construction area had been delimited and the infrastructure project partially initiated, lacking resources and capacities it might end up being postponed until state authorities realized that the cost of actually removing the growing number of illegal residents was too high. Either way, it would be difficult for the residents not to gain from the process if only they kept their eyes on the state apparatus, whose growing weaknesses were a source of both immense frustration and relative stability.

The Flipside of "Accumulation by Dispossession"

In her studies of messy global capitalism in Indonesia and beyond, Anna Tsing (2000, 119) proposes that natural-resource extraction is also a "scale-making project," that is, it produces by itself the scales ("local," "global," etc.) by which it is to be imagined and enacted. More precisely, Tsing argues, natural-resource extraction in Indonesia might be conceived of as three overlapping "scale-making projects," namely "the globe-making aspirations of finance capital, the nation-making coercions of franchise cronyism, and the region-making claims of frontier culture. . . . Globalist, nationalist, and regionalist dreams linked to enunciate a distinctive economic program, the program of spectacular accumulation" (141). The effect of these overlapping scale-making projects is a "frontier culture" that has captured the imaginations of both foreign entrepreneurs and local residents to such an extent that "a spreading of frontier culture is created. It is a culture dedicated to the obliteration of local places, local land and resource rights, local knowledges of flora and fauna" (132).

Returning to the Catembe Peninsula, it is relevant to ponder what "scale-making projects" are imagined and enacted through the Chinatown project and what the implications might be for the people involved, such as those residents currently occupying plots of land in the area previously owned by the Emodraga company. Following Tsing, we might take scaling to signify precisely those framing activities that produce the specific spatial dimensionality of social life necessary "for a particular kind of view, whether up close or from a distance" (120). Still, as Tsing also reminds us, scales are not neutral frames that lend themselves to an objective viewing of the world. On the contrary, "scale(s) must be brought into being: proposed, practiced, and evaded, as well as taken for granted" (120). In the case of the Catembe Bridge and Chinatown projects, the spatial dimensioning at hand seemed to be imagined as an urban frontier ripe for "surgical intervention," to paraphrase Bergesen (2008), where the place rather than the people was considered to be useful. Mozambican state officials involved in the project worked from layouts and blueprints designed by their Chinese counterparts, and it is truly quite remarkable that these documents did not map out existing buildings and housing units in the projected construction zone. In fact, from the documents that Bunkenborg and Nielsen examined while in Mozambique, it seems that the construction site was envisioned as a completely blank slate. The planned roadnet and buildings were overlaid on a topographical map that outlined differences in altitude and a geotechnical description of soil conditions but did not contain any reference to existing physical constructions, such as individual houses.

To be sure, while it was rare that the urban initiatives launched by the Mozambican government reflected the needs and priorities of residents living under fragile conditions (cf. Castel-Branco 2015), their existence was usually acknowledged. During interviews with Mozambican officials, Nielsen would bring up the striking "purification" (cf. Latour 1993) that seemed to be built into these formal layouts. "We have been wondering about that as well," a young municipal architect admitted. "I am not even sure that they (the Chinese planners) know that there are people living in the construction zone." According to the official, given that the Chinese planners did not include existing buildings in their layouts of the area, it was impossible for their Mozambican counterparts to know exactly which housing units would be removed. Judging from the material submitted to the Mozambican officials by the Chinese engineers, it was clear that existing maps had not been used for reference when designing the project layout. Several months prior to commencing the building project, Chinese topographers had visited the area to determine its topographical characteristics; these had apparently been used as the only basis for the layouts. The Mozambican officials therefore had to decipher the Chinese layout by comparing it with available geographical data at the Maputo municipality. As officials at the municipality told Nielsen, the two did not really tally. Large parts of the construction zone were occupied by residents and small-scale farmers, and it was a challenge to mark off its boundaries, which often traversed individual plots and houses. In order to establish some form of workable alignment between the Chinese layout and the actual situation on the ground, the Maputo municipality had ordered the local authorities in Catembe to physically mark all housing units with either a *p* for those that could (probably!) be preserved and an *x* for those that would eventually be demolished.

In *The New Imperialism* David Harvey (2005) makes a convincing diagnosis of contemporary forms of capitalism. Based on an updated reading of the Marxist idea of "primitive accumulation," Harvey explores the myriad forms of privatization by which capitalist expansion has been able to produce new realms of proletarianization and private appropriation of public property. Since the end of the Fordist era, Harvey claims, capitalism has been caught by the problem of "overaccumulation" where "surpluses of capital . . . lie idle with no profitable outlets in sight" (149). In order to continue accumulating, capitalism therefore requires something "outside of itself," such as "non-capitalist social formations or some sector within capitalism . . . that has not yet been proletarianized" (141). Crucially, if such assets do not lie ready at hand, capitalism must somehow produce them by itself. A primary vehicle for this kind of capitalist expansion continues to be state-supported investments in markets throughout the world and an accompanying denial of access to their own markets for those countries that refuse to accept such strategies. According to Harvey, when international agencies, such as the World Bank and the IMF, implement measures that seek to open up local markets, the result is a "limited crisis" leading to the "periodic creation of a stock of devalued, and in many instances undervalued assets . . . which can be put to profitable use by the capital surpluses that lack opportunities elsewhere" (150). This phenomenon is what Harvey defines as "accumulation by dispossession, which release(s) a set of assets (including labor power) at very low (and in some instances zero) costs" (149).

When thinking through the situation in the Catembe Peninsula with Harvey's Marxist-inspired analysis of global capitalism, the forcing open of the territory to politically orchestrated urban development at first glance seems like a good example of "accumulation by dispossession." Privatization, say, of public land, has in recent decades been the major force that capitalism has used to create something "outside of itself," as Harvey describes it, that it can then appropriate (Castel-Branco et al. 2003; Mains 2012; Verdery 2004; Manji 2012). In many regions of the world (sub-Saharan Africa and Latin America being the most prominent examples), public land has been opened up to private investments with the effect of producing new fields for over-accumulation to seize upon as well as generating a landless proletariat that has few or no possibilities of accessing land unless by activating capitalist mechanisms that are based on private property rights. Through the forced eviction of residents in Catembe that was being planned at the time of Nielsen and

Bunkenborg's fieldwork, large sections of the peninsula were going to be released into the "privatized mainstream of capital accumulation," allowing new entrepreneurial agents, such as the Chinese investors planning to build a Chinatown, to capitalize on the process. Following Harvey (2005, 150), we might therefore consider this process as leading to the "periodic creation of a stock of devalued . . . assets" (such as land, infrastructure—and even residents), which would be put to profitable use by capital interests. What had previously been an expanding habitational zone, in which property relations were imagined and regulated in accordance with moral economies and bureaucratic structures that were partly or fully detached from the logics of the market, was "re-scaled" (*pace* Tsing 2005) in order to conjure a provisional urban frontier available for capitalist expansion. It could be argued, then, that at the core of the capitalist "surgical operation" (Bergesen 2008) was a fundamental lack: as Harvey reminds us, faced with the paradox of over-accumulation, an "outside" always has to be created in order for capitalism to feed upon it. This re-scaling requires a devaluation—or could we say, an "unseeing"—of specific exterior elements and agencies. Not unlike Tsing's (2000, 132) troubling account from Indonesia, where a "frontier culture" can be imagined precisely through the obliteration of local places and knowledges, capitalism enforces upon an "outside" a particular reading that only distinguishes certain qualities and traits, while others (persons, places, ideas) are relegated to a status of obscure insignificance (Simone and Nielsen 2021). In a nutshell, what is seized upon is what is also defined (or re-scaled) by a lack of value.

What is striking about the Catembe Peninsula, however, is that the capitalist process of making something "outside of itself" seems to cut both ways. Rather than a classical example of capitalist expansion where marginal people are overlooked and dispossessed, as Harvey would have it, the Catembe case suggests that the potential victims may choose to strategically ignore or "unsee" the agents of dispossession. In order for the residents in Catembe to gain from their relationship with the weak state apparatus in either one of the two ways already mentioned, the Chinese agents have to be removed from the equation. Whereas in Harvey's account of capitalism, the dispossessed are devalued and "unseen," for the dispossessed in Catembe, it is through a similar operation, but aimed at the Chinese agents, that they continue to engage in productive negotiations with the Mozambican state cadres. Had they counted on the Chinese agents as a factor in determining their future, they would in all likelihood still be living under worse conditions somewhere outside the construction site.

Gateway Encounters

During a visit to Catembe, Nielsen accompanied José, the community chief's assistant in KweKwe, on a trip around the peninsula to interview residents living in houses that had already been marked either for preservation or demolishment. While the majority of affected residents were still puzzled by the spray-painted signs on their houses, none had approached the officials to ask why they had been singled out in such a visible manner. "I came home after work one day to find my house painted," Nielsen was told by a perplexed resident. "But I didn't want to push the matter further. . . . This is my plot, and if they have something to talk with me about, they need to come to me!" Walking across the peninsula, Nielsen heard several versions of this response, which initially seemed to indicate a lack of interest in knowing about the causes and possible implications of the markings. "Why didn't they immediately approach Alberto Costa (the head of the local municipal urbanization department)?" Nielsen wondered when he sat down with Bunkenborg to discuss the Catembe residents' disinterested responses. "I mean, . . . several of the residents didn't even bother to find out what the signs on their houses meant!" Ignoring Nielsen's question, Bunkenborg launched into a lecture on the gradual emergence of intimate distances in social relations between Chinese and Mongolians and a detailed comparison between the Catembe and the projected site for a Chinese-built power plant that he had visited outside of Ulaanbaatar together with Pedersen (see Pedersen 2017). Nielsen was somewhat annoyed with his colleague's know-it-all attitude. Was it not completely obvious that Catembe was characterized by the absence of any interaction between the Chinese planners and the local residents? Most of the residents currently living within the construction zone would eventually have to be resettled on the outskirts of the city, where there was still vacant land to be found. However, if they were to confront state or municipal agencies directly involved in the process, it might still be possible to postpone or perhaps even prevent forced eviction. And, as Nielsen concluded, even the planning agencies might benefit from further information about the situation. If the Chinese planners had taken into account the fact that the area was already inhabited by several thousand people, a collective process of urban development might have been launched that could potentially prevent many conflicts about rights of occupancy, which Nielsen foresaw as a probable but unfortunate outcome of the current situation. From the case of the Chinese oil company in Mongolia, Bunkenborg and Pedersen had learned that certain forms of infrastructure reduced an initially messy social interaction to a polite and minimal relationship between two opposing sides. Surely, it was the same process going on in Catembe, Bunkenborg insisted, and he proceeded to relate an anecdote from a recent field trip to Catembe in order to lend ethnographic substance to his interpretation.

In Maputo there was talk of a Chinese cement factory being constructed on the Catembe peninsula, and on a sunny day in July 2011, Bunkenborg decided to drive south to investigate the matter. The road was pretty much one continuous

FIGURE 4.2. The gate of the future Chinese cement factory on the Catembe peninsula. March 2009.

pothole with inconvenient creases of asphalt here and there. When Bunkenborg finally found the fenced construction site after hours of extremely bumpy driving, the brake caliber on the right front wheel had come loose. The inscription in Chinese and English on the large blue gate proclaimed that a cement factory was being built with the goal of furthering "cooperation," a "win-win situation," and "cherishing China-Mozambique friendship."

It was time for lunch, and while Bunkenborg waited outside the gate for Mr. Wang, the senior Chinese manager, a group of Mozambican workers lined up to exit the gate one by one. The Chinese guards at the gate amused themselves by commenting on the appearance of the workers. "Your hat is pretty cool," one of the guards said in Chinese and pulled at the green hat worn by a grey-haired Mozambican man.[4] Probably not to be outdone, the other Chinese guard tugged at a pocket that was coming loose on the man's jacket and said in Chinese, "You better mend that when you get home." The elderly man was clearly baffled by the antics of the guards, but he didn't respond. The next worker in line was a young, muscular Mozambican who decided to give one of the guards a hefty handshake. "You're strong," the Chinese guard remarked in Chinese and felt the young man's biceps. The young Mozambican then took hold of the Chinese man's upper arm and said disapprovingly in English, "No power!" Unable to understand, the Chinese looked to Bunkenborg for a translation and then turned to the young

Mozambican to explain, in Chinese, that he was twenty-five years senior and couldn't be expected to have the muscles of a young man. The young Mozambican didn't understand a word of this, but he couldn't be bothered to wait for a translation and simply walked off with a laugh.

The guards stepped deferentially aside when Mr. Wang, a thickset Chinese man in his late forties, exited the gate with a small retinue and walked briskly up to Bunkenborg to inform him that it was quite impossible to admit visitors. "Construction sites are dangerous," he said, pointing to the white hard hat he was wearing by way of explanation. No doubt Mr. Wang intended to dismiss Bunkenborg out of hand, but he appeared somewhat mollified when Bunkenborg complained in Chinese about the rough drive. Mr. Wang finally consented to a brief interview on the spot. "As it says on the gatepost," Mr. Wang explained, "we are constructing a 5,000-ton-a-day cement factory, and we have a contract on this strip of land, roughly three kilometers wide. The people living here now will be removed. Then we'll strip off the topsoil, extract the clay, and put back the topsoil. There are no serious environmental problems in this; it's a little dusty, but we do our best to minimize that."

"At least there will be some jobs for the locals," Bunkenborg suggested in a feeble attempt to energize the interview.

"Well, not really," Mr. Wang replied, "you see, it is a fully automated plant, and it won't be necessary to employ any locals. You make the same mistake as the local government here by focusing on employment. You should think of this factory as a locomotive. You shouldn't ask, 'How many people can sit in the locomotive?' Obviously, there is only room for the driver on the locomotive itself. What you should be asking is 'How many cars and passengers can this locomotive pull?'" Mr. Wang then launched into a long description of all the local economic activity that would prosper from the cement production—transportation, brick making, construction, etc.

Having said goodbye to Mr. Wang, Bunkenborg fiddled with the unstuck brake caliber, feeling a little sorry for the local residents who were to be removed from their land and then left to latch on to Mr. Wang's locomotive and create their own jobs as best they could. A young Mozambican walked up and offered to help. Johnny, as he introduced himself, had a friend with a repair shop in the nearby village, and they set off to find replacements for the missing bolts. "Do you know what 'win-win' means in Chinese?" Johnny asked and pointed to the inscription on the gate. "It means I beat you twice—'win, win.'" It turned out that Johnny used to work for the Chinese, but he became dissatisfied with the terms of employment and found a job elsewhere. With the Chinese it was always three-month contracts with pauses in between; they only paid the minimum wage; and there was no free food. "They have no respect for other people," Johnny said. "They spit on the floor right next to you when you're eating!" Bunkenborg explained that spitting was quite common in China and not a sign of disrespect, but Johnny did not seem entirely convinced: "Well, that's exactly what they said, when we workers complained and called for a meeting to stop the spitting." Johnny estimated that there were two hundred Chinese and seventy Mozambicans working on the construction site. Originally, all the workers were Chinese; the construction company only employed local workers now because the local government insisted. Johnny explained how messy things had been when the Chinese first arrived. Chinese workers would walk into people's houses, lift the lids on the cooking pots, and spit on the floor as if they were disgusted by the food. There were also reports of workers prowling for local girls. "The government wouldn't tolerate that, and now the Chinese workers get arrested if they leave the construction site," Johnny explained with a satisfied grin on his face.

There were no spare bolts to be found, and as Bunkenborg edged homeward with a screeching brake caliper, he had plenty of time to muse upon the significance of the fence next to the road. Was it built to keep the locals out, as Mr. Wang claimed? Or was Johnny right in his assumption that it served to contain the Chinese? Having spoken to both Chinese and Mozambicans around the future cement plant, Bunkenborg came to the conclusion that both sides contributed to a gradual segregation of social worlds and that they were learning to strategically ignore the other, much as he had witnessed with Pedersen in Mongolia. Mr. Wang appeared to imagine that Mozambicans would be happy to sit in the passenger seat and leave the driving to Mr. Wang and his company. In this narrow sense the Chinese entrepreneurs could, indeed, be described as the "locomotive" of progress, but at the cost of excluding any local people from an active role on it. The socioeconomic conditions in Mozambique could indeed be considerably improved, but this would—paradoxically—require a radically reduced involvement of Mozambicans in the process. But if the Chinese were trying to "unsee" and remove the Mozambicans from the equation, or at least relegate them to the passive passenger seat, the conversation with Johnny suggested that some Mozambicans were equally eager to eliminate, or at least contain, the Chinese presence. Much like the situation around the fluorspar mine in the Gobi Desert, where Chinese miners were not so much trying to insulate themselves from the local Mongolians as being forced to contain themselves and hide in their camp, some of the Mozambicans seemed to be very much in favor of the fences erected around the Chinese cement plant. The gradual reduction of interaction to an absolute minimum followed from a broad range of awkward exchanges between Chinese and Mozambicans, which now only took place at the gateway during the brief moments when the Mozambican workers were entering or leaving the compound. As Bunkenborg interpreted the situation, the sparse and disjointed verbal exchanges between the collaborating partners functioned as a residual manifestation of an original awkwardness that was now being ritualized into something like a joking relationship, "a relational infrastructure" by which to steer everyday intimate distances (*pace* Simone 2004).

Nielsen was not entirely satisfied with this interpretation. Thinking back on the unstable situation in the section of Catembe set aside for the new bridge and Chinatown, it was really not a question of the Chinese planners and the Mozambicans gradually minimizing interactions and learning to ignore each other, as Bunkenborg had suggested. In order to extract from the land its latent potential, Nielsen thought, Chinese and Mozambican residents in the area were attempting to engineer a complete "unseeing" of each other; in different and opposing ways they were seeking to completely devalue the social importance of one another. When the Chinese engineers were preparing to launch their infrastructural plans, they were operating on the basis of a geographical map depicting an empty space without people and houses. Whether intentional or not, the effect of this planning maneuver was that the Mozambican state authorities in charge of overseeing the process were left with the responsibility of making sure that the physical space would reflect the emptiness of the Chinese engineers' map. In other words, the state authorities were forced to orchestrate the resettlement of all residents living in the construction zone instead of integrating within the project design some degree of adaptation to the existing social and physical conditions of the area. At the same time, the Mozambican residents were attempting to conceptually eliminate the Chinese construction agents from the social landscape in order to achieve a minimum form of security of occupancy from the Maputo municipality. Most residents in Catembe, such as Felizardo and even Lourdes Simango, the community chief, had little or no interest in knowing what the Chinese were actually up to. Based on their longtime experiences with a highly dysfunctional and erratic state apparatus, many residents had come to the realization that the most productive and feasible strategy was to leave aside what could not be controlled and instead focus on consolidating and securing one's position as best as possible. It is in this sense that these simultaneous strategies of "unseeing" could be considered as a doubled version of "accumulation by dispossession" (Harvey 2005). From both sides, it seemed, attempts were made to capitalize on the process by creating an "outside" that was strategically devalued and unseen.

Crucially, this double process of "unseeing" did not require physical interactions—such as the quotidian encounters at the gateway—in order to become operational. Lourdes Simango made it abundantly clear that there was absolutely no need to inquire further about the reasons for the Chinese visit in Catembe. And as far as we know, no Chinese engineer was ever in contact or dialogue with local residents or local authorities during the entire preparation phase leading up to the construction process. Could it be, Nielsen pondered, that Bunkenborg had the situation upside down? In a sociopolitical setting where interacting agents are strategically seeking to "unsee" the Other, physical encounters do not orient or steer the relational dynamics. For both parties, the significance of the Other was so fundamentally devalued that a physical encounter (if it were to take place) would appear irrelevant. In fact, as Nielsen thought about the matter, the gateway encounters were like the "underbelly" of intimate distances. The brief meetings were merely a series of physical approximations between two parties who were systematically attempting to reduce the importance of the other to an absolute minimum. To both Chinese construction agents and Mozambican authorities and residents, the Other was first and foremost figured as an absence and as a subject of avoidance. The scattered, infrequent and always awkward encounters between the two sides were to be viewed as aberrations, Nielsen argued, not a form of "relational infrastructure."[5]

"I think I get it," Bunkenborg said as he returned to the narrow balcony with another pair of cold Laurentinas. "The analysis you're aiming for sounds like something out of a sci-fi novel called *The City and the City*." In this book, Bunkenborg explained, two different cities overlap and occupy the same geographical space. The inhabitants of both cities are trained to identify and conscientiously "unsee" everything that pertains to the other city. Noticing the other city—including people, vehicles, buildings, and events—in any way is illegal, and "breaching," as it is called, will get people into serious trouble with the authorities. It is possible to move legally between the two cities, but one must go through a gateway called the Copula, the only place that exists under the same name in both cities. At the Copula border crossers exit exactly where they enter, but they are in a different city. "This is exactly the situation in Catembe," Bunkenborg continued. "The Chinese planners 'unsee' the existing buildings and residents, the residents 'unsee' Chinatown, and the two are connected and severed by gateways like the one I described at the cement factory. The funny thing is that you yourself, Nielsen, have been 'unseeing' the Catembe Chinatown. You haven't believed in any of the information I found in Chinese!" "Well," Nielsen retorted. "I could say the same about you. The only reason you spoke to a Mozambican worker was that your car broke down and you couldn't repair it without getting oil on your white shirt. And your analysis doesn't apply to this case because clearly there is no training involved. Here the residents and the Chinese planners manage to unsee each other before they even meet!"

Unseeing as Intimate Distance

The state-promoted process of urbanizing the Catembe Peninsula clearly generated a need for defining the area as a new capitalist frontier, the corollary being the planned eviction of the current residents. In parallel, residents in Catembe sought to wrest away from this process of dispossession productive imaginaries of the area that would allow them to maintain or acquire secure rights to land either in the peninsula or elsewhere near the city center or alternative, equally viable imaginaries where the state would never be capable of actually realizing its ambitious project and the residents would remain there indefinitely. In a continuation of the state-orchestrated attempt at "re-scaling" the area as a new zone of urban property investment, residents in the projected construction zone participated in conjuring up an imaginary of the peninsula in which it was the place rather than the people that was imbued with value. The difference was that in the former case, it was the residents who were omitted from the conceptual and material mapping of the area, while in the latter it was the Chinese investors who were being devalued or "unseen" by the same communities of locals. In so doing, residents were at least momentarily able to maintain a certain directionality and force in their ongoing attempts to establish relatively secure rights of occupancy. By provisionally denying the significance and indeed the very existence of the Chinese investors, the residents' claims were directed and channeled toward those formal governmental agencies responsible for administering the everyday pragmatics of urban planning in Maputo.[6] While these agencies were not formally authorized to administer the use of land within the projected construction zone, they continued to do so throughout the planning process. The administrative procedure was short-circuited for many reasons: the coordination of urban planning activities in Maputo is hampered by a general lack of human and financial resources, and the administrative structures are not geared toward accommodating large-scale building projects, such as the planned Chinatown. The immediate but brief effect of this short-circuiting was that residents' claims successfully activated an administrative domain that operated in parallel to that of the Chinese investors, both sharing the contested land in the Catembe Peninsula as a matter of concern.[7]

To Bunkenborg's Chinese and Nielsen's Mozambican interlocutors—as well as the two anthropologists themselves—"unseeing" became a particular kind of intimate distance that figured the Other as "irreducibly enigmatic." By relating to significant others through strategic acts of devaluation and "unseeing," it became possible to play out different parallel but unconnected scenarios structured by the need to avoid immediate or direct confrontations between contrasting realms of experience. There is no doubt that the shadow cast by the Chinese building project in Catembe irrevocably transformed, or "re-scaled," social life and kinship-property relationships on the peninsula as well as the parameters of the relationship between residents and cadres working within the dysfunctional administrative system of Maputo municipality. "I don't understand why we are kept in the dark (*no escuro*)," Lourdes Simango noted with overt frustration when Nielsen last spoke to her on the phone in the fall of 2015. "Now I have to read about Catembe in *Noticias*. Nobody tells me anything anymore, Morten!"[8] Apparently, the municipal architects allegedly keeping the Catembe residents "in the dark" were as puzzled about the situation as Simango was. On a hot Sunday afternoon in May 2012, Nielsen met up with Costa in the city center, where he was living with his family. After a few introductory comments about the ruthless heat, Costa gave Nielsen an update on the current situation in Catembe. "It looks as if the Chinese are taking over the peninsula. I really didn't think that the project would be realized but here we are." Nielsen asked what would happen to the residents in the projected construction zone. "Ah! They will have to leave. It's a new reality (*nova realidade*). Now the Chinese are doing what we never managed to do ourselves."

ENCLAVES AND ENVELOPES

Cutting and Connecting Relations in
Sino-Mozambican Workplaces

There was no doubt that the palm of Mr. Zou's right hand connected audibly
with Célio's forehead, but it was impossible to judge whether the odd gesture was
intended as a friendly pat or an angry slap. Célio emitted a very short laugh of
surprise and embarrassment, then his smile disappeared, and he told Mr. Zou
in Portuguese, "You shouldn't do that. That's not ok." Mr. Zou leaned forward
again and made as if to repeat the gesture; then he laughed, apparently choosing
to ignore the seriousness evident in Célio's words and demeanor. This awkward
exchange took place in the office of a sawmill in Montepuez, in the northernmost region of Mozambique. For quite a while Nielsen and Bunkenborg just sat
silently in their white plastic chairs and pretended to watch the Chinese action
movie playing at low volume while their brains churned to grasp the implications
of the exchange they had just witnessed. Having entered the gate in the morning, Bunkenborg had gone straight to the office in the big house at the center of
the walled compound and spent two hours in conversation with Mr. Zou, who
was stationed at the sawmill as a machinist and general caretaker. Meanwhile,
Nielsen had spent the morning in a small cubicle next to the machine shop where
he interviewed Célio, who was employed as foreman for the Mozambican team
of workers. Having pursued their individual lines of enquiry, Bunkenborg and
Nielsen expected to wrap up with an amicable joint session, but instead they
became witnesses to this charged physical exchange between their informants.
Despite the increasingly heated discussion that ensued and a return visit to the
compound later in the day to interview the protagonists separately about the

event, they have never quite been able to agree upon exactly what happened. For Nielsen, things were crystal clear—it was a slap in the face; an act of aggression by an insensitive Chinese manager, and judging from Célio's reaction, it was nothing less than a moral aberration, especially given that it was framed within an asymmetrical power relationship between a foreign "master" and an African "subject." Without disputing that the gesture could well be highly offensive to local sensibilities, Bunkenborg insisted on a different interpretation. Mr. Zou was clearly rattled by the very serious breach of etiquette that had occurred when Célio walked into the restricted area of the office without asking for permission, threw himself in a chair, and left the menial task of organizing seats for the other visitors to his nominal superior, Mr. Zou. Far from random aggression, Mr. Zou's gesture was a physical manifestation of an intense discomfort caused by Célio's transgression of the boundaries and norms that Mr. Zou considered proper and necessary.

The interaction between Célio and Mr. Zou was deeply disturbing to all, and the logging compound had suddenly proved to be a far more tense and unpredictable place than either Bunkenborg or Nielsen had imagined, as if a wedge had severed the shared understanding between the two ethnographers. Where Nielsen saw a slap in the face expressing Mr. Zou's inability to see and relate to Célio as a person capable of interacting with strangers and representing the company, Bunkenborg saw a nudge stemming from Célio's evident disregard for the spatiotemporal order of a Chinese workplace and his failure to fulfill his assigned role as a worker. The interaction between Mr. Zou and Célio, then, revealed two radically different ideas about how to deal with strangers in a social environment only partially known and decipherable. In the unexpected social context of receiving visitors, Mr. Zou felt that security vis-à-vis intrusive outsiders like the nosy ethnographers could best be achieved by strict adherence to the hierarchy and order of the compound. Célio, conversely, seemed to be attempting to step out of his role as a subordinate worker in this Chinese-defined hierarchy; he expected to be seen and treated as "a person" (*uma pessoa*) capable of conversing both with Nielsen and Mr. Zou on a basis of mutual respect and the maintenance of proper physical as well as social distance (Nielsen 2010). For Bunkenborg, "the nudge in the face," as the event eventually came to be referred to between the two ethnographers, seemed to confirm the impression that the Chinese informants attempted to establish distinct spatiotemporal orders that could disentangle their operations from what they perceived as a chaotic environment. For Nielsen it confirmed that a characteristic feature of Sino-Mozambican relations was the attempt and failure of Mozambican workers to establish proper interpersonal relations with their employers. For the two ethnographers, the incident represented a sudden juxtaposition and strangely disturbing connection between these two distinct strategies for dealing with alterity that recurred in many of the Chinese-owned workplaces they visited in Mozambique.

It was in Maputo that Bunkenborg and Nielsen first developed their disparate takes on Sino-Mozambican relations. Strolling through the dilapidated colonial streets of downtown Maputo, they came across dozens of Chinese operations, ranging from unimposing shoe shops and Chinese restaurants to full-blown supermarkets crammed with Chinese goods. After seeing numerous fenced construction sites where Chinese and Mozambican workers, sometimes in identical uniforms and hard hats, were engaged in some of the many projects that Chinese construction companies have undertaken in and around Maputo in recent years, the two ethnographers decided that one of these construction sites, the national football stadium, seemed the most promising for a case study of the relations between Chinese and Mozambican interlocutors.

The large football stadium with a capacity of 42,000 people was then under construction in Zimpeto, on the outskirts of Maputo, as part of China's global "stadium diplomacy," (Will 2012) which has seen Chinese companies undertaking the construction of sports venues financed or supported by the Chinese state. The football stadium was considered by both Chinese informants and local politicians alike to be the epitome of friendly and mutually rewarding Sino-Mozambican collaboration. Employing approximately 300 Chinese and 300 locals, the gated construction site afforded optimal conditions for

FIGURE 5.1. The National Stadium in Zimpeto. Entrance to the construction site. February 2009.

implementing the Dual Perspective Approach guiding the overall research project. So Bunkenborg and Nielsen started their simultaneous exploration of Sino-Mozambican relations in the workplace at the stadium.

The Chinese workers at the football stadium lived and worked in guarded compounds; apart from dealing with the Mozambican workers on site, they had little occasion to interact with local society. As in Mongolia, the Chinese contingent was largely self-contained, and from the Chinese perspective the integrity of the workplace and the safety of the workers seemed to hinge on various infrastructure measures that set these spaces apart from their surroundings. Based on his initial fieldwork in Chinese workplaces in Mongolia, work on "enclave capitalism" (Ferguson, J. 2005), and the literature describing Chinese projects in Africa as self-contained or even as "surgical" (Bergesen 2008), Bunkenborg was quick to conceive of this and other Chinese projects in Mozambique as "enclaves." Following Appel's (2012a, 442) ethnographic study of offshore oil extraction in Equatorial Guinea, he saw enclaving as a process of ongoing disentanglement from local circumstances where "the work-intensive disentanglement from responsibility for life outside enclave walls, the building of spatial and phenomenological distance in which the enclaves are at once in and not in Equatorial Guinea, is itself a form of violence." In both Equatorial Guinea and Mongolia, Bunkenborg reasoned, it required a great deal of infrastructure, hard work, and possibly even violence to ensure that enclaves were cordoned off from local social worlds, the same kind of work, he now assumed, that also allowed Chinese workers and bosses to think of their workplaces as islands of order in a Mozambican sea of chaos. When Mr. Zou's hand connected with Célio's forehead, Bunkenborg first saw it as an attempt to preserve the social order of the enclave, but Célio's intense bewilderment and anger made it clear that there was more to the nudge in the face than a predictable assertion of established social norms.

Through discussions with Mozambicans working for Chinese employers on the football stadium and elsewhere, Nielsen learned that these employees did not share the Chinese employers' view of their workplaces as islands of order in a sea of chaos. On the contrary, the Mozambican workers expressed confusion about the unpredictable behavior of their employers and the opaque rules that determined their salaries. As in the example from the Montepuez sawmill, the Mozambican workers insisted that the stability of their social existence was predicated on being seen as persons with lives and obligations outside the workplace, and their discontent at being considered only as workers took the emblematic form of complaints about the way the Chinese employers paid the local workers by counting out cash in public.

In Mozambique, as in many other African contexts, patronage relations are an integral part of everyday social life. As Cahen (2011) aptly describes with historical references to both Portuguese colonialism and the initial post-independence period of Frelimo's Marxist-Leninist rule, "In hard conditions of subalterity, people need a Master who will be feared and loved" (see also Geffray 1991; Wiegink 2015). During colonial rule a Portuguese boss or the head of a household was referred to as *patrão*, which implied unequal bonds of reciprocity between patron and client, ruler and ruled. In addition to paying salaries, the patrão could provide the client or employee with additional support, such as information about other job opportunities, housing, or advances on the next salary. In return, the patrão relied on the client's unambiguous loyalty and labor. Still, dependence on others for securing one's social stability goes beyond vertical links of economic and social support. In southern Mozambique alliances are forged by way of relational conduits, such as shared names (*xará*), that allow for mutual recognition and reciprocal responsibility to be established and reproduced even in volatile social environments (Pina-Cabral 2010). Presenting wages enclosed in an envelope would have suggested a similar kind of recognition of status, not simply as employees or anonymous representatives of the Mozambican chaos but as "persons" (*pessoas*) with whom it was possible to forge proper interpersonal relations (see also Laheij 2018). By choosing to count and disburse cash salaries in public, the Chinese employers unknowingly destroyed the illusion that the employer-employee relationship was one that the Mozambican workers could perceive as a "proper" interpersonal exchange between mutually recognized persons. Noting the importance of these missing envelopes, Nielsen conceptualized the Mozambican worker's attempts to construct predictable and reciprocal relations with the Chinese employers as a strategy of envelopment—and not, as Bunkenborg conceived of the Chinese side, as a strategy of enclaving.

Based on their work at the football stadium, Bunkenborg and Nielsen were well on their way to formulating separate analyses in which Chinese expatriates dealt with Mozambicans through enclaving and Mozambicans tried to handle the Chinese through enveloping, but the two ethnographers were stopped in their analytical tracks by the nudge incident. In keeping with their methodological demands and the graphic representation of their research fields as triangles that run parallel without ever meeting (see figure 0.2), Bunkenborg and Nielsen had been conducting their interviews as if they were worlds apart even when they were literally next door to each other. Their shock and disagreement about the incident in the sawmill was no doubt caused by the physical contact and subsequent collapse of the neatly circumscribed ethnographic worlds they had each been constructing. Put otherwise, Bunkenborg and Nielsen had been studiously "unseeing" each other's fields, but now they faced a breach in which the two distinct analytical ideas of enclaving and enveloping were simultaneously revealed as two inherently partial accounts of Sino-Mozambican relations. Hammered out in endless discussions sparked by the nudge in the face, the initially inchoate ideas about enclaving and envelopment were dislodged from their ethnographic particularity and allowed to travel laterally between fields so that Bunkenborg set out in search of strategies of envelopment among the Chinese, while Nielsen set out to find the Mozambican equivalent of enclaving. Having exchanged analytical registers, Bunkenborg and Nielsen came to realize that there were operations of relational cutting and connecting on both sides. As suggested by other workplaces as well, the Chinese tended to see the enclave as the only possible response to a situation where attempts to establish personal relations had already failed, while the Mozambicans eventually came to see the envelope and the relation it enfolded as a necessary step toward a future where their work had produced the material surplus that would allow them to finally cut their relation to the Chinese employers.

Strategies of Enclaving

The construction of Mozambique's new national football stadium was well underway in 2010 when Bunkenborg first approached the construction site. A Chinese man sporting the purple uniform of Sogecoa, a subsidiary of the Chinese construction company[1] responsible for the stadium, was guarding the entrance. The managers were out, he claimed, so Bunkenborg sat down on a bench outside the gate, and the two of them struck up a conversation. The gatekeeper turned out to be a forty-seven-year-old electrician from rural Anhui in central China, who was temporarily posted to the gate as work on the electricity and surveillance systems had not yet commenced. He had more than a year left on his two-year contract in Mozambique, and he assured Bunkenborg that he liked his life on the construction site:

> Right now, there aren't that many people, so it's one or two per room, but once we are many, it will be four people to a room, just like in school. The rooms are very clean, there's air-con, and the managers often do inspections. Bedclothes must be folded, shoes have to be placed correctly, and clothes should be on hangers. . . . It's all very orderly. Every morning, we stand in line for briefings. The managers make sure that every aspect of your daily life is systematic, logical, and orderly. . . . We get up at five thirty, and after eating breakfast at six, we jog and sing our song [he starts singing a in low voice, but struggles to remember the words]:
>
> *Construct a better world, strive hard for global peace.*
> *We are envoys of aid, that means friends of the world.*
> *Struggle for a peaceful world, dispel the troubles of the poor.*

FIGURE 5.2. Compound for Chinese workers in Maputo. February 2009.

As the electrician described his life on the construction site, everything proceeded according to a schedule. In the morning work started at seven o'clock, and at eleven o'clock it was time for lunch in the canteen and a midday nap. In the afternoon work started at two o'clock, and at six o'clock it was time for dinner in the canteen. The Chinese workers on site had all brought computers from home so they generally spent their evenings online, chatting with family members back home, browsing the news, or watching Chinese television—much as Bunkenborg and Pedersen had found to be the case at the state-owned Chinese oil field in far eastern Mongolia.

Finding it hard to believe that life on the construction site could be so entirely self-contained and prison-like, Bunkenborg asked whether the Chinese workers ever ventured out for dinner. "Well," the electrician responded, "security enforcement here in Mozambique is not quite as mature as in China, so we don't go out on our own, but the managers sometimes invite us to a Chinese restaurant for dinner." As for shopping, the electrician claimed that he had brought what he needed. "I brought enough from home. Shorts, shampoo, soap, toothpaste, toothbrushes, and soap. A bar of soap will generally last one month, so I brought twenty-some bars of soap. A toothbrush lasts three months. A tube of toothpaste lasts two months."

"But you just told me about the price of shoes in Mozambican markets, so you must have ventured outside," Bunkenborg protested.

"I have seen such markets," the electrician replied, "but I have never actually bought anything there. I don't know the language, and I might offend someone. That would be bad for me and bad for China's image abroad. Because of the language barrier, we try to have everything ready before we leave China, and if we have to buy something here, we go to the Sogecoa supermarket. After all, we work for Sogecoa." Racking his brains to come up with other scenarios that might make it necessary for the Chinese workers to leave their compound, Bunkenborg asked what they did in case of illness, but even that could be handled without interacting with the locals. Apparently, a team of Chinese doctors worked in the central hospital in Maputo as part of the Chinese state's long-standing efforts to provide medical aid to third-world countries (Bunkenborg 2014). Not surprisingly, they were much in demand among the Chinese nationals in Maputo.

Driving home that afternoon, Bunkenborg managed to convince himself that the Chinese worker's description of the regulated and industrious life on the construction site was not just a careful rehearsal of the image that his Chinese managers wanted to project. The electrician's appreciation of the safe routines that unfolded on the construction site seemed perfectly genuine and, as offensive to liberal sensibilities as the idea of spending two years more or less confined to a construction site might seem, the man really seemed to like the fact that the company took care of everything, so that he didn't just work in the Sogecoa uniform, but also took all his meals in the Sogecoa canteen, slept in tidy Sogecoa accommodations, and did his shopping in the Sogecoa supermarket.

Nielsen, on his side, found it impossible to believe that anyone could enjoy such a regulated life where time could be measured in toothbrushes and bars of soap. "Are you joking? Those guys must be idiots!" Nielsen exclaimed when Bunkenborg later relayed the story of the Sogecoa workers singing a song about development and world peace every morning. Nielsen simply refused to believe that life inside the enclave was so entirely regulated or that anyone might actually like that sort of setup. "He must be hiding something. Are you absolutely sure they're not convicts?" Nielsen asked. "Many of the Mozambicans I talked to claim that the Chinese workers are actually prisoners who have chosen to work here instead of serving time in China." Bunkenborg insisted that the idea of Chinese convicts working in Africa was rubbish[2] and that it was eminently possible to organize a construction site along the lines indicated by the electrician. Launching into a detailed description of the socialist work unit in China, the *danwei* (单位) which has been the subject of numerous books and articles (Bray 2005; Lu and Perry 1997), Bunkenborg tried to explain to his skeptical collaborator that it might be this particular form of social organization that served as a point of reference for middle-aged Chinese workers like the electrician. Conceptualized as an island of order in a sea of chaos, Bunkenborg lectured, the state socialist Chinese work unit was typically a walled compound where life was deemed to be safe and predictable because the work unit took care of housing, food, and pensions—in the heyday of socialism, a retiring couple could even pass their jobs on to their children. "That's extremely interesting," Nielsen said with more than a hint of irony, "but the construction site couldn't possibly be so organized and insulated—one of the Mozambican interpreters told me that a Chinese employee was caught burning the insulation off the company's copper wires and selling it as scrap metal. That's the sort of stuff we need to know about to get behind the facade!"

Returning to the site the next day in search of more information, Bunkenborg found a secluded storage area guarded by another man wearing the company's purple uniform, Mr. Lin. Like the electrician, he hailed from Anhui Province, but he was a few years older and spoke more freely of his experiences in Mozambique. In the small room he shared with a younger colleague, Mr. Lin had a laptop with a headset but little in the way of furniture—a couple of rough beds, two stools, and a scruffy table with two jam jars, one serving as a tea mug, and one full of cigarette butts. Apart from a few months of vacation back home in Anhui with his family every second year, Mr. Lin had spent the past seven years on construction sites in Uganda, Grenada, and Suriname; the company had transferred him directly from a job in Madagascar to work as a painter for the construction of the national stadium in Maputo.

Mr. Lin was generally quite happy with the terms of his employment, he told Bunkenborg, but he would have liked to have provisions for overtime and holidays. Some Chinese managers would give their workers a day off now and then, but they were not required to, and Mr. Lin's present manager seemed incapable of or unwilling to finding substitutes. Mr. Lin had thus been on the job every day and night for months without a day off, and he felt he deserved a rest. His younger colleague assented and added additional causes of discontent, including unclear terms of employment and long periods of low-paid training: "Even before you have finished reading the contract, they will say, 'Hurry up and put your signature there,'" the electrician sighed. "If you don't sign up, someone else will. . . . The company has all the contracts. They say that they just want to keep them safe, but that's not really the case because you don't get to see the contract." Not only did the company keep the contents of the contracts secret, they also required the workers to consent to a period of so-called training that might last as much as a year. "Nobody likes training. They call it training, but actually you are just working for less than a normal salary. . . . You have to do well and be obedient and the wages are pitiable. A normal wage in China is more than RMB 100 a day, but while you're in training, they only pay you around RMB 50 a day."

According to Mr. Lin, he and his younger colleague earned the equivalent of US $700 a month. Like most of the Chinese workers Bunkenborg talked to in Mongolia and Mozambique, the terms of their employment were such that their wages were paid out as a lump sum on their return to China. Even the additional monthly allowance of US $100 for living expenses worked as an account; accommodation and safety gear on the construction site was free, but meals and daily necessities—such as Chinese cigarettes ordered through the company—were docked against the allowance account. Mr. Lin and his peers thus had very little money to spend during their stay in Mozambique, but this didn't seem to trouble them at all. Mr. Lin in particular seemed to relish the fact that he hardly spent any money. He was looking forward to a substantial paycheck of more than RMB 100,000 when he returned home. Doing a quick calculation, he estimated that he would get an additional RMB 5,300 because he had only spent half his allowance. The standard wage level for Chinese blue-collar workers in Mozambique was RMB 5–6,000 a month at the time of Bunkenborg and Nielsen's fieldwork, and most of the workers seemed quite satisfied with that. Wages in China were going up, but even if it was possible to make RMB 7,000 in a good month in China, it was hard to do so month after month, Bunkenborg was told. What Mr. Lin and the other Chinese workers seemed to appreciate about working abroad was not only the relatively high wages, but also the fact that their income was entirely predictable and their expenses minimal. Being cut off from ordinary social life and obligations to kin and friends made it possible to accumulate capital at a rate that would have been impossible at home. For the electrician and Mr. Lin, it was a question of financing marriages for their sons. The goal of the younger men was usually real estate investments, and many of them kept an eye on the housing market back home, worrying that the value of their savings was being undercut by rising prices. For the Chinese workers on a two-year contract, the job represented a temporal and spatial bracketing of normal life that facilitated the quick accumulation of money.

The story of Mr. Lin was by no means unique; very few of the Chinese workers Bunkenborg met in Mozambique (or Mongolia) expressed any desire to stray from their construction sites. That said, it is worth noting that they were subjected to structural constraints that prevented them from wandering off. Much as Bunkenborg had seen in Mongolia, the Chinese companies operating in Mozambique took the workers' passports "for safekeeping" (保管) as soon as they arrived. It was possible to wander around Maputo without a passport, but the local police would frequently accost foreigners in the street in order to check their passports; as seems to be the case in Tanzania (Sheridan 2019), the Chinese felt they were easy targets. If the documents were not in order, the police demanded a fine to be paid on the spot. Even when the documents were perfectly in order, the unfortunate civilians approached by local policemen might be asked for money to "buy a soda" (*comprar um refresco*) (i.e., a small bribe to avoid further hassle). Small wonder, then, that a general understanding had crystalized among the Chinese workers that the world outside the construction site was dangerous: If you were walking around without a passport, it made little difference whether you were waylaid by robbers or by the police. The safekeeping of passports restricted the Chinese workers' freedom of movement dramatically, but it was regarded as part and parcel of life on a construction site abroad, and none of the workers seemed particularly upset about it. For the duration of their stay, Mozambique remained opaque, incomprehensible, and vaguely threatening, a darkness surrounding the predictable and safe existence on the construction site.

Compared to, for instance, the offshore oil rigs in West Africa discussed by Hannah Appel, the Chinese workplaces in Mozambique—sawmills, shoe shops, and construction sites—were small and hard to insulate from the local settings in which they operated. But even if they did not amount to enclaves in the strict sense discussed above and in the introduction, there were, Bunkenborg began to realize, distinct strategies of enclaving to be observed in and extrapolated from the physical layout of the Chinese workplaces. Compounds with walls, construction sites with fences and floodlights, and even shoe shops with guards posted at the door and Chinese employers perched on high chairs to survey the actions of both customers and employees were, it seemed to him, attempts to carve out small, well-lit zones of security and visibility in a milieu that the Chinese largely viewed as an opaque chaos. In short, Bunkenborg told Nielsen, he had come to the conclusion that the Chinese working in Mozambique tended to conceive of the local chaotic and potentially threatening environment as one that was best dealt with in an impersonal way by carving out tiny but numerous enclaves of order. Building walls around workplaces, policing boundaries, and establishing orderly regimes of visibility and calculation not only served to keep out thieves and induce workers to perform on the job, but also ensured that the lives of Mozambican employees outside the workplace were kept from view and that it was unnecessary to relate to locals as persons with families and obligations beyond the walled enclave.

While the Chinese workers were largely detached from local society for reasons both structural (the terms of their employment) and psychological (fears of robbers and police), many supervised teams of local workers on a daily basis and what they dismissed as Mozambican chaos invariably asserted itself inside the supposedly snug, safe haven of their compounds. Posted on the wall in Mr. Lin's modest office-cum-bedroom was a list with the names of a dozen Mozambican employees. Bunkenborg was puzzled to see that many of them bore Chinese names. "I have learned a little Portuguese," Mr. Lin explained. "Useful words like 'good morning,' 'good evening,' and 'faster,' but it's hard for us to tell the local workers apart, and their names all sound the same, so we gave them names in Chinese. Otherwise we couldn't get their pay slips right." This list of Sinicized names might be an interesting crack in the otherwise hermetically tight enclave, Bunkenborg thought to himself as he took leave of Mr. Lin. The Chinese workers and managers often had little to say about the lives of the Mozambicans they worked with, but perhaps the pay slips could be interpreted as a potential opening through which the Mozambican workers came to acquire a Chinese identity, so to speak, and then became visible inside the enclave as persons with a legitimate demand for wages that reflected their individual contributions. Nielsen would no doubt appreciate this half-baked analytical idea of the Sinicized name as a sort of "cloak of visibility," Bunkenborg mused as he walked home to learn from Nielsen what the Mozambican workers thought about working on the Chinese construction sites.

Strategies of Envelopment

Felix was part of a group of Mozambican welders hired by the Chinese construction company AFECC to work on the football stadium's massive iron framework. When Nielsen met Felix in 2009, he was having a quick lunch in a hot-food stall (*baraca*) before returning to the construction site for the afternoon shift. Only minutes into their conversation, it was obvious that Felix was far from enthusiastic about his Chinese employers, the wage policy being the most salient point of critique. "The thing is," Felix held Nielsen's arm as if to focus his attention on his words. "They (the Chinese employers) don't tell us how they calculate our monthly pay. You just go there at pay day, and they give you what they think is sufficient. . . . As employers, they ought to say, 'Hey, your daily pay is this and after eight hours of work, your salary goes up to this.' But that's not how it works; none of us know what we make from thirty days of work." To make matters worse, Felix told Nielsen, salaries were paid out from a movable stall placed in the middle of the construction site. At payday all Mozambican workers would line up and receive their salaries from a Chinese accountant handing out wads of money through an open window. "No one likes that!" Felix thumped his index finger on the bar counter several times. "They really ought to put the money in an envelope, you know. In this situation, that would be the proper way to do it."

To many Mozambican workers involved in the construction project, such as Felix, quotidian interactions with the Chinese were fraught with uncertainty. As Nielsen was constantly being told, it was completely impossible to decipher the actions of the Chinese coworkers, which buttressed the already widespread feeling of being radically different. Elísio, a young man from a nearby neighborhood, worked as a bricklayer at the stadium site. A few days after Nielsen's meeting with Felix, he elaborated on the Mozambican workers' perceptions of the Chinese. "We don't speak to them," Elísio said with conviction, "because their way of doing things (*a maneira deles*) doesn't even seem human. I don't know. . . . The Chinese, . . . they aren't human. They aren't persons to whom you can actually talk. . . . They don't respect you. . . . They are really racists, you know. They don't consider the negro as a human being."

To Nielsen, the explanation was clear. Placed in an unknown social and material microcosmos constructed and governed by what they perceived to be radically different and potentially malevolent Others who, at the same time, were also crucial for maintaining their socioeconomic livelihood, the key issue for Elísio and his peers was how to establish stable and (relatively) predictable forms of social interaction with their Chinese coworkers (cf. Nielsen 2012a). And as Elísio and many of his colleagues saw it, a paper envelope for delivering their salaries would play a central role in accomplishing that goal. This was clear to Nielsen when Elísio explained the importance of the envelope by outlining the consequences of its absence. "Anyone can see that they are handing out money," Elísio argued. "It's like taking money off the street." Without the discretion of the envelope, Elísio and his colleagues felt increasing exposure; they were fundamentally prevented from acquiring a well-defined social identity. In southern Mozambique, people are essentially what their relations to others make them (Paulo, Rosário, and Tvedten 2007, 4; Pina-Cabral 2010). Similarly, without the envelope to conceal and contain the cash, recipients are thrown into and defined as anonymous, which invariably minimizes their ability to act as social agents—there is nothing to demarcate the parameters of relationships.

As a consequence of lacking the "envelopment of the relationship" with their foreign superiors, Nielsen told himself, it was impossible for people like Elísio to figure out how to ensure that their interactions with the Chinese would not end up being harmful to them. Felix made this point in response to Nielsen's question about teaching the Chinese workers some basic Mozambican words. "No, no, no!" Elísio shook his head energetically. "Why should you teach them any words at all? In the future, they'll use those same words against you; they'll use them to insult you (*começa ti insultar com ela*)." This suggested to Nielsen that, from the perspective of the Mozambican workers at the stadium site, social interactions with the Chinese were automatically defined as potentially dangerous, requiring a carefully organized form of proximity to enable coexistence. As Elísio, Felix, and their peers saw it, the envelope would have established a form of proximity to certain important but potentially dangerous Others at the other end of the "relational contract" established by the enclave. Without fully eliminating the widespread sense of uncertainty pertaining to their Chinese employers and social life in general, it would have compartmentalized the always lurking dangers at the construction site and other social spaces so that these would take the form of defined relations, rather than coincidental occurrences and random shapes. As Nielsen told Bunkenborg, it was just this organized and relatively stable form of proximity that was seen as absent in the present case.

But why, one might ask, did the local Mozambican construction workers not consider the money they received by their Chinese superiors as proper salaries? It could be imagined, after all, that the money was perceived to constitute "real" (albeit very low) salaries, similar to those the young Mozambicans workers had previously earned when working for local (non-Chinese) companies—indeed, this was the line of thinking adopted by Bunkenborg in response to Nielsen's analysis. Still, the local Mozambican workers insisted that they had come to experience in very concrete ways such radical differences between themselves and their Chinese employers that the likelihood of establishing viable reciprocal relationships was miniscule. This point was made even clearer during a prolonged conversation between Nielsen and Ináncio (a young construction worker) a few days later, in a dimly lit bar close to the building site.

INÁNCIO: A salary has value because someone was working.

NIELSEN: What kind of value?

INÁNCIO: A symbolic value because he [the employer] is rewarding me for my efforts. He has to respect (*considerar*) me like I respect him for being in charge.

NIELSEN: So, in order to be valued in that way, you have to be paid a proper salary?

INÁNCIO: Yes. You have to be paid in a proper manner (*tem que ser pago de boa maneira*).

NIELSEN: And are you paid in a proper manner by the Chinese?

INÁNCIO: Ihh! (Makes a high-pitched sound.) Never!

Within the specific setting of the stadium construction site, Nielsen gradually came to conclude that the envelope constituted a way in which social life could be organized so that viable forms of proximity were established with significant but potentially dangerous others. Had the workers received money in sealed envelopes from their Chinese superiors, they would probably have acted on the assumption that the latter were acknowledging them as proper persons with whom social interactions were not only possible but also necessary. The envelope would thus provisionally establish a secure domain and stabilize the relationship between the Chinese superiors and the Mozambican workers both temporally and spatially. But that was not how things were done at the Chinese construction site.

"Why can't the Chinese just show a little consideration for local sensibilities and learn to put the wages in envelopes?" Nielsen asked Bunkenborg after a long harangue about the way Mozambican workers were treated by their Chinese employers. "Well, it does seem a little odd," Bunkenborg replied, still unconvinced by Nielsen's insistence on the "inhuman" nature of the relationships established through transactions in raw cash. "I have always been taught to put money in an envelope in China. Obviously, you can buy things and hand out small tips openly, but money that means something—wages, loans, and gifts—is usually wrapped in envelopes to underscore that there is more than a simple monetary transaction at stake." Perhaps, Bunkenborg ventured, "the Chinese construction companies have some sort of misguided idea about conforming to international standards?" Upon learning from his fellow ethnographer that cash was generally put in envelopes in China also, Nielsen felt doubly outraged on behalf of his Mozambican interlocutors—apparently presenting "raw money" wasn't just wrong by Mozambican standards, it was even wrong by Chinese standards!

Bunkenborg speculated that the Chinese employers might simply be trying to be professional and practice transparency by handling wages as cash payouts in the open, but Nielsen immediately dug out his cell phone and showed him a series of photos documenting how the hours were penned in with Chinese characters on the pay slips that determined how much the workers were paid. "If they are trying to be transparent," Nielsen fumed, "why do they write the basis for calculation in a language no one understands!"

Unable to reach a consensus about the nature of the Sino-Mozambican encounter on the construction site on the basis of their individual fieldwork, Bunkenborg and Nielsen decided to continue their investigations together and arranged an interview with Severinho, the Mozambican interpreter whose office was inside the walled compound. Unfortunately, the planned interview never got beyond a few introductory pleasantries about the comfortable, fat sofas in his nicely ventilated office. Severinho was called aside by his Chinese boss, a uniformed Mozambican security guard took up a position next to the exit, and Bunkenborg and Nielsen were politely asked to remain seated and await the arrival of the senior Chinese manager. With mounting apprehension, the two sat in the sofa, overhearing the argument in the adjacent room where Severinho was first scolded loudly and then summarily fired for having invited two foreigners, probably journalists, inside the compound without clearing it with his superiors first. When the senior Chinese manager arrived, Bunkenborg and Nielsen tried to make polite conversation to smooth things over. Later that evening Nielsen phoned Severinho who, to the great relief of the two anthropologists, confirmed that he had not been fired after all. As interesting as this visit to the construction site had been, Bunkenborg and Nielsen decided that they couldn't very well return and risk getting people fired. More detailed information on the lives of Chinese workers on construction sites in Mozambique would have to come from elsewhere.

The two ethnographers failed to bridge their respective analyses despite their frequent conversations about dealing with uncertainty on the construction site. Bunkenborg elaborated on the happily confined and radically routinized lives of the Chinese workers, and Nielsen described the Mozambican workers' experiences of unfulfilled and perplexing relationships with their Chinese superiors. For the duration of their ethnographic case study of the Maputo football station, they treated the social worlds of their Chinese and Mozambican interlocutors as if they were entirely disjointed and separate from one another and therefore failed to reach a shared anthropological interpretation of them. But several months later, as an unexpected side effect of their heated discussion about the nudge incident, the two otherwise separate ethnographic worlds suddenly connected.

A Nudge in the Face

One of the unintended consequences of the Dual Perspective Approach in joint fieldwork was that we often found ourselves taking sides with our respective interlocutors. The nudge incident in the sawmill was one of the most extreme of many occasions where misunderstandings between Chinese and locals proved to be contagious and came to be reproduced and amplified within our research team. Immediately after that incident, Bunkenborg and Nielsen went to a nearby food stall for lunch and started discussing the dramatic occurrence at the logging compound. Nielsen was adamant that Mr. Zou had struck Célio in the face, but Bunkenborg found the gesture to be more of nudge. Having talked to Mr. Zou for two hours before Célio and Nielsen walked in, Bunkenborg tried to explain to Nielsen that Mr. Zou was not the arrogant Chinese boss that Nielsen made him out to be but basically a decent person who was terribly out of his depth in Mozambique. Mr. Zou had repaired machinery and electronics in rural Anhui before he and his wife ended up in Montepuez through family connections. The couple had been left to take care of the company during the rainy season while the boss was in China, and over the last four months they had only left the compound twice. On one of these occasions, the local police had detained Mr. Zou. When his wife turned up with his documents and scolded the police in Chinese, she was also detained and had to wait several hours for a Portuguese-speaking Chinese friend who could set things straight. Like the gardening Chinese managers that Bunkenborg and Pedersen encountered in the Mongolian desert (see chapter 2), the couple had started cultivating a garden inside the compound. They were thus largely self-sufficient when it came to vegetables, and they sent a Mozambican employee for the only things they needed to buy locally—eggs and tomatoes. As for staple foods, condiments, and other necessities, they had a substantial stock and when they ran out of particular things, they notified the boss in China, who made sure to add these items to the next container sent from China.

Mr. Zou was deeply worried about robbers and relayed to Bunkenborg how on several occasions he had fired his gun into the air to scare off intruders at night. Actually shooting someone would cause too much trouble with the police, Mr. Zou surmised. Asked to explain which aspects of living in Mozambique had made the deepest impression upon him, he responded with two words: "chaos" (乱) and "corruption" (腐败). Far from being a powerful and authoritarian boss in the style of a colonial patrão, Mr. Zou and his wife seemed to Bunkenborg to be two Chinese farmers who were incapable of operating independently in Mozambique and pretty much scared out of their wits at the thought of leaving the compound. Evidently Mr. Zou lacked both the linguistic and social skills required to manage the complex relations with Mozambican officials and the local population outside the walls; the only way he could feel secure in the "Mozambican chaos" was by carving out an enclave within which he could police space and time.

Bunkenborg's attempt to explain his Chinese interlocutor's behavior to Nielsen was totally in vain. Nielsen stubbornly refused to moderate his interpretation of the event at the sawmill no matter how much contextual information Bunkenborg provided. After several hours of heated discussion, they were nowhere near an agreement as to how the incident might be interpreted ethnographically. On the verge of giving up, they finally decided to return to the compound to get the views of Mr. Zou and Célio, the two primary stakeholders. This did not settle the issue, however.

Mr. Zou tried to dismiss the whole thing as a joke at first, but then he admitted that he felt Célio should know better than to barge into the office, throw himself in a chair, and pretend to be the boss:

> BUNKENBORG: The Mozambican who walked in together with my friends, Célio, what's your relation to him?
>
> MR. ZOU: Oh. Célio, he just works here, he's a worker. I wouldn't call it a relation. He works, he gets paid, that's it.
>
> BUNKENBORG: Was there a disagreement between the two of you just now, or were you just joking?
>
> MR. ZOU: We were joking, it was a joke. He measures wood here in the mill, he is our employee. I know him, otherwise I wouldn't joke like that.
>
> BUNKENBORG: I couldn't make out whether he counted as a guest or a host.
>
> MR. ZOU: He doesn't count as a guest. He's neither host nor guest. . . .
>
> BUNKENBORG: He sat down before we did.
>
> MR. ZOU: He doesn't understand the rules. We are friends, so I couldn't really throw him out. But if the boss were here, he wouldn't even dare to enter the door, he wouldn't be allowed inside. . . .
>
> BUNKENBORG: So you were dissatisfied with his conduct, because he doesn't follow the rules. I had a hunch that you were both joking and . . . a little angry?
>
> MR. ZOU: You're damn right. It's ok for people who come here as guests. I invited you inside, didn't I? But he's a worker, how is he better than us?
>
> BUNKENBORG: So he doesn't know the rules, he doesn't know about Chinese conventions?

MR. ZOU: He doesn't know any rules, whatsoever. If you went to visit
him in his home, he wouldn't invite you inside, he would let you
stand and bring a bench outside. . . .
BUNKENBORG: Have you ever explained Chinese conventions to him?
MR. ZOU: He knows.
BUNKENBORG: How?
MR. ZOU: He knows. He's worked here for a year. He has a little bit of
education and he thinks he is above the other workers, but he should
state his business and stay outside the door. You have to be careful,
even with the best of friends. If you have a cell phone or money lying
around, it will disappear.

Much like the more or less generalizing and stereotypical views held by Chinese mid-level mining managers and foremen about their Mongolian counterparts, Mr. Zou's attempt to explain what had happened was full of reversals and
contradictions. Initially, he tried to dismiss the nudge in Célio's face as a harmless
joke, but then his temper flared and the incident turned out to be highly serious. Mr. Zou's failure to describe Célio with any degree of consistency was also
revealing. On one hand, he stated that his relation to Célio was purely economic:
Célio simply worked for money and was therefore effectively to be considered a
"nonrelation." On the other hand, less than a minute later Mr. Zou claimed that
they were friends. Célio was neither host nor guest; he was a worker, but then
again, given that he had some education, he thought that he was better than the
other workers. He knew the rules but refused to act the part. He was a friend,
but he was also, at least potentially, a thief. Mr. Zou was particularly worked up
about Célio's transgression of spatial boundaries, which constituted a breach of
the compound's safety since Célio was not normally allowed to enter the office.
Célio did not fit in the office, nor did he fit comfortably into any of the categories
that Bunkenborg and Mr. Zou tried to apply to him in the course of the interview.
His behavior thus subverted all sorts of distinctions. Almost as an incarnation of
imagined Mozambican chaos, Célio threw himself in a chair in Mr. Zou's office,
effectively defying and exploding from within everything that Mr. Zou considered right and proper.

While Bunkenborg was conducting his follow-up interview with Mr. Zou,
Nielsen sat down with Célio in his small cubicle near the entrance of the compound
to discuss the incident. As Célio carefully explained to Nielsen, in Mozambique
relations between employer and employee are marked by mutual and respectful
recognition (*respeito*), where it is crucial that each person involved in the relationship is treated as an important counterpart. As in the ethnographic examples
from the football stadium, unless this mutual recognition is made sufficiently

visible it is, from a Mozambican view, highly problematic if not impossible to work together (Nielsen 2012b; 2013). Understood in this way, the incident earlier that day was a particularly grave example of the "Chinese anomaly" (*anomalia Chinês*), which is how Célio summarized what he saw as his foreign employers' near-total lack of respect for their local employees and their overt and offensive disregard for social norms. "In Mozambique, bosses never touch the workers' bodies!" Célio emphasized to Nielsen with a headshake. "That would signal a complete lack of respect, you know! But the Chinese don't care about that." Célio slapped himself on the forehead with his right hand to imitate Mr. Zou's gesture earlier in the day: "They treat us as if we weren't even human beings, . . . like dogs or cats to be kicked around at will."

So far from solving or reducing their disagreement, Nielsen and Bunkenborg's follow-up interviews only complicated things further. The two never managed to reach an agreement as to what had actually happened that morning. Nevertheless, in retrospect, the event in question came to perform an analytically critical, productive role in the collaborative study conducted by the three of us of Chinese globalization. When Mr. Zou's hand connected with Célio's forehead, the gesture came to reverberate with the concepts of "enclaving" and "enveloping" that Bunkenborg and Nielsen had been formulating (but which were still vaguely defined assumptions without explicit arguments). In that sense the "nudge in the face" became the turning point in our analysis. Both concepts, essentially fragile and permeable, collapsed precisely because they were devised for and enacted in a social setting that neither of the interacting parties could fully master.

It eventually became clear to both Bunkenborg and Nielsen that the incident had changed their interpretation of their respective ethnographic data from the football stadium. In fact, as it dawned on Bunkenborg and Nielsen when they embarked upon the joint analysis of the stadium case study and conjoined their previously separate analyses, the nudge in the face precipitated the crystallization of enclaving and envelopment as their primary analytical concepts and opened a passage for ethnographic and analytical traffic between social and cultural worlds that the two anthropologists had hitherto regarded as radically separate. By allowing the incident from northern Mozambique to reconfigure their separate analyses of data from the stadium, it became possible for Bunkenborg and Nielsen to pursue new and productive analytical trajectories that would otherwise have remained invisible and uncharted.

We now describe in further detail the methodological and analytical process that eventually led the two anthropologists to realize that their concepts of enclaving and envelopment could only partially capture the encounter between local workers and Chinese at the stadium site and possibly elsewhere in Mozambique and sub-Saharan Africa as a whole. While all the material that goes into the following sections is based on Bunkenborg and Nielsen's fieldwork in Mozambique, the account is stitched together from disparate field sites and situations that are analytically connected by the fact that "the nudge" in each case allowed for a more nuanced ethnographic description and a more sophisticated anthropological theorization of the Sino-Mozambican relationships under investigation.

The History of the Enclave

Analyzing Sino-Mozambican relations in the workplace as the outcome of processes of enclaving tallies well with the growing literature on Chinese workplaces in Africa (Arsene 2014; Dobler 2008; Giese and Thiel 2012; Haugen and Carling 2005; Lee 2009). Yet the image of calculating Chinese businessmen failing to establish personal relations with locals does not really fit with the rich ethnographic literature from China itself, where the establishment and affirmation of the interpersonal relations known as *guanxi* (关系) through gifts, favors, and banquets, is generally presented as a crucial part of life (Kipnis 1997; Wank 1999; Yang 1994; Yan 1996; Gold, Guthrie, and Wank 2002), In the absence of a clear legal framework in the first decades of economic reforms, Chinese entrepreneurs sought to produce trust through personal relations instead, and it was quite surprising to Bunkenborg to hear both Western academics and Mozambican workers describe Chinese businessmen as unwilling to engage in interpersonal relations (Lee 2009). After all, Bunkenborg pondered, if the cultivation of personal relations had been shown to constitute a recipe for success in the uncertain business environment of reform-era China, why would Chinese businessmen suddenly change their strategies and start to cordon off their enterprises once they were in Africa? It could be argued that the socialist work unit in China was a precedent for the contemporary enclave culture of Chinese expats, just as one could point to language barriers or even racial prejudices as factors that might lead Chinese businessmen to curtail the cultivation of interpersonal relations in Africa. Even so, Bunkenborg's interlocutors' proclivity to sever their lives and work from their surroundings was hardly a logical necessity, and in practice it seemed impossible. As he and Pedersen had also found to be the case in Mongolia, foreign companies in Mozambique are required by national labor law to employ local labor. As the nudge incident had clearly hammered home, there was no surgical neatness about the divide between Chinese and locals in this country either. Instead, Mozambique and Mozambicans seemed to be always already inside the enclave-like spaces forged by the Chinese as these local employees demanded to be seen and remunerated as real persons. Constantly badgered by Nielsen's questions about the absence of envelopes and other manifestations of personal relations with Mozambican employees in Chinese work places, Bunkenborg patiently reiterated that Chinese businessmen were in fact renowned for their cultivation of interpersonal relations and that relations between employers and employees in China were generally construed as having an element of "emotion" (感情). Much like a Mozambican boss (*patrão*), who acts as patron in a vertical relationship of support, Bunkenborg insisted that a proper Chinese "boss" (老板) is expected to act the part of a pater familias and take a personal interest in the well-being of the employees in a small business. Unimpressed by Bunkenborg's speculations, Nielsen challenged him to investigate whether small Chinese business operations managed to produce mutually satisfying personal relations, and Bunkenborg spent the next two weeks among the Chinese shoe traders they had discovered in downtown Maputo.

One of the first things that he noticed was a young Mozambican man with a baton and a shotgun slung over his shoulder, who had been posted at the entrance to one of the small, crowded shoe shops. The middle-aged Chinese couple who turned out to own the business did not seriously believe that the guard would contribute much to their security. Nevertheless, as they explained to Bunkenborg, after having been robbed at gunpoint a week earlier, they felt that something had to be done. Business was pretty brisk in the shoe shop on the day of Bunkenborg's visit. A new container of shoes had come in, and the customers were lined up on the street outside the shop. Whenever the shop became too crowded, Mr. Huang said, thieves would take off with the shoes on display, so the guard was instructed to close the door whenever there were six customers inside. "All the shoes on display are for the right foot," Mr. Huang added, casting a tired glance over his reading glasses at the metal grate where the shoes were tied up, "but even that hasn't helped, the thieves steal them anyway." The majority of the customers were Mozambican street vendors, and some had set up shop on the pavement right outside the store. In China such a thing was unthinkable, Mr. Huang explained, but Mozambique was so disorganized that there was nothing that could be done about it. While the street vendors were making profits that might have gone into Mr. Huang's pockets, they were also saving him the trouble of retail sales.

Only a couple of the stores in the neighborhood had signs indicating Chinese ownership, but, as Bunkenborg eventually learned, Mr. Huang's shop was but one among a score of Chinese shops in the area, most specializing in shoes. Some of the shop owners claimed to have made quite a bit of money before the influx of Chinese competitors and the fluctuation of exchange rates curtailed their profits, but the shops were unassuming affairs in run-down premises rented from own-ers of Indian or Pakistani descent. As inconspicuous as the Chinese shops were, almost half of them had been hit by a gang of armed robbers in the summer of 2011. One of the shop owners had fired a gun into the air when the robbers took off, but the round in the chamber proved to be too old, and the strangled sound from the dud bullet caused a great deal of mirth among the bystanders. Another elderly Chinese shop owner dryly remarked to Bunkenborg that this was prob-ably the extent of the resistance the robbers would encounter—the police were inefficient, and even if the culprits were apprehended, the laws of the country seemed to favor local robbers over foreign victims. "To really solve the prob-lem, it would be necessary to build a high-rise, concentrate the Chinese and have them open their shops there, side by side to ensure everyone's safety. Like a Chinatown!"

The elderly shoe trader was not the only Chinese businessman who would have liked to build a Chinatown; closed enclaves and increased policing of spatial boundaries at first glance seemed to be the gut response to real or imagined secu-rity concerns among Chinese businessmen, even among those who depended upon Mozambican customers. But once again, the Mozambican chaos, as Mr. Zou called it, could not be entirely shut out. Chinese shop owners needed to employ Mozambicans as guards and assistants, just as they were forced to relate to any locals who worked or visited on the inside. Accordingly, how to manage relations with locals—and particularly relations with employees—was some-thing that seemed to constantly puzzle most Chinese shop owners. Mr. Tao, for instance, was fluent in Portuguese and had spent ten years in Maputo, but he was still struggling to understand how money and affect were imbricated in his relations with locals. He was doing pretty well from his three small stores with shoes and bags in the run-down center of Maputo. With net profits approach-ing MZM 300,000 a month, there was enough money to cover the rising cost of dealing with local officials and the constant losses due to theft, but Mr. Tao wasn't planning to stay. "If I could find a true friend in Mozambique, I really might stay, but I don't have any, and you can't live without friends all your life. I find it so tiring that everyone approaches you with a purpose." Having done poorly on his university entrance exams in Beijing, Mr. Tao figured that it would be hard to get ahead in China and went to Mozambique with his father, who was then working in the timber industry. Mr. Tao really seemed to have made a life for himself in Maputo. His wife was four months' pregnant, and his brother-in-law had come out to help with the business, but even so, he was not entirely happy. "Apart from making money, there is no point in staying here," he lamented. "Even after all these years, my relations to black people are 'money relations' (金钱关系)."

Like most of the other Chinese shoe traders, Mr. Tao was not just concerned with robberies, but also with the constant pilfering carried out by employees. "We used to sell panties in the shop, but some of the female employees would go to the toilet, put on ten pairs, and hide them under their own underwear. I have gotten used to it over the years, let them steal and rob, as long as they don't kill me. Nothing surprises me any longer."

He felt that he tried hard to be good to his employees, and he was personally affronted by the many instances of theft in his shop. He even discussed the issue with his staff. "The girl over there has worked in my shop for four years and never stolen anything from me. Once I asked her, 'I am so good to you employees, so how does it occur to you to steal my stuff?' She said 'When you're hungry, you don't consider how well a person has treated you, you just think about ways of stealing his things.'"

Mr. Tao admitted to Bunkenborg that he only paid the minimum salary of MZM 2,950, and he recognized that it was hard to survive on that. Most of the employees came from the north and tried to send some of their wages back home, but food was expensive in the city and even a very basic room with electricity in Maputo cost MZM 600–900 a month. Mr. Tao had visited some of his employees where they lived and seemed to be well aware of the difficulties they were facing. Instead of increasing the wages, he provided extras such as occasional meals and expected them to appreciate anything he did in excess of his contractual obligations as gifts that ought to elicit reciprocal gifts and affective attachment. Much to Mr. Tao's surprise, his attempts to minimize theft and produce security through paternalistic benevolence toward his employees tended to backfire:

> If you give them something, they just take it for granted, and they don't feel that they ought to give you something in return out of politeness. To give you an example, I brought food for an employee. I do that quite often, but as a newcomer, he didn't know that. One day I didn't bring food, and he asked, "Boss, why didn't you bring me any food today?" I said, "I didn't cook today, so why should I give you food?" He said, "You gave me food yesterday, so you should give me food today." Then I didn't give him anything, and after a few days, he started stealing. The big guy over there is a good fellow, and he told me: "Boss, he is stealing." "Why is he stealing?" I asked. He said, "It's because you didn't give him anything to eat." I said, "Well, I can't bring food every day, and you haven't stolen anything." He said, "That's because I know you're a good person." Sometimes it's really difficult to understand their way of thinking.

Like many of the Chinese shoe traders Bunkenborg spoke to, Mr. Tao complained about the ingratitude of the Mozambicans. The local employees were unable to see a gift for what it was, and they never reciprocated as expected. On the contrary, they would steal things.

> I have been really nice to them all along, but they still do their best to steal my things. I understand that, after all, it's a relation between a boss and an employee, and that we may not be entirely of one mind. But speaking from an emotional point of view, if they judged my heart by their own hearts, they shouldn't act like that toward me. I have had to fire scores of workers over the years. . . . Actually, I was hoping that I might become friends with my employees. It's just that they get their wages from me every month. In every other respect, I feel that we could become friends.

Accusing the Mozambican employees of ingratitude could be interpreted as an easy way of justifying and excusing what was in fact an exploitative labor regime, but Mr. Tao seemed genuinely frustrated by his failure to establish an affective relationship with his employees. Bunkenborg had no doubt that Mr. Tao and other Chinese shop owners felt that they had made a real effort in this respect, only to end up sorely disappointed. Indeed, the fraught relations between Chinese and locals that Mr. Tao had witnessed in his shop are hardly exceptional in the African context (or other regions of the world as we also saw in the first part of this book), and though it is possible to find counternarratives and examples of successful cooperation between Chinese and locals (Arsene 2014; Haugen and Carling 2005), the ethnography on Chinese shops in Africa give the impression that relations between Chinese employers and local employees are not exactly harmonious (Dobler 2008; Giese 2013; Giese and Thiel 2015; French 2014; Lampert and Mohan 2014). A study of Chinese traders and their Ghanaian employees in Accra by Giese and Thiel (2012) (conducted in a "two-sided" fashion partly resembling our Dual Perspective Approach) suggests that mismatched expectations and different social logics are at stake:

> Deprived of gifts and allowances or concessions with regard to social obligations, Ghanaian employees feel that their Chinese employers lack any understanding of and empathy for the vulnerability that many of them perceive as threatening their social and material survival. Without alternatives for generating income, they strive for the recognition of their existential fears by extorting additional monetary benefits (tips, extras, theft) from their employers, where the latter fail to perform expected symbolic acts that would signify their willingness to protect their subordinates. Without being related to their employees by kinship ties or other bonds of affection, the Chinese merchants, however, do not

recognize themselves as providers of fully fledged social security, nor do they feel obliged to take up responsibilities that are usually attributed to close relatives according to their own social logic (16).

Chinese shop owners are presented here as trying to reduce their relations to Ghanaian employees to something purely economic; one could easily get the impression that the Chinese shop owners in Africa do not really care about their local employees. Yet Giese and Thiel's "two-sided" study tends to sympathize with the employees without really exploring the existential fears of the employers or their experiences of relations with employees. Judging by the frustrations expressed by Mr. Zou and Mr. Tao, and other of Bunkenborg's interlocutors, there is reason to doubt that the absence of kinship ties between employers and employees precludes attempts to form relations based on affect and mutual obligation. When relations between Chinese employers and Mozambican employees turned sour, Bunkenborg concluded, it was not because the deeds and words of the two sides reflected fundamentally different "social logics." Both sides claimed that they had sought to initiate exchanges meant to produce mutual recognition, if not friendship and affection; when relations turned sour, as they frequently did, it was often due to misunderstandings that brought the progression of exchanges out of sync. A Chinese employer like Mr. Tao thought he was doing his employee a favor by providing work, paying the minimum wage, and serving an occasional free lunch on the job. The employee thought he was doing Mr. Tao a favor by working for a measly wage, and he saw the free lunch as his due. The outcome was that both sides were disappointed, much as if they were waiting for a return gift that never materialized. Not unlike the tragicomical example of the Chinese fluorspar workers who ended up hiding inside their refitted nomadic tents, Bunkenborg mused, the wallbuilding of his Chinese friends in Mozambique was never a goal in itself but a response to frustrated attempts at forging relations with social and cultural Others who sometimes seemed to willfully misunderstand and misconstrue earnest gestures of respect and friendship.

"That's what I told you. The Chinese don't relate to their Mozambican employees; they really don't understand how things are done here." Nielsen sneered when Bunkenborg tried to share his new-found insight that relations with local staff in the Chinese shoe shops were not affectionate because of frustration and disappointment, not lack of will. "But you are missing the point completely," Bunkenborg protested. "You keep speaking of the Chinese employers as if they only think about profits, but the problem is not that they are incapable of establishing personal relations to their employees, whether here in Mozambique or back home in China. On the contrary, all the Chinese talk of disappointment and ingratitude suggests that the problem is caused by an initial excess of affective expectations on their side, not a lack. Can't you see it? It's like Mr. Jia, the Chinese entrepreneur in Mongolia that I am constantly talking about. Enclaving is not a goal in itself for my Chinese interlocutors but a response that is elicited from a perception that local embedding, or in your terms 'envelopment,' fails—that's also what Pedersen and I found to be the case in Mongolia. So, from the Chinese vantage point, your envelope is the history of their enclave."

The Future of the Envelope

Mr. Tao was not the only Chinese employer who told Bunkenborg about failed attempts to establish closer relations with local employees. Even if these narratives mostly took the form of past disappointments, it was clear to Bunkenborg than the concept of strategies of enveloping could in fact be deployed in order to reach a more sophisticated understanding of the relationship between his interlocutors and the local Mozambicans. The question, then, was whether the concept of the enclave could similarly be mobilized to enhance Nielsen's interpretation of his interlocutors. Were the Mozambican workers really as intent on establishing a personal and respectful relationship to their Chinese bosses? Or could they sometimes be said to pursue a strategy of enclaving in order to allow for a relational detachment from their foreign employers?

As Nielsen had seen things until now, the Mozambican workers sought to deal with alterity via strategies of envelopment, whose purpose was to enhance their employers' recognition of them as persons with relations and obligations that reached beyond the workplace. As he had told Bunkenborg in no uncertain terms on more than one occasion, the sort of relationship to his boss that the Mozambican worker deemed desirable was not a strictly contractual relation where economic relations were separated from the rest of social life. Still, Nielsen began asking himself, why would Mozambican workers, cast in an unknown social universe peopled by Others with whom communication rarely exceeded bodily gestures and a few phrases in English or Portuguese, consistently emphasize the need for establishing social relations with these Others? One might assume that the distinct sociality of the Chinese compound would be considered so radically different from the outside world that even widely held ideas of how to establish viable social relationships could be ignored.

For the Mozambican workers the wages received from their Chinese employers sufficed only for purchasing basic foodstuff. In that sense it was similar to money picked up from the street or alms given to a beggar. As Nielsen eventually discovered, however, even limited amounts of money that was, in narrow economic terms, considered as being of no or little value might eventually gain significance if it could catapult his young interlocutors into a form of livelihood beyond the untenable conditions of the construction site. Once this was accomplished, then the money received would be considered a proper salary and the hardship involved in earning it could be retrospectively endured as an unfortunate but necessary component of the employer-employee relationship. Given the lack of mutual recognition between the Chinese employers and their Mozambican workers from the latter's perspective, it was clear that this money represented a distinct kind of value, understood as not indexing a reciprocal relationship of the sort one would ideally have with a Mozambican boss. This other kind of value had less to do with actual monetary value but was underwritten by the potential capacity of these salaries to help manage or even eliminate the untenable connection to the Chinese superiors. "With a salary, I would start building a house in order to live in a better way," Alex explained to Nielsen. "It could be a cement house or just a 'bedroom and living room' (*quarto e sala*) in order for me to have a memory (*para ter uma lembrança*) of having worked in this place. That would enable me to have a life until I die." Nielsen asked him whether the salary received from the Chinese could also be considered as a memory. "It might become a memory (*ia tornando lembrança*)." Alex nodded several times before continuing. "We consider it as a memory only when the money can be used for commencing a construction project." Here, it seems, the potential future (such as a construction project) that "proper salaries" could make possible was predicated on the money that the Mozambicans received from their Chinese superiors. Given the perceived lack of recognition from the latter, however, this "future memory," as one might call it, was no longer predicated upon a mutually respectful relationship between employee and boss. Rather, the moment that the salary could pay for construction materials, a new connection would be established between a future house-building project and the stadium the workers were presently building. Alex explained, "We wish that we had a memory (*nós desejíamos que nós teíamos uma lembrança*). What would we then remember? The football stadium! . . . That we have a great football stadium here in Mozambique. I would have a memory of living in a house that I built, . . . living a quiet life knowing that I purchased these things while I was working."

In a sense the significance of the salaries here emerges by moving backward from an imagined moment in the future toward its current manifestation in the present (see Nielsen 2011; Pedersen 2012). In those instances where the received money allowed Alex and his fellow workers to imagine and possibly even plan viable future scenarios, then the present (which was then imaginatively considered as the past) could be considered as a proper "memory" (*lembrança*). To Alex and many other young Mozambican workers that Nielsen spoke with, the untenable relationship with their Chinese superiors, whose recognition was deemed impossible to obtain, would then cease to have a paralyzing effect on their current lives by virtue of the latent futures lodged in the concreteness of purchased construction materials. By shifting their focus from the dysfunctional relation to the material gains achieved from having worked at the construction site, the lacking envelope would become nothing but a momentary hindrance on a path toward a viable future.

"So, . . . what you are basically suggesting is that the lacking envelope within the context of cash payment from their bosses is not just a sign of a missing interpersonal relation, but also a vehicle by which the Mozambican workers can imagine a strategy for future detachment from the Chinese?" Bunkenborg had listened in silence while Nielsen, in his usual energetic fashion, presented his new interpretation, but now he demanded some clarification.

"Exactly!" Nielsen nodded several times while pacing the uneven balcony floor. "And for that to happen, they have to convert the raw cash into a different value entirely. The moment they manage to gather enough money to buy building materials for their cement houses, the fraught relationship between employer and employee is annulled." While Bunkenborg was intrigued by Nielsen's geeky analysis of the football stadium case as an example of an obviation of relations in Roy Wagner's sense (1981), it did not seem plausible to him that a temporal displacement of one set of symbols with another could provide the Mozambican workers with a mode of security to adequately replace their perceived lack of respect and sociability in the relationship between them and their Chinese employers. Nielsen waved his arms around as if to stop Bunkenborg's line of thought. "Of course, the Mozambican workers acknowledge the presence of the Chinese bosses, man! I am not implying that these guys have somehow entered a mythic realm where the Chinese are magically transformed into sacks of cement and steel mesh. But it is this sequence of symbolic displacements that enable them to endure the hardships of their current job. The moment they buy building materials for a cement house, they realize that their relationship with the Chinese bosses is insignificant. . . . It has become irrelevant."

From the Nudge to a Productive Analytical Collapse

Based on ethnography from different Chinese workplaces and construction sites in Maputo and northern Mozambique, we have examined Sino-Mozambican relations in locations where Chinese and Mozambicans met and interacted and where both sides were forced to deal with each other because their livelihoods depended on it. In similar contexts in Mongolia, we saw that both Mongolian and Chinese actors sought to turn a messy sociality into a singular, distant, and seemingly more manageable relationship by setting up infrastructures of roads and walls. Bunkenborg suspected that something similar might be taking place in Mozambique. Surrounded by walls, the Sino-Mozambican workplaces that he and Nielsen encountered called to mind the "enclaves" described in the anthropological and social-scientific literature. In line with Appel's account of offshore oil production in West Africa and how such work involves a constant disentanglement from local contexts, it initially seemed to Bunkenborg and Nielsen that the many attempts to establish a sense of security among Chinese expats in Mozambique involved a similar dynamic. However, it gradually became clear that, unlike the Mongolian case, where the strategy of managers and sometimes workers was to detach the latter maximally from the Chinese, Nielsen's Mozambican interlocutors were skeptical about the techniques of material and social distance imposed by the seemingly relentless Chinese quest for order, security, and predictability. Experienced as opaque zones governed by mysterious rules, these spaces defied the Mozambican workers' attempts to establish personal relations of respect with their employers in accordance with established Mozambican norms. The preliminary conclusion from Bunkenborg and Nielsen's joint study of Sino-Mozambican workplaces was thus that the two sides used radically different strategies—one side trying to disentangle itself from local obligations by pursuing a strategy of enclaving and the other attempting to produce attachment by pursuing a strategy of envelopment.

Had it not been for the nudge incident, this could have been their final interpretation. However, the intense disagreement about what actually happened when Mr. Zou's palm connected with Célio's forehead forced Bunkenborg and Nielsen to question their conceptual vocabularies and to reorganize and rethink some of the fundamental tenets and assumptions undergirding their ongoing study. As a consequence, Bunkenborg began to look for Chinese attempts to establish personal relations to Mozambicans, while Nielsen started looking for local Mozambican practices of enclaving that might complement and therefore also show the limits of "envelopment" as a strategy among his Mozambican informants.

In this way, Bunkenborg and Nielsen's disagreements about how to understand "the nudge incident" served as a wedge that caused what had until then seemed two neatly compartmentalized strategies of enclaving and envelopment to sustain an analytical collapse. As a result, the two ethnographers found it necessary to reexamine "enclaving" and "envelopment" as connected and complementary strategies that might be relevant for both the Mozambican and the Chinese sides. A relationship where one side is always trying to make things personal and the other side constantly seeks to make them economical could hardly give the intense or intimate quality to the distances perceived to exist between Chinese and Mozambicans, and it would be unlikely to result in exchanges as unpredictable and emotionally charged as the nudge in the face.

Even as it gradually became apparent to Bunkenborg and Nielsen that both the Chinese and the Mozambicans were involved in social and material processes of relational cutting as well as relational connecting, there were clearly differences in the temporal orientation of their respective groups of interlocutors. Asking questions about Chinese attempts to forge close personal relations to Mozambicans, Bunkenborg was presented with narratives of failed attempts to establish relations of trust. Strategies of enclaving were presented as a regrettable but inevitable response to a situation where close interpersonal relations had proven to be impossible. When Nielsen identified strategies of enclaving in his Mozambican interlocutors' actions and words, it turned out they did not see the forging of personal relations with their Chinese employers as an end in itself but as a necessary step toward a proper future livelihood that would enable them to sever all relations to the Chinese. Both sides were involved in practices and strategies of both cutting and connecting relationships. When concrete relations between Chinese employers and Mozambican workers turned out to be intimately distant, this was not necessarily because they had radically different strategies for dealing with unknown others but because they were asynchronous in the temporal organization of these strategies. Both sides seemed to be engaged in the same dance, but the Chinese took their cue from the past and the Mozambicans took it from the future. Their steps were necessarily out of sync.

ALTERITY IN THE INTERIOR

Tree Scouts, Spirits, and Chinese Loggers
in the Forests of Northern Mozambique

In late autumn of 2012, Nielsen accompanied two local *olheiros* (tree scouts) hired by a Chinese timber company as they made their way through the forests of Cabo Delgado, Mozambique's northernmost region, in order to locate certain kinds of rare hardwoods later to be cut and exported to China as unprocessed trunks (figure 6.1). Several times, they had to cross vast fields of wildly growing elephant grass. Almost without exception, Nielsen would end up falling desperately behind, struggling through the dense vegetation until, somewhat disoriented, he was led back on track by his patient travelling companions. By contrast, the two *olheiros* never seemed to lose their sense of direction even when passing through areas that were still relatively unknown to them. With little or no verbal communication, Jaime Paguri led the small group and cleared a path through the tangled undergrowth using the rusty machete he had owned since his early youth. At sixty-six, he was the most experienced of the local should be in italics every time *olheiros* is mentioned and was often sought by young aspirants wanting to work for the increasing number of Chinese timber companies that were active in the area.

Such was the case for Taquinha, the twenty-two-year-old former bricklayer who walked between Paguri and Nielsen. For nearly a year, Taquinha had worked with Paguri as an assistant (*adjunto*) while doing some infrequent tree scouting for local loggers. During their trips into the forests north of Montepuez, Nielsen often wondered whether Paguri's sense of direction was as flawless as his determined movements through the landscape seemed to suggest. For the trip they embarked on in the autumn of 2012, Paguri had invited Nielsen

FIGURE 6.1. Jaime Paguri and Taquinha walking through the forest heading for the *umbila* trees that Paguri had spotted the previous year. May 2012.

into the forest to locate some *umbila* trees that he remembered having spotted toward the end of the previous season.[1] They decided to do the initial part of the journey in the Toyota 4x4 that Nielsen was renting and drive as far into the forest as possible before getting out to walk the final distance. Heading in, the vegetation soon became increasingly dense, and they had to go entirely by Paguri's directions. After a while the thick undergrowth became virtually impossible to penetrate, and they consequently stopped the car and continued the journey on foot.

Nielsen had been wondering about how to document Paguri's movements through the forest, and he decided to track the journey using a GPS-supported app on his iPhone. The umbila trees, Nielsen thought, would make an excellent orientation marker in relation to which one could subsequently identify deviations and detours. When returning to the car, Nielsen checked his iPhone and immediately realized that Paguri had, in fact, led him and Taquinha directly to the trees and back. After having left the car somewhere in the lush forest, they had walked in a straight line toward the umbilas that Paguri had allegedly seen only once, while working in the area with a group of loggers more than six months ago. Without any detours they had then returned to the car and driven back toward Paguri's house, some twenty-odd kilometers away. During the hour-long drive, Nielsen tried to encourage Paguri to explain his trade. In particular, Nielsen was eager to learn more about how *olheiros* acquired the navigational skills that allowed them to cross several kilometers of dense vegetation as if following a straight line. Hoping for an extended lesson on how to survive in the forest, Nielsen turned on the tape recorder and waited for Paguri to enlighten him. The elderly tree scout's response was as puzzling as it was short. "Well, Morten, we do it the Chinese way. Before they came to our land (*a nossa terra*), we didn't even know where the trees were."

Here we explore the crucial albeit contested status that the *olheiro* had for some Mozambican communities and Chinese timber companies alike at the time of Nielsen and Bunkenborg's fieldwork in northern Mozambique. Having come into prominence with the increased Chinese economic activities in Cabo Delgado and other heavily forested areas in Mozambique, many if not most *olheiros* made a living from working for Chinese loggers. Coincidentally, they had also come to assume the ritually important and prestigious responsibility of appeasing and being in continuous dialogue with the ancestral spirits controlling the forest where the hardwood was being cut. This key politico-religious role was otherwise performed only by local chiefs, but since the hardwood desired by the Chinese was growing in the deep forest at a considerable distance from the villages where the chiefs lived, the *olheiros* had over time assumed this responsibility on site. Given their crucial importance to Chinese and locals alike, it was surprising that many *olheiros* were looked upon with a sense of reserved skepticism. For some reason, they did not seem to quite fit in. During the yearly commemorative ceremonies in honor of deceased ancestors, who are perceived to protect the local community, for example, the Chinese timber agents (those with proficient language skills, that is) would only hesitantly engage in conversation with the *olheiros* who coordinated and carried out these all-important rituals. Likewise, relationships between *olheiros* and other residents of the local *aldeias communiais* (communal villages) in which most of them lived and worked were often tenuous, with conflicts erupting even over relatively minor disagreements. As we discovered, a primary reason for these tensions was precisely the fact that circumstances had thrown the *olheiros* into a political and ritual role for which they were ill prepared.

By focusing on the cosmological role and capacities of the *olheiro* figure, we wish to draw out a puzzling aspect of the Sino-Mozambican (and more generally Sino-xeno) relationship that has so far received very little attention: the striking similarities in the ways Mozambicans and Chinese "other" each other as Others.

Why is it, we ask, that the *olheiros* were generally met with reserved skepticism by the Mozambican loggers as well as the Chinese timber merchants encountered by Nielsen and Bunkenborg? Could it be that the figure of the tree scout for locals and Chinese alike represented an internalization of the Other, in the form of the mechanism that Michael Taussig (1993, 130) has called "interiorized alterity"? Two things need to be taken into account in order to make this argument. Firstly, the *olheiros'* capacity for locating the much-coveted hardwood, as demonstrated by Paguri's skills, was perceived to inhere from an almost occult understanding of and affiliation with the Chinese timber agents. Prior to working for Chinese timber merchants, the large majority of *olheiros* had struggled to make a living as small-scale farmers, with additional income from hunting and trapping birds and small game. It was precisely in this capacity as hunters that they had initially been approached by timber agents: Living off the forest, they knew the area like no one else. But it was only after being approached by Chinese timber merchants that their unique capacities for scouting trees (in addition to game) were discovered. Secondly, the skillful *olheiro* was understood to be under the guidance and protection of powerful ancestral spirits on whose benevolence he relied. Together with the fact that the *olheiro's* capacities for scouting trees was perceived to be enhanced by his central position in the network of more or less tenacious Sino-Mozambican relations (as per the first issue), might there be a sense in which his actions were understood to be underwritten by Sinicized spirit forces? We may conceive of the skepticism with which the *olheiros* were met as "caused" by an interiorized, Chinese alterity.

In the ethnographic analysis that follows, our overarching theme and concept of "intimate distances" will emerge as a configuration of forces that are "internally opposed." Although we focus on the "interior otherings" of Chinese and Mozambicans, this dynamic was not unique to their specific relationship. In another, and no less "awkward encounter" (Tsing 2005) the professional relation between Bunkenborg and Nielsen as anthropologists was challenged by the former relationship's encroachment upon the "ethnographic space" of the latter. This incident came to significantly and irreversibly affect the relationship between the two fieldworkers and to serve as a model for exploring the dynamics of Sino-Mozambican relationships more generally.

How to Ruin a Good Entrance

Intrigued by a report on the timber industry in Mozambique as a "Chinese takeaway" (Mackenzie 2006), Bunkenborg and Nielsen decided to look into the subject during their first joint fieldwork in Mozambique in 2010. Shortly after their

arrival in Maputo, Nielsen met António Colombo, a Mozambican in his late forties who owned a sawmill in Pemba, the regional capital of Cabo Delgado. It
was clear that Colombo knew a great deal about his Chinese competitors, and
he promised to explain what was "really going on" in the timber industry. He
also pledged to inflict physical violence upon Nielsen, if the latter revealed how
he knew about the set-up in Pemba. Charmed by the secrets, the paranoia, and
even the latent violence embodied in Colombo, Nielsen managed to convince
Bunkenborg that Pemba was the perfect base for a study of Chinese timber companies, and a week later, Bunkenborg and Nielsen found themselves up north.
The initial visits to half a dozen Chinese sawmills went smoothly. Precisely as
had been the case during Bunkenborg's time in Mongolia, the Chinese managers
were sufficiently puzzled by the appearance of a Chinese-speaking foreigner to
open the gates to their otherwise seclusive compounds. While the Chinese were
busy chatting to Bunkenborg, Nielsen could wander around the different sites
and talk to the Mozambican employees. But then something that may have been
a mere slip of the tongue disrupted the smooth collaboration between the two
ethnographers, infecting their relation with a degree of tension and suspicion
akin to the fraught relations between Mozambicans and Chinese.

For days Bunkenborg had tried in vain to get in touch with Stanley, who was
not only the general manager of CADEL but also the head of a business association for Chinese logging companies in Pemba.[2] When Stanley finally returned
Bunkenborg's calls, the first thing he asked was how Bunkenborg knew his number. Without hesitation Bunkenborg explained that he and Nielsen had stopped
at a number of sawmills on their way into town in order to locate the local Chinese outfits. At the Maxingo sawmill someone had suggested that they get in
touch with Stanley as he was the head of the Chinese business association.

Picking out the word "Maxingo" from Bunkenborg's conversation in Chinese
with Stanley, Nielsen started gesticulating wildly, and a heated argument ensued
once the telephone conversation had ended. There was no doubt, Nielsen complained, that Bunkenborg must have understood enough of the conversation
between Nielsen and Colombo back in Maputo to know that it was of the utmost
importance to keep the latter's name secret. By revealing to Stanley how he got
his number, Nielsen felt that Bunkenborg had traded an important secret that
he had obtained from a key Mozambican interlocutor in order to get an interview with a key Chinese gatekeeper. Bunkenborg protested that it was crucial to
answer the question about the phone number and that he had made the connection to Colombo's company sound so casual that no one would get into trouble.
In the event, it turned out Nielsen was right. While the two were still quarrelling, Colombo texted them, stating in no uncertain terms that Bunkenborg and
Nielsen were "complete idiots" and had best keep their distance from him if they

wanted to leave Pemba alive. Apparently, an official from the Department of Agriculture and Forestry, whom Nielsen had also interviewed, had already called Colombo to ask whether he had anything to do with the nosy anthropologists. The officials had also informed Stanley of their suspicions. Immediately after his conversation with Bunkenborg, Stanley called Colombo to say he was well aware that Colombo was the one passing information to the visiting foreigners.

In this atmosphere of illegality and secrecy, it took only two days before Bunkenborg and Nielsen's attempt to gain a deeper understanding of Chinese involvement in the logging industry fell apart. Bunkenborg had gambled with sensitive information and ruined Nielsen's relation to Colombo in a bid to cultivate his own relation to a potential Chinese informant. A gradually widening fissure and increasing divergence of interests began deepening between them. Bunkenborg and Nielsen were becoming a liability rather than an asset to each other, a problem further underlined that evening when Nielsen sat down to conduct an interview with a Mozambican worker just outside one of the Chinese sawmills they had visited earlier in the day. After half an hour, the Chinese manager emerged from the compound and shouted to the worker in broken Portuguese that he had better shut up and get inside if he wanted to keep his job. This time it was Bunkenborg's turn to come up with an excuse for Nielsen's behavior, while the manager listened politely, it was clear that he found the whole thing highly suspicious and that he would not allow either of the two foreign instigators inside the compound again.

Sensing that the logging companies in Pemba were rapidly closing their doors and somewhat uneasy about threats of physical violence, Bunkenborg and Nielsen decided to temporarily abandon Pemba as a field site and instead head inland toward the deep forests of northernmost Cabo Delgado to investigate and see with their own eyes exactly how the chain saws met the trees. But over the coming days and weeks, Nielsen could not escape the nagging sensation that his colleague and friend had invaded his field site and in this process done irremediable damage to the tenuous relationships with local loggers that he had been trying to consolidate. Eventually, the two returned to Pemba, but the repercussions of the "Colombo incident," as they sometimes called the unfortunate occurrence, came to structure their subsequent research in the sense that they now worked in separate Chinese and Mozambican networks. Making a conscious effort to avoid each other, Bunkenborg continued his visits to sawmills, where he met and conversed with Chinese loggers, while Nielsen headed deeper into the forest to explore how local communities were affected by logging. On one of these journey Nielsen met Jaime Paguri, the middle-aged *olheiro* who showed Nielsen the umbila trees.

A Chinese Takeaway?

Jaime Paguri had first started scouting for precious hardwood in the mid-1990s, when South Africans and Israelis were competing with Mozambican companies to dominate the local timber industry. In 1992 a viable peace agreement was finally reached between the ruling Frelimo party and Renamo, a guerilla movement supported by South Africa (Abrahamsson and Nilsson 1995). Not long after, the government attempted to gradually increase timber production by granting Mozambican nationals so-called simple licenses, which allowed them to cut up to 500 cubic meters of wood per year. From the mid-1980s Mozambique had gradually opened up to outside investors. With the peace agreement timber export by the government was described as a viable means of "generating significant foreign currency with minimal capital investment" (Sun et al. 2008, 124). During the 1990s Paguri had worked for Maxingo Ltd., a Mozambican timber company that bought and processed hardwood at its sawmill on the outskirts of Pemba. As António Colombo, the owner of Maxingo Ltd., told Nielsen, for those relatively few Chinese timber agents active in the area during that period, the common strategy was to buy hardwood from South African and Mozambican timber companies and ship it to China. In contrast to other sectors of Mozambique's economy in which Chinese companies were intensely involved the late 1990s (such as the construction sector), the Mozambican timber industry had not been a priority for China. Although forestry was frequently mentioned in memoranda signed by the Chinese and the Mozambican governments, the companies in question were privately owned. Not until just prior to Nielsen and Bunkenborg's fieldwork had those companies formed an association to establish cooperation with the Chinese government through the embassy in Maputo.[3]

According to Daniel Ribeiro of Justica Ambiental (a Mozambican NGO focusing on environmental politics), the Chinese timber industry in Cabo Delgado was established through private companies operating individually. "It wasn't part of a national strategy," Daniel explained to Nielsen during an interview in the fall of 2012 at his small Maputo office, "the forestry sector was essentially passed aside, and there was never sufficient information for the big Chinese companies to become interested in the Mozambican market." From the late 1990s, however, the Chinese government began making loans available to companies wanting to invest in the Mozambican timber industry. According to Daniel Ribeiro, a second influx of Chinese timber companies some years later was further facilitated by the emerging network of smaller Chinese operators already active in the area. "The timing was excellent! After having struggled with the South Africans and the Israelis, an increasing number of small Chinese operators had settled in Cabo Delgado, and they paved the way for the larger companies arriving in Mozambique around 2000." In what almost appears as explicit encouragement to further increase the involvement of foreign agents, a Forestry and Wildlife Law (Law no. 10/99), which specified rules for timber operations in the country, was passed by the Mozambican government in 1999. According to the new legislation, nationals could still apply for "simple licenses" to cut 500 cubic meters per year with renewal of the approval required each year. But of particular relevance to the Chinese timber companies, the Forestry and Wildlife Law also introduced a novel harvesting and logging business model based on concessions of up to 10,000 hectares with a fifty-year renewable management period. In contrast to the "simple licenses" that had regulated the timber industry for several decades, both nationals and foreigners were now eligible for concessions with no specific annual cut quotas. According to the Forestry and Wildlife Law, "the holder of the concession permit . . . must guarantee the processing of the forest products harvested in accordance with the regulatory terms" (art. 16, 2). The concessionaire was therefore required to submit a management plan to the regional department of agriculture outlining in detail the particulars of the production setup. In order to establish a mutually beneficial collaboration with local stakeholders, the grant of a forest concession must be preceded by a consultation with the affected communities (art. 17, 2). This prioritization of local stakeholders was also emphasized in the 2002 regulations to the Forestry and Wildlife Law, which stipulated that 20 percent of the tax revenues must be reinvested in the affected communities (Assembleia da República 2002).

Thus, at the turn of the century, Mozambique began welcoming foreign agents in the local timber industry. The invitation was soon accepted by a number of Chinese timber companies responding to a growing need for hardwoods in China (Environmental Investigation Agency [EIA] 2012). A quick inspection of the formal documentation of wood exported to China provides an initial sense of China's rapid rise as a primary export destination of Mozambican hardwood. By 2001 China had replaced South Africa as Mozambique's largest buyer of forest products, receiving approximately 85 percent of the 430,000 cubic meters of logs shipped from Mozambique from 2001 to 2005 (EIA 2012, 18; Sun et al. 2008). Since then, China's share of Mozambique's timber export has remained impressively stable. In 2013 Mozambique became China's biggest supplier of African logs, culminating in 2018 when 93 percent of all the country's exported timber went to China (Macqueen 2018; see also China-Lusophone Brief 2018; German and Wertz-Kanounnikoff 2012). Conversely, in 2005, Mozambique's export of all wood to China amounted to merely 0.12 percent of the total value of timber imports (Sun et al. 2008, 138). In other words, whereas China at the time of Nielsen and Bunkenborg's fieldwork had unquestionably become Mozambique's most important trade partner, in terms of timber, Mozambique's importance to China was minimal.

One of the first Chinese timber companies established in Cabo Delgado was the Cabo Delgado Logging Consortium, Ltd. (CADEL). While many of the Chinese companies in the northern region essentially operated as timber merchants during Nielsen and Bunkenborg's fieldwork, CADEL had invested in a production setup in Mozambique, and the owner also had a factory in Guangzhou where the wood was processed and marketed. Bunkenborg never managed to meet the owner of CADEL, a Guangzhou man known as Wang Guoqiang, but he did speak to a number of Chinese and Mozambican employees, including Stanley, its general manager, in his spacious home.[4]

Though the house was still under construction, the living room was spotless, most likely due to the efforts of the Chinese maid who answered the door and served Bunkenborg tea while he waited, perched on a beautiful hardwood chair. Stanley turned out to be a tall and vivacious man in his forties, and the ensuing conversation was highly interesting. According to Stanley, the business venture had started when Wang Guoqiang, dining in a restaurant in Beira, ran into the governor of Cabo Delgado. Wang Guoqiang was looking for timber, and the governor was looking for investors, so the latter urged the former to start up in Cabo Delgado. CADEL was accordingly set up in 2000. By 2010 the company had 65,000 hectares of concessions and employed a score of Chinese as well as 700–800 local workers. As the first Chinese company with an impact in Cabo Delgado, CADEL was widely known, and Stanley claimed that locals would often shout out "CADEL!" whenever they saw an Asian person driving past. After two or three years, Stanley told Bunkenborg, the new arrivals had learned the ropes in Mozambique and started to get "oily" (油) and difficult to control. Then they were asked to move on, and many of them found employment as managers in other Chinese companies or started their own business ventures.

CADEL had also played a central role in setting up the Chinese Business Association of Pemba（彭巴华人商会）, which mainly catered to the Chinese timber industry. As Stanley explained to Bunkenborg, the association not only organized social events but also helped companies in relation to the local authorities and with liaison with the Chinese embassy in Maputo.

> Not every Chinese manager has the language skills to negotiate with
> the local authorities, and there are all sorts of problems with various

departments such as agriculture, police, and traffic. You know African countries, they won't act like this when they see a white man, but when they see a Chinese they think they can get some money by helping to solve the problem. Treating Chinese in this way has become a bad habit that causes a lot of friction. Seeing that there were many Chinese around, I thought we should have an association to help with these problems, that all the Chinese should unite.

Stanley complained that the embassy had never before taken an interest in the many Chinese companies operating in the north, but once the association was set up, he had contacted the embassy, and the ambassador had started to phone on a regular basis. Of course, he explained, the Chinese companies competed, but the business association made it possible for them to act in concert, and CADEL played a central role in this since he was not just the association's elected head but also its general manager. Many of the Chinese employed by CADEL had only the most rudimentary command of Portuguese, but Stanley— who was fluent—insisted that things worked out despite the language barrier. As to precisely how and why things were done, however, Stanley was as mystified as everyone else.

> At first they don't understand each other, but after a while they come to understand even though they don't speak the same language. Take the drivers, for instance, they will have a local worker accompanying them. The driver only speaks a tiny bit of Portuguese, he is trying to learn, and the local worker doesn't understand what the driver is talking about. But after a while, they start to understand. People from the upper class here ask me, 'How do your workers communicate with our people?' and I think it is a mystery. I don't know how they communicate. But they get things done.

Stanley himself evidently knew enough Portuguese to do business and cultivate lasting relations with members of the local elite, a highly useful skill in a business climate as precarious and unpredictable as the Mozambican one. But, Bunkenborg had learned, there was no policy in this company (or possibly other Chinese logging firms) that required or encouraged Chinese workers to learn Portuguese, even when they were in charge of teams of Mozambican workers. Getting things done, it seemed, did not necessarily depend on the acquisition of formal language skills but involved an extended process of intimate adaptation that made it possible for *olheiros* and other local employees to intuitively understand what the Chinese wanted.

Finding the Trees

In 2011 Nielsen visited Felizardo Tiago, a former CADEL manager, and asked him how many *olheiros* were currently employed by the company. "Well, you can't do it without the *olheiros* . . . (*olheiros nunca podem faltar*), it's as simple as that." Felizardo paused and thumped the table several times. "But how many? . . . They are often quite complicated individuals so we generally leave it up to the local team leaders to deal with the *olheiros*."

Jaime Paguri was one of these "complicated individuals." Having worked for Maxingo Ltd. for more than a decade, in May 2006 he gave António Colombo, the company's owner, a notice of resignation and returned to his family, who was living in a small, wooden house outside Nairoto, north of Montepuez. Despite having no alternative income strategy, Paguri had decided that the unsatisfactory work conditions with Maxingo Ltd. could no longer be ignored. Sitting in the shade outside his mud house while his wife and two daughters were shelling a huge pile of *feijão manteiga* (butter beans), Paguri explained his decision to Nielsen. "I built my house while I was working for Colombo, and I didn't even make enough money to buy a wooden door; it's all bamboo!" Paguri roared with laughter and repeated several times that it was, indeed, "all bamboo."

During their walks in the forest, Nielsen had several times inquired about the Maxingo period, but he rarely got more than a monosyllabic response. In his more familiar setting, however, Paguri enthusiastically shared his experiences from nearly two decades of working as a tree scout:

> During the first period with Colombo, I continued to set up traps in the forest to catch *galinhas do mato* (helmeted guinea fowls). That's what I have always done, you know. But Colombo didn't like that: he thought that I ought to work only for my patrão (boss). To be an *olheiro* is to work for a patrão and you have to fear your patrão. And the money. . . . He never paid us enough money. We received [MZM] 1200 or maybe 1800 per month. That's not really worth the trouble . . . (*não vale a pena*).

After resigning from Maxingo, Paguri returned to his *machamba* (cultivated field) and resumed cultivating crops and trapping in the forest as he had always done, supplementing his wages with money made from selling meat and pelts. During the same period, his household was augmented when his two grand-daughters came to live in the small house. For several months, Paguri's son had unsuccessfully been trying to find a job; without financial means, he decided to entrust Paguri with the responsibility of providing for his daughters. Realizing the need for a stable income, Paguri approached his longtime friend, Acacio Tuende, who was head of CADEL's work crew hauling hardwood in the forest. Acacio had been working for the Chinese company for more than five years, and he was generally well respected among his superiors. After a few introductory conversations, Paguri was hired as CADEL's main *olheiro* in the Nairoto area. During their prolonged conversation in the shade outside his house, Nielsen asked Paguri whether he found the work conditions at CADEL different from his prior job with Maxingo. "Well, Colombo never really paid us anything," Paguri told Nielsen with a headshake. "But in some ways, it was even worse with the Chinese. With Colombo, our pay depended on the number of trees being cut whereas the Chinese pay per cubic meter. So we might find, say, 1,000 *pau preto* and still not make MZM 300 per month [laughs]."

With the Forestry and Wildlife Law of 1999, the Mozambican government aimed to strengthen the national timber industry by requiring the domestic processing of all but two sorts of precious hardwoods (art.12, 1; art. 12, 2). In other words, all timber industries, both national and international, were legally required to process the logs and ship them off as sawn timber. To the majority of timber companies, however, these rules weakened the possibility of selling Mozambican hardwood in the Chinese market where there had been little or no interest in sawn timber (Mackenzie and Ribeiro 2009, 38–42). When making high-quality furniture and carvings, the grain of the wood is of paramount importance, so Chinese craftsmen demand unprocessed logs. There was also an import duty on timber that did not apply to logs, and governmental support for local industries also played a role in maintaining a widespread preference for logs rather than sawn timber. At the time of Nielsen and Bunkenborg's fieldwork, Chinese demand for precious hardwood had been growing rapidly prompted by an increasing wealthy middle class willing to spend considerable money on exotic furniture. According to Mackenzie and Ribeiro (2009, 38), Mozambican timber has predominantly been used for reproductions of Ming and Qing dynasty furniture (especially sought-after species are *pau ferro, mondzo, pau preto,* and *jambire*), as well as for solid-wood flooring veneers and carvings that are sold both domestically and internationally (here *jambire* and *chanfuta* are the preferred woods).

Despite the Mozambican government's attempts to regulate international transactions in precious hardwood, many timber companies had continued to export unprocessed logs illegally to China.[5] By scrutinizing trade data in Mozambique and China, EIA estimated that China imported 11.8 million cubic meters of illegal logs in 2011 (worth US \$2.7 billion), of which 183,000 cubic meters came from Mozambique (2012, 7).[6] Twenty years after the implementation of the Forestry and Wildlife Law, it is therefore probably no exaggeration to conclude that the forestry sector in Mozambique is still out of control (cf. Lemos and Ribeiro 2007). In 2012 Chinese authorities registered 323,000 cubic meters of Mozambican log imports, whereas Mozambique's total registered global log exports during the same period amounted to merely 41,543 cubic meters (EIA 2013). Such a staggering discrepancy indicates systematic underreporting of the actual volume of timber exported to China and elsewhere. It would be missing the point, however, if these irregularities were simply written off as a sign of a dysfunctional customs system. Rather, it seems that the timber industry in Mozambique as such operates with little or no measures to secure the observance of existing laws and regulations. In 2011 Nielsen visited Felizardo Tiago, then the highest-ranking Mozambican employee at CADEL. At the time there was a persistent but unconfirmed rumor that the minister of agriculture had both personal and financial interests in CADEL. Reluctant to ask about the relationship directly, Nielsen made some vague remarks about the impressive efficiency of Chinese companies in a political landscape with so many overlapping interests. Tiago looked at him for a few seconds before replying. "Disregarding the risk that this creates for me, let me say that CADEL currently ships off between 100 and 200 containers each month that are packed with "processed logs." As a distinguished partner, we have the minister of agriculture. So you tell me, do you think that there are any obstacles or any doors closed for this company?"

Still, there were occasional hiccups in the otherwise smooth operations of CADEL and other Pemba-based logging firms. A few weeks prior to Bunkenborg and Nielsen's visit to Pemba in May 2011, the port authorities boarded a freighter preparing to leave for China and seized more than one hundred containers of unprocessed logs belonging to CADEL. For a while, the incident seemed to create a heightened awareness of the massive plundering of forest resources by a predatory Mozambican elite colluding with Chinese timber operators. CADEL was fined for attempting to smuggle precious hardwood to China, and more than half the forestry agents at the regional department for agriculture and forestry were fired. During their return visit less than a year later, however, the two anthropologists found that CADEL seemed to be up to speed again. Through personal ties to the local party elite, the company had managed to repossess the seized logs, which were now awaiting shipment to China. At the Department of Agriculture and Forestry, new cadres had already been hired; according to several timber operators in Pemba, they seemed quite willing to continue what had previously been a relationship based on "mutual benefits" (i.e., one hand washes the other, *uma mão lava a outra*). "You know, Morten, we are all too small to do anything about it. Since the seizure, nothing has happened!" Nielsen had tried for some days to meet up with Nelson Sîtoe, the owner of a small local logging company, but it was only on the final day of his 2011 stay in Pemba that there was a chance to discuss the seizure of CADEL's hundred-odd containers. Nelson continued while lighting a cigarette, "Nothing has happened, but that sure as hell doesn't mean that the government is in better control now or that the Chinese have stopped stealing our hardwood for that matter. What it means is that the system is happy. And when the system is happy, nothing will be changed."

"Without *Olheiros*, There Is No Timber!"

In late May 2012, Nielsen went with a group of young Mozambicans working for CADEL into the forest near Xilungo in the western part of Cabo Delgado (figure 6.2). The day before, the company's logging team had felled more than twenty *muanga* trees, which were now to be loaded onto a truck and hauled back to the company's main camp in Balama, some thirty kilometers east of Xilungo. En route to the muanga trees, the crew stopped for a few hours in the small *aldeia* (village) where the logging team was staying during the cutting season. While the

FIGURE 6.2.   A CADEL work crew carrying a log across an opening in the forest cleared by the *picadeiros* (trail makers). May 2012.

Mozambican workers tried to fix the truck's somewhat unstable engine, Nielsen sat down with Alberto, CADEL's *olheiro* in the area, to learn more about what a tree scout does.

> The *olheiro* walks in the bush (*no mato*). That's what he does. It's like in the army. In the army, it's called reconnaissance (*reconhecimento*). Only . . . we don't use maps and compasses. We never received any maps. Our map is our eyes and what we know in our hearts about where to go next.

Before working for CADEL, Alberto used to catch antelopes and helmeted guinea fowls with traps set in the forest near his house. Based on his regular hunting trips he had been more or less able to provide meat for his family and to occasionally supplement his meager income by selling a few animals. "The bush practically belongs to the *olheiros*!" Alberto cast a sideways glance toward the forest that encircled the aldeia. "We have been walking in the forests for a very long time, . . . setting up our traps in order to catch *galinhas do mato* and that's how we discovered what's an umbila and what's a pau preto. So when a boss (*patrão*) asks me whether there are any umbila or pau preto, I'll tell him where they are."

Back in 2012 the majority of *olheiros* were hired by Chinese timber companies through community chiefs (*líderes comunitário*) acting as intermediaries. "They wanted someone who knew the forest," Alberto explained. "And that's why the community chief chose me. He told me to sort things out with them [the Chinese] and then get to work." Now entering his third season working for CADEL, Alberto imagined that he would continue as their main *olheiro* in the area west of Xilungo until all the precious hardwood was gone.

At the time of Nielsen and Bunkenborg's fieldwork in 2010 and 2011, the work conditions and salary agreements for *olheiros* varied considerably depending on the individual timber operator. Whereas Chinese timber companies such as CADEL paid approximately MZM 300 (US $9.8) for one cubic meter of hardwood, most Mozambican concessionaires calculated salaries based on the number of logs hauled back to the main camp, or approximately MZM 150 (US $4.9) per log. According to Alberto, it was much more difficult to maintain a stable income when working for Chinese timber companies. Given the size of the trees that the Chinese timber companies were interested in, it was significantly harder to make a cubic meter of hardwood than it was to spot two pau preto or jambire. Without viable alternatives, Alberto had nevertheless accepted the work conditions at CADEL and immediately started preparing for the logging season when he was first asked in early April 2010. In the northern part of Mozambique, the rainy season ends in late April or early May; shortly afterward, the timber companies start setting up provisional work camps as close to the concession areas as possible. In mid-April Alberto went to CADEL's work camp and made an initial plan for the coming months with the manager of the work crew. Most of the timber companies were relatively rigid hierarchical organizations with work activities coordinated from above. In the case of CADEL, the cutting season started when the head of the local company branch in Montepuez received the annually renewed concession papers from the Department of Agriculture. Based on the work specifications defined by the administration in Pemba (e.g., the kinds of hardwood to focus on and when to haul the logs back to Pemba), the head of the Montepuez branch then communicated with the main camp in Nairoto, and from there the orders finally reached the cutting crew.

Despite this hierarchical organization of work tasks, all the different agents involved in the logging process expressed unequivocal dependency on the *olheiro*. Irrespective of position and work obligations, or ethnicity and cultural background, both the quantity and the quality of timber was perceived to reflect the scouting skills of *olheiros* like Alberto and Jaime Paguri.[7] According to Felizardo Tiago, the high-ranking Mozambican CADEL employee, the forests were dangerous to outsiders without the *olheiro*'s thorough knowledge of the area. "If you and I were to enter the forest alone, we might end up going in circles without ever finding a single tree," Tiago explained. "We would never work here if we didn't have *olheiros*, you know." Small wonder, then, that Alberto seemed well aware of the crucial importance and value ascribed to his work by his colleagues and employers, be they Mozambicans or Chinese. "Well, I knew that he (the manager of the local crew) would have to work with me. Without *olheiros*, there's no timber (*sem olheiros, não há madeira*)!"

Taking into account local differences in managerial strategies, the logging process in the forest might be divided into four consecutive phases: scouting, trailmaking, cutting, and transportation.[8] The *olheiro* is always the first person to enter the forest and will use at least two or three days to get an initial sense of the concession area and to identify an appropriate site from which to haul the hardwood. Depending on the efficiency of the work crew, either the *olheiro* or his assistant then returns to the provisional camp to coordinate subsequent activities with the manager of the cutting crew, which usually consists of chain saw operators, *picadeiros* (trail makers), and tractor drivers. [9] After the rainy season the forest vegetation is particularly dense and humid, making it difficult for tractors and trucks to enter. The *olheiro* or his assistant therefore accompanies a group of picadeiros while they open a trail to the logging site by cutting down plants and trees with machetes and crosscut saws. The improved accessibility allows the tractor to reach the logging site with the chain saw operators and their small work crew. During Nielsen's trips into the forests, the chain saw operators cut an average of thirty trees per day; the number was only smaller when chain saws repeatedly misfired or the work crew had difficulty reaching a location identified by the *olheiro* (cf. Mackenzie 2006, 49).[10] In each location the crew manager would choose an appropriate site for stacking the hardwood. As soon as all selected trees were felled and the branches removed, the tractor driver would start hauling the logs together using chains and heavy rope. This was often a tiresome and difficult process in which the workers had to manually drag the logs through dense and tangled undergrowth.

When the felled logs were stacked, the work crew either returned to the provisional camp or, depending on the distance between the camp and the cutting site, proceeded to the next location. The manager of the work crew in Namalala then notified the main camp in Nairoto where all the logs were stored, and they were transported to Pemba. CADEL had two trucks with open bodies in Nairoto, which were used to transport the logs from the forests and, later in the season, to Pemba. As soon as all selected trees were felled, both trucks were sent into the forest with at least twenty or thirty workers to haul and load the logs onto the truck bodies before returning to the main camp. Timber companies kept only top-quality trees, discarding logs with visible defects like holes or knots, so a great deal of usable timber was left as waste.[11] Once, Jaime Paguri stopped and pointed to a small heap of muanga logs almost buried by wildly growing bushes and elephant grass. He told Nielsen that he had found the trees toward the end of the previous cutting season and asked the chain saw operators to cut them, but he never informed the truck driver. "Ah! I was tired," Paguri admitted with a smile. "And I knew that they [CADEL] would probably not even want the trees. . . . Look at those curved trunks and all the knots."

Sino-Mozambican Resemblances

Logging companies like CADEL used the *olheiros* to identify marketable species of trees in the forest, but the close collaboration also had an effect on the Chinese. One conversation Bunkenborg conducted in Cabo Delgado offered a particularly interesting perspective on the gradually shifting relations between Chinese and Mozambicans. Having banged loudly on the metal gate, Bunkenborg was admitted to the walled compound by one of the Mozambican workers, who led him to a cement house with a roof of corrugated iron. With a view of the machine shack and the logs and vehicles in the compound through the window, the house served both as the office and the makeshift living quarters of Mr. Jiang, a former geography teacher from Beijing. Employed to measure and assess the value of the timber that was brought in, Mr. Jiang had little to do so early in the cutting season and clearly welcomed the distraction of talking to

Bunkenborg. Having found it increasingly difficult to make ends meet on RMB 2000 a month in Beijing, Mr. Jiang decided to leave China when a relative offered to double his salary by working in a sawmill in Montepuez. By the time Bunkenborg met him in 2011, Mr. Jiang had spent four years in Mozambique. And yet, like many of his countrymen working in Africa, he almost never went out, preferring instead to stay within the compound and devote himself to an all-absorbing interest in football. Indeed, while Mr. Jiang claimed to take a particular interest in the German Bundesliga, his knowledge of football was truly encyclopedic; in the course of their conversation, Bunkenborg was treated to an extraordinarily detailed account of the exploits of the Danish National team at the 1986 World Cup in Mexico. Mr. Jiang also took an interest in history, or at least Chinese history, and was surprised when Bunkenborg mentioned the civil war in Mozambique as a possible explanation for the low level of education of the workers. It soon transpired that Mr. Jiang had until this point operated under the assumption that nothing had really happened in Mozambique since the Portuguese "made a mess of things and left" in 1975. Mr. Jiang didn't want to speculate too much on the legacy of colonialism, he confided to Bunkenborg, but he was rather worried about the unequal power relations being forged in the timber business in Mozambique.

> MR. JIANG: It's as if we are masters and they are servants. And the majority of Chinese take this sort of relation for granted. I don't. Maybe the reason why my attitude is different is that I come from one of the best places in China. I am better educated and I believe that all men are equal, including poor people and criminals. Obviously, it happens that they haven't done their work properly, and even I get angry and scold them. But many of the Chinese come from the countryside, they are used to being bullied, but now they have "stood up" (翻身 *fanshen*)[12] and become masters and it seems they get a kick out of that. . . . I have even quarreled with a number of Chinese because of this. I think that no matter what, Mozambicans should be treated with respect. Take the two of us drinking tea, for instance, I will pour the tea myself, but others will order a Mozambican to pour the tea. I find that unnecessary, the tea is right there, and it's easy to pour it yourself.
>
> BUNKENBORG: You said you have quarreled with Chinese over this sort of thing. Could you give a specific example?
>
> MR. JIANG: For the midday rest, for instance . . ., some Chinese will call a Mozambican over from quite a distance to move the bed into the shade. Actually, they could easily move it themselves. That sort

of thing happens all the time, and one day I finally had enough and said, "Why have someone run over from a such distance for a small thing that you could just do yourself?" When he didn't accept that, I asked him, "Did your hands rot? Did your feet rot? Why can't you do it?" I am generally very patient, but that day I just couldn't stand it any longer. If the man was right there, smoking a cigarette, and you asked him to lend a hand, that would be fine, but getting someone to run over from a distance to move your bed a few inches, that's really unnecessary. In the end, it's a lack of culture, and that's the attitude of the majority of the Chinese. None of the bosses are like that, it's the temporary workers. Once they're here, they think they are no longer peasants, they think they are superiors.

Apparently, Mr. Jiang had managed to learn some phrases in Portuguese that he used to communicate with the Mozambican workers, but he claimed that on the rare occasions when he ventured outside the fenced perimeter of the sawmill, people didn't seem to understand him. He had eventually come to the conclusion that his own workers had simply learned to guess what he wanted without really understanding what he was actually trying to say. The only thing Mr. Jiang felt he had learned during his years in Mozambique was to assess the quality of logged timber. However, he would not be able to identify the right species in the forest as he had only been on two short visits to a logging camp at Nairoto. Feeling somewhat different from them because of his education and urban origins, Mr. Jiang was puzzled by the way some of his Chinese colleagues had started to behave like colonial masters; he suggested that they must be "uneducated peasants who did not fully embody Chinese culture" and would begin to behave in ways that seemed to him decidedly "un-Chinese."

Other Chinese timber operators had learned to speak Portuguese, however, and collaborated much more intensely with the locals. For example, the manager of CADEL's main camp in Nairoto until 2012 was a middle-aged Chinese timber merchant named Martin, who was not only fluent in Portuguese but had even mastered a few key phrases in Makua.[13] Yet, despite his ability to effortlessly communicate with local staff, Martin had apparently never been interested in understanding Mozambican work ethics. "Martin is bad, he is really bad! (*Martin é mau, é mau mesmo*)." Taquinha repeated the expression to Nielsen as if to remind himself of his former employer's questionable character. After a long and bumpy drive to the main camp in Nairoto, Nielsen had invited Jaime Paguri and Taquinha to a nearby liquor stall to discuss the work conditions at CADEL. Earlier that day Nielsen had overheard a conversation between Taquinha and Acacio, the manager of the cutting crew for the sawmill, about Martin's lack of respect for the Mozambican workers. Not knowing Martin, Nielsen suggested an afternoon meeting to discuss their relationship with this particular Chinese timber merchant. As the manager of a local work camp, Martin was legally required to use resident labor when assembling cutting teams at the beginning of each season. Even so, Nielsen was told, it was often workers from Martin's previous work camp in Chiúre who ended up cutting and hauling the hardwood. "Martin prevented us from doing our jobs," Paguri sighed. "He didn't consider us as proper workers; that was the problem, you know. The only thing he really valued (*valorizou*) was the MZM 50 note [laughs]. Even after having worked from five in the morning until eight at night, he would still say that the salary for a day's work was MZM 50." It seemed as if Martin's alleged blatant lack of respect for Mozambican work ethics was surprisingly familiar to Paguri and other local Mozambicans who had met or worked with him. "He has been here for a long time," Paguri explained, "and he has already habituated himself with the Mozambican way of life. So, his characteristics, rather than being those of a Chinese, are those of a Mozambican (*já a característica dele em vez de ser dum chinês é dum mocambicano*). In fact, it's more than that. He's a mobster (*mafioso*)." Taquinha bellowed with laughter while nodding several times, confiding to Nielsen, "If you talked to Martin and heard him speak Portuguese, you really wouldn't believe that he is actually Chinese. . . . Ihh! [makes a high-pitched sound] Martin is bad!"

Nielsen's interlocutors' description of Martin's refusal to acknowledge them as "proper workers" closely echoed what Nielsen had previously heard from a number of young Mozambicans hired by AFECC, the Chinese construction consortium, to work on the national football stadium on the northern outskirts of Maputo (Pedersen and Nielsen 2013). In ways surprisingly similar to the relationship between the Chinese employer and the Mongolian workers discussed in chapter 2, the Chinese ganders were seen as unable to recognize and respect their Mozambican employees as proper persons with whom reciprocal social relationships might be established. To the young construction workers in Maputo, the failure to be recognized as proper persons had only seemed to further confirm that their Chinese superiors were, indeed, too alien and dangerous for viable social relations, but to Paguri and Taquinha it seemed to be the other way around: in this case, the "mobster-like" behavior of Chinese managers like Martin suggested a peculiar similarity between themselves and some of their Asian counterparts. In a sense, one might say, his unjust treatment of local workers paradoxically seemed to configure Martin as a fellow Mozambican in their eyes—not just another Chinese manager. Precisely because of his excessive and repeated misuse of power, Martin seemed to appear as a sort of intensified version of (morally reprehensible) "Mozambican-ness" (recalling Paguri's last statement that Martin was "more than that. He's a mobster"). Martin's lack of respect for basic work conditions supposedly set him aside from most of the Mozambican employers that Paguri and his peers had worked for. Mozambican bosses are known to generally recognize the hardships that their workers face in order to allow for some negotiation and flexibility in terms of work hours and the need for people to do occasional odd jobs. In this regard, Martin was totally inflexible and never open to negotiating work agreements (either formally or informally) with his local workers. At the same time, however, he was known to be obsessed with money and to do whatever it took to make as much as possible. To Nielsen's informants, it was in order to maximize profits—not because he had any real interest in Mozambique or its people—that Martin had acquired such amazing Portuguese language skills and knowledge of local customs. Yet Paguri and his colleagues could easily relate to Martin's desire to make money; perhaps they even admired this quality in their Chinese boss. Accordingly, Nielsen concluded, Martin was not just "bad" in the sense of being alien and incomprehensible; he was also "bad" in a manner eerily similar to themselves.

While further pondering Paguri and Taquinha's reflections that night, Nielsen was reminded of a previous conversation with an *olheiro* working more than five years for another Chinese-owned timber company in the area around Nacololo. During a visit to the company's concession area in 2011, Nielsen had enquired about the *olheiro*'s impressions of his Chinese superiors.

> OLHEIRO: Well . . . even though the Chinese are whites, their character-istics are just like ours (*os chineses só embora eles são brancos, mas a característica é tal e qual como nós*).[14]
>
> NIELSEN: Why do you think that the characteristics of the Chinese are similar to those of the Mozambicans?
>
> OLHEIRO: China is a poor country, you know. And if you ask them where they lived before, they'll tell you that they lived in the bush (*no mato*). They don't even try to hide it! And they are not hygienic at all. They could take a shit right here (*cagar*) and still sleep on the floor. Have you seen their food? They will boil the meat and keep it until it rots. And they won't even throw it away; they'll offer it to you!

Recalling the tendency of the young Mozambican workers to distance them-selves from their Chinese superiors by emphasizing seemingly insurmount-able differences and the latter's lack of respect and humanity, it was puzzling to Nielsen that the *olheiros* agreed on their likeness to their Chinese counterparts. How was it possible for the Mozambican workers to detect similarities while they also acknowledged that the Chinese way of treating their local employees was in stark opposition to most employer-employee relationships in Mozambique? The appropriate question, Nielsen concluded, might be how "Chineseness" ended up as an "interiorized alterity" (cf. Taussig 1993) to the *olheiros* working for Chinese timber companies in northern Mozambique? To explore this crucial question and its implications, we need to unpack the social and economic effects of Chinese timber operations in Cabo Delgado, particularly how those operations have reconfigured the already tenuous relations between *olheiros* and certain members of their local communities.

"*Furtivos*" and Forest Spirits

It should now be clear that, around 2012, logging in Cabo Delgado not only included a number of interconnected businesses, it also involved a wide range of differently positioned agents, Chinese as well as Mozambican, who sought to benefit in various, often contradictory ways. For example, Chinese timber companies increasingly bought hardwood from local loggers to eliminate several tiresome steps (cutting, hauling, etc.) in the process from tree to timber and thereby increase their profit (German and Wertz-Kanounnikoff 2012, 41). While this strategy created a more cost-efficient process for the timber operators, a side effect was the emergence of a booming illegal market for small-scale loggers, who cut without licenses and sometimes even stole hardwood from concession areas.[15] According to several legal license holders, around 2012 the situation was becoming so critical that they considered cutting trees illegally before outside loggers entered their areas to steal the logs (Ribeiro 2010, 159).[16] The unlicensed loggers, known as *furtivos* (literally, "poachers"), not only cut and sold the hardwood themselves but also started to buy logs directly from local villagers and community chiefs in search of small profits.[17] As a consequence of this development, although community chiefs were formally obliged to ensure that all logging requirements were observed, they often came to function as gatekeepers for outside furtivos seeking to purchase cheap hardwood from local villagers. In this way they assisted in concealing the basic illegality of the operation by imprinting all logs with the initials of the Chinese timber companies, making it virtually impossible to trace their dubious history.

Needless to say, illegal logging is a potentially risky enterprise, particularly stealing hardwood belonging to concessionaires and individual license holders. Many furtivos living near the cutting areas reduced this risk by using the less noisy crosscut saws and by asking buyers to haul the logs from the cutting site themselves. These small-scale illegal loggers were usually local farmers living off their land while generating an additional income from occasional sales of hardwood to larger timber operators. By contrast, outside furtivos (*furtivos da fora*) were organized loggers who used chainsaws and tractors to cut and haul the hardwood. As Bunkenborg and Nielsen discovered during several trips into the forests near Nairoto, many outside furtivos operated as de facto franchises of Chinese timber companies that lend them equipment and sometimes even personnel in return for exclusive purchase rights to the hardwood (see also German and Wertz-Kanounnikoff 2012, 41). Whereas local loggers relied on their intimate knowledge of the land to find and cut the hardwood themselves, the outside furtivos needed collaborators with in-depth knowledge about potential cutting sites. At the time of Bunkenborg and Nielsen's fieldwork, a number of experienced *olheiros* had become of paramount importance to the illegal loggers—not only had they worked in or around the designated cutting areas, they also knew the planned logging activities of legal concessionaires and license holders.

Consider the following example: In 2010 Jaime Paguri was contacted by an outside furtivo who needed help in locating jambire hardwood for a Chinese timber operator without concession rights in the area. Not wanting to dishonor his agreement with CADEL, Paguri initially turned down the furtivo but promised to reconsider the offer at the end of the cutting season. "I should have accepted the offer to begin with," Paguri later admitted to Nielsen. "The Chinese are no good. . . . Even if you really work hard and comply with their rules, the pay is still bad." As the forests near CADEL's provisional logging camps were cleared of usable hardwood, Paguri and his assistant had to walk longer distances to locate possible cutting sites. As fewer and fewer trees were found, their salaries diminished accordingly. Paguri had tried to explain to his Chinese superiors that the current situation was untenable; he had even asked for a change of salary policies (fixed salaries rather than commission), but to no avail. According to the manager at CADEL, the increased competition among timber operators in the area necessitated immediate budget cuts, including salaries and commissions for cutting teams and *olheiros*. Increasingly dissatisfied with the work conditions at CADEL, Paguri went back to the furtivo, who was still looking for an experienced tree scout, and agreed to start moonlighting as soon as the rainy season was over. Since Paguri did not want to give up his affiliation with CADEL, their initial agreement was to do the illegal tree scouting during weekends and work holidays. This arrangement was soon to change, however, as Paguri began planning to leave CADEL altogether. During their last conversation in May 2012, Paguri told Nielsen that he had decided to work exclusively for the furtivo, even if this implied a temporary reduction of income. "You know, Morten, we Mozambicans are poor, and we do want to work. But to work without getting paid, that's not really work (*trabalhar sem ganhar não é trabalho*)."

Jaime Paguri was not the only *olheiro* to leave the Chinese timber companies to work exclusively for local or outside furtivos. As the timber industry increased the pace of its production and more and more *olheiros* were needed to spot the desired hardwood, new opportunities arose for making money on illegal logging. Not surprisingly, those *olheiros* who already had experience working for the major Chinese companies were particularly coveted by illegal loggers searching for immediate marketing possibilities. In fact, as Nielsen was told in 2012 by an illegal outside logger, only *olheiros* who had worked for Chinese timber companies were capable of finding trees that could later be sold to these very same companies. "Why do you think that they always find the trees? If I go into the bush (*mato*), there don't seem to be any trees at all." Before giving Nielsen a chance to respond, he proceeded to answer himself: "The *olheiros* think like the Chinese; that's for sure. Ah! The Chinese. . . . They are a bunch of ugly, worn-out old men who only know how to eat (*só sabem comer*)." In a certain sense, the furtivo's comments on the scouting skills of local *olheiros* were not entirely off the mark. As Nielsen was repeatedly told by Paguri and his colleagues, it was only after being hired by Chinese timber companies that they managed to find the precious hardwood. Alberto, one of CADEL's local *olheiros*, described the enhanced sense for hardwood that came with his new position working for the Chinese timber company: "Originally, the *olheiro* wasn't even aware that other people might be needing the wood. That started only after the Chinese (*os chinês*) told us that they needed *chamfuta, pau preto, muanga* [species of precious hardwood]".

To many *olheiros*, the value of precious hardwood (both in monetary and relational terms) changed as they were approached by Chinese timber operators in need of their scouting skills: the seemingly intimate relationships between Mozambican *olheiros* and Chinese timber operators came to feed into and affect the increasing number of collaborations between *olheiros* and illegal loggers. As more and more *olheiros* found additional revenue opportunities working for illegal loggers—a situation which in itself was an effect of the increasing presence of Chinese timber operators in the area—they gradually came to be perceived as imbued with a particular capacity for locating precious hardwood.[18] When the *olheiros* were approached by illegal loggers, this capacity was made visible (cf. Strathern 1992, 180) in the process of making the latter consider the former as useful collaborators. A viable collaboration between tree loggers and tree scouts could only be activated if a capacity for locating hardwood could be turned into the object of the relationship between *olheiro* and furtivo. The majority of the *olheiros* that Nielsen spoke to had been approached by illegal loggers wanting to hire them on the basis of their alleged (but not confirmed) scouting skills. However, the furtivos ended up getting more than they had bargained for. While acknowledging the *olheiros'* superior ability to find precious hardwood, several furtivos also expressed skepticism regarding the nature of the relationships between these tree scouts and the Chinese timber operators and, particularly, the effects those relations had on the social and cosmological well-being of the communities in which they worked and lived. We see how the perceived capacity for locating hardwood was not merely a practical skill that anyone could in principle learn to master. Quite on the contrary, a gifted *olheiro* was also perceived to be able to control the malevolent spirit forces that, as Nielsen was told many times, had often injured or even killed inexperienced loggers during the cutting season. Since many *olheiros* had acquired or optimized their powerful skills through work relations with Chinese timber operators, the control of local forest spirits had most likely been taken over by Chinese forces.[19]

In April 2011, Nielsen witnessed the yearly commemorative ritual (*makua: sadaka* or *ipepha ontholoni*) to appease the ancestor of a local community chief that always occurs before the cutting season. During conversations with some of the participants, Nielsen became aware of the aforementioned consequences of the reciprocal relationships between *olheiros* and Chinese timber operators. Throughout Mozambique, clan leaders are traditionally considered as the true owners of land, and this privilege is maintained after their physical death (Menezes 2001). Before cutting and hauling hardwood that in the last instance belongs to deceased clan leaders, incumbent community chiefs must ask permission to do so by presenting the ancestral spirits with traditional offerings such as locally brewed beer, wine, goat meat, and fried chicken. The particular ritual that Nielsen witnessed took place near the impressive baobab tree that graced the entrance to the *machamba* where the family of the deceased clan leader had grown crops for more than eighty years. Corropa, the deceased clan leader, was now "resting" in the shade under the baobab tree from where he controlled the lives of his descendants and successors. All invited guests stood in a disorganized semicircle around Corropa's eldest son, Isténio, the area's main healer (*curandeiro*). Isténio knelt in front of the baobab, a plastic can in his right hand from which he poured wine on the ground while asking for Corropa's permission to cut hardwood in the forest during the coming season. During the ritual Nielsen was standing next to Babo, a local farmer who was also working as a furtivo in the forests near the village. Shortly after the ritual started, Babo moved closer in order to speak without being heard by anyone else. "You know that Alberto paid Isténio to speak to Corropa, right?" Babo nodded toward Alberto, CADEL's *olheiro* in the area, who was standing quite close to the community leader. "But I wonder why Corropa accepted the money," he continued in a soft voice. "Perhaps he couldn't see that it was Chinese money."

As Nielsen was soon to find out, Alberto had been moonlighting for Babo and another local furtivo while keeping his day job with CADEL. As the local representative for the Chinese timber company, he had donated a small amount of money for Isténio's wife to prepare food and wine to be consumed during the ritual. It was not uncommon for Chinese managers to participate in such commemorative rituals (even though their role was usually only that of a silent spectator), but this year no Chinese superior had shown up, and it was up to Alberto to represent CADEL, a fact that seemed to slightly worry Babo. By accepting Alberto's donation (through his widow), Corropa had signaled his approval of the *olheiro's* activities on his land and thereby of the spirit forces that enabled Alberto to locate the hardwood. Whereas the benevolence of the landowner (living or dead) was required in order for the *olheiro* to operate in the forest, the capacity for locating hardwood was considered the result of one's own spirit forces (cf. Feliciano 1998, 269–70). As Babo reminded Nielsen, although nearly all the *olheiros* knew the forests from hunting helmeted guinea fowls and antelopes, their capacity for finding precious hardwood was an unintended effect of their liaison with the Chinese timber operators. In that sense, these Mozambican *olheiros*, in order to improve their scouting skills, had invited and allowed powerful Chinese forces to operate through them, perhaps even to take control of the ancestral spirits that oriented their everyday lives. As one of the illegal loggers had commented, "The *olheiros* think like the Chinese; that's for sure," but being *olheiro* was not merely a matter of thinking like the Chinese. To Babo and his peers, the more worrying question was to what extent the tree scouts were becoming Chinese.

"The Chinese Are the Fishermen and We Are the Hooks"

To most of the Mozambicans that Nielsen got to know over the four visits he made to Cabo Delgado between 2009 and 2012, death was not the end of a person's existence. When one died and the body was buried, ancestral spirits remained in the lives and bodies of the descendants as "the effective manifestation of his or her power and personality" (Honwana 1997, 296; see also West 2005, 116–17; Nielsen 2012a). In "Spiritual Agency and Self-renewal in Southern Mozambique" (1996), Alcinda Honwana describes how "humans and spirits become one single entity because spirits possess people, live and grow in people and are there on a permanent basis. Thus, humans and spirits become part of the same agency as they share a combined and integrated existence" (2). Honwana focuses on the southern part of Mozambique, but her apt description of the human-spirit relationship equally captures the cosmological dynamics of many communities in Cabo

Delgado. The special kind of agentive force established through these human-spirit relationships is limited both by the strikingly human-like affects of the spirits (jealousy, suspicion, anger, love) and the kinship-based relationality through which it asserts itself. A living individual can be affected—or governed—only by the force of those spirits to which he or she has a consanguine relation. During a short visit in Nairoto in 2012, Nielsen asked a retired hunter whether he had ever been guided by spirit forces outside his family when setting up traps. "Never! (*nada*)". He made a sweeping gesture with his arm as if to embrace the entire community. "You cannot ask Ngungunyane to help you here; only those of your own land can help you."[20] How, then, are we to make sense of the seeming paradox that "Chinese spirits" were understood to guide the *olheiros* in their search for precious hardwood?

Before becoming affiliated with Chinese timber operators, Alberto and his colleagues had worked as small-scale farmers. While they sometimes supplemented their meager income by selling a few animals caught in the forest, they claimed to have had little or no knowledge of the different species of hardwood. The efficiency with which they were now capable of finding hardwood was perceived to prove beyond any doubt the influence of powerful spirits. According to outside furtivos and local farmers alike, these abilities had to be of Chinese origin. The effects of this unusual involvement in local matters by outside spirits were glimpsed in a variety of ways. As we heard earlier, Corropa's spirit protected the land against harmful intrusions, such as the cutting of hardwood without proper acknowledgment of his historical ownership rights to all natural resources in the area. As in other parts of Mozambique, however, ancestral spirits assert themselves predominantly within a cosmological universe constituted by kinship-based relationships and attack only those individuals considered somehow affiliated to his or her clan (Nielsen 2012a). On an earlier occasion Nielsen had asked Taquinha whether forest spirits might attack Chinese loggers. Apparently, the Chinese were only affected indirectly: "The Chinese are the fishermen and we are the hooks. The forest spirits only cause trouble by attacking the hooks, not the fishermen." People were surprised to learn, then, that a Chinese logger had recently been attacked by some unidentified spirit force while cutting in the forest near the home of Corropa, the deceased but still active clan leader. According to Babo, the Chinese logger had been working in the area for an extended period of time, but during recent years he had failed to reciprocate Corropa for allowing him to cut hardwood on his land. As the Chinese logger had come to know the area quite well, he would often go into the forest without *olheiros*. "And that is just stupid!" Babo sneered. "How can you cut a tree without anyone to tell you if it's ok?" One day while walking in the forest, the unfortunate Chinese logger fell down and was carried to the local hospital, where the doctor diagnosed his illness as thrombosis. Yet, to most of the people Nielsen spoke to, the attack on the Chinese logger had been a worrying occult occurrence somehow connected to his intimate collaboration with local *olheiros*. Although it was impossible to know with certainty the nature of that collaboration, it had certainly optimized the *olheiro*'s capacities for finding hardwood while later allowing the Chinese logger to operate independently in the forest.

In *Mimesis and Alterity* (1993), Taussig discusses the building of the Panama Canal and the "hierarchy of alterities within a colonial mosaic of attractions and repulsions" that emerged through encounters between white Americans, black workers, and local Cuna Indians (144). Dictated by white-defined imageries of work discipline and efficiency, a "culture [was] stitched together" (145) in which blacks were inferior to both white Americans and the Cunas. More precisely, Taussig suggests, the working of an invisible but "minutely orchestrated color line, traced remorselessly throughout everyday life" (148) had a continuous effect on the Cuna Indians' view of both blacks and whites: "Interesting and disturbing about the Cuna case are the strange complicities achieved between whites and Indians despite the enormity of cultural misunderstanding that existed, complicities in which the positive and negative poles of savagery, as defined by white culture, were meticulously stitched into Indian cosmologies of cultural identity-formation through mirroring and alterizing" (150).

With Taussig's account of this "mosaic of alterities" in mind, we can understand why eerie similarities were sometimes perceived to exist between Mozambicans and Chinese in and around Pemba at the time of Bunkenborg and Nielsen's fieldwork. Local *olheiros* viewed both the Chinese and fellow Mozambicans as excessively greedy. Our question was how this space of resemblance might have come into being in the first place.

As in the Panama described by Taussig, postcolonial Mozambique is home to "hierarchies of alterity within a colonial mosaic of attractions and repulsions," imprinted through centuries of enforced obedience to the Portuguese colonial regime (Allina 2012; Penvenne 1995). After the celebration of independence in 1975, the ruling Frelimo party sought to "decolonise individual minds" and reconstruct a national identity based on a "scientific socialism" devoid of the vices of capitalist-imperialist exploitation (Cahen 1993, 48; West 2001, 121). Only a decade later, however, the government made an irrevocable "turn toward the West" (Hanlon 1996), agreeing to implement a series of economic structural-adjustment programs as a condition for immediate financial aid. Despite its compliance with the conditions imposed by international lending institutions, Frelimo has since succeeded in reproducing a political discourse of national superiority based on a revolutionary past (Coelho 2013; Dinerman 2006; cf. Nielsen

2017). Talking to people in northern Mozambique, however, Nielsen noticed that Frelimo's decolonial language was rarely mentioned. Instead, people expressed strong feelings of racial inferiority linked to memories of colonial subjugation. "There is a difference between negros and whites," Alberto once said. "The whites help each other whereas the negroes. . . . I suppose it's because negroes are closer to the apes; why else do we have so many problems?" Nielsen heard similar comments regarding "the black race" from Mozambican construction workers in Maputo. In 2011 he visited Raimundo, a young construction worker, and his family in their small reed hut on the city's outskirts. The wife was trying to get their youngest daughter to sleep. "It was Raimundo who destroyed (*estragou*) her with his dark color," she told Nielsen in a low voice so as not to wake up the child. "I almost couldn't look at her right after she was born." Raimundo laughed and shook his head. "Yeah, this color is shit. It's not worth the trouble (*não vale a pena*)."

As should be clear by now, when Jaime Paguri and his peers claimed to recognize in their Chinese employers certain negative traits characteristic of Mozambican people, the nature of these supposed traits echoed deep-seated experiences and discourses of racial inferiority. However, it is still remarkable that these traits were here extended to what they perceived as radically different Others, namely the Chinese. In a sense, the relationship between the Mozambican workers and the Chinese superiors seemed to double itself: The fraught relationship between Chinese bosses and locals reflected deep-seated colonial hierarchies between "whites" (*brancos*) and locals, in the sense that the Chinese superior became for the Mozambican workers a sort of mirror of his or her own value (cf. Zizek 1989, 24). As a result of the intensification of scouting capacities via a transfer of a new mode of visibility from Chinese logging agents to Mozambican *olheiros*, an otherwise exterior relationship revealed itself to operate on the inside of a local cosmos of "attractions and repulsions in which some alters exert positive, and others negative, charges" (Taussig 1993, 144).

This, then, might explain the intimate distant form assumed by the Chinese Other in the present case. On the one hand, the Chinese were perceived as too uncannily familiar to neatly fit into and remain fixated within prevailing postcolonial hierarchies and logics. On the other hand, they were seen as too fundamentally incomprehensible, different, and alien to fit into the same subjectivity space as the Mozambicans. Perhaps when Jaime Paguri and his peers gazed skeptically at their Chinese counterparts, their reserve was not a reflection of a mimetic desire to obtain the properties of a distant other (Ferguson, J. 2006, 155–65); perhaps their reaction expressed the disturbing realization of seeing into the unknown eyes of themselves.

More than Local and Less than Global

"It never ends (*nunca para*). We will never govern our own country. . . . Now it's the Chinese, who are running Mozambique. . . . When you come back here, you will have to talk to a Chinese community chief." Nielsen was about to leave Paguri's house when the old *olheiro* summarized his analysis of living side by side with Chinese loggers. Now, several years later, Paguri's words still speak to social, political, and ethnic tensions pertaining to natural resource extraction in the northernmost parts of Mozambique. The local community chiefs are still Mozambican; indeed, at the time of Nielsen and Bunkenborg's fieldwork, the managers of the Chinese logging companies were already planning to move on as they foresaw that the hardwood resources in Mozambique would be exhausted in a few more years. The many years of unrestricted maneuvering room given to external logging agents have destabilized and sometimes fundamentally ruptured local residents' relationship to the territories they continue to occupy. The entrenched weaknesses of the Mozambican state administration not only make possible but almost seem to encourage the misuse of power and the illegal appropriation of public goods for private gain.

To residents like Jaime Paguri, that was not overly surprising. After decades of encounters with corrupt state cadres and a gradually weakened state administration, the misuse of public office was something he and his fellow residents had come to see as just the way things were. More worrisome for local people was the way that free-roaming foreigners, in their view, have disrupted the stability and functioning of social life at its very core. In a social environment scarred by recurrent national and international sociopolitical conflicts (including most recently a militant Islamic insurgence in the Cabo Delgado province beginning in 2019), people in northern Mozambique have become used to living through unstable times. But the infringement of community territories, the illegal cutting down of hardwood, and the control of labor relations by Chinese logging companies in collusion with local elites have caused more than momentary disturbances. Excessive natural resource extraction significantly reconfigures the workings of social life beyond a passing sense of disequilibrium. Nowhere is this clearer than in the interiorization of alterity whereby the growing appetite for hardwood in mainland China through a series of symbolic transformations has become sedimented in the minds and bodies of Mozambican tree scouts several thousand kilometers away. As such, the *olheiro* is the personification of a tension that is more than local and less than global, a tension that operates by constantly shifting the coordinates of peoples' relationship to one another and the territories they inhabit. The *olheiro* figure is inherently ambiguous; his relationship to the Chinese and how he acquires his almost occult capacity to find the much-coveted hardwood is unclear. In the ongoing process through which people in northern Mozambique try to figure out their relation to the land and the invisible and opaque forces that govern it, the *olheiro* has become the symbolic operator through which these seemingly irresolvable issues are worked out.

Bunkenborg and Nielsen returned to Pemba in 2012 with the intention of exploring the extent to which these forms of interiorized alterity might structure the wider Sino-Mozambican encounter. Since the "Colombo incident," Bunkenborg and Nielsen had worked on separate Chinese and Mozambican networks in Pemba. Not wanting to further hamper their possibilities for accessing crucial information (and informants), they had tacitly decided to stay out of each other's way and only rarely discussed in detail their ethnographic findings pertaining to the logging companies and their murky relationships to regional and national stakeholders and authorities. In keeping with this practice, Bunkenborg on his side now reconnected with Stanley, the CADEL manager, while Nielsen decided to approach the officials at the local branch of the Directorate of Land and Forests (DLF) in order to discuss the legislative framework with local timber agents. Soon, however, both Bunkenborg and Nielsen realized that their access to these and other crucial informants had been drastically reduced in comparison to their previous trip to the north. For more than a week, Nielsen returned every day to the DLF office in the hope of setting up appointments with active officials, but he never succeeded in speaking to any employee other than the front-office secretary. Making appointments with Mozambican officials is often an arduous process involving long hours of waiting in damp office halls, but this was the first time during more than eight years of ethnographic research in Mozambique that Nielsen had completely failed in making an appointment with officials working for a state department. During this frustrating period of refusals and deferrals, Nielsen also tried contacting two local timber companies; in both instances the outcome was as discouraging as with the DLF. Although Bunkenborg succeeded in setting up another meeting with Stanley and other Chinese working in the Pemba timber world, he also sensed that he was being kept politely at arm's length, and the conversations were little more than repetitions of things he already knew.

Six days after returning to Pemba, Nielsen had dinner with a local journalist who had investigated the weaknesses and growing illegalities of the Mozambican logging industry for many years. With overt frustration Nielsen explained the sudden lack of access to key informants in Pemba. The journalist paused and leaned toward Nielsen. "Perhaps there is no more information for you to get here. Colombo wasn't joking, you know. . . . He knows a lot of people in Pemba." As the journalist went on to explain, it was likely that Nielsen and Bunkenborg were meeting only closed doors as a direct consequence of having disappointed Colombo earlier on. Colombo was still collaborating with CADEL and other Chinese timber agents, but he had also recently initiated a parallel enterprise of selling hardwood to national timber merchants in Maputo in order to gain some independence from the Asian distributors. Whether Colombo found Bunkenborg and Nielsen's research activities interesting or not, he could not risk being associated with them. Being an influential and well-known figure in and around Pemba, he had probably advised his colleagues (Chinese and Mozambican) to avoid them as well. After a few more days with little or no progress, Bunkenborg and Nielsen packed up and returned to Maputo. Reluctantly, they had to admit that the journalist had been correct in concluding that "there is no more information for you to get here." Although it was impossible for them to know exactly how it had happened, their initial falling-out with Colombo had reverberated in the local social environment in such a way that this part of the research project was no longer feasible.

This collaborative collapse has implications for our wider arguments of collaborative damage in this book. While Bunkenborg and Nielsen's fieldwork and subsequent analyses had benefited from "productive misunderstandings" in Tsing's sense (2005) and shared ways of "getting it wrong" in other cases during their joint fieldwork in Mozambique (as in the case of the Maputo football stadium), the Colombo incident suggested a limit to this "method." During previous instances, new and vital anthropological insights had been gained from the mirroring within their own relationship as scientific collaborators of the external relationship between their Sino-Mozambican interlocutors. Through this obfuscation of the distinction between ethnographer and ethnography, the object of their study had infused the internal dynamics of their collaboration via a mimesis of the Sino-Mozambican tensions that they had been seeking to keep at what would normally be considered an appropriate analytical distance. But the Colombo incident led to no new analytical insights; far from being "productive," in the sense discussed earlier in this book, the misunderstandings between Bunkenborg and Nielsen led only to analytical dead ends. Could it be that this incident in northern Mozambique had provided them with a glimpse into the "dark side" of the Dual Perspective Approach (see figure 0.2) and anthropological collaboration more generally? Neither one felt that the incident in question—understood by Nielsen as an invasion by Bunkenborg of his research field and his relations of trust with his informants, and by Bunkenborg as an unfortunate leak of information that would probably have occurred anyway—had contributed productively to their joint research. Rather than generating new insights into the "intimate distances" between Mozambicans and Chinese, the incident had left a distinct form of intimate distance between them, one marked by a lack of dialogue and engagement with each other's findings. In the period following the Colombo incident, the relationship between Bunkenborg and Nielsen had become characterized by avoidance; they had worked hard to stay out of each other's way so as to do as little harm to one another's research as possible. As their respective fieldwork progressed, this strategy of avoidance became a way of structuring their collaboration. If Bunkenborg was in the midst of exploring a certain Chinese timber merchant, Nielsen would refrain from looking into these issues; considering instead other, sometimes less obviously relevant research trajectories. By adjusting their individual research activities so that they did not interfere or overlap, a distinct mode of collaborative ethos emerged that operated by deflection. A given issue or problem was made ethnographically visible and possible to study by one of the anthropologists through the other's deliberate deflection of his own ethnographic research away from the former's analytical agenda.

On their return to Maputo from the final trip to Pemba in 2012, Bunkenborg and Nielsen went to the same coffee shop where Nielsen had initially met up with Colombo. Having both tried in vain to put a happy spin on the logging case, Bunkenborg finally summed up the discussion. As he saw it, the Colombo incident produced a rule of avoidance that prompted his colleague to shift his research into the communities in the forest, while Bunkenborg remained ensconced in the Chinese compounds. It was only from these two vantage points that certain marginal figures like the "Chinese" Mozambicans and the "un-Chinese" Chinese became ethnographically visible to them. Instead of crossing back and forth between the two sides, Bunkenborg went on, "we were forced to take up positions in different camps, which enabled us to see how some Mozambicans and Chinese were crossing the lines—it was only from there that 'interior alterity' could emerge as a topic." "But how is that different from classic fieldwork?" Nielsen suddenly looked uncharacteristically tired. Pulling off his sunglasses, he called for the bill and ended the conversation. "Perhaps we should just conclude that in some instances of collaborative damage, the collaborative bits are less evident than the damage."

Conclusion

One person's infrastructure is another's difficulty.

—Susan Leigh Star, 1999

We are going to become a Chinese colony. An economic colony.

—Taxi driver, Ulaanbaatar, Mongolia

In the end, it was Nielsen who found it. Lying on its back in the bushes behind the National Museum of Art in Maputo, it looked like an exhausted giant that had finally found a shady place to rest at a comfortable distance from the city's hectic street life. The remarkable ten-meter-high sculpture of stainless steel had briefly stood tall and prominent in front of the entrance to the Chinese-built national stadium that we discussed in chapter 5, but it disappeared just before the opening ceremony. Over the following months, the hunt for the missing statue became a competitive side project for Nielsen and Bunkenborg as both of them began asking around, embarking on one wild goose chase after the other. Most of Bunkenborg's Chinese informants claimed that they had never heard of the statue; the construction company declined to comment upon the matter; at the consular office a junior employee tittered with embarrassment behind her hand and refused to say anything except that there had been "some sort of misunderstanding" (某种误解) about the statue. Bunkenborg finally struck gold when an official at the Ministry of Sports suggested he pay a visit to the National Museum of Art. After a thorough but futile search of the museum halls, Bunkenborg persuaded the museum guard to unlock the basement, where there was, in fact, a Chinese statue. It was not the ten-meter-high sculpture that once graced the entrance to the national football stadium, however, but a beautifully carved wooden statue of Guan Gong (关公), which had been moved there when the buildings and religious paraphernalia owned by the Chinese Association in Maputo were nationalized in 1975. While Bunkenborg was sidetracked

FIGURE 7.1.   The statue in the garden behind Mozambique's National Museum of Arts. May 2012.

by the story of the incarcerated god of war, Nielsen had also found his way to the museum. On this occasion, the guard suddenly remembered having witnessed "a huge metal thing" being off-loaded behind the museum at some point during the early months of 2011. After a quick inspection, Nielsen and the guard concluded that the statue was not in the backyard so they proceeded to check the wildly growing garden behind the museum building. And there it was! While neither the guard nor the museum inspectors knew anything about the complicated and (as we shall see) fraught history of the statue, including why it had ended up in the museum in the first place, they had decided that it would be too bothersome to have it transported to the junk yard. And so it happened that the *Spirit of Eternity* (永恒的精神), known to a bewildered Mozambican public as *The Chinese Goddess (Deusa Chinesa)*, ended up being dumped in the garden behind the National Museum of Arts.

We begin with this snapshot from Bunkenborg and Nielsen's quest to discover the whereabouts of the missing Chinese statue as a reminder of the overarching purpose of this book, namely, a comparative ethnographic study of Chinese globalization from the inside out, as the three of us witnessed, documented, and debated it over a decade of collaborative research and writing.

What originally prompted us to embark on this collaborative endeavor more than a decade ago was a series of questions about not just Chinese globalization but also about how one might study it ethnographically. How do Chinese nationals work with local people and state cadres and institutions in Mozambique and Mongolia, in and around resource extraction, construction, and trade? Can the sum of the countless and variegated Chinese projects around the globe be said to constitute an empire-in-the-making? Is it possible to conduct an ethnographic investigation of something as large as an emerging empire? As we have sought to demonstrate, "collaborative damage" is simultaneously the long and short answer to these questions. It is, on the one hand, the title of this anthropological monograph that presents the findings from an empirical study of Chinese globalization in the aftermath of the Great Recession. On the other hand, "collaborative damage" denotes a theoretical abstraction—a conceptual shorthand for the multifarious processes, practices, things, and discourses linking diverse participants in Chinese globalization—Chinese, Mozambican, Mongolian, and Danish—in intimately distant relations characterized by attraction, incomprehension, suspicion, desire, and repulsion. Before we conclude by summarizing what this focus on collaborative damage has taught us about China in the world, however, we return to the statue. Satisfying as it was for Bunkenborg and Nielsen to find the missing statue, it was also a somewhat pointless exercise, since the statue in and of itself could answer none of their broader questions. But if the statue itself had little to contribute to their individual and collaborative research, it was for almost a year the center of an escalating conflict at the Chinese football stadium project that came to encapsulate in condensed form some of the key traits of what we take collaborative damage to mean.

"A Lasting Monument to Eternal Friendship"

Thoroughly annoyed that it was Nielsen who succeeded in locating the missing statue, Bunkenborg attempted to deflate his colleague by dismissing the competitive hunt as an insignificant prank. In fact, Bunkenborg ventured, Nielsen's discovery of the statue and his photographs of its ignominious fate might even be counterproductive, because they provided a false ending to a larger, much more interesting story that continued to unfold. What was interesting about the statue was not the physical object itself but rather the way its appearance affected the Chinese and Mozambican nationals working on the football stadium construction project and the ways it continued to reverberate across various Sino-Mozambican relations even after it was removed. The story of the statue,

Bunkenborg insisted, was inherently collaborative and open-ended, and accordingly this was how it should be written.

The "Bunkenborgesque" version of the story began with the arrival of several large wooden containers from China at customs control in Maputo harbor during the summer of 2009. Unlike other shipments destined for the national stadium, the wooden containers had not previously been registered at the Ministry of Sports, nor had the Chinese engineers at the construction site informed their Mozambican counterparts of their arrival. Even more puzzling, however, was the content of the wooden containers. According to the ministry officer present at the customs office when the first box was opened, it contained several curved pieces of stainless steel. "I knew immediately that it was certainly not something to be used by the engineers," the officer told Nielsen. "It looked more like something that belonged in a Chinese church, I suppose." Still, since the metal pieces appeared entirely harmless, a decision was made to resolve the issue swiftly; the wooden containers were formally registered and transported to the construction site. The mystery of the containers was soon forgotten, but over the summer a massive cement pedestal coated in black marble was erected in the middle of the huge square in front of the stadium building. A white marble plaque with an inscription in both Chinese and Portuguese, praising the eternal friendship between China and Mozambique, was placed in front. A ten-meter-high statue made of the pieces of curved stainless steel that the ministry official first saw at the Maputo harbor a few weeks earlier was set atop the pedestal.

The public consternation caused by the appearance of an enormous "Chinese Goddess" in front of the national stadium came as a complete surprise to the Chinese engineers working at the football stadium. Even if the statue's eight arms did have a superficial resemblance to representations of Guanyin, the goddess of mercy, the sculptor, Xu Xiaohong (徐晓虹), apparently intended the statue as an abstract symbol of enduring friendship. On an earlier visit to Mozambique, he had described his art as a conduit for mutual understanding and proclaimed that "the sweat of hard work has irrigated the friendship between China and Mozambique. I made many Chinese and Mozambican friends there and the friendship between us was linked up through the artwork" (Xu 2003, 56). This time, however, the alien and possibly religious iconography of his sculpture suggested a complete misreading of Mozambican political aesthetics. The sculptor came to realize that his statue was not so much an emblem of friendship as a catalyst for fundamental and divisive misunderstandings between Chinese and Mozambican collaborators.

"I could see right away that something was wrong!" Paulino Coelho, a municipal architect and member of the national steering committee for the stadium, told Nielsen. "I really have no idea what goes on inside their heads! Because we had never asked them to build that thing, you know. Never! But then again, that just proved to us what working with the Chinese is like. They nod at everything we say but then, when it is time for action, they end up doing something altogether different and strange (*estranho*). The Chinese, . . . I tell you, they are a mystery (*mistério*) to me!" The statue had not been described in any blueprint or mentioned in official documents before it was suddenly revealed in front of the stadium, and Coelho and his colleagues had questioned their Chinese counterparts to no avail. "They just don't want to communicate," Coelho sneered. "They know it's wrong, but they see Africa as their private playground. That's probably why they seem to think that they can do whatever they want." Nielsen suggested that a workable solution might be simply to incorporate the statue within the existing plan based on its aesthetic or symbolic qualities, but this suggestion was flatly refused. In no way did the statue evoke national Mozambican symbolism, and its blatant voluptuousness and goddess-like curves suggested something quite alien. "In Mozambique, we don't worship religious things like that," Coelho argued frantically. "That is simply too much!" So, the statue had to be removed—preferably as soon as possible. Removing the statue was, however, not as easy as the Mozambican officials had first imagined. From the ministry's minutes, it appears that the subject of the statue was brought up at nearly every meeting with the Chinese engineers, but all kinds of problems continued to postpone its removal. (Nielsen could not get copies of the minutes, but state officials allowed him to go through them while taking notes). Several blueprints existed, but only the Chinese versions contained descriptions of the statue. Consequently, the Chinese engineers steadfastly maintained that confirmation from the company headquarters in China was required before removal of the statue could be initiated. The Mozambican officials demanded to inspect the Chinese blueprints until they realized that everything was written in Chinese; their strategy soon reverted to polite political pressure and forceful argumentation. It was during this period of tense negotiations over the statue that many Mozambican officials realized what their Chinese counterparts were really up to. "It's all going to be China here," a municipal surveyor told Nielsen and Bunkenborg during a visit to the football stadium. "They build walls around their construction sites, and when they open the doors again, it's all China with their statues and silly hats. This is exactly the stuff that we need to avoid, you know." Nevertheless, despite the explicitly stated demand to have the statue removed, for the next several months it remained in front of the stadium building as a physical reminder of the fraught relationships between Chinese engineers and Mozambican officials.

Amid the rising tension over the "Chinese Goddess," Xu Xiaohong visited Mozambique to oversee the installation of his works at the stadium. According to a biography by Wu Xianfei (伍先飞), the sculptor insisted on visiting the construction site on September 1, 2010, and was surprised to see that "none of the workers on the construction site were working. Instead, they were arguing in small groups about something that Xu Xiaohong didn't understand. When the workers saw him, they weren't cordial as they used to be and the expression in their eyes seemed different" (Wu 2017). Xu Xiaohong noticed that there was thick, dark smoke rising in the vicinity. Suddenly the sound of gunfire and explosions around the stadium made the workers throw down their tools and rush out "as if they had taken stimulants" (Wu 2017). Making his way to the top of the stadium through smoke and tear gas, the sculptor looked out on a city where demonstrators and police clashed around numerous makeshift roadblocks made from burning vehicles and felled trees. Counting himself lucky that the stadium was walled and that the police were still guarding the gate, he stayed there until nightfall. In the evening the Chinese embassy persuaded the Mozambican police to escort the sculptor to the airport, and he was extracted by three cars and twelve officers. Threading their way through roadblocks and burning vehicles in a city without electricity, their cars were rocked by firebombs and peppered with bullets along the way, but after four hours they reached the airport unscathed, and the Chinese sculptor made his escape. After describing the general strike as something akin to a full-blown civil war, the biography adds, "After his return, Xu Xiaohong learned that in addition to factors internal to Mozambique, one of the important reasons behind the riots might well [have been] that that opposition party in Mozambique was extremely displeased that a giant statue in front of the national stadium was made by a Chinese. They claimed that the statue was a hidden Chinese cultural influence that eroded their culture" (Wu 2017).[1]

Despite the general strike, the statue was still in place in 2011 as the date for the formal delivery of the football stadium from the Chinese to the Mozambican government was drawing near. The local officials were becoming increasingly frustrated. "We had to get rid of it," Paulino Coelho explained to Nielsen. "Imagine the president having to walk past a Chinese goddess on the inauguration night. He could just as well hand over his country to the Chinese ambassador!" When the project was finally handed over, however, the Mozambican dignitaries were met by the impressive sight of the ten-meter-high metal statue still gracing the entrance.

Having realized that they could not force their Chinese counterparts to remove the statue, the Mozambican officials decided to wait until the project was formally handed over to them and then quickly remove both statue and pedestal. Not long after the ceremonial delivery of the project, Mozambican workers quickly removed the metal statue and began to take down the black marble over the pedestal only to realize that its base was made of cement. Two options were considered: use heavy equipment to tear the base apart, possibly destroying parts of the surrounding square that had been carefully covered by flagstones, or simply leave the pedestal where it was.

On April 23, 2011, the new National Stadium of Mozambique, with seating for 42,000 spectators, was inaugurated by President Armando Guebuza and a delegation from the Chinese embassy. The stadium gradually filled in anticipation of the evening's main event, a football match between Mozambique and Tanzania. More than 1200 school children lined up on the grass, some dressed in multicolored sports clothing and some equipped with masks, spears, and shields in preparation for a traditional dance. After the president's brief opening, the Chinese ambassador delivered a fifteen-minute-long speech in fluent Portuguese, praising the collaborative spirit pervading all phases of the construction process. "With efficiency and hard work," he bellowed with more than a hint of the socialist jargon so familiar to most Mozambicans, "we have created a lasting monument to the eternal friendship between our two nations."

FIGURE 7.2. The Chinese ambassador speaking at the inaugural ceremony of Mozambique's National Football Stadium. The photo is taken at the precise moment when the projector system broke down and the monitors showed a screen saver image of colorful flowers. April 2010.

Impressive and pompous as the opening ceremony was, it was not free of glitches. Just when the Chinese ambassador shouted his message of eternal friendship, the huge monitors at each end of the stadium suddenly went black and then displayed a screensaver of colorful interlaced flowers (see figure 7.2). This sparked a great deal of mirth among the audience. Until the problem was fixed a few minutes later, every shift of the screensaver image was followed by a rhythmic and surprisingly enthusiastic chant of "China!" that somehow seemed more derisive than celebratory. In keeping with his role as a critic of all things Chinese, Nielsen took an almost perverse pleasure in the jeering. Losing no opportunity to point out to Bunkenborg every little crack in the stadium walls, claiming that they were caused by "the poor quality of the cement imported from China," Nielsen had a field day when it became apparent that there was an equally disturbing—although more entertaining—problem with the weak metal structures supporting the plastic seats at the stadium. Nearly all the seats in the VIP area collapsed during the inauguration night, and the plastic wreckage was scattered throughout the spacious aisles where the party elite had been sitting. "Our bosses are too fat," Nielsen's friend Fernando Sitoe said with a deadpan expression. "The Chinese are all so small and bony. They only build chairs for themselves—not for us." Any mention of the statue was studiously avoided by both Mozambican and Chinese participants, but as Bunkenborg and Nielsen filed out of the stadium through the main entrance that evening, it was immediately apparent that the pedestal in the floodlights at the entrance was in fact empty. It was then that they decided that the *Spirit of Eternity* had to be found.

When the hunt for the missing statue came to a successful end and Bunkenborg was trying to curb Nielsen's gloating, he pointed out that finding the statue was actually of little significance and that the story would keep rolling even in its absence. As an iconic form of contentious materiality, the statue's brief appearance and subsequent disappearance from its pedestal in front of the stadium served, he suggested, as an anchor for an accumulation of Sino-Mozambican misunderstandings that had not so much been resolved as unleashed with its removal to a forgotten corner of a museum garden. Much to the surprise of Bunkenborg and even to himself, Nielsen grudgingly agreed with his fellow ethnographer for once. Still, it was not so much Bunkenborg's arguments as a field trip to Maputo in 2012 that finally convinced Nielsen of the enduring significance of the statue. During a meeting with Sérgio, a municipal surveyor who had been involved in the construction project since the beginning, Nielsen noticed a small, framed photo of Armando Guebuza, the Mozambican president, taken just as he bent forward to read the inscription on the pedestal. Nielsen nodded toward the photo, and Sérgio picked it up with a grin on his face. "Yeah, our president is making *ku phahla*[2] in honor of his Chinese ancestors. . . . Didn't you see it?" Oftentimes, when the president visits important national sites, he commemorates local ancestral spirits by making a *ku phahla* ceremony with local leaders. According to Sérgio's interpretation, rather than merely reading the inscription, the Mozambican president was honoring the Chinese goddess, which thereby acquired the status of a spiritual force. A few days later, Nielsen described to Paulino Coelho what Sérgio had suggested. Coelho roared with laughter. "Yeah, man! Guebuza is our Chinese president, that's for sure. Didn't you also hear the Chinese ambassador?" Coelho continued. "His Portuguese was better than my mother's. Well, that's just strange. Now people are saying that Guebuza also speaks Chinese. . . . I mean, . . . What is going on (*o que passa*)?"

In many ways, the story of the *Spirit of Eternity* encapsulates the central argument of this book. As an iconic example of a particularly tense "zone of awkward engagement" in Anna Tsing's terms (2005), the tragicomic tale of the erection and subsequent removal of the statue from the square in front of the national football stadium in Maputo offers an apt illustration of the "intimate distances" that characterized relations between Chinese and locals during the period of our research. At the same time, the case represents a paradigmatic example of

FIGURE 7.3.   The statue-less pedestal that still graces the entrance to the football stadium. September 2014.

"collaborative damage." Starting with a seemingly trivial faux pas concerning the desirability of symbolic ornamentation, misunderstandings between Chinese and Mozambicans escalated to a point where they divided up and, by so doing, structured an entire social field, affecting not just the Chinese and local interlocutors directly involved in the project but also the ethnographers documenting this process. Despite their initial plan to document all aspects of the unfolding case study and develop a collective interpretation of it, Bunkenborg and Nielsen got tired of the limited perspectives of the other and as their efforts to locate the missing statue became more competitive, their collaboration became little more than a polite pretense.

For the three of us, the fact that the collaboration between Chinese and locals turned out to be far from seamless was hardly a shocking discovery, but the realization that the repercussions of these misunderstandings and tensions reverberated within our team and came to recalibrate the dynamics of our internal relations was truly unexpected. Indeed, as we have shown in the preceding six chapters, the collapse of the distinction between ethnographic discoveries (data) and collaborative research approach (methodology) recurred with different intensity and consequence across all our case studies of Chinese globalization. As such, the story of the statue has a wider relevance, not just for Sino-local encounters in Mozambique, Mongolia, and elsewhere, but also for social scientific collaboration.

Collaborative Damage

As middle-aged, male, white, heterosexual anthropologists from Denmark, the three of us have obviously been provided with a particular perspective on and positioning in the world that is at one and the same time enormously privileged, extremely limited, and irreversibly and uncomfortably tarnished by Western (including Danish) legacies of colonialism. We have made no secret of these challenges. By inserting ourselves into the narrative in ways that may have come across as if making a virtue of our naivety, ignorance, and sometimes plain selfishness and egoism, we have sought to insert into the analytical narrative an explicit self-critique of the biases inherent in this research setup. But there has also been an important if unexpected side effect of this almost perverse socioeconomic sameness and cultural homogeneity that took us by surprise and that we have therefore made a concerted effort to register. We are referring to the persistent undercurrent to this book's chapters, namely our accounts of and reflections about our own mutual positioning and relationships as researchers, including the growing disagreements among us, which came to significantly affect the ways that we envisioned the project's analytical and methodological challenges and potentials. Through the fault lines reflected by our different language skills, previous fieldwork experiences, and theoretical proclivities, we have sought to highlight (again, indeed make a virtue of) how the accelerating positional divergences that emerged in the course of our collaboration led key characteristics of what we experienced as Chinese globalization to be incorporated and reenacted within our research team itself.

While this insight turned out to be the key that unlocked our analysis and our understanding of Chinese globalization, it did not arise from a series of detached analytical deliberations conducted from the safe haven of the office or the armchair. It was only when we realized that we were ourselves invariably caught in the same webs of tensions, misunderstandings, and ambiguities that tied Chinese and locals together in particular configurations of intimate distances that the theme of "collaborative damage" became an overarching concern that guided our ongoing research activities. By sticking to the fixed analytical scale delineated by the Dual Perspective Approach (DPA), we ended up with significant ethnographic data that denies rather than confirms the commensurability between the different social realities that we studied both individually and collectively. It has been by keeping one analytical scale steady through a series of consecutive events that we have come to identify the noncomparability of the same ethnographic phenomena that initially seemed to lend themselves to comparison. If the DPA design turned out to be too rigid a methodological device for doing this collaborative research, it was perhaps our insistence on using it that turned out to be the most "productive misunderstanding" of all. It was because we stubbornly attempted to organize our comparative and collaborative efforts into a neat tripartite structure of separate fieldwork, imagined as touching only tangentially along the edges, that we discovered an unforeseen analytical possibility at the core of our collaborative project, namely, the fact that our own internal disagreements and misunderstandings could be a point of departure for further anthropological insights and new comparative knowledge—not an aberration to be eradicated. Instead of being dismissed as excrescent aberrations from failed meetings or mediations between preexisting cultural forms, the social and material disconnections at the heart of this book can be conceived of as being constitutive of a particular kind of fraught and awkward relationality, which we have conceptualized as "intimately distant."

During our joint research in Mozambique and Mongolia, we gradually came to realize that the very procedures whereby we attempted to wrest from local ethnographic contexts analytical concepts that, according to conventional understanding of inductive and comparative methods, ought to allow us to develop a more general account of a global Chinese empire in the making severed from all local relational contexts, were themselves part of our primary object of study. What gradually dawned upon us was that the relational forms we had sought to extract from the mesh of social life did not offer coherent conceptual configurations that seamlessly replicated themselves; instead, they were, to use Paul Rabinow's (2007, 39) expression, a "space of problems" that sustained incommensurable positions in their incommensurability within an often dysfunctional and conflict-ridden relational infrastructure. Across our different empirical data sets and analytical insights, we found a capacity for maintaining difference and detachment, but we were incapable of merging this insight into broader generalizations.

As such the concept of intimate distances and its sister concept of collaborative damage are nothing more than heuristic analytical props devised by the three of us to denote awkward relationships and real or latent conflicts between our Chinese, Mozambican, and Mongolian interlocutors as well as among ourselves. As much as suggesting a possible analytical trajectory, these concepts have served as a reminder of the absent holism that we have structured the project around. Through the realization that misunderstandings were not to be avoided but emphasized and further intensified, our research project ceased to be guided by the overall ambition of constructing a unified scaffold that would somehow bring our different ethnographic sets of data together. By systematically focusing on the relational strategies of our interlocutors—but always abstaining from generating any ethnographic or analytical whole detached from these—we have tried to operationalize a dynamic, nonlinear analytic scale that was not independent of our data. Small wonder, then, that we eventually had to discard any ambition of generating a holistic account integrating and generalizing our different data sets into a tightly knit analytical whole. In acknowledging our blatant failure to generate self-similar data sets via the DPA research design, we also noticed that our mutual misunderstandings and tendencies to get each other wrong (and to get in each other's way) reverberated in ways surprisingly similar to what we were witnessing among our interlocutors. There was a symmetrical incommensurability to our misunderstandings that ended up being constitutive to our wider analysis. By keeping our analytical gaze fixed on the same abstract object (Chinese globalization), while laterally extending and expanding our insights and concepts from one ethnographical context to another (Boyer and Howe 2015), a series of productive incommensurabilities came into being between our individual positions and our joint fieldwork in Mozambique and Mongolia.

Our insights about globalizing China have emerged from a constant process of shifting back and forth between two analytical modalities that have permeated and continued to relativize each other as they shifted from figure to ground and back. For all intents and purposes, the distinction between theory and method ended up collapsing, opening up instead a different way of doing ethnographic descriptions and anthropological analyses, where endemic misunderstandings and irresolvable disagreements became the main object of study. We might go as far as suggesting that the ultimate unit of study in this book is not just misunderstandings, but misunderstandings *of misunderstandings* (see also Wagner 1981). Our interlocutors often disagreed, and sometimes they even seemed to disagree about what they disagreed about. More often than not, these individuals or groups of Chinese, Mongolians, and Mozambicans entertained radically divergent perspectives about what mattered in their mutual relationship, sometimes to the point where they appeared to fundamentally disagree about the quality and nature of this social relationship, or indeed any social relationship. Then, these relationships between our interlocutors were also perceived and interpreted in fundamentally different ways by us as researchers. In light of this doubling and repetition of the form of their relationships among our relationships, we could reverse another apt formulation by Roy Wagner (1981, 20) and argue that while their misunderstandings of us are not the same as our misunderstandings of them, we did misunderstand each other with similar intensity so that their misunderstandings of us are also at the same time our misunderstandings of them.

To many readers who do not happen to be committed to the discipline of anthropology and its recent theoretical and methodological debates, the above deliberations may come across as obtuse navel-gazing. We have insisted on including them because they bring home what we take to be this book's greatest insight. It is the nature of this finding that defines our approach and analysis as fundamentally different from that of Ching Kwan Lee and other social or political scientists who have sought to theorize about China's political-economic intervention in Africa and elsewhere in the Global South since the turn of the millennium. The truth about contemporary Chinese globalization, and its future imperial potentialities, is not just located "out there." It is also and has been since the beginning of our collaborative endeavor, present between and within the three of us. We too are the Chinese empire, but we only found out—we only discovered the secret of globalizing China—when we started arguing about it!

If "collaborative damage" and "intimate distances" have been the two overarching concepts we have developed and deployed to probe into the heart of Chinese interventions in Mozambique and Mongolia, their capacity for capturing key facets of a Chinese empire derives as much from how this analysis came to be written as what it ended up being written about. The foregoing meta-methodological and meta-analytical reflection has not just reminded us about the fundamentally situated nature of ethnographic and all other social science research. It also shows why and how a bottom-up ethnographic study of a handful of different empirical cases can give unique insight into the nature of globalization.

Imperial Potentialities

In the introduction we promised to tackle some issues: Is there a sense in which the growing Chinese political-economic intervention in the Global South that took its beginning around the turn of the millennium amounts to a new empire in the making, and if so, what kind of empire would this be? We now offer a distinctly anthropological answer. First of all, we believe it is reasonable to conclude that there *are* specific characteristics and logics to contemporary Chinese globalization, and that one *can* speak of a Chinese empire in the making. As we have shown, contemporary Chinese globalization amounts to a unique relational infrastructure that is manifest in specific social and material forms. In that sense, we may define the incipient Chinese empire as a social and material "hyper-object" (Morton 2013) that comes into being when mishaps and minor disagreements—often tied to material props and vestiges such as statues, roads, envelopes, tree trunks, and walls—escalate to a point where they make erstwhile collaborators intimately distant, locked in intense and asymmetrical relations of mutual incomprehension. We have found the defining features of Chinese globalization and empire to depart in equal measure from the breezy laissez-faire image of empire espoused by conservative historians like Niall Ferguson and from the poststructuralist anticapitalists like Hardt and Negri. Both these models of empire also put great emphasis on the unintentional and decentralized aspects of past and present imperial formations. But what we have presented fundamentally diverges from this and other social and political scientific scholarship on empire. Other scholars of empire (from Gibbon to the Marxists to recent scholarship about empire) have hardly been oblivious of the role of conflict and contradiction in the making and the unmaking of imperial polities, historical or contemporary. What makes our account of empire stand out is the extent to which we have treated contradictions, conflicts, and constraints as integral to the meaning of this concept, rather than as something it is affected by and refracted through. To illustrate this point, compare our approach and findings with one of the few—if not the only—other ethnographic studies of Chinese globalization, Ching Kwan Lee's *The Specter of Global China: Politics, Labor, and Foreign Investment in Africa* (2017).

In *The Specter of Global China*, Lee presents not just a detailed ethnography of Chinese mining and construction projects in Zambia but a broader theoretical argument about the public and scholarly debate on China in Africa and its wider ramifications. Rather than siding with prevailing interpretations of the Chinese presence in Africa as either concerted neocolonialism or run-of-the-mill exploitative capitalism, she asks, "Is Chinese state capital a different kind of capital?" (26). Lee's response is that this is indeed the case since it prioritizes political capital over immediate profits, stable production over speculative windfalls, and a management ethos characterized by ascetic collectivism over individual careerism.[3] On the face of it, this argument is close to ours. In several of our case studies, we have presented the reader with the image of a highly centralized and planned mode of state capitalist production less focused on agility, leanness, and surplus than on stability, harmony, and demand. On closer inspection, however, there are substantial differences between Lee's findings and ours. For one thing Lee does not want to label the Chinese presence in Africa as an empire. As she puts it, "Rather than hastily applying an ill-defined concept purporting to be a historical formation that is out of proportion to the contemporary phenomenon at hand, a more productive strategy is to recognize outbound state investment from China for what it is—a type of capital" (154). Willfully ignoring what is undeniably heavy theoretical baggage and conceptual plasticity, we have used the concept "empire" heuristically to capture the spatiotemporal particularities of a global configuration of social and material forms and forces that crystallize, sediment, and coalesce as particular infrastructure and resource extraction projects abroad adapt—or fail to adapt—to local imponderabilia and global market flows.

Secondly, Lee's approach represents a fundamentally different understanding of the relationship between ethnography and theory in anthropological analysis. For Lee, the purpose with ethnographic data is to provide empirical support for general inferences about an object of study (Chinese globalization, capital, etc.), whose nature is imagined to exist independently of the form of inquiry at hand. By contrast, as we gradually allowed the ethnographic investigation and its mishaps to define the parameters of our analysis, we made a point and a virtue of collapsing the boundary between analytical object and analyzing subject. While *The Specter of Global China* traces Chinese globalization back to a general and single logic of Chinese state capital subsequently inflected by local forms of "eventful capitalism," here we have sought instead to develop an analytics that can move along with the nonlinear dynamics of Chinese globalization as its paradoxical form takes shape from concurrent sociomaterial processes in different parts of the globe. Importantly, many of the differently positioned agents contributing to this potential empire in the making are also struggling (even more intensely, perhaps, than we) to figure out what exactly it is that they are part of.

In this way our study is different from not just Lee's account of Chinese globalization but also from recent social and political scholarship on past and present empires. Far from being imbued with the seamless, invisible, and spectral features so often associated with the flow and potency of capital in the late twentieth century, the incipient Chinese empire whose form we have unearthed is characterized by *not* fitting more or less seamlessly and invisibly into its surroundings. Clearly, the infrastructure and resource extraction projects studied by us in Mozambique and Mongolia are a far cry from the ghostly shadows of global capital theorized by neo-Marxist anthropologists (e.g., Comaroff and Comaroff 1999). On the contrary, the Chinese footprint on local communities and places and sometimes entire national economies in the Global South, is, in our rendering, hypervisible and maybe even hyperreal: what makes globalizing China distinct from other past and present empires in Africa and inner Asia is the fact that it is *too* visible. Think back on some of the starkest, strangest, and most troublesome images conveyed over the preceding pages, including not just the "not-road" with which we began this book, but also the pompous gates with inscriptions in Chinese letters that greeted us whenever we entered the detached worlds of Chinese enclaves in the Gobi Desert and the forests of Cabo Delgado. Globalizing China is not so much "empty" as overly "full" (Bunkenborg and Bregnbæk 2017). Indeed, the first thing that comes to mind here is not exactly the "shadowy" or "spectral" quality of global China. In many ways we are left with precisely the opposite impression: loud, clunky, and imposing material forms that do not so much operate under the surface as on top of it.

* * *

As we write, the world is battling the consequences of the Covid-19 pandemic and entering an era of new economic and political uncertainties. Little more than a decade has passed since we began our ethnographic study on Chinese globalization, but we now live in a very different time with different problems (health, race, climate). Considering that this study began against the backdrop of the 2008 financial crisis and the great recession that followed in its wake, it is nonetheless oddly, maybe even morbidly appropriate that our collaborative project reaches its end as the world is thrown into a new major crisis that threatens to take millions of lives and to disrupt and shatter families across the globe. As national economies grind to a halt, national borders shut down, and geopolitical relations and alliances are reshuffled, China could once again emerge from the crisis one step ahead. The fact that China seemingly contained the outbreak where many democracies failed is touted by its government as another clear sign of the superiority of the Chinese model. The near-collapse of health care systems in some parts of the United States and Europe has featured prominently in state media along with stories of donations of Chinese medical equipment flown to distant countries in need. "The pandemic won't make China the world's leader" a headline in *Foreign Affairs* insisted (Green and Medeiros 2020), as if the authors were trying to make a case against an already established fact.

While China's ostensibly successful fight against the virus inspired admiration in some corners of the globe, many politicians and media in the United States and Europe were eager to criticize the belated reporting of the virus and the draconian measures taken by the Chinese government. But the tough Western stance towards China was evident long before the Covid-19 outbreak. The first attempts toward a decoupling of Chinese and Western economies have been underway for some time as the political pushback against China gained traction both in the United States and the European Union. The recent trade war between the United States and China that started in 2018; the labeling of China as a "systemic rival" by the European Union in 2019; Western support for the Hong Kong protests, including the recent British offer of citizenship to several millions of Hong Kong residents; and President Trump's threat to "cut off the whole relationship" all indicate an increasingly volatile geopolitical climate, which the belligerent rhetoric from China's new coterie of "wolf warrior" diplomats coupled with the Trump administration's hardliners only fuel further. Some might be tempted to predict that we are entering an era of deglobalization where tariffs, borders, public-health concerns, and political ill will make it impossible for China to become the new empire it seemed on track to become a decade ago when public and private Chinese investors were "buying up Africa" and other parts of the world. Based on our findings, we predict the very opposite. Rather than slowing down the speed and the impact of Chinese globalization, endemic tensions and fraught relations will continue to be the means by which a Chinese empire is brought into being.

Notes

INTRODUCTION

1. The text to the right of the gate listed the company values: Trustworthy, law-abiding, united and dedicated; truthful, pragmatic, pioneering and innovative (诚信 守法 团结 奉献 求真 务实 开拓 创造). The vertical couplet was strange even in Chinese: Greatly unfold an imposing presence overseas (展海外雄风，大也). Plant the great tree of monumental achievement in Mozambique (树莫桑丰碑，巨木).

2. Joining the chorus of anxious pundits, the *Economist* in November 2010 launched a front cover to the same effect: "Buying up the World: The Coming Wave of Chinese Take-overs."

3. As Peter Nolan (2012) points out, the sum total of Chinese investments abroad has been dwarfed by the share of the Chinese economy controlled by foreign companies. Using figures from 2010, David Shambaugh (2013) notes that the OFDI of US $68.8 billion from China pales in comparison to the 328.9 billion from the United States and that the US $317 billion worth of foreign assets owned by Chinese companies was a far cry from the US $4 trillion of OFDI stock accumulated by US companies (179).

4. The *New York Times* (2007) chimed in by describing China as "the patron of African misgovernment" and criticizing its support for Mugabe's rule in Zimbabwe and its oil investments in war-torn Sudan. United by a paroxysm of China anxiety, journalists from both ends of the political spectrum settled on a simplistic narrative of "an essentially well-intentioned West (Dr. Livingstone), and the amoral, greedy, and coldly indifferent Chinese (Fu Manchu) battling over a corrupt and/or helpless Africa (the Dark Continent)." (Mawdsley 2008).

5. Not surprisingly, things did not exactly turn out in this way. While the mining sector added a big boost to the Mongolian economy in the decade from 2005 to 2015, it also brought economic imbalances and insecurities familiar from other resource-extraction-dependent countries (Baatarzorig, Galindev, and Maisonnave 2015) and a severely negative environmental impact (Farrington 2015; McIntyre et al. 2016). For more ethnographic details on the political, economic, and environmental ramifications of the booms and bust of the Mongolian economy, see High 2017; Plueckhahn and Dulam 2018; Abrahms-Kavunenko 2019; Empson 2020; Dulam 2020; Plueckhahn 2020. See also Højer and Pedersen 2019.

6. Identical figures about Chinese FDI in Mongolia are hard to come by, but these numbers are mentioned in several sources, including Javzandorj and Dehong (2012), and World Economics (2011). Interestingly, there is a substantial discrepancy between the figures reported by the Chinese Ministry of Commerce and the figures reported by the Mongolian National Chamber of Industry and Commerce (MNCIC); the figures provided by the latter are 30–40 percent higher for the period between 2004 and 2010. In an article citing both Chinese and Mongolian statistics Fang Fang and Tumenqiqige (2010) speculate that many of the Chinese companies investing in Mongolia are probably individually owned or small- and medium-size enterprises that have not registered their investments with the authorities in China. Mongolian statistics indicate that 51 percent of the cumulative FDI into Mongolia from 1990 to 2010 came from China. By mid-2012 China's share of the cumulative FDI dropped to 31.71 percent as more than US $4 billion was poured into Mongolia from RioTinto in conjunction with the construction of the massive Oyo Tolgoi gold and copper mine. Even so, China was still the greatest investor in Mongolia

at the time of Bunkenborg and Pedersen's fieldwork. In terms of foreign companies registered in Mongolia, it also ranked first. In the period from 1990 to mid-2012, 49 percent (5951) of the foreign companies registered in Mongolia were Chinese. Statistics from the period 1990–2008 suggest that the majority, 64.75 percent, registered as "trade and catering services," 5.06 percent as "engineering, construction, and production of construction materials," and only 2.55 percent as "geological prospecting, oil exploration, and mining." However, mining was—and still is—where the real money was invested. "Geological prospecting, oil exploration, and mining" thus accounted for 67.43 percent, "trade and catering services" for 20.84 percent, and "engineering, construction, and production of construction materials" for 2.15 percent.

7. Rather than participating in high-profile mining projects involving so-called strategic deposits (such as the controversial Oyo Tolgoi mine that has been hyped as the world's biggest untapped gold-and-copper deposit, Chinese FDI in Mongolia has been focused on the purchase of small- and medium-sized mines and firms (although there are exceptions, including the PetroChina oil field discussed in chapter 3). However, with the economic downturn from 2012, the Mongolian government began "welcom[ing] Chinese state-owned enterprises, i.e., Shenhua Group, Sinopec Group, China National Petroleum Corporation, and Chalco, investing in major mining and developmental projects . . . [having] previously been reluctant to approve large-scale investments from China" (Mendee 2015).

8. Additional examples from other interviews include the following: Example 1: "The members of parliament and other leaders are robbing us of our wealth in collaboration with businessmen and foreign companies. Our resources are being sold at a price that is far too low. Around here, the price of coal is MT 150,000 per ton, but in China it is sold for RMB 300–500, I have heard. Why is it so cheap here? Some people—Chinese—are making a lot of money, which ought to go to the Mongolian people! There are only three million of us, and they are two billion people. So why are we selling our land so cheaply? I wonder why this is so, and I wonder about what our members of parliament are doing" (herdsman from Central Gobi province, August 2010). Example 2: "All the goods sold at our markets are from China. Some Chinese traders told me, 'We will occupy you soon.' When I asked why, they said because Mongolia has no factories. It made me think a lot, and I realized they are right" (minibus driver, September 2011).

9. As he elaborates, "Some scholars have argued that the general Chinese ethical principle appears the same as the western Golden Rule, but it differs essentially in the philosophical presuppositions wherein western philosophy sees in terms of subjectivity, but the Chinese in terms of other-ness. The Bible's golden rule, 'do unto others as you would have them do to you' sounds promising, but it would encounter challenges and difficulties when other hearts are taken into account. The other-ness of the other heart is something absolute and transcendent, so the other heart might reasonably want a different life. In terms of other-ness, the Chinese ethical principle thus runs: 'let others reach their goals if you reach yours. . . .' Here we see the difference between the western and Chinese ethics: western philosophy sees humanity through the eyes of subjectivity, while the Chinese sees it through the eyes of other-ness" (Zhao, 2006, 35–36).

10. One of the earliest and to this date most sophisticated attempts to offer a remedy to this impoverished theorization of relationships within anthropology and cognate disciplines is the so-called New Melanesian Ethnography (NME) promulgated by Roy Wagner (1972, 1977), Marilyn Strathern (1988, 1999), and followers (Leach 2003; Reed 2004; Crook 2007; Mosko 2010; for two recent overviews, see Holbraad and Pedersen 2017; Strathern 2020). Far from representing, as some critics have suggested (Bessire and Bond 2014), an antirelational perspective, NME explorations of "relations that separate"

(Strathern 1988), seek to widen the concept of the relation to encompass also those forms of social engagements (such as antagonisms, conflicts, or mutual disinterestedness) that cannot be described as "connections" in the simplified and, one might argue, fetishized sense (Pedersen 2013) favored by many anthropologists and sociologists. Still, there are inevitable limitations to the NME model, including the fact that discontinuity and instability tend to be sidelined at the expense of continuity and stability (Robbins 2007; Højer & Pedersen 2019). Indeed, while the possibility for exploring radically heterogeneous and capricious social forms of the sort encountered by us in Mozambique and Mongolia is certainly present in this approach, most relational anthropologists (barring a few such as Kelly 2011; Nielsen 2011; Walford 2012; Pedersen 2017) have done research in tribal and rural contexts, and no one has to our knowledge done a systematic comparative study of something as "big" as globalizing China and related imperial imaginaries.

11. We deliberately write dynamics in the plural, as we take to be an open-ended ethnographic question what it means for something to be intimately distant in a given context. Indeed, it is possible to identify a raft of relational forms in our data that in their own way adhere to the above definition but are at the same time imbued with so much specificity that they call for further theoretical deliberation. Other examples and kinds of intimate distances may be thus identified in the gifts and offers of friendship proffered by Chinese investors in both Mongolia and Mozambique (chapters 1 and 5), just as various seemingly mundane artifacts—such as paycheck envelopes used by Chinese managers in Mozambique (chapter 5) and in Mongolian road projects (chapter 3)—will emerge as material instantiations of and scaffolds for intimate distances. Put together, this catalogue of intimate distances adds up to a relational infrastructure amounting to the "mode of existence" (Latour 2013) of an potential Chinese empire. Of course, another study done elsewhere at another time by another team of scholars would produce another catalogue of intimate distances and thus also another relational infrastructure. Nevertheless, in our capricious constellation of partly disconnected fieldwork events and data sets gathered over a decade of often fraught collaborative work, a generic logic of globalizing China is made visible.

12. We have here in mind, for example, the writings of Paul Rabinow and several of his colleagues on biogenetic research and the ethics of collaboration (Rabinow and Stavrianakis 2013), the work by Anne Tsing and colleagues on Matsutake worlds and other global flows (Choy et al. 2009), and more recent works about the nature of the Anthropocene (Swanson et al. 2015), as well as recent work attempting to decolonize anthropology (Harrison, 1997; Todd 2016).

1. FRIENDSHIP EMPIRE

1. The exact extent of his holdings remains unclear, but a Chinese newspaper article from 2009 suggested that the value of his various investments added up to some RMB 40 million (Li 2009).

2. During Bunkenborg and Pedersen's fieldwork, there were many news reports in China about Mongolia's mining boom as a new "frontier of capitalism," an upcoming Asian "wolf economy" promising spectacular riches based on "untapped" resources in a "pristine land" abroad; calling to mind past and present Western colonial discourses (Tsing 2000; Kragelund 2009).

3. No currency was specified, but presumably it was MT 30,000,000. The US $500 million mentioned below was supposedly a gift presented by Chinese Premier Wen Jiabao on his 2010 state visit to Mongolia, but the figure is an exaggeration or perhaps a misreading of the figure of RMB 50 million.

2. WHOSE WALLS?

1. According to Pasternak and Salaff (1993, 170–71), "Although Han [Chinese] and Mongols have both adopted to the pastoral way of life, in crucial ways they are still culturally and socially apart. . . . Whereas the Han live in town with their cows, Mongols prefer life with their flocks on open grassland. The yurt is still the principal dwelling for twenty-nine percent of all Great Pasture Mongols. Some Han own and use yurts as well, but none call them home."

2. Since 2000 fluorspar has emerged as an important commodity in the Mongolian resource extraction industry, especially within the context of the smaller- and middle-sized mines that have generally been able to operate under the radar in comparison with megaprojects like the Oyo Tolgoi mine and other so-called strategic deposits. Certainly, as Lahiri-Dutt and Dondov note, "relatively less attention has so far been paid" to Mongolian fluorspar mining in comparison with coal and especially gold mining (e.g., Murray 2003; High 2017). This is despite the fact that in 1997, "Mongolia was the third largest producer of fluorspar in the world" (Wu 1997, 3) and the fact that, in terms of numbers employed, "fluorspar comes second in importance to gold" (1997, 4). See also Baatar and Grayson (2009) for an extended mapping of Mongolian fluorspar mines based on Google Earth data.

3. Based on visits to Mongolian-owned mines in Central Gobi, Lahiri-Dutt and Dondov (2017, 9) offer a vivid description: "The environment is extremely dusty, forcing the women and men to learn to cover their faces to stop swallowing dust. . . . The fluorspar mountain is being quarried for ore using heavy machinery. Three excavators are working to extract ore from the ridge for three groups, each of whom has its own allocated land based on a local approval. . . . The loaders wait patiently until the earth movers dig out material from their allotment, and hop onto the trucks after the ore is trucked out of the quarry site. The material is then transported to the dumping site, where the same group manually sort the material into ores of different richness. The selection is purely visual and the sorting is manual, often done squatting on the ground or bending." While these observations stem from an open-shaft mine, its general gist—including the great degree to which the mining process depends on hard manual labor—calls to mind what Pedersen and Bunkenborg observed during their visits to Chinese fluorspar mines in the same area (see also Purevjav 2011 and High 2017 on gendered divisions of labor and moral economies among Mongolian artisanal miners).

4. Ching Kwan Lee (2009) makes a similar observation about Chinese industrial sites in Africa. "More profound than the communication barrier is the gap between what managers call 'work ethics' and workers see as 'exploitation.' Chinese managers have come to Africa with personal career experience in reformed state-owned enterprises, and have now basically rejected the socialist firm as a viable form for economic development. They often attribute China's lift from backwardness and poverty to its abandonment of the 'iron rice bowl' mentality and practice. They demand of their African workers the same work ethics and sacrifice they believed have allowed the Chinese to develop, and have yet to be found among the African workforce" . . . "Zambian and Tanzanian workers, on the other hand, appeal to the moral economic standards and labour rights that were established during the 'government periods' and insist that foreign investors today should at least match those conditions of service" (654). See chapter 5 for a discussion of similar issues in the context of Chinese investments in Mozambique.

5. The injunction to "respect the customs and traditions of the people of Mongolia" is explicated in the Foreign Investment Law of Mongolia (including 2008 revisions), chap. 3, art. 10, ¶ 2.4 (http://erc.gov.mn/web/en/download/172).

3. ROADS THAT SEPARATE

1. According to the Law of Foreign Investment in Mongolia (including 2008 amendments), "Business entities with foreign investment shall primarily employ citizens of Mongolia. Foreign citizens may be hired for jobs requiring special or high qualifications. Issues on importing labor forces and experts shall be regulated by the relevant legislation of Mongolia" (http://erc.gov.mn/web/en/download/172). The proportion of a company's work force allowed to be of foreign nationality according to different laws, their amendments, and conflicting interpretations was a topic of hot debate among Pedersen's interlocutors generally and in the context of the PetroChina oil field in particular. There was widespread agreement among local people as well as journalists and NGOS that a loophole in the regulation enabled PetroChina to employ thousands of Chinese workers by subcontracting elements of the oil exploration and exploitation process to Chinese companies. As the following excerpt from a March 2019 article published in *Mongol Messenger* indicates, the question of foreign versus Mongolian workers was also very high on the agenda during meetings between top officials from the Chinese company and the Mongolian government: "PetroChina Daqing Tamsag Mongol LLC president, Mr. Fang Baacai . . . briefed the PM on the company and requested it be exempt from the payment of employment permits for company workers from China. . . . He said company policy was to hire more Mongolian workers; however a shortage of qualified Mongolian workers forced him to use Chinese employees" (http://www.olloo.mn).

2. Another example was reported in the English-language newspaper *UB Post* in 2008 when a "brawl" had taken place at the Mongolian-Chinese border. "Workers from Junyuan, a drilling company subcontracted by the petroleum mining company Petro-China Daqing Tamsag Mongolia LLC are accused of attacking border guards in Dornod aimag [region]. . . . According to Dornod aimag's governor, the Junyuan workers entered a prohibited area on the border and ignored the border guards' numerous warnings to exit the premises. The workers then refused to show guards their documents and began taking photos while arguing with the guards. After the border patrol said that photos were not allowed in the area and again asked for documentation, the conflict escalated to blows. . . . Speaking for PetroChina, [Zhao] Zhenglun . . . agreed that ultimately the guilt or innocence of the workers would be determined by the ministry of justice, saying that PetroChina would take serious action if the ministry found that the workers were at fault. However, he said, the incident was likely caused by misunderstandings, exacerbated by the language barrier. . . . The company, Zhenglun said, is taking a lesson from this case and will take steps to demonstrate its responsibility" (hhttp://ubposgt.mongolia news.mn).

3. Available on PetroChina's website: http://www.petrochina.com.cn/Ptr/Society_and_Environment07/.

4. In addition, the vice president of PetroChina Daqing Tamsag listed these "difficulties": "(1) unstable legal environment, (2) conflicts for PSC created by frequent new laws and amendments to laws, (3) lack of specialized labor force, (4) lack of support and knowledge of the significance of the middle and low echelons of government institutions, and (5) lack of consistency between decisions made by different institutions."

5. Local cadres did not restrict their criticism to the Chinese but expressed dissatisfaction with "politicians in Ulaanbaatar" and, in particular, what they considered to be the ill-conceived 1993 oil law, the basis of the 2006 product-sharing agreement between PetroChina and the ministry of oil. Indeed, as frequently reported in Mongolian newspapers, blogs, and TV stations over the four years we monitored this case (2009–2012), several prominent Matad community members (and two MPs representing the Dornod region)

publicly lamented how little the district (and the region) had benefited from the millions of US dollars paid by PetroChina Daqing Tamsag to the Mongolian state in taxes and revenues. Probably more than the Chinese company itself, it was dissatisfaction with the centralization of power and revenue in Ulaanbaatar that led six Matad residents to submit a formal petition to the national parliament.

6. Interestingly, this particular solution is highlighted as an example of good practice in a report concerned with local-level agreements in Mongolia's resource sector (2017): "Under the cooperation agreement between Matad District of Dornod Province and PetroChina Dachin Tamsag, local businesses and herders have preferential access for supplying goods to the company. Procurement notices are regularly posted on district government information boards" (https://resourcegovernance.org/sites/default/files/documents/nrgi-mongolia-agreement-briefing-english.pdf).

7. As a 2019 article from the official Mongolian news agency shows, the relationship between the oil company, the local community, and the state has remained characterized by the same dynamic of broken promises and retaliation that Bunkenborg and Pedersen first observed a decade ago: "Prime Minister U. Khurelsukh met with the authorities of the company and exchanged views on possibilities of further cooperation, current situation and prospects of the extraction. 'Petro China Daqing Tamsag' company has been producing 7.5 million tons of oil since the Production Sharing Agreement was signed in 2005. . . . 2015 was the peak year of oil extraction, reaching 1 million tons, however the extraction amount is decreasing in recent years with annual average extraction of 800.000 tons, reported the company. Still, the company officials said that they can supply oil to the refinery to be built by increasing the oil extraction. During the PM's visit, the Professional Inspection Agency introduced the results of the inspection, made in the company. According to the inspection, 'Petro China Daqing Tamsag' company should secure chemical hazardous waste storage and waste water from the environment and make amendments to the Production Sharing Agreement. In addition, the Professional Inspection Agency considers it necessary to charge royalty on oil extraction, to alter customs tax exemptions of companies and subcontractors and to make foreign labors [sic] pay social security premium to Mongolia" (https://www.montsame.mn/en/read/206455).

8. Http://web.worldbank.org/WBSITE/EXTERNAL/COUNTRIES/EASTASIA PACIFICEXT/EXTEAPREGTOPTRANSPORT/0,contentMDK:20767661~menuPK:206 9306~pagePK:34004173~piPK:34 003707~theSitePK:574066,00.html.

9. Following a protracted process of geopolitically motivated twists and turns, planning Mongolia's first oil refinery began in 2018 in the regional capital, Sainshand, although the site of the refinery has since been shifted to a district in the same province (https://www.montsame.mn/en/read/233619). Originally based on bilateral aid from the Chinese government, the US $700 million cost (including US $264 million for pipelines) will supposedly be paid by the Import-Export Bank of India, which took over from the Chinese following their temporary falling-out with the Mongolian government after the Dalai Lama's visit to Mongolia in 2016 (https://www.livemint.com/Industry/g7DRl6eT5 HX6IHJTFEhyjP/Mongolia-pegs-1-billion-from-India-for-oil-refinery-pipeli.html; and https://www.business-standard.com/article/pti-stories/mongolia-builds-first-refinery-to-ease-russian-fuel-dependence-118062200907_1.html).

10. At first blush, then, local disappointment with the oil company would seem to reflect a perception that too little infrastructure investment was made by the Chinese owners, but for many people, it may be more accuate to say that there was *too much* infrastructure, or at least infrastructure of the "wrong" kind, given that "too many" Chinese people, trucks, pipes, and wells were seen to have had detrimental effects on the lives of both herders and animals and local livelihood more generally.

11. See, e.g., Star 1999; Jensen and Winthereik 2013; Harvey, Jensen, and Morita 2016) for STS, and Humphrey 2005; Larkin 2013; Chu 2014; Anand 2017; and Carey

and Pedersen 2017 for anthropology (on Mongolia specifically see, Nielsen and Pedersen 2015; Pedersen 2017).

12. Consider the conventional depiction of a "relation" in the social sciences—a line connecting two separate points. One might ask what this formalized abstraction of a social relationship resembles, other than a flat stretch of desert road in Mongolia? Understood in these terms, the roads at hand were themselves enactments of the Sino-local intimate distances they calibrated. Of course, it would be naïve to assume that the herdsman had any interest in these "conceptual affordances" (Holbraad 2012; Holbraad and Pedersen 2017) of the road along which he and his family had temporarily pitched their ger indeed, he would probably find our attempt to turn this ordinary infrastructure into an analytical concept very strange. But this is beside the methodological point we are making here: although roads were certainly a matter of ethnographic concern in the Gobi and Tamsag context (everyone agreed that roads were central to the Sino-Mongolian relations at hand), their usefulness as theoretical tools was not. It is we, as anthropologists, who are responsible for turning the road into an analytical concept, not they, as our interlocutors.

4. STRATEGIES OF UNSEEING

1. In 2011 the ruling Frelimo government signed a memorandum with the Chinese government on the financing of a suspension bridge between the Maputo city center and the Catembe Peninsula. Less than a year later, an official loan agreement was signed, and on September 20, 2012, the first brick was laid for the largest public works project to be initiated in Mozambique since the country's independence in 1975. The project was implemented by Maputo Sul, a state institution created for realizing the Catembe Bridge and a new ring road encircling Maputo, in collaboration with the China Road and Bridge Corporation as part of the project of building a new highway from Maputo to Ponta do Ouro (a distance of 209 kilometers). Construction work continued until November 10, 2018, when the Maputo-Catembe Bridge was finally inaugurated by Filipe Nyusi, the president of Mozambique. With a total length of 680 meters and towers 135 meters high, the suspension bridge is one of the largest on the continent.

2. Maputo Sul was the now closed state institution responsible for coordinating the building of the Catembe Bridge and the Maputo Ring road.

3. In this chapter we purposefully omit any clear definition of the term "Chinatown" and follow our Mozambican interlocutors' vague usage of the notion to capture the mysterious and oftentimes worrying activities going on in the Catembe Peninsula, activities that might—and might not—result in the making of an entirely new city. In Chinese, the project was usually referred to as the "Catembe New Urban District" (卡腾贝新城区) or simply "New City" (新城).

4. "Wearing a green hat" (戴绿帽子) means "being a cuckold" in Chinese, and the color of the hat no doubt contributed to the mirth of the Chinese guards.

5. As Geschiere (2013, 28) has argued in his study of the Maka in southeast Cameroon, in situations marked by societal and cosmological insecurity, a key challenge is how to "fence oneself off" in order to maintain productive distances from others who are both crucial and potentially detrimental to one's social existence. Relations carry the potential for enhancing one's social capacities as well as the threat of existential annihilation when a functional distance between interacting agencies can no longer be maintained.

6. Recall Lourdes Simango's persistent visits to the Department for Urban Planning at the Maputo municipality.

7. "Brief" in the sense that the bridge was in the end actually built!

8. *Notícias* is the largest national newspaper in Mozambique.

5. ENCLAVES AND ENVELOPES

1. Anhui Foreign Economic Construction Group (AFECC) (安徽省外经建设集团).

2. The rumors of Chinese prison labor in Africa have been debated and debunked by Yan Hairong and Barry Sautman (2013). See also Lee 2017, 104.

6. ALTERITY IN THE INTERIOR

1. Umbila is a local form of precious hardwood used mainly for furniture and decorative veneer.

2. Cabo Delgado Logging Consortium, Ltd. (CADEL). CADEL is a Chinese-owned logging company whose history and importance are discussed below.

3. This information is based on personal communication with Mozambican state officials involved in these processes.

4. If Wang Guoqiang was somewhat wary of talking to foreign researchers, it was not without reason. In 2012 investigators involved in the EIA research posed as timber buyers and exposed one of Wang Guoqiang's compatriots in the final report, which contains a clandestine photo and relates how he bragged about his government contacts and his one million hectares of concessions.

5. The extent of this trade at the time of fieldwork is further corroborated by seizures by Mozambican authorities. In 2006, more than 170,000 cubic meters of illegally cut wood were seized in Nampula, and in 2007, it was discovered that CADEL had stacked more than 1,000 logs of precious hardwood at the port of Pemba in Cabo Delgado awaiting shipment to China (Ribeiro 2010). Less than two years later, in January 2009, the head of the Cabo Delgado Provincial Forestry and Wild Life Service announced that 958 cubic meters of precious hardwood had been seized at the port of Pemba (allAfrica.com 2009). Apparently, the unprocessed logs had already been loaded onto a container ship before the illegal activities were discovered. In February 2011, the National Directorate of Land and Forests canceled the licenses of sixteen timber companies who were caught attempting to export not only logs but also ivory and "other natural resources" to China (*Zimbabwean* 2011b). Although comprising 11,097 cubic meters of unprocessed logs in 807 containers, the Mozambican Tax Authority later discovered that little more than 5,000 cubic meters of wood had been declared by the companies involved in the illegal activities. Finally, in July 2011, 508 containers of precious hardwood were seized in the northern port of Nacala (*Zimbabwean* 2011a). It did not take long, however, before the valuable timber was back in the hands of the culprits. According to Mozambican legislation, despite having been convicted of attempting to illegally export precious hardwood, timber companies can reacquire the wood subsequent to the seizure. By paying a price of MZM 15.8 million (US \$517,186), the eight companies involved avoided losing the hardwood at a public auction, which would otherwise have been the most likely outcome.

6. Environmental Investigation Agency (2012, 7); according to EIA, major exporters of illegal logs include Russia (5.6 million cubic meters), Papua New Guinea (2.5 million cubic meters), Solomon Islands (1.5 million cubic meters), Myanmar and Congo Brazzaville (500,000 cubic meters each), Equatorial Guinea (270,000 cubic meters), and Mozambique (183,000 cubic meters).

7. In Mackenzie and Ribeiro's (2006) study of Chinese logging activities in Mozambique, the importance of *olheiros* is also emphasized. The authors argue that "felling teams work through the forests relying on the memories of the tree spotters [i.e., *olheiros*], cutting timber where they find it" (48; see also Sun, Chen et al. 2008, 146).

8. The following description of the logging process pertains only to timber companies and not to individual license holders and furtivos.

9. The difference lies in the quality of the machinery. If the work crew has access to powerful chain saws and a stable means of transportation (tractor and truck), the *olheiro* will often continue scouting for trees while his assistant returns to the provisional camp. All these work tasks are carried out by Mozambican employees.

10. A crucial factor in determining the efficiency of the work crew is the quality and number of chain saws. To all logging crews operating in the forests, the handheld chain saw constitutes the single most valuable item, and it is handled with great reverence and extreme care. When Nielsen visited the work crews in their provisional camps near the concession areas, it was rarely possible for him to commence a conversation with the *olheiro* before having marveled at the operators' capacity for igniting the chain saws again and again.

11. Cabo Delgado was one of the provinces that contributed most to the national forestry trade when Nielsen examined the numbers in 2012. The productive forests covered three million hectares (36 percent of the region's total area), and the value of trees in Cabo Delgado was estimated to represent approximately US $97 million (Sun, Chen et al. 2008). It was reasonable to infer that within a relatively short time the forestry industry would irrevocably collapse. According to a series of studies (EIA 2012; 2013; Mackenzie 2006; Mackenzie and Ribeiro 2009; Ribeiro 2009; 2010; Sun, Chen et al. 2008), if the illegal trade in precious hardwood maintained the pace described here, it would likely push Mozambique's forests beyond their maximum sustainable yield in the not-distant future. The problem was worsened by the fact that the majority of Chinese timber companies cut trees that had not yet reached maturation (forty centimeter diameter depending on the species), threatening the necessary regeneration of the forest. According to calculations made by Daniel Ribeiro, Justica Ambiental (personal communication), for each log of precious hardwood that is cut, seven additional nonprecious trees (forty centimeter diameter or more) are removed by picadeiros and truck drivers.

12. Part of Chinese revolutionary vocabulary, the term *fanshen* (翻身) literally means "to turn over," but in the context of land reforms it came to describe the process of freeing oneself from the dominance of landlords and acquiring land, livestock, and housing.

13. Makua (also spelled "Makhuwa") is the primary Bantu language spoken by three million people living in the northern part of Mozambique.

14. "Whites" (*brancos*) is frequently used as a plural generic term.

15. In 2009, 87,000 cubic meters of timber, worth approximately MZM 71 million (US $2.3 million) was cut without a license (German and Wertz-Kanounnikoff 2012, 39).

16. Illegal cutting here implies cutting more than 500 cubic meters per year or, equally likely, cutting in an area belonging to another concessionaire.

17. In general, sellers (such as villagers and community chiefs) make approximately MZM 100 (US $3.2) for a log, which is later sold at a price between US $120–450 (Mackenzie and Ribeiro 2009, 16).

18. One could perhaps say that, hidden behind and enveloped by a simple reciprocal monetary relationship (of salaries and profits) between employer and employee, there was an equally crucial transaction of hardwood and skills. As the furtivo reminded Nielsen, the existence of precious hardwood was predicated on the *olheiros*' abilities to find it; conversely, the ability of the *olheiros* to find the hardwood in the first place was predicated on their being hired by Chinese timber companies. Conceived of in these terms, the *olheiros* became capable of locating the coveted hardwood by virtue of their employer-employee relation with the Chinese, not because of some innate or acquired capacity for tree scouting.

19. Rather than manifesting an object of the collaboration between *olheiro* and furtivo, one might say that the tree-scouting capacity "eclipsed" a prior relationship between

Chinese timber operators and *olheiros* that was now asserting its power too close to home. This use of the concept of eclipsing is based on the idea that the "content of whatever reading is eclipsed is present in the content of whatever is foregrounded. A view of the sun in eclipse is still a view of the sun, not the moon, though it is the moon one sees" (Gell 1998, 92).

20. Ngungunyane (ca. 1850–1906) was the last emperor of Gaza; he rebelled against and was later defeated by the Portuguese colonial regime (Liesegang 1996).

CONCLUSION

1. Actually, the popular uprising that took place in Maputo on September 1–2, 2010, probably had little to do with the *Spirit of Eternity*. For two days several major Mozambican cities were converted into battlefields as crowds of frustrated and angry urbanites captured main urban spaces where they "burned off heaps of tyres as barricades on main roads" and looted shops and warehouses (Berthelsen 2014, 28; see also Buur 2015). The immediate reason for the popular uprisings was an increase in fuel and bread prices, but the event was, equally importantly, a moment of almost carnivalesque "effervescence," where dispossessed urbanites experimented with new forms of political subjectivities and ideological imageries (Bertelsen 2014).

2. In xiChangana, a Bantu language widely spoken in the southern part of Mozambique, *ku phahla* is an annual commemorative ritual generally carried out by traditional leaders and diviners in honor of those deceased ancestors who guide the lives of the living (Honwana 1996; Nielsen 2012a).

3. It should be noted, however, that in locating Chinese state capital as the heart of Chinese globalization, Lee (2017, xiv) at the same time stresses that it is highly difficult to distinguish Chinese state capital from other forms of capital labeled as Chinese on cultural or ethnic grounds and that global China takes "myriad forms" that are not necessarily manifestations of state capital.

References

Abrahamsson, Hans, and Anders Nilsson. 1995. *Mozambique: The Troubled Transition*. London: Zed Press.

Abrahms-Kavunenko, Saskia. 2019. *Enlightenment and the Gasping City: Mongolian Buddhism at a Time of Environmental Disarray*. Ithaca, NY: Cornell University Press.

Alden, Chris. 2005. "China in Africa." *Survival* 47: 147–64.

——. 2007. *China in Africa*. London: Zed Books.

Alden, Chris, and Sérgio Chichava. 2014. *China and Mozambique: From Comrades to Capitalists*. Auckland Park, Johannesburg, South Africa: Jacana Media.

Alden, Chris, and Daniel Large, eds. 2018. *New Directions in Africa—China Studies*. Boca Raton, FL: Routledge.

Alden, Chris, Daniel Large, and Ricardo Soares de Oliveira. 2008. *China Returns to Africa: A Rising Power and a Continent Embrace*. London: Hurst.

allAfrica.com. 2009. "Timber Companies Fined over Illegal Exports." Accessed 10 May 10, 2013. http://allafrica.com/stories/200901090867.html.

——. 2019. "Mozambique: Trade with China Up by over a Third." Accessed February 3, 2020. https://allafrica.com/stories/201902010980.html.

Allina, E. 2012. *Slavery by Any Other Name: African Life under Company Rule in Colonial Mozambique*. Charlottesville: University of Virginia Press.

American Anthropological Association. 2009. *Code of Ethics of the American Anthropological Association*. Accessed 10 May 10, 2021. http://ethics.americananthro.org/category/statement/

Anand, Nikhil. 2017. *Hydraulic City: Water and the Infrastructures of Citizenship in Mumbai*. Durham, NC: Duke University Press.

Andersen, Jørgen E., Paul Jenkins, and Morten Nielsen. 2015a. "Who Plans the African City? A Case Study of Maputo: Part 1—The Structural Context." *International Development Planning Review* 37 (3): 331–52.

——. 2015b. "Who Plans the African City? A Case Study of Maputo: Part 2—Agency in Action. *International Development Planning Review* 37 (4): 423–44.

Appel, Hannah C. 2012a. "Offshore Work: Oil, Modularity, and the How of Capitalism in Equatorial Guinea." *American Ethnologist* 39 (4): 692–709.

——. 2012b. "Walls and White Elephants: Oil Extraction, Responsibility, and Infrastructural Violence in Equatorial Guinea." *Ethnography* 13 (4): 439–65.

Arsene, Codrin. 2014. "Chinese Employers and Their Ugandan Workers: Tensions, Frictions and Cooperation in an African City." *Journal of Current Chinese Affairs* 43 (1): 139–76.

Asche, Helmut. 2008. "Contours of China's 'Africa Mode' and Who May Benefit." *China Aktuell, Journal of Current Chinese Affairs* 3: 165–80.

Assembleia da República. 1999. "Lei no. 10/99." *Boletim da República* no. 27, (I Series), 4th Supplement, July 12, 1999.

——. 2002. "Regulamento da Lei de Florestas e Fauna Bravia." *Boletim da República* no. 22, (I Series), 2nd Supplement, June 6, 2002.

Baabar.mn. 2010. "NGOs Request Investigation in Petrochina." March 22, 2010. http://www.baabar.mn/article/1623.

Baatar, C. E., and R. Grayson. 2009. "Remote Sensing of the Coal Sector in China and Mongolia." *World Placer Journal 9*: 24–47.

Baatarzorig, Tsolmon, Ragchaasuren Galindev, and Hélène Maisonnave. 2018. "Effects of Ups and Downs of the Mongolian Mining Sector." *Environment and Development Economics* 23 (5): 527–42.

Bacevich, A. J. 2002. *American Empire: The Realities and Consequences of U.S. Diplomacy*. Cambridge, MA: Harvard University Press.

Batbuyan, B., and Maria E. Fernández-Giménez. 2012. "Law and Disorder: Local Implementation of Mongolia's Land Law." *Development and Change* 35 (1): 141–66.

Bateson, Gregory. 1958. *Naven, a Survey of the Problems Suggested by a Composite Picture of the Culture of a New Guinea Tribe Drawn from Three Points of View*. 2d ed. Stanford, CA: Stanford University Press.

Bawden, Charles R. 1989. *The Modern History of Mongolia*. 2nd ed. London: Kegan Paul International.

Benwell, Ann F. 2009. *Keeping Up Appearances: Gender and Ideal Womanhood in Postsocialist Mongolia*. PhD diss. University of Copenhagen.

Bergesen, Albert. 2008. *The New Surgical Colonialism: China, Africa, and Oil*. American Sociological Association Annual Meeting, Boston, MA, July 31.

Bertelsen, B. E. 2014. "Effervescence and Ephemerality: Popular Urban Uprisings in Mozambique." *Ethnos* 81 (1): 25–52.

Bessire, Lucas, and David Bond. 2014. "Ontological Anthropology and the Deferral of Critique." *American Ethnologist* 41 (3): 440–56.

Betar Consultores. 2012. *Estudo de Pré-viabilidade Ambiental e Definicão do Âmbito e dos Termos de Referência do Estido de Impacto Ambiental*. Maputo, Mozambique: Maputo Sul.

Billé, Franck. 2008. "Faced with Extinction: Myths and Urban Legends in Contemporary Mongolia." *Cambridge Anthropology* 28 (1): 34–60.

——. 2013. "Indirect Interpellations: Hate Speech and 'Bad Subjects' in Mongolia." Accessed May 10, 2021. https://aspace.repository.cam.ac.uk/bitstream/handle/1810/245386/Bill-xC3-xA9.%202014.%20Indirect%20interpellations%20%28pre-print%29.pdf?sequence=1&isAllowed=y.

——. 2014. *Sinophobia: Anxiety, Violence, and the Making of Mongolian Identity*. Honolulu: University of Hawaii Press.

Blandy, S. 2006. "Gated Communities in England: Historical Perspectives and Current Developments." *Geojournal* 66 (1/2):15–26.

Bodomo, Adams. 2010. "The African Trading Community in Guangzhou: An Emerging Bridge for Africa, China Relations." *China Quarterly* 203: 693–707.

Boyer, D., and C. Howe. 2015. "Portable Analytics and Lateral Theory." In *Theory Can Be More than It Used to Be*. edited by J. D. Faubion and G. E. Marcus, 15–38. Ithaca, NY: Cornell University Press.

Brady, Anne-Marie. 2003. *Making the Foreign Serve China: Managing Foreigners in the People's Republic*. Lanham, MD: Rowman & Littlefield.

Brautigam, Deborah. 1998. *Chinese Aid and African Development: Exporting Green Revolution*. International Political Economy Series. New York: St. Martin's Press.

——. 2009. *The Dragon's Gift: The Real Story of China in Africa*. Oxford: Oxford University Press.

——. 2015. *Will Africa Feed China?* Oxford: Oxford University Press.

Bray, David. 2005. *Social Space and Governance in Urban China: The Danwei System from Origins to Reform*. Stanford, CA: Stanford University Press.

Bruun, Ole. 2006. *Precious Steppe: Mongolian Nomadic Pastoralists in Pursuit of the Market.* Oxford: Lexington Books.

Bruun, Ole, and Ole Odgaard, eds. 1996. *Mongolia in Transition: Old Patterns, New Challenges.* Surrey, UK: Curzon.

Bulag, Uradyn Erden. 1998. *Nationalism and Hybridity in Mongolia.* Oxford Studies in Social and Cultural Anthropology. Oxford: Oxford University Press.

——. 2002. *The Mongols at China's Edge. History and the Politics of National Unity.* Lanham, MD: Rowman & Littlefield.

——. 2009. "Mongolia in 2008: From Mongolia to Mine-golia." *Asian Survey* 49 (1):129–34.

——. 2010. *Collaborative Nationalism: The Politics of Friendship on China's Mongolian Frontier.* Lanham, MD: Rowman & Littlefield.

Bunkenborg, Mikkel. 2014. "All Part of the Master Plan? Ethnographic Encounters with the Chinese in Mozambique." In *China and Mozambique: From Comrades to Capitalists,* edited by Chris Alden and Sergio Chichava, 50–66. Johannesburg, South Africa: Jacana.

Bunkenborg, Mikkel, and Susanne Bregnbæk. 2017. "Introduction." In *Emptiness and Fullness: Ethnographies of Lack and Desire in Contemporary China,* edited by Susanne Bregnbæk and Mikkel Bunkenborg, 1–13. London: Berghahn.

Bunkenborg, Mikkel, and Morten Axel Pedersen. 2012. "The Ethnographic Expedition 2.0: Resurrecting the Expedition as a Social Scientific Research Method." In *Scientists and Scholars in the Field: Studies in the History of Fieldwork and Expeditions* edited by K. H. Nielsen, M. Harbsmeier, and C. J. Ries, 415–29. Aarhus, Denmark: Aarhus Universitetsforlag.

Burton, Paul J. 2011. *Friendship and Empire: Roman Diplomacy and Imperialism in the Middle Republic (353–146 BC).* Cambridge: Cambridge University Press.

Buur, L. 2015. "Sovereignty, Riots, and Social Contestation." *Conflict and Society: Advances in Research* 1 (1): 165–81.

Cahen, Michel. 1993. "Check on Socialism in Mozambique—What Check? What Socialism?" *Review of African Political Economy* 20 (57): 46–59.

——. 2011. "The Enemy as Model. Patronage as a Crisis Factor in Constructing Opposition in Mozambique." OXPO Working Papers. Oxford: University of Oxford.

Caldeira, Teresa Pires do Rio. 2000. *City of Walls: Crime, Segregation, and Citizenship in São Paulo.* Berkeley: University of California Press.

Callahan, William A. 2004. "Remembering the Future—Utopia, Empire, and Harmony in 21st-Century International Theory." *European Journal of International Relations* 10 (4): 569–601.

Callon, Michel. 1998. "Introduction: The Embeddedness of Economic Markets in Economics." In *The Laws of the Markets,* edited by Michel Callon, 1–57. Oxford: Blackwell.

Campbell, Ben. 2010. "Rhetorical Routes for Development: A Road Project in Nepal." *Contemporary South Asia* 18: 267–79.

Campi, Alicia J. 2004. *Modern Mongolian-Chinese Strategic Relations: Challenges for the New Century.* Burke, VA: U.S.-Mongolia Advisory Group.

——. 2013. "The Bumpy Path to Sino-Mongolian Cooperation in the Mining Sector." *China Brief* 13 (3). https://jamestown.org/program/the-bumpy-path-to-sino-mongolian-cooperation-in-the-mining-sector/

——. 2014. "Transforming Mongolia-Russia-China Relations: The Dushanbe Trilateral Summit." *Asia-Pacific Journal* 12 (1). https://apjjf.org/2014/12/45/Alicia-Campi/4210.html

——. 2017. "Mongolian Foreign Relations Under 25 Years of Democracy." In *Routledge Handbook of Asia in World Politics,* edited by Teh-Kuang Chang and Angelin Chang, 61–104. London: Routledge.

Candea, Matei. 2010. "'I Fell in Love with Carlos the Meerkat.' Engagement and Detachment in Human-Animal Relations." *American Ethnologist* 37 (2): 241–58.

——. 2015. "Going Full Frontal, or, the Elision of Lateral Comparison in Anthropology." CRASSH Sawyer Seminar September 25. Accessed February 15, 2016. http://www.mateicandea.net/?p=962.

——. 2018. *Comparison in Anthropology: The Impossible Method.* Cambridge: Cambridge University Press.

Candea, Matei, Joanne Cook, Catherine Trundle, and Tom Yarrow, eds. 2015. *Detachment: Essays on the Limits of Relational Thinking.* Manchester, UK: Manchester University Press.

Carey, Mathew, and Morten Axel Pedersen. 2017. "Introduction: Infrastructures of Certainty and Doubt." *Cambridge Journal of Anthropology* 35 (2): 1–7. https://doi.org/10.3167/cja.2017.350203.

Castel-Branco, C. N. 2015. "Growth, Capital Accumulation and Economic Porosity in Mozambique: Social Losses, Private Gains." *Review of African Political Economy* 41 (1): 26–48.

Castel-Branco, C., C. Cramer et al. 2003. "Privatization and Economic Strategy in Mozambique." In *From Conflict to Recovery in Africa*, edited by Tony Addison, 155–70. Oxford: Oxford University Press.

Chichava, Sérgio. 2008. "Mozambique and China: From Politics to Business?" Discussion Paper No. 05/2008. Maputo, Mozambique: Instituto de Estudos Sociais e Económicos.

China-Lusophone Brief. 2018. "Mozambique Tackles Illegal Logging." Accessed April 27, 2020. https://www.clbrief.com/mozambique-tackles-illegal-logging/.

Choy, Timothy, Lieba Faier, Michael Hathaway, Miyako Inoue, and Anna Tsing. 2009. "A New Form of Collaboration in Cultural Anthropology: Matsutake Worlds." *American Ethnologist* 36(2): 280–403.

Chu, Julie Y. 2010. *Cosmologies of Credit: Transnational Mobility and the Politics of Destination in China.* Durham, NC: Duke University Press.

——. 2014. "When Infrastructures Attack: The Workings of Disrepair in China." *American Ethnologist* 41 (2): 351–67.

Clifford, James. 1983. "On Ethnographic Authority." *Representations* 1: 118–46.

——. 1986. "Introduction: Partial Truths." In *Writing Culture: The Poetics and Politics of Ethnography*, edited by James Clifford and George E. Marcus, 1–26. Berkeley: University of California Press.

——. 1988. *The Predicament of Culture: Twentieth-Century Ethnography, Literature, and Art.* Cambridge, MA: Harvard University Press.

Clifford, James, and George E. Marcus, eds. 1986. *Writing Culture: The Poetics and Politics of Ethnography.* Berkeley: University of California Press.

Coelho, J.P.B. 2013. "Politics and Contemporary History in Mozambique: A Set of Epistemological Notes." *Kronos* 39 (1): 20–31.

Comaroff, Jean, and John Comaroff. 1999. "Occult Economies and the Violence of Abstraction: Notes from the South African Postcolony." *American Ethnologist* 26 (3): 279–301.

Comaroff, John L. 1989. "Images of Empire, Contests of Conscience: Models of Colonial Domination in South Africa." *American Ethnologist* 16 (4): 661–84.

Cooper, Frederick, and Ann L. Stoler, eds. 1989. *Tensions of Empire: Colonial Cultures in a Bourgeois World.* Berkeley: University of California Press.

Corsín Jiménez, Alberto. 2018. "A Data Governance Framework for Ethnography v. 1.0." *Spanish National Research Council*, November 2018. http://digital.csic.es/bitstream/10261/172227/3/data%20governance%20framework%20181115

Crook, Tony. 2007. *Anthropological Knowledge, Secrecy and Bolivip, Papua New Guinea: Exchanging Skin*. Oxford: Oxford University Press.

Currier, Carrie L., and Manocher Dorraj, eds. 2011. *China's Energy Relations with the Developing World*. New York: Continuum.

Dalakoglou, D., 2010. "The Road: An Ethnography of the Albanian and Greek Cross-border Motorway." *American Ethnologist* 37 (1): 132–49.

Davaakhuu, Oyunbadam, Kishor Sharma, and Yapa M.W.Y. Bandara. 2014. "Foreign Direct Investment in a Transition Economy: Lessons from the Experience of Mongolia." *Global Business Review* 15 (4): 663–75.

Delaplace, Grégory. 2009. "A Sheep Herder's Rage: Silence and Grief in Contemporary Mongolia." *Ethnos* 74 (4): 521–41.

——. 2010. "Chinese Ghosts in Mongolia." *Inner Asia* 12 (1):127–41.

——. 2012. "Parasitic Chinese, Vengeful Russians: Ghosts, Strangers, and Reciprocity in Mongolia." *Journal of the Royal Anthropological Institute* 18: 131–44.

Demirbag, Mehmet, Ekrem Tatoglu, and Adiya Oyungerel. 2005. "Patterns of Foreign Direct Investment in Mongolia, 1990–2003: A Research Note. Eurasian Geography and Economics 4: 247–259

Detienne, Marcel. 2008. *Comparing the Incomparable*. Translated by Janet Lloyd. Stanford, CA: Stanford University Press.

Di Cosmo, Nikolai. 2010. *Ancient China and Its Enemies: The Rise of Nomadic Power in East Asian History*. Cambridge: Cambridge University Press.

Dinerman, A. 2006. *Revolution, Counter-Revolution and Revisionism in Postcolonial Africa: The Case of Mozambique, 1975–1994*. Oxon, UK: Routledge.

Dobler, Gregor. 2008. "Solidarity, Xenophobia and the Regulation of Chinese Businesses in Namibia." In *China Returns to Africa: A Rising Power and a Continent Embrace*, edited by Chris Alden, Daniel Large, and Ricardo Soares de Oliveira, 237–55. London: Hurst.

——. 2009. "Chinese Shops and the Formation of a Chinese Expatriate Community in Namibia." *China Quarterly* 199: 707–27.

Dulam, Bumochir. 2020. *The State, Popular Mobilisation and Gold Mining in Mongolia: Shaping 'Neo-Liberal' Policies*. London: UCL Press.

Dutton, Michael. 1998. *Streetlife China*. Cambridge: Cambridge University Press.

Economist. 2010. "Buying up the World: The Coming Wave of Chinese Take-overs." November 12, 2010.

——. 2012. "Booming Mongolia: Mine, All Mine." January 21, 2012.

——. 2020. "Belt and Road: A Special Report." February 8, 2020.

Elverskog, Johan. 2006. *Our Great Qing: The Mongolians, Buddhism, and the State in Late Imperial China*. Honolulu: University of Hawai'i Press

Empson, Rebecca. 2020. *Life in the Gap: Subjective Lives and Economic Transformations in Mongolia*. London: UCL Press.

Environmental Investigation Agency [EIA]. 2012. *Appetite for Destruction. China's Trade in Illegal Timber*. London: EIA.

——. 2013. *First Class Connections. Log Smuggling, Illegal Logging, and Corruption in Mozambique*. London: EIA.

Escobar, Artudo. 1995. *Encountering Development: The Making and Unmaking of the Third World*, Princeton: Princeton University Press.

European Commission. 2018. *Ethics and Data Protection*. November 14, 2018.

Fabian, J. 1995. "Ethnographic Misunderstanding and the Perils of Context." *American Anthropologist* 97 (1): 41–50.

Fang Fang 芳芳 and Tumenqiqige 图门其其格. 2010. "中国对蒙古国直接投资的现状及音响分析" [Analysis of the Present Situation and Influence of Chinese Direct Investment in Mongolia]. 内蒙古财经学院学报 *Journal of Inner Mongolia College of Finance and Economics* 4: 52–57.

Farrington, John D. 2015. "The Impact of Mining Activities on Mongolia's Protected Areas: A Status Report with Policy Recommendations." *Integrated Environmental Assessment and Management* 1 (3): 283–89.

Feliciano, J. F. 1998. *Antropologia Económica dos Thonga do Sul de Moçambique.* Maputo, Mozambique: Arquivo Histórico de Moçambique.

Ferguson, James. 1994. *The Anti-politics Machine: "Development," Depoliticization, and Bureaucratic Power in Lesotho.* Minneapolis: University of Minnesota Press.

——. 1999. *Expectations of Modernity: Myths and Meanings of Urban Life on the Zambian Cobberbelt.* Berkeley: University of California Press.

——. 2005. "Seeing Like an Oil Company: Space, Security, and Global Capital in Neoliberal Africa." *American Anthropologist* 107 (3): 377–82.

——. 2006. *Global Shadows. Africa in the Neoliberal World Order.* Durham, NC: Duke University Press.

Ferguson, Niall. 2003. *Empire: How Britain Made the Modern World.* London: Allen Lane.

Ferme, Mariane C., and Cheryl M. Schmitz. 2014. "Writings on the Wall: Chinese Material Traces in an African Landscape." *Journal of Material Culture* 19 (4): 375–99. https://doi.org/10.1177/1359183514551118.

Fioratta, Susanna. 2019. "A World of Cheapness: Affordability, Shoddiness, and Second-best Options in Guinea and China." *Economic Anthropology* 6: 86–97.

Fischer, Andrew M. 2014. *The Disempowered Development of Tibet in China: A Study in the Economics of Marginalization.* Oxford: Lexington Books.

Fiskesjö, Magnus. 2006. "Rescuing the Empire: Chinese Nation-Building in the Twentieth Century." *European Journal of East Asian Studies* 5: 15–44.

Flower, John M. 2004. "A Road Is Made: Roads, Temples, and Historical Memory in Ya'an County, Sichuan." *Journal of Asian Studies* 63: 649–85.

Flyvbjerg, Bent. 1999. *Rationalitet og Magt.* Vol. 1. Det Konkretes Videnskab. København: Akademisk Forlag.

Freeman, Carla, and Drew Thomson. 2011. *China on the Edge. China's Border Provinces and Chinese Security Policy.* Baltimore, MD: Center for the National Interest and Johns Hopkins SIAS.

French, Howard W. 2014. *China's Second Continent: How a Million Migrants are Building a New Empire in Africa.* New York: Alfred A. Knopf.

——. 2017. *Everything under the Heavens: How the Past Helps Shape China's Push for Global Power.* New York: Alfred A. Knopf.

Ganzorig, B. 2009. "Mongolian Foreign Investment Legal Environment, Current Development of Development of Regional Foreign Investment, Further Trends and Opportunities." Paper presented at the FIFTA Conference, Choibalsan, August 2009.

Geffray, Christian. 1991. *A Causa das Armas. Antropologia da Guerra Contemporânea em Moçambique.* Translated by Adelaide Odete Ferreira. Porto, Portugal: Edições Afrontamento.

Gell, Alfred. 1998. *Art and Agency. An Anthropological Theory.* Oxford, Clarendon Press.

German, L. A. and S. Wertz-Kanounnikoff. 2012. *Sino-Mozambican Relations and Their Implications for Forests: A Preliminary Assessment for the Case of Mozambique.* Bogor, Indonesia: CIFOR.

Geschiere, Peter. 2013. *Witchcraft, Intimacy and Trust. Africa in Comparison.* Chicago: University of Chicago Press.

Giese, Karsten. 2013. "Same-Same But Different: Chinese Traders' Perspectives on African Labor." *China Journal* (69):134–53.

Giese, Karsten, and Alena Thiel. 2012. "The Vulnerable Other—Distorted Equity in Chinese–Ghanaian Employment Relations." *Ethnic and Racial Studies*: 37 (6): 1101–20.

——. 2015. "The Psychological Contract in Chinese-African Informal Labor Relations." *International Journal of Human Resource Management* 26: 1807–26.

Gladney, Dru. 2004. *Dislocating China: Muslims, Minorities, and Other Subaltern Subjects*. Chicago: University of Chicago.

Gledhill, John. 2008. "'The People's Oil': Nationalism, Globalization, and the Possibility of Another Country in Brazil, Mexico and Venezuela." *Focaal* 52: 57–74.

Gold, Thomas, Doug Guthrie, and David L. Wank. 2002. *Social Connections in China: Institutions, Culture, and the Changing Nature of Guanxi*. Structural Analysis in the Social Sciences. Cambridge: Cambridge University Press.

Góralczyk, Bogdan. 2017. "China's Interests in Central and Eastern Europe: Enter the Dragon." *European View* 16 (1): 153–62.

Gottlieb, Alma. 1995. "Beyond the Lonely Anthropologist: Collaboration in Research and Writing." *American Anthropologist* 97 (1): 21–26.

Grant, Andrew. 2018. "China's Double Body: Infrastructure Routes and the Mapping of China's Nation-state and Civilization-state." *Eurasian Geography and Economics* 59 (3–4): 378–407.

Green, Michael, and Evan S. Medeiros. 2020. "The Pandemic Won't Make China the World's Leader: Few Countries Are Buying the Model or the Message From Beijing." *Foreign Affairs*, April 15, 2020.

Guardian. 2006. "Beijing's Race for Africa." Accessed June 19, 2020. http://www.the guardian.com/commentisfree/2006/nov/01/world.china.

Han, Enzel, and Christopher Paik. 2017. "Ethnic Integration and Development in China." *World Development* 93: 31–42.

Hanlon, Joseph. 1991. *Mozambique. Who Calls the Shots?* Bloomington: Indiana University Press.

——. 1996. *Peace without Profit: How the IMF Blocks Rebuilding in Mozambique*. Oxford: James Currey.

——. 2016. "Following the Donor-Designed Path to Mozambique's US $2.2 Billion Secret Debt Deal." *Third World Quarterly*: 1–18.

Hardt, Michael, and Antonio Negri. 2000. *Empire*. Cambridge, MA: Harvard University Press.

Harrison, Faye V. 1997. *Decolonizing Anthropology: Moving Further toward an Anthropology for Liberation*. 2nd ed. Arlington, VA: American Anthropological Association.

Harrison, Simon. 2003. "Cultural Difference as Denied Resemblance: Reconsidering Nationalism and Identity." *Comparative Studies in Society and History* 45 (2): 343–61.

Harvey, David. 2005. *The New Imperialism*. Oxford, Oxford University Press.

Harvey, Penelope, Casper Jensen, and Atsuro Morita, eds. 2016. *Infrastructures and Social Complexity: A Companion*. London: Routledge.

Harvey, Penelope, and H. Knox. 2008. "'Otherwise Engaged': Culture, Deviance and the Quest for Connectivity through Road Construction." *Journal of Cultural Economy* 1 (1): 79–92.

——. 2015. *Roads: An Anthropology of Infrastructure and Expertise*. Ithaca, NY: Cornell University Press.

Haugen, Heidi Østbø. 2012. "Nigerians in China: A Second State of Immobility." *International Migration* 50 (2): 65–80.

——. 2019. "The Social Production of Container Space." *Environment and Planning D: Society and Space* 37: 868–85.

Haugen, Heidi Østbø, and Jørgen Carling. 2005. "On the Edge of the Chinese Diaspora: The Surge of Baihuo Business in an African City." *Ethnic and Racial Studies* 28 (4): 639–62.

Herzfeld, Michael. 2005. *Cultural Intimacy: Social Poetics in the Nation-state*. 2nd ed. New York: Routledge.

High, Mette. 2017. *Fear and Fortune. Spirit Worlds and Emerging Economies in the Mongolian Mining Boom*. Ithaca, NY: Cornell University Press.

Holbraad, Martin. 2012. *Truth in Motion. The Recursive Anthropology of Cuban Divination*. Chicago: University of Chicago Press.

Holbraad, Martin, and Morten Axel Pedersen. 2009. "Planet M: The Intense Abstraction of Marilyn Strathern." *Anthropological Theory* 9 (4): 371–94.

——. 2017. *The Ontological Turn: An Anthropological Exposition*. Cambridge: Cambridge University Press.

Honwana, Alcinda. 1996. "Spiritual Agency and Self-renewal in Southern Mozambique." PhD diss., University of London.

——. 1997. "Healing for Peace: Traditional Healers and Post-War Reconstruction in Southern Mozambique." *Peace and Conflict: Journal of Peace Psychology* 3 (3): 293–305.

Huang, Mingwei. 2019. "The Foreign and the Familiar: Reading the China Bag in South Africa." *International Journal of Cultural Studies* 22: 536–57.

Humphrey, Caroline. 1987. "The Host and the Guest: One Hundred Rules of Good Behaviour in Rural Mongolia." *Journal of the Anglo-Mongolian Society* 10 (1): 42–54.

——. 1998. *Marx Went Away—But Karl Stayed Behind*. Ann Arbor: University of Michigan Press.

——. 2005. "Ideology in Infrastructure: Architecture and Soviet Imagination." *Journal of the Royal Anthropological Institute* 11: 39–58.

Humphrey, Caroline, and D. Sneath. 1999. *The End of Nomadism? Society, State and the Environment in Inner Asia*. Cambridge: White Horse Press.

Højer, Lars. 2019. *The Anti-Social Contract: Injurious Talk and Dangerous Exchanges*. New York: Berghahn Books.

Højer, Lars, and Morten Axel Pedersen. 2019. *Urban Hunters: Dealing and Dreaming in Times of Transition*. New Haven, CT: Yale University Press.

InfoMongolia.com. 2010a. "The Transportation of Petro China Datsan Tamsag Is Terminated." Accessed August 5, 2011.

InfoMongolia.com. 2010b. "Prime Minister Gave a Notice to Petro China Daqing Tamsag LLC." Accessed August 5, 2011.

Iphofen, Ron. 2013. *Research Ethics in Ethnography/Anthropology*. European Commission. http://ec.europa.eu/research/participants/data/ref/h2020/other/hi/ethics-guide-ethnog-anthrop_en.pdf.

Isaacman, A. F., and B. S. Isaacman. 2013. *Dams, Displacement, and the Delusion of Development: Cahora Bassa and Its Legacies in Mozambique, 1965–2007*. Athens: Ohio University Press.

Jackson, Sara L. 2015a. "Imagining the Mineral Nation: Contested Nation-building in Mongolia." *Nationalities Papers* 43 (3): 437–56.

——. 2015b. "Dusty Roads and Disconnections: Perceptions of Dust from Unpaved Mining Roads in Mongolia's South Gobi Province." *Geoforum* 66: 94–105.

Jackson, Sara L., and Devon Dear. 2016. "Resource Extraction and National Anxieties: China's Economic Presence in Mongolia." *Eurasian Geography and Economics* 57 (3): 343–73.

Jansson, J., and C. Kiala. 2009. *Patterns of Chinese Investment, Aid and Trade in Mozambique*. Stellenbosch: University of Stellenbosch, Center for Chinese Studies.

Javzandorj, Ariunzul, and Lu Dehong. 2012. "Factors Contributing to Foreign Direct Investment in Mongolia." *European Researcher* (30) 9–3: 1559–64.

Jenkins, P. 2001. "Strengthening Access to Land for Housing for the Poor in Maputo, Mozambique." *International Journal of Urban and Regional Research* 25 (3): 629–48.

——. 2013. *Urbanization, Urbanism and Urbanity in an African City*. New York: Palgrave Macmillan.

Jensen, Casper B., and Brit R. Winthereik. 2013. *Monitoring Movements in Development Aid: Recursive Partnerships and Infrastructures*. Cambridge, MA: MIT Press.

Joniak-Lüthi, Agnieszka. 2016. "Roads in China's Borderlands: Interfaces of Spatial Representations, Perceptions, Practices, and Knowledges." *Modern Asian Studies* 50: 118–40.

Kapferer, Bruce. 1989. "Nationalist Ideology and a Comparative Anthropology." *Ethnos* 54 (3–4): 161–99.

Kelly, Jose A. 2011. *State Healthcare and Yanomami Transformations: A Symmetrical Ethnography*. Tucson: University of Arizona Press.

Kipnis, Andrew B. 1996. "The Language of Gifts: Managing Guanxi in a North China Village." *Modern China* 22 (3): 285–314.

——. 1997. *Producing Guanxi: Sentiment, Self, and Subculture in a North China Village*. Durham, NC: Duke University Press.

Kirsch, Stuart. 2014. *Mining Capitalism: The Relationship between Corporations and Their Critics*. Berkeley: University of California Press.

Kleveman, Lutz. 2003. *The New Great Game: Blood and Oil in Central Asia*. New York: Atlantic Monthly Press.

Kotkin, Stephen. 1997. *Magnetic Mountain: Stalinism as a Civilization*. Berkeley: University of California Press.

Kragelund, Peter. 2009. "China's Investments in Africa." In *The New Presence of China in Africa: The Importance of Increased Chinese Trade, Aid and Investments for Sub-Saharan Africa*, edited by M. P. van Dijk, 83–101. Amsterdam: Amsterdam University Press.

——. 2012. "Bringing 'Indigenous' Ownership Back: Chinese Presence and the Citizen Economic Empowerment Commission in Zambia." *Journal of Modern African Studies* 50 (3): 447–66.

Kynge, James. 2006. *China Shakes the World. The Rise of a Hungry Natio*n. London: Phoenix.

Labour Arbitration Center. 2007. *Labour Law*. Maputo, Mozambique: Mozlegal/ Centro de Arbitragem Laboral.

Laheij, Christian. 2018. "Dangerous Neighbours: Sorcery, Conspicuous Exchange and Proximity among Urban Migrants in Northern Mozambique." *Africa* 88 (S1): S31–S50.

Lahiri-Dutt, K., and H. Dondov. 2017. "Informal Mining in Mongolia: Livelihood Change and Continuity in the Rangelands." *Local Environment* 22 (1): 126–39.

Lampert, Ben, and Giles Mohan. 2014. "Sino-African Encounters in Ghana and Nigeria: From Conflict to Conviviality and Mutual Benefit." *Journal of Current Chinese Affairs* 43: 9–39.

Lan, Shanshan. 2017. *Mapping the New African Diaspora in China: Race and the Cultural Politics of Belonging*. Routledge: New York.

Larkin, Brian. 2013. "The Politics and Poetics of Infrastructure." *Annual Review of Anthropology* 42: 327–43.

Latour, Bruno. 1993. *We Have Never Been Modern*. Cambridge, MA: Harvard University Press.

———. 2013. *An Inquiry into Modes of Existence: An Anthropology of the Moderns*. Cambridge, MA: Harvard University Press.

Lattimore, Owen. 1962. *Inner Asian in Frontiers in China*. Boston, MA: Beacon.

Leach, James. 2003. *Creative Land: Place and Procreation on the Rai Coast of Papua New Guinea*. New York: Berghahn Books.

Lee, Ching Kwan. 2009. "Raw Encounters: Chinese Managers, African Workers and the Politics of Casualization in Africa's Chinese Enclaves." *China Quarterly* 199: 647–66.

———. 2017. *The Specter of Global China: Politics, Labor, and Foreign Investment in Africa*. Chicago: University of Chicago Press.

Lemos, A., and D. Ribeiro. 2007. "Taking Ownership or Just Changing Owners?" In *African Perspectives on China in Africa*, edited by F. Manji and S. Marks, 63–70. Cape Town, South Africa: Fahamu.

Li, Qiang 李强. 2009. "菏泽人蒙古国演绎闯关东" [Heze Man in Mongolia on Going North-East] 菏泽日报 [*Heze Daily*], March 18, 2009.

Liesegang, G. J. 1996. *Ngungunyane. A figura de Ngungunyane Nquamayo, rei de Gaza 1884–1895 e o desaparecimento do seu Estado*. Maputo, Mozambique: ARPAC.

Low, S. 2003. *Behind the Gates: Life, Security, and the Pursuit of Happiness in Fortress America*. London: Routledge.

Lu, Xiaobo, and Elizabeth J. Perry. 1997. *Danwei: The Changing Chinese Workplace in Historical and Comparative Perspective, Socialism and Social Movements*. Armonk, NY: M. E. Sharpe.

Lutz, Catherine. 2006. "Empire Is in the Details." *American Ethnologist* 33 (4): 593–611.

Macauhub.com. 2016. "China the Top Investor in Mozambique in 1st Half-year." Accessed September 29, 2016. https://macauhub.com.mo/2016/08/10/china-the-top-investor-in-mozambique-in-1st-half-year/.

———. 2018. "China: An Indispensable Partner for Mozambique." Accessed February 3, 2020. https://clubofmozambique.com/news/china-an-indispensable-partner-for-mozambique/.

Mackenzie, C. 2006. *Forest Governance in Zambézia, Mozambique: Chinese Takeaway!* Maputo, Mozambique: FONGZA.

Mackenzie, C., with D. Ribeiro. 2009. *Tristezas Tropicais: More Sad Stories from the Forests of Zambézia*. Maputo, Mozambique: Justica Ambiental/ORAM.

Macqueen, D., ed. 2018. *China in Mozambique's Forests. A Review of Issues and Progress for Livelihoods and Sustainability*. London: IIED.

Mains, D. 2012. "Blackouts and Progress. Privatization, Infrastructure, and a Development State in Jimma, Ethiopia." *Cultural Anthropology* 27 (1): 3–27.

Manji, A. 2012. "The Grabbed State: Lawyers, Politics and Public Land in Kenya." *Journal of Modern African Studies* 50 (3): 467–92.

Marcus, George E. 1986. "Contemporary Problems of Ethnography in the Modern World System." In *Writing Culture: The Poetics and Politics of Ethnography: A School of American Research Advanced Seminar*, edited by J. Clifford and G. E. Marcus, 165–93. Berkeley: University of California Press.

Marcus, George E., and Michael M. J. Fischer, eds. 1986a. *Anthropology as Cultural Critique. An Experimental Moment in the Human Sciences*. Chicago: University of Chicago Press.

———. 1986b. "Introduction." In *Anthropology as Cultural Critique. An Experimental Moment in the Human Sciences*, edited by George E. Marcus and Michael M. J. Fischer, 1–6. Chicago: University of Chicago Press.

Mathews, Gordon. 2015. "Africans in Guangzhou." *Journal of Current Chinese Affairs* 44: 7–15.

Mawdsley, Emma. 2008. "Fu Manchu versus Dr Livingstone in the Dark Continent? Representing China, Africa and the West in British Broadsheet Newspapers." *Political Geography* 27 (5): 509–29.

McIntyre, Neil, Nevenka Bulovic, Isabel Cane, and Phill McKenna. 2016. "A Multi-disciplinary Approach to Understanding the Impacts of Mines on Traditional Uses of Water in Northern Mongolia." *Science of the Total Environment* 557–58: 404–14.

Mehta, Uday Singh. 1999. *Liberalism and Empire. A Study in Nineteenth-Century British Liberal Thought*. Chicago: University of Chicago Press.

Mendee, Jargalsaikhany. 2015. "Mongolia's Dilemma: A Politically Linked, Economically Isolated Small Power." *Asan Forum* 4: 6. http://www.theasanforum.org/mongolias-dilemma-a-politically-linked-economically-isolated-small-power/.

Menezes, C. 2001. "Mito e Cosmogonia na Concepcão do Assentamento Mocambicano." In *Um Olhar para o Habitat Informal Mocambicano: De Licinga a Maputo*, edited by J. Carrilho, S. Bruschi, C. Menezes and L. Lage, 58–65. Maputo, Mozambique: Faculdade de Arquitectura e Planeamento Fisico, UEM.

Menhas, Rashid, Shahid Mahmood, Papel Tanchangya, and Muhammad Nabeel Safdar. 2019. "Sustainable Development under Belt and Road Initiative: A Case Study of China-Pakistan Economic Corridor's Socio-Economic Impact on Pakistan." *Sustainability* 11 (21): 6143.

Miyazaki, Hirozaki, and Annelise Riles. 2005. "Failure as an Endpoint." In *Global Assemblages: Technology, Politics and Ethics as Anthropological Problems*, edited by A. Ong and S. J. Collier, 320–32. Oxford: Blackwell.

Mohan, Giles. 2013. "Beyond the Enclave: Towards a Critical Political Economy of China and Africa." *Development and Change* 44 (6): 1255–72.

Monson, Jamie. 2008. "Liberating Labour? Constructing Anti-Hegemony on the TAZARA Railway in Tanzania, 1965–76." In *China Returns to Africa: A Rising Power and a Continent Embrace*, edited by Chris Alden, Daniel Large, and Ricardo Soares de Oliveira, 197–219. London: Hurst.

Montsame. 2018. "PetroChina Daqing Tamsag Assigned to Cooperate with Local Administration." August 5, 2018. Accessed May 31, 2021. https://www.montsame.mn/en/read/134964.

Morton, Timothy. 2013. *Hyperobjects: Philosophy and Ecology after the End of the World*. Minneapolis: University of Minnesota Press.

Mosko, Mark. 2010. "Partible Penitents: Dividual Personhood and Christian Practice in Melanesia and the West." *JRAI* 16 (1): 215–40.

Murray, William. 2003. "Informal Gold Mining and National Development: The Case of Mongolia." *International Development Planning* Review 25 (2): 111–28.

Murray Li, Tania. 2007. *The Will to Improve: Governmentality, Development, and the Practice of Politics*. Durham, NC: Duke University Press.

———. 2014. *Land's End. Capitalist Relations on an Indigenous Frontier*. Durham, NC: Duke University Press.

Myadar, Orhon. 2011. "Imaginary Nomads: Deconstructing the Representation of Mongolia as a Land of Nomads." *Inner Asia* 13 (2): 335–62.

Needham, Rodney. 1975. "Polythetic Classification: Convergence and Consequences." *Man* 10: 349–69.

New York Times. 2007. "Patron of African Misgovernment." February 19, 2007.

Nielsen, Morten. 2010. "Contrapuntal Cosmopolitanism: Distantiation as Social Relatedness among House-builders in Maputo, Mozambique." *Social Anthropology* 18 (4): 396–402.

——. 2011. "Inverse Governmentality. The Paradoxical Production of Peri-Urban Planning in Maputo, Mozambique." *Critique of Anthropology* 31 (4): 329–58.

——. 2012a. "Interior Swelling. On the Expansive Effects of Ancestral Interventions in Maputo, Mozambique. "*Common Knowledge* 18 (3): 433–50.

——. 2012b. "Roadside Inventions: Making Time and Money Work at a Road Construction Site in Mozambique." *Mobilities* 7 (4): 467–80.

——. 2013. "Analogic Asphalt. Suspended Value Conversions among Young Road Workers in Southern Mozambique." *HAU: Journal of Ethnographic Theory* 3 (2): 79–96.

——. 2017. "Ideological Twinning: Socialist Aesthetics and Political Meetings in Maputo, Mozambique." *Journal of the Royal Anthropological Institute* 23 (S1): 139–53.

Nielsen, Morten, and M. A. Pedersen. 2015. "Infrastructural Imaginaries: Collapsed Futures in Mozambique and Mongolia." In *Reflections on Imagination: Human Capacity and Ethnographic Method*, edited by M. Harris and N. Rapport, 237–62. Surrey, UK: Ashgate.

Niigmiin Tol'. 2010. "Petrochina Dachin Tamsag Has Been Sued." Translated by M. A. Pedersen. October 22, 2010.

Nolan, Peter. 2012. *Is China Buying the World?* Cambridge: Polity Press.

Nyíri, Pál. 2006. "The Yellow Man's Burden: Chinese Migrants on a Civilizing Mission." *China Journal* (56): 83–106.

Nyíri, Pál, and Joana Breidenbach. 2008. "The Altai Road: Visions of Development across the Russian–Chinese Border." *Development and Change* 39: 123–45.

Oates, John. 2006. "Ethical Frameworks for Research with Human Participants." In *Doing Postgraduate Research*, edited by Stephen Potter, 200–22. London: Sage.

Ong, Aihwa. 2004. "The Chinese Axis: Zoning Technologies and Variegated Sovereignty." *Journal of East Asian Studies* 4 (1): 69–96.

——. 2006. *Neoliberalism as Exception: Mutations in Citizenship and Sovereignty.* Durham, NC: Duke University Press.

Ong, Aihwa, and Stephen J. Collier. 2005. *Global Assemblages: Technology, Politics, and Ethics as Anthropological Problems.* Malden, MA: Blackwell Publishing.

Önöödör. 2001. "Interview with J. Vashon, President of SOOS." Translated by M. A. Pedersen. December 7, 2001.

Osburg, John. 2013. *Anxious Wealth: Money and Morality Among China's New Rich.* Stanford, CA: Stanford University Press.

Park, Yoon Jung. 2008. *A Matter of Honour: Being Chinese in South Africa.* Auckland Park, South Africa: Jacana.

Pasternak, Burton, and Janet W. Salaff. 1993. *Cowboys and Cultivators: The Chinese of Inner Mongolia.* Boulder, CO: Westview Press.

Paulo, Margarida, Carmeliza Rosário, and Inge Tvedten. 2007. *"Xiculungo"—Social Relations of Urban Poverty in Maputo, Mozambique.* Bergen, Norway: Chr. Michelsen Institute.

Pedersen, Morten Axel. 2003. "Networking the Landscape: Place, Power and Decision Making in Northern Mongolia." In *Imagining Nature: Practices of Cosmology and Identity*, edited by A. Roepstorff, N. Bubandt, and K. Kull, 238–59. Aarhus, Denmark: Aarhus University Press.

——. 2007. "'Public' and 'Private' Markets in Postsocialist Mongolia." *Anthropology of East Europe Review* 26 (1): 64–72.

——. 2011. *Not Quite Shamans: Spirit Worlds and Political Lives in Northern Mongolia.* Ithaca, NY: Cornell University Press.

——. 2012. "The Task of Anthropology Is to Invent Relations: For the Motion." *Critique of Anthropology* 32 (1): 59–65.

——. 2013. "The Fetish of Connectivity." In *Objects and Materials. A Routledge Companion*, edited by P. Harvey, E. C. Casella, G. Evans, H. Knox, C. Mclean, E. B. Silva, N. Thoburn, and K. Woodward, 197–207. London: Routledge.

——. 2017. "The Vanishing Power Plant. Infrastructures and Ignorance in Ulaanbaatar." *Cambridge Journal of Anthropology* 35 (2): 79–95.

Pedersen, Morten Axel, and Mikkel Bunkenborg. 2012. "Roads That Separate: Sino-Mongolian Relations in the Inner Asian Desert." *Mobilities* 7 (4): 555–69.

Pedersen, Morten Axel, and L. Højer. 2008. "Lost in Transition: Fuzzy Property and Leaky Selves in Ulaanbaatar." *Ethnos* 73 (1): 73–96.

Pedersen, Morten Axel, and Morten Nielsen. 2013. "Trans-temporal Hinges: Reflections on an Ethnographic Study of Chinese Infrastructural Projects in Mozambique and Mongolia." *Social Analysis* 57 (1): 122–42.

Pels, Peter. 2018. "Data Management in Anthropology: The Next Phase in Ethics Governance?" *Social Anthropology* 26 (3): 391–96.

Penvenne, J. M. 1995. *African Workers and Colonial Racism. Mozambican Strategies and Struggles in Lourenco Marques, 1877–1962.* Portsmouth, NH: Heinemann.

Perdue, Peter. 2006. *China Marches West. The Qing Conquest of Central Asia.* Cambridge, MA: Harvard University Press.

Pina-Cabral, João de. 2010. "Xara: Namesakes in Southern Mozambique and Bahia (Brazil)." *Ethnos* 75 (3): 323–45.

Piot, C. 2010. *Nostalgia for the Future: West Africa after the Cold War.* Chicago: University of Chicago Press.

Plueckhahn, Rebekah. 2020. *Shaping Urban Futures in Mongolia Ulaanbaatar: Dynamic Ownership and Economic Flux.* London: UCL Press.

Plueckhahn, Rebekah, and Bumochir Dulam. 2018. "Capitalism in Mongolia: Ideology, Practice and Ambiguity." *Central Asian Survey* 37 (3): 341–56.

Povinelli, Elizabeth A. 2006. *The Empire of Love: Toward a Theory of Intimacy, Genealogy, and Carnality.* Durham, NC: Duke University Press.

——. 2016. *Geontologies: A Requiem to Late Liberalism.* Durham, NC: Duke University Press.

Powell, Bill. 2009. "It's China's World (We Just Live in It)." *Forbes Magazine*, October 8, 2009. Accessed May 21 2020. http://archive.fortune.com/2009/10/07/news/international/china_natural_resources.fortune/index.htm.

Purevjav, Bolormaa. 2011. "Artisanal and Small-Scale Mining: Gender and Sustainable Livelihoods in Mongolia." In *Gendering the Field: Towards Sustainable Livelihoods for Mining Communities*, edited by Kuntala Lahiri-Dutt, 197–211. Canberra, Australia: ANU Press.

Rabinow, Paul. 1986. "Representations Are Social Facts: Modernity and Post-Modernity in Anthropology." In *Writing Culture: The Poetics and Politics of Ethnography*, edited by James Clifford and George E. Marcus, 234–61. Berkeley: University of California Press.

——. 2007. *Marking Time: On the Anthropology of the Contemporary.* Princeton, NJ: Princeton University Press.

Rabinow, Paul, and Anthony Stavrianakis. 2013. *Demands of the Day on the Logic of Anthropological Inquiry*. Chicago: University of Chicago Press.

Radchenko, Sergey. 2013. "Sino-Russian Competition in Mongolia." *Asan Forum*. http://www.theasanforum.org/sino-russian-competition-in-mongolia/.

Ramo, Joshua Cooper. 2004. *The Beijing Consensus: Notes on the New Physics of Chinese Power*. London: Foreign Policy Centre.

Reed, Adam. 2004. *Papua New Guinea's Last Place. Experiences of Constraint in a Postcolonial Prison*. Oxford: Berghahn Books.

Reeves, J., 2011. "Resources, Sovereignty, and Governance: Can Mongolia Avoid the 'Resource Curse'?" *Asian Journal of Political Science* 19 (2): 170–85.

——. 2017. "Infrastructural Hope: Anticipating 'Independent Roads' and Territorial Integrity in Southern Kyrgyzstan." *Ethnos* 82 (4): 711–37.

Revistamacau. 2006. "O regresso dos chineses." Accessed November 17, 2017. http://www.revistamacau.com/2006/06/30/mocambique-o-regresso-dos-chineses/.

Ribeiro, D. 2009. *Levantamento Preliminar da Problematic das Florestas de Cabo Delgado*. Maputo, Mozambique: Justica Ambiental.

——. 2010. "Disappearing Forests, Disappearing Hope: Mozambique." In *Chinese and African Perspectives on China in Africa*, edited by A. Harneit-Sievers, S. Marks, and S. Naidu, 155–62. Cape Town, South Africa: Pambazuka Press.

Robbins, Joel. 2007. "Continuity Thinking and the Problem of Christian Culture: Belief, Time, and the Anthropology of Christianity." *Current Anthropology* 48 (1): 5–38.

Robinson, David A. 2012. "Chinese Engagement with Africa: The Case of Mozambique." *Portuguese Journal of International Affairs* 6: 3–15.

Roque, Paula Christina. 2009. *China in Mozambique: A Cautious Approach. Country Case Study*. Johannesburg: South African Institute of International Affairs.

Sanders, Todd, and Harry G. West. 2003. "Power Revealed and Concealed in the New World Order." In *Transparency and Conspiracy. Ethnographies of Suspicion in the New World Order*, edited by H. G. West and T. Sanders, 1–37. Durham, NC: Duke University Press.

Sautman, Barry, and Hairong Yan. 2007. "Friends and Interests: China's Distinctive Links with Africa." *African Studies Review* 50 (3): 75–114.

——. 2008. "The Forest for the Trees: Trade, Investment and the China-in-Africa Discourse." *Pacific Affairs* 81(1): 9–29.

——. 2009. "African Perspectives on China–Africa Links." *China Quarterly* 199: 728–59.

Scott, James. 1998. *Seeing Like a State. How Certain Schemes to Improve the Human Condition Have Failed*. New Haven, CT: Yale University Press.

Segal, Lotte Buch. 2016. "Ambivalent Attachment: Melancholia and Political Activism in Occupied Palestine." *Ethos* 44 (4): 464–84.

Shambaugh, David L. 2013. *China Goes Global: The Partial Power*. New York: Oxford University Press.

Sheridan, Derek. 2018. "'If You Greet Them, They Ignore You': Chinese Migrants, (Refused) Greetings, and the Inter-personal Ethics of Global Inequality in Tanzania." *Anthropological Quarterly* 91: 237–65.

——. 2019. "Weak Passports and Bad Behavior." *American Ethnologist* 46: 137–49.

Shi, Qiting 石奇亭 and Chang Fangyuan 常方元. 2009. "北边邻国也有个北大荒。贾鑫升：走，到蒙古种地去！[The Neighbouring Country to the North Also has a Great Northern Wilderness. Jia Xinsheng: Let's Go, To Farm in Mongolia!] 大众日报 *Masses Daily*, March 18, 2009.

Simone, AbdouMaliq. 2004. "People as Infrastructure: Intersecting Fragments in Johannesburg." *Public Culture* 16 (3): 407–29.

Simone, AbdouMaliq, and M. Nielsen. 2021 (forthcoming). "Urban Chiaroscuro: Plunging into the Obscurity of the City." *L'Afrique Contemporaine*.

Singh, Bhrigupati. 2011. "Agonistic Intimacy and Moral Aspiration in Popular Hinduism: A Study in the Political Theology of the Neighbor." *American Ethnologist* 38 (3): 430–50.

Sitoe, B. 2011. *Dicionário Changana-Português*. Maputo, Mozambique: Texto Editores.

Siu, Helen F., and Mike McGovern. 2017. "China–Africa Encounters: Historical Legacies and Contemporary Realities." *Annual Review of Anthropology* 46: 337–55.

Smith, Marissa. 2015. "Treasure Underfoot and Far Away: Mining, Foreignness, and Friendship in Contemporary Mongolia." PhD diss., Princeton University.

Smith, Neil. 2003. *American Empire: Roosevelt's Geographer and the Prelude to Globalization*. California Studies in Critical Human Geography. Berkeley: University of California Press.

Smith, Vanessa. 2010. *Intimate Strangers: Friendship, Exchange and Pacific Encounters*. New York: Cambridge University Press.

Sneath, David. 1993. "Social Relations, Networks and Social Organisation in Post-Socialist Rural Mongolia." *Nomadic Peoples* 33: 193–207.

——. 2000. *Changing Inner Mongolia: Pastoral Mongolian Society and the Chinese State*. Oxford: Oxford University Press.

Snow, Philip. 1989. *The Star Raft: China's Encounter with Africa*. Ithaca, NY: Cornell University Press.

Soni, Sharad K. 2009. "China's Periphery Policy: Implications for Sino-Mongolian Relations." *India Quarterly* 65 (3): 251–69.

——. 2018. "China–Mongolia–Russia Economic Corridor: Opportunities and Challenges." In *China's Global Rebalancing and the New Silk Road*, edited by B. R. Deepak, 101–17. Singapore: Springer.

Ssorin-Chaikov, N. V. 2003. *The Social Life of the State in Subarctic Siberia*. Stanford, CA: Stanford University Press.

Star, Susan L. 1999. "The Ethnography of Infrastructure." *American Behavioral Scientist* 43 (3): 377–91. http://doi.org/10.1177/00027649921955326

Stasch, Rupert. 2003. "Separateness as a Relation: The Iconicity, Univocality and Creativity of Korowai Mother-in-law Avoidance." *Journal of the Royal Anthropological Institute* 9: 317–37.

——. 2009. *Society of Others. Kinship and Mourning in a West Papuan Place*. Berkeley: University of California Press.

Stein, Rolf. 1990. *The World in Miniature: Container Gardens and Dwellings in Far Eastern Religious Thought*. Stanford, CA: Stanford University Press.

Stengers, Isabelle. 2010. *Cosmopolitics I*. Minneapolis: University of Minnesota Press.

Stocking, George W. 1995. *After Tylor: British Social Anthropology 1888–1951*. Madison: University of Wisconsin Press.

Stoler, Ann Laura. 2002. *Carnal Knowledge and Imperial Power: Race and the Intimate in Colonial Rule*. Berkeley: University of California Press.

Strathern, Marilyn. 1988. *The Gender of the Gift: Problems with Women and Problems with Society in Melanesia*. Berkeley: University of California Press.

——. 1992. "Qualified Value: The Perspective of Gift Exchange." In *Barter, Exchange and Value: An Anthropological Approach*, edited by C. Humphrey and S. Hugh-Jones, 169–91. Cambridge, Cambridge University Press.

——. 1999. *Property, Substance and Effect: Anthropological Essays on Persons and Things*. London: Athlone Press.

——. 2004. *Partial Connections*. Updated edition. Oxford: Altamira Press.

——. 2020. *Relations: An Anthropological Account*. Durham, NC: Duke University Press.

Strauss, Julia C. 2009. "The Past in the Present: Historical and Rhetorical Lineages in China's Relations with Africa." *China Quarterly* 199: 777–95.

Strauss, Julia C., and Ariel C. Armony. 2012. *From the Great Wall to the New World: China and Latin America in the 21st Century. China Quarterly*. Special Issues. Cambridge: Cambridge University Press.

Strickland, Michael. 2010. "Aid and Affect in the Friendships of Young Chinese Men." *Journal of the Royal Anthropological Institute* 16 (1):102–18.

Sun, Chanjin Liqiao Chen, Lijun Chen, and Steve Bass. 2008. *Global Forest Product Chains: Identifying Challenges and Opportunities for China through a Global Commodity Chain Sustainability Analysis*. Winnipeg, Canada: International Institute for Sustainable Development.

Swanson, Heather Anne, Nils Bubandt, and Anna Tsing. 2015. "Less than One but More than Many: Anthropocene as Science Fiction and Scholarship-in-the-Making." *Environment and Society: Advances in Research* 6 (1): 149–66.

Swider, Sarah Christine. 2015. *Building China: Informal Work and the New Precariat*. London: ILR Press.

Taussig, Michael. 1993. *Mimesis and Alterity: A Particular History of the Senses*. New York: Routledge.

Taylor, Ian. 2006. *China and Africa. Engagement and Compromise*. London: Routledge.

——. 2011. *The Forum on China-Africa Cooperation*. Routledge Global Institutions. London: Routledge.

Thunø, Mette. 2007. *Beyond Chinatown: New Chinese Migration and the Global Expansion of China*. Copenhagen: NIAS Press.

Todd, Zoe. 2016. "An Indigenous Feminist's Take on the Ontological Turn: 'Ontology' Is Just Another Word for Colonialism." *Journal of Historical Sociology* 29 (1): 4–22.

Trindade, J. C. 2006. "Rupture and Continuity in Political and Legal Processes." In *Law and Justice in a Multicultural Society: The Case of Mozambique*, edited by B. d. S. Santos, J. C. Trindade, and M. P. Meneses, 31–62. Dakar, Senegal: Council for the Development of Social Science Research in Africa.

Tsing, Anna L. 2000. "Inside the Economy of Appearances." *Public Culture* 12 (1): 115–42.

——. 2005. *Friction: An Ethnography of Global Connection*. Princeton, NJ: Princeton University Press.

UB Post. 2008. "After Brawl at Border, China Offers Apology." July 31, 2008.

Verdery, K. 2004. "The Obligations of Ownership: Restoring Rights to Land in Post-socialist Transylvania." In *Property in Question: Value Transformation in the Global Economy*, edited by K. Verdery and C. Humphrey, 139–60. Oxford: Berg.

Wagner, Roy. 1972. *Habu: The Innovation of Meaning in Daribi Religion*. Chicago: University of Chicago Press.

——. 1977. *Lethal Speech: Daribi Myth as Symbolic Obviation*. Ithaca, NY: Cornell University Press.

——. 1981. *The Invention of Culture*. Chicago: University of Chicago Press.

Walford, Antonia. 2012. "Data Moves: Taking Amazonian Climate Science Seriously." *Cambridge Anthropology* 30 (2): 101–17.

Wang, Bijun, and Kailin Gao. 2019. "Forty Years' Development of China's Outward Foreign Direct Investment: Retrospect and the Challenges Ahead." *China & World Economy* 27 (3): 1–24.

Wang, Gungwu. 2006. "Tianxia and Empire: External Chinese Perspectives." Inaugural Tsai Lecture, Harvard University, May 4, 2006.

Wank, David L. 1996. "The Institutional Process of Market Clientelism: Guanxi and Private Business in a South China City." *China Quarterly* 147: 820–38.

———. 1999. *Commodifying Communism: Business, Trust, and Politics in a Chinese City.* Structural Analysis in the Social Sciences. Cambridge: Cambridge University Press.

Wastell, Sari. 2001. "Presuming Scale, Making Diversity." *Critique of Anthropology* 21 (2): 185–210.

West, Harry G. 2001. "Sorcery of Construction and Socialist Modernization: Ways of Understanding Power in Postcolonial Mozambique." *American Ethnologist* 28 (1): 119–50.

———. 2005. *Kupilikula. Governance and the Invisible Realm in Mozambique.* Chicago: University of Chicago Press.

White, Thomas. 2020. "Domesticating the Belt and Road: Rural Development, Spatial Politics, and Animal Geographies in Inner Mongolia." *Eurasian Geography and Economics* 61 (1): 13–33.

Wiegink, Nikkie. 2015. "'It Will Be Our Time to Eat': Former Renamo Combatants and Big-Man Dynamics in Central Mozambique." *Journal of Southern African Studies* 41 (4): 869–85.

Will, Rachel. 2012. "China's Stadium Diplomacy." *World Policy Journal* 29 (2): 36–43.

Williams, Dee Mack. 2002. *Beyond Great Walls.* Stanford, CA: Stanford University Press.

Wissink, Bart, Ronald van Kempen, Yiping Fang, and Si-ming Li. 2012. "Introduction—Living in Chinese Enclave Cities." *Urban Geography* 33 (2): 161–66.

Wong, Bernard P., and Chee-Beng Tan. 2013. *Chinatowns around the World: Gilded Ghetto, Ethnopolis, and Cultural Diaspora.* Leiden: Brill.

World Economics. 2011. "The Importance of FDI." Accessed May 31, 2021. https://www.worldeconomics.com/papers/Investing%20in%20Mongolia_c93dbdb0-1a04-4e33-b331-51c25d21d47a.paper.

Wu, John C. 1997. "The Mineral Industry of Mongolia." In *Minerals Yearbook*, vol. 3. The Bureau, pp: R1–R3. U.S. Department of the Interior: U.S. Geological Survey.

Wu, Keping. 2020. "Building Infrastructure and Making Boundaries in Southwest China." In *It Happens among the People: Resonances and Extensions of the Work of Fredrik Barth*, edited by Keping Wu and Robert P. Weller, 82–103. New York: Berghahn.

Wu, Xianfei 伍先飞. 2017. 大师之路:探寻中国当代著名雕塑家徐晓虹成长之路 [The Way of a Master: Exploring the Coming of Age of the Renowned Contemporary Sculptor Xu Xiaohong]. http://artist.artron.net/20170427/n927038.html.

Xu, Xiaohong 徐晓虹. 2003. "情系非洲: 赴莫桑比克创作小记" [Feelings for Africa: Brief Note on Visiting Mozambique] 雕塑 *Sculpture* 5: 56–57.

Yan, Hairong, and Barry Sautman. 2012. "Chasing Ghosts: Rumours and Representations of the Export of Chinese Convict Labour to Developing Countries." *China Quarterly*: 398–418.

———. 2013. "'The Beginning of a World Empire?' Contesting the Discourse of Chinese Copper Mining in Zambia." *Modern China* 39 (2): 131–64.

Yan, Hairong, Barry Sautman, and Yao Lu. 2019. "Chinese and 'Self-segregation' in Africa." *Asian Ethnicity* 20: 40–66.

Yan, Yunxiang. 1996. *The Flow of Gifts: Reciprocity and Social Networks in a Chinese Village*. Stanford, CA: Stanford University Press.

Yang, Mayfair Mei-hui. 1989. "The Gift Economy and State Power in China." *Comparative Studies in Society and History* 31 (1): 25–54.

——. 1994. *Gifts, Favors, and Banquets: The Art of Social Relationships in China*. Wilder House Series in Politics, History, and Culture. Ithaca, NY: Cornell University Press.

Yeh, Emily T. 2016. "Introduction: The Geoeconomics and Geopolitics of Chinese Development and Investment in Asia." *Eurasian Geography and Economics* 57 (3): 275–85.

Zang, Yaohong 臧耀红. 2008. "民营企业国外种地" [Private Company Farming Abroad]. 菏泽日报 [*Heze Daily*], August 20, 2008.

Zhang, Li. 2001. *Strangers in the City: Reconfigurations of Space, Power, and Social Networks within China's Floating Population*. Stanford, CA: Stanford University Press.

Zhao, Tingyang. 2006. "Rethinking Empire from a Chinese Concept 'All-under-Heaven' (Tian-xia)." *Social Identities* 12 (1): 29–41.

Zhou, Min. 1992. *Chinatown: The Socioeconomic Potential of an Urban Enclave*. Philadelphia, PA: Temple University Press.

Zhou, Yongming. 2013. "Branding Tengchong: Globalization, Road Building, and Spatial Reconfigurations in Yunnan, Southwest China." In *Cultural Heritage Politics in China*, edited by Tami Blumenfield and Helaine Silverman, 247–59. New York: Springer.

Zimbabwean. 2011a. "Illegal Logs Sold Back to Timber Companies." Accessed March 11, 2013. http://www.thezimbabwean.co.uk/news/africa/55022/mozambique-illegal-logs-sold-back.html.

——. 2011b. "Timber Companies Lose Their Licences." Accessed March 11, 2013. http://www.thezimbabwean.co.uk/news/africa/54235/mozambique-timber-companies-lose-their.html.

Zizek, S. 1989. *The Sublime Object of Ideology*. London, Verso.

Index

Page numbers followed by letter *f* refer to figures.

ethnographers' fieldwork in, 65–68, 69, 74–75; road infrastructure in, 124
ultranationalist movements, in Mongolia, 92, 93–94
United States: concerns about Chinese competition in Africa, 9; contemporary empire of, scholarship on, 20; Covid-19 pandemic and, 237; end to hegemony of, predictions regarding, 18; offshore oil production in Equatorial Guinea, 24, 110; oil exploration in Mongolia, 101, 112; outward foreign direct investment (OFDI) by, 239n3; political pushback against China, 238
unseeing: in Catembe construction projects, 147, 149, 156; in collaborative ethnographic research, 137, 139, 155, 162; in Sino-Mozambican relations, 135–37, 153, 154–55, 156; strategies of, 137–38

violence: against Chinese transgressors in Mongolia, 91, 93–94; and enclaving, 161; in Mongolian cultural context, 91; threats of, against Chinese operations in Mongolia, 58, 59, 94, 96; threats of, against ethnographers, 193, 194; tree-planting project as form of, 110

Wagner, Roy, 186, 234
wall(s), Chinese: around Bountiful Nature Mine, Mongolia, 71, 72, 75f, 76, 96; motivations for building, 96, 97, 98. See also compound(s)
Wank, David, 49

water resources, competition over, 83–84
wealth: Chinese, and corruption of Mongolian officials, 114, 115, 118; Chinese, stereotypes about, 65, 80; Chinese demonstration of, as offensive, 63–64, 65, 68; of Mongolian homeland, resource extraction companies seen as depleting, 105–6
Wen Jiabao, visit to Mongolia, 57–58, 241n3
workers. See Chinese employees; Mongolian workers; Mozambican workers
World Bank, 8, 124, 148

Xi Jinping, 8
Xu Xiaohong, 225, 226–27

Yan, Hairong, 5, 246n2
Yang, Mayfair, 49
yos (custom), Mongolian: Chinese behavior with respect to, 76–77, 88, 104; within ger, 76, 128–29
yurt. See ger(s), Mongolian

Zambia, Chinese projects in, 235–36
Zhao Tingyang, 1, 19–20, 240n9
Zhao Zhenglun, 108, 243n2
Zheng He, 50
zinc mine, at Baruun-Uurt, Mongolia, 72
zone(s): of awkward engagement, 20–21, 89; construction, accumulation by dispossession in, 145–46, 156; of exception, China's transition to capitalism and, 23, 24; of security and order, Chinese compounds as, 168–69, 175–76

CPSIA information can be obtained
at www.ICGtesting.com
Printed in the USA
LVHW021649110522
718482LV00004B/506